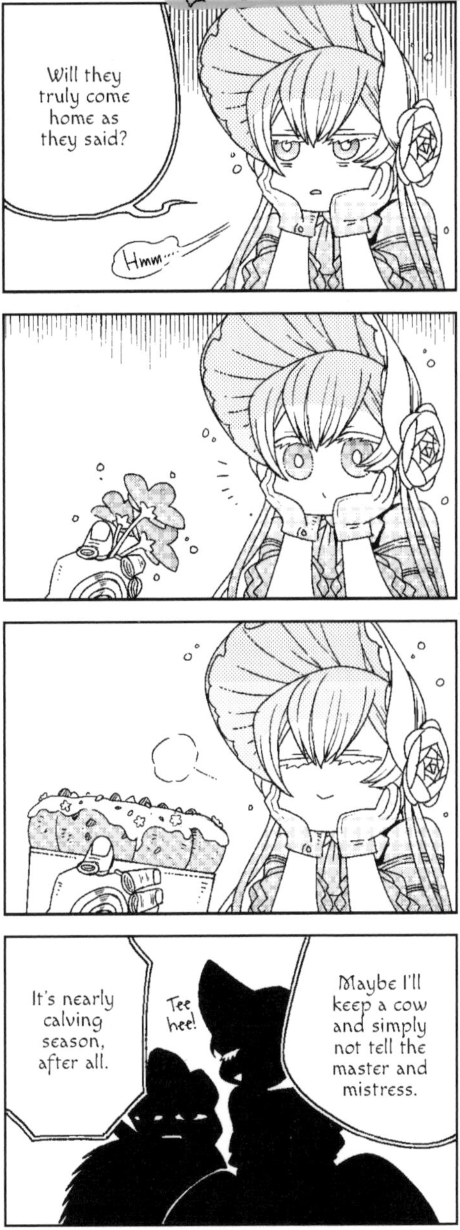
Will they truly come home as they said?
Hmm....
Maybe I'll keep a cow and simply not tell the master and mistress.
Tee hee!
It's nearly calving season, after all.

Silky's Diary 18

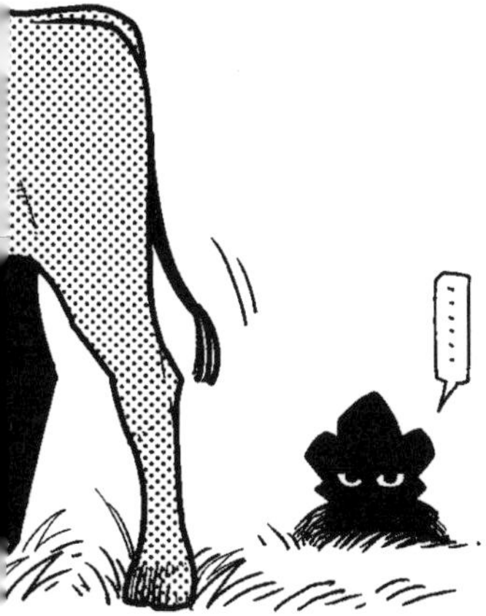
......

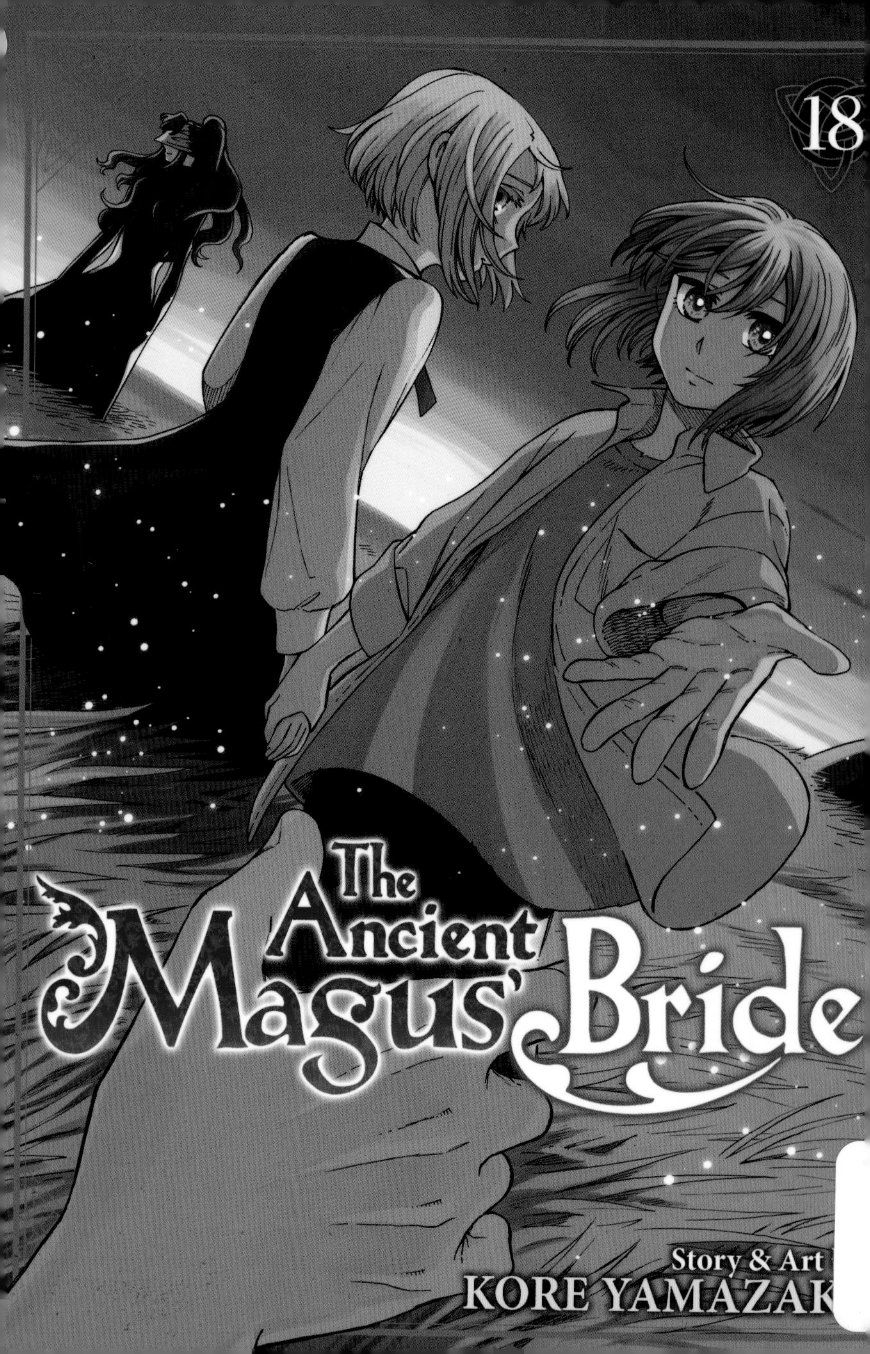
18
The Ancient Magus' Bride
Story & Art
KORE YAMAZAK

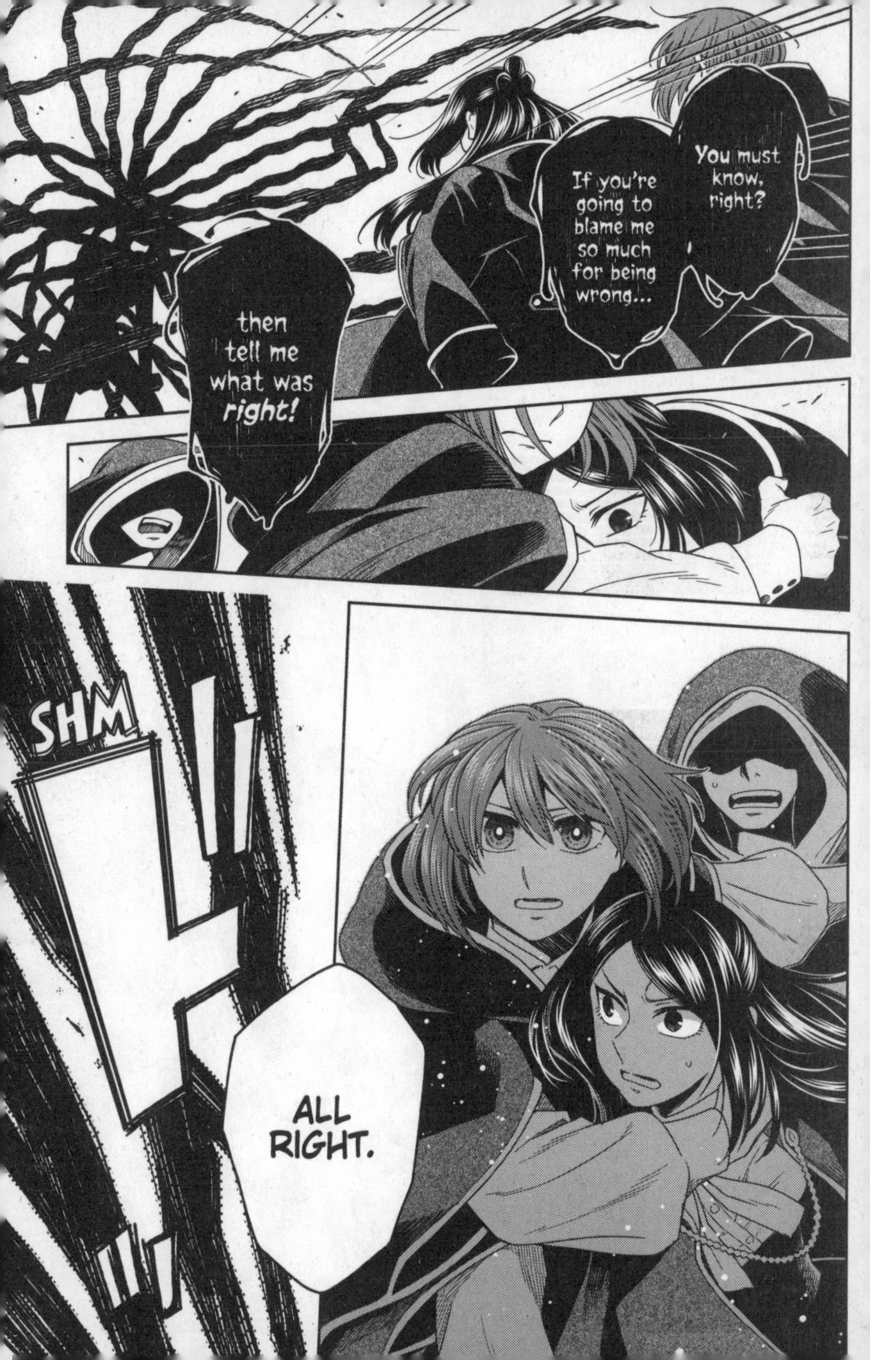
You must know, right?
If you're going to blame me so much for being wrong...
then tell me what was right!
SHM
ALL RIGHT.

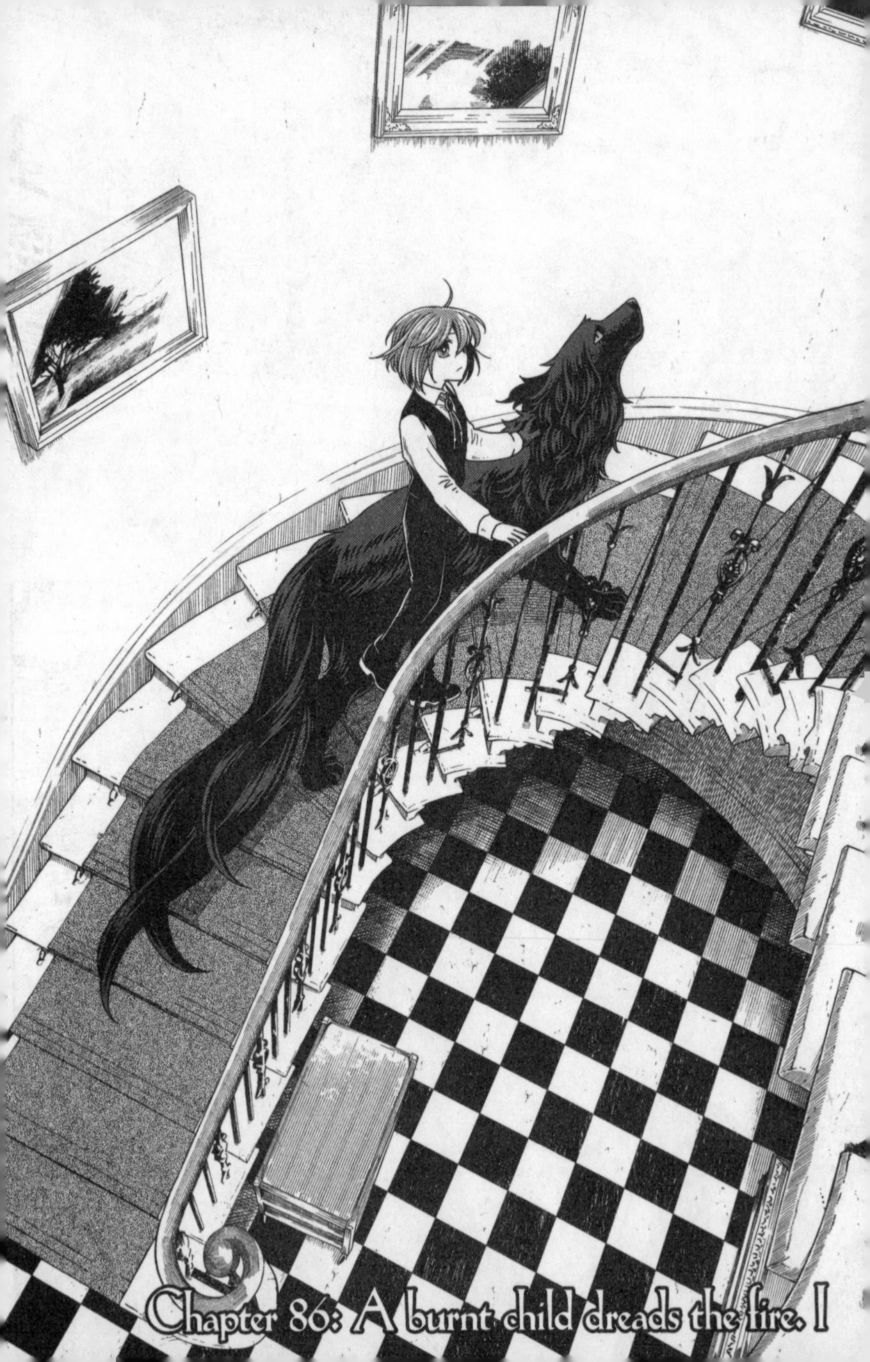

Chapter 86: A burnt child dreads the fire. I

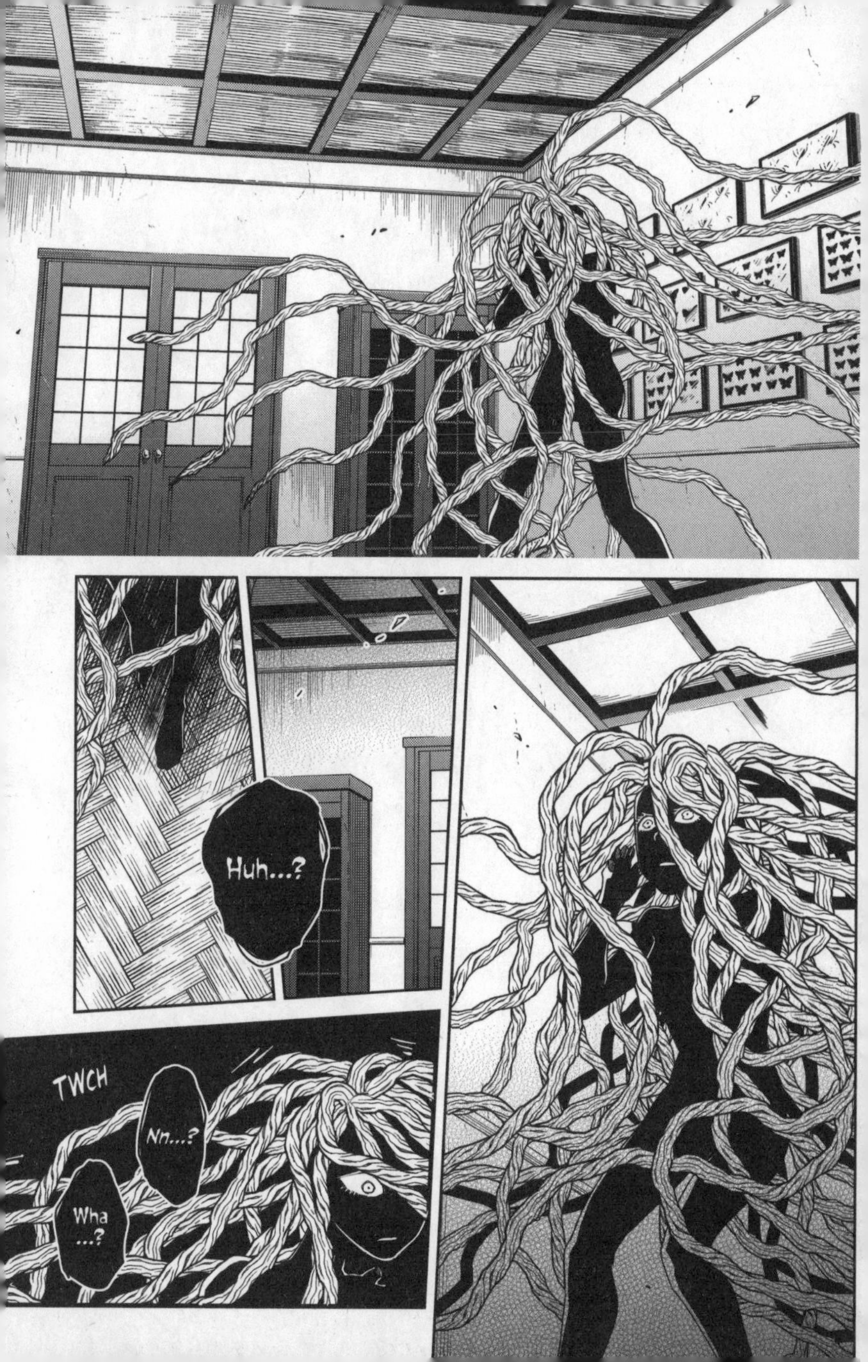
Huh...?
Nn...?
TWCH
Wha
...?

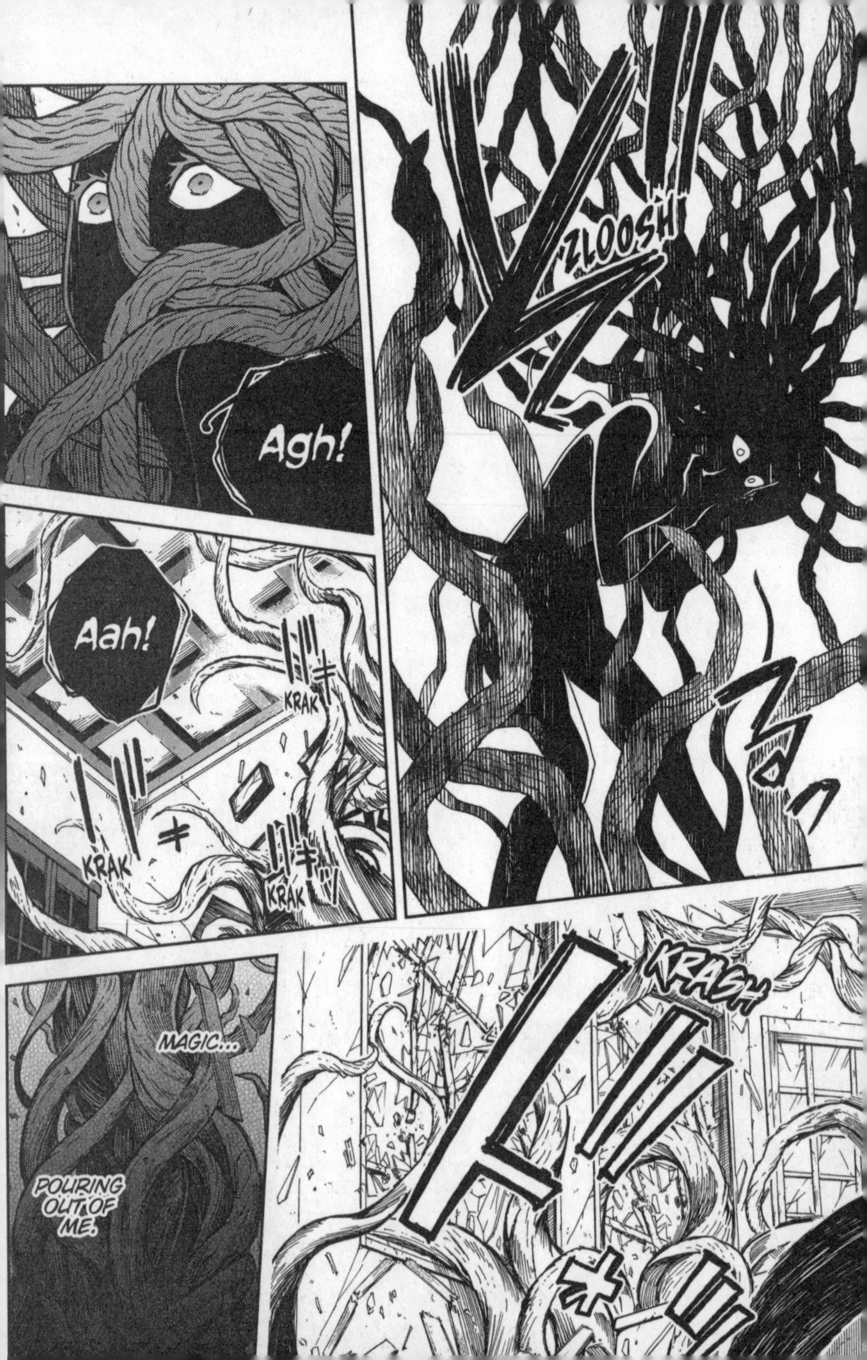
ZLOOSH
Agh!
Aah!
KRAK
KRAK
KRAK
KRASH
MAGIC...
POURING OUT OF ME.

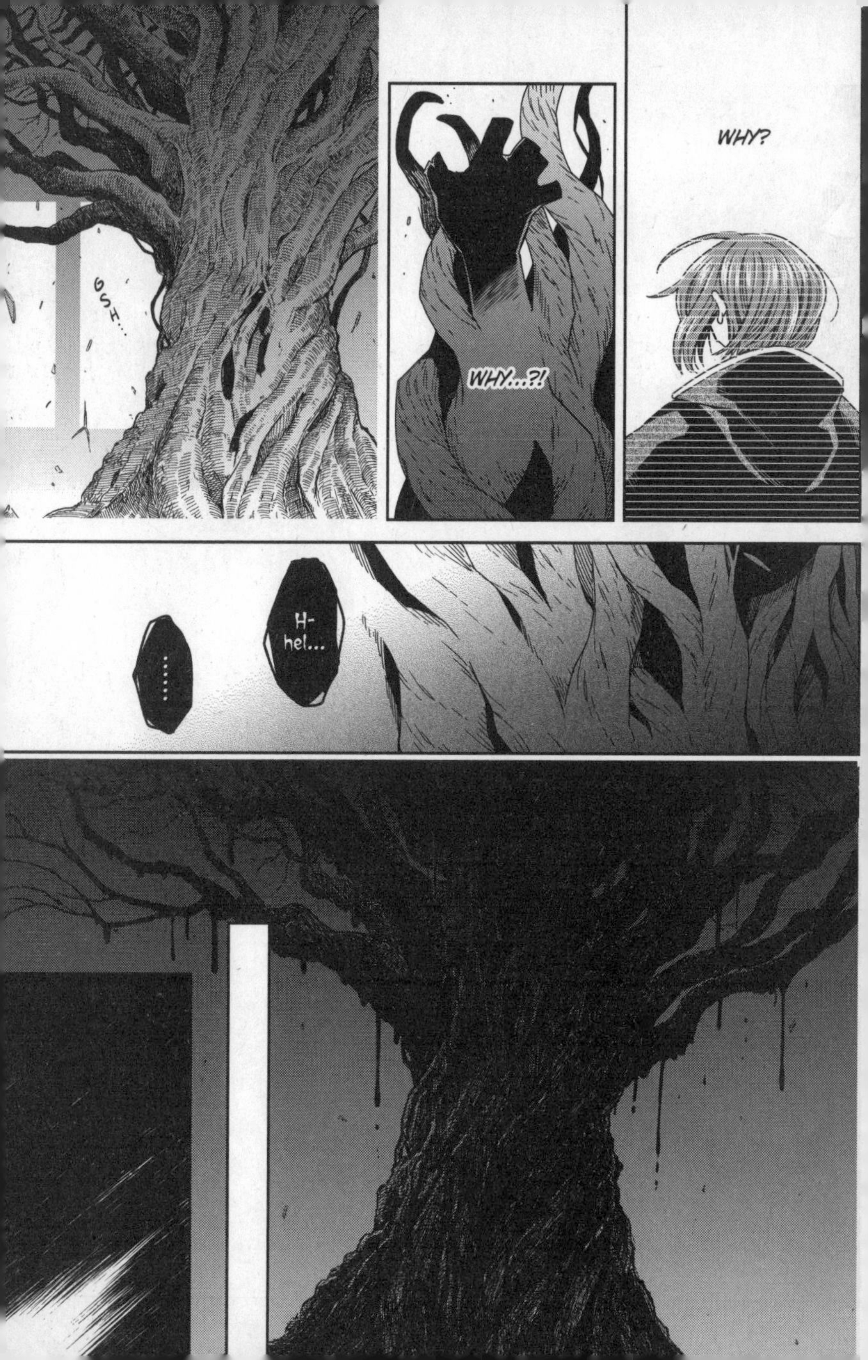
WHY?
WHY...?!
GSH...
H-hel...
......

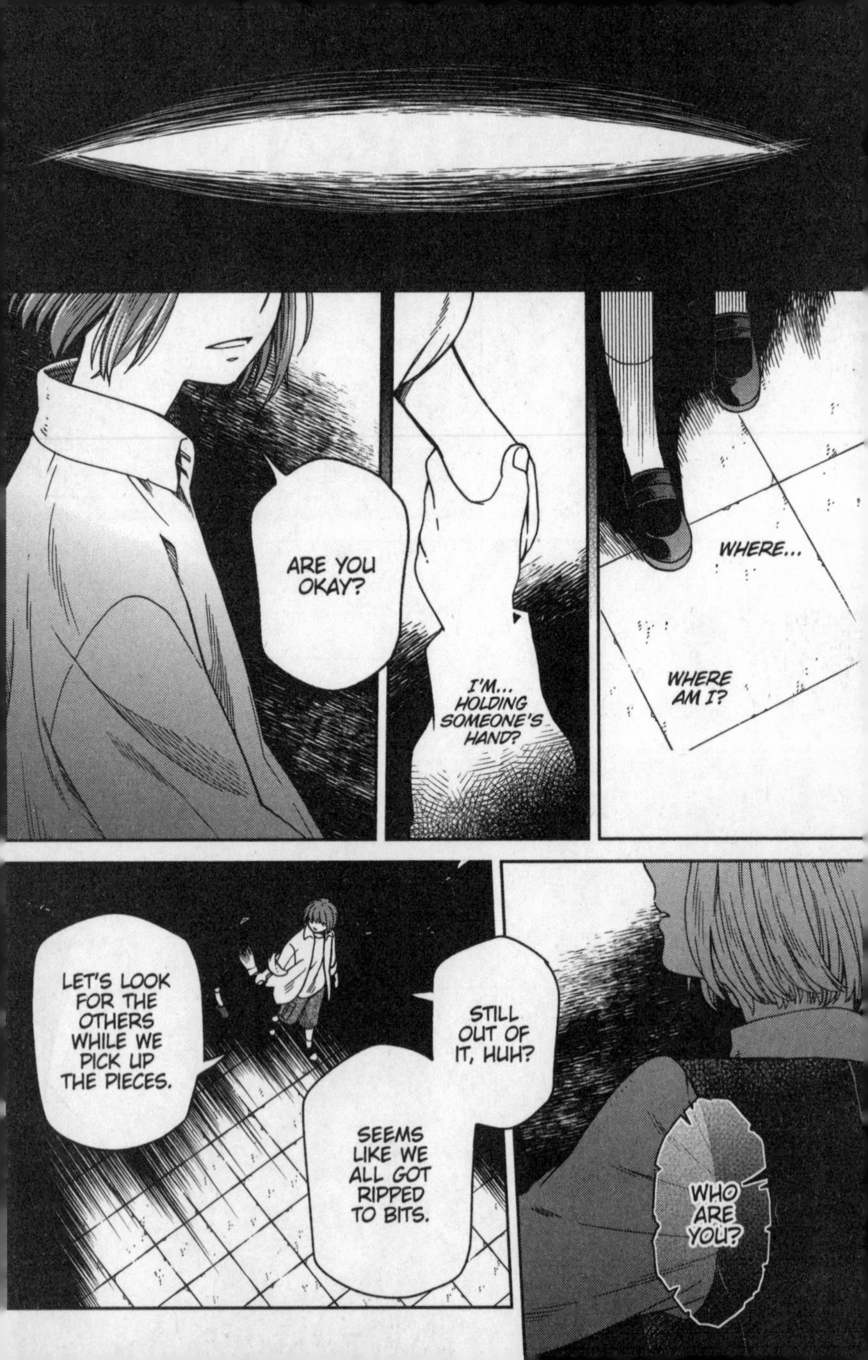
WHERE...
WHERE AM I?
I'M... HOLDING SOMEONE'S HAND?
ARE YOU OKAY?
WHO ARE YOU?
STILL OUT OF IT, HUH?
SEEMS LIKE WE ALL GOT RIPPED TO BITS.
LET'S LOOK FOR THE OTHERS WHILE WE PICK UP THE PIECES.

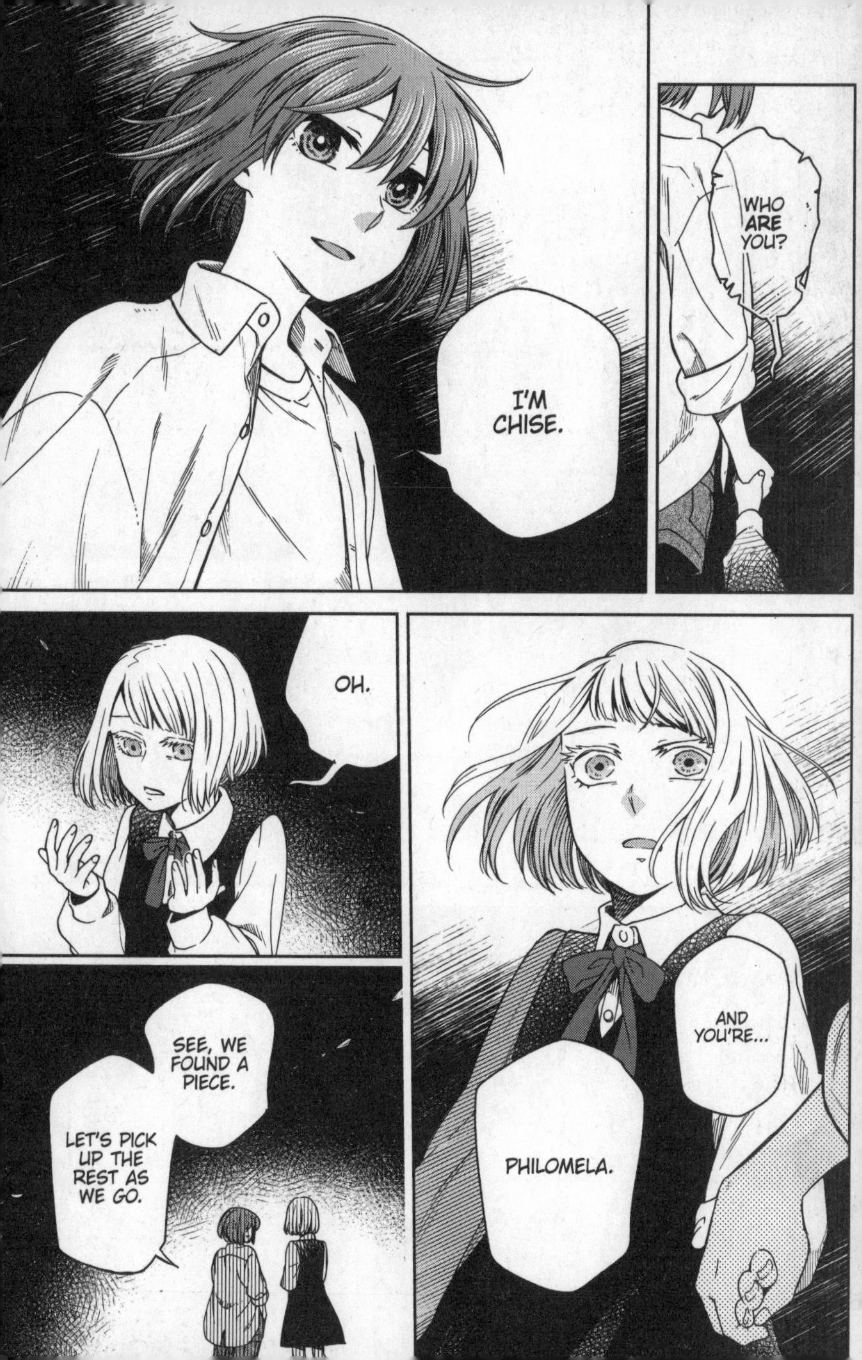
WHO ARE YOU?
I'M CHISE.
AND YOU'RE...
PHILOMELA.
OH.
SEE, WE FOUND A PIECE.
LET'S PICK UP THE REST AS WE GO.

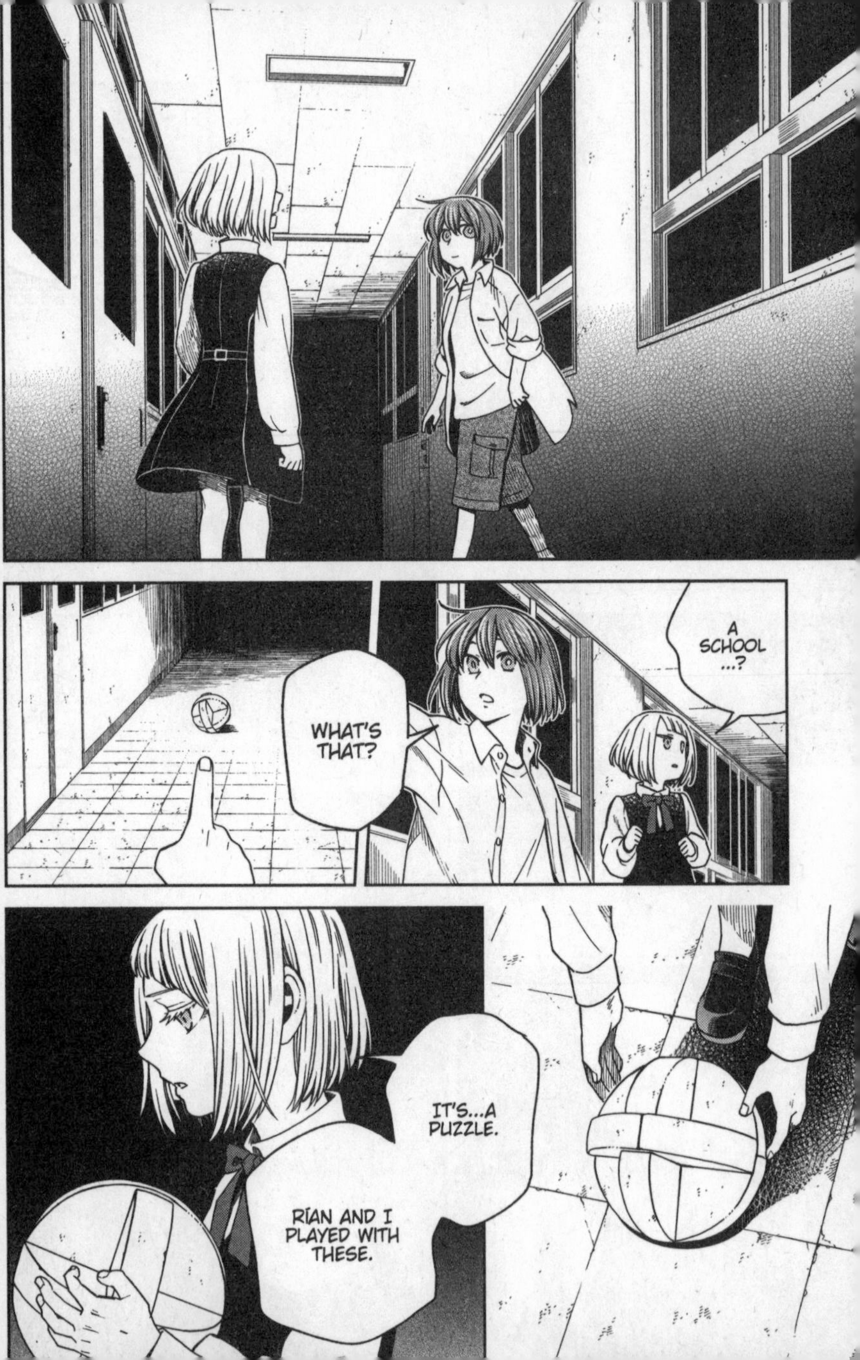
A SCHOOL ...?
WHAT'S THAT?
IT'S...A PUZZLE.
RÍAN AND I PLAYED WITH THESE.

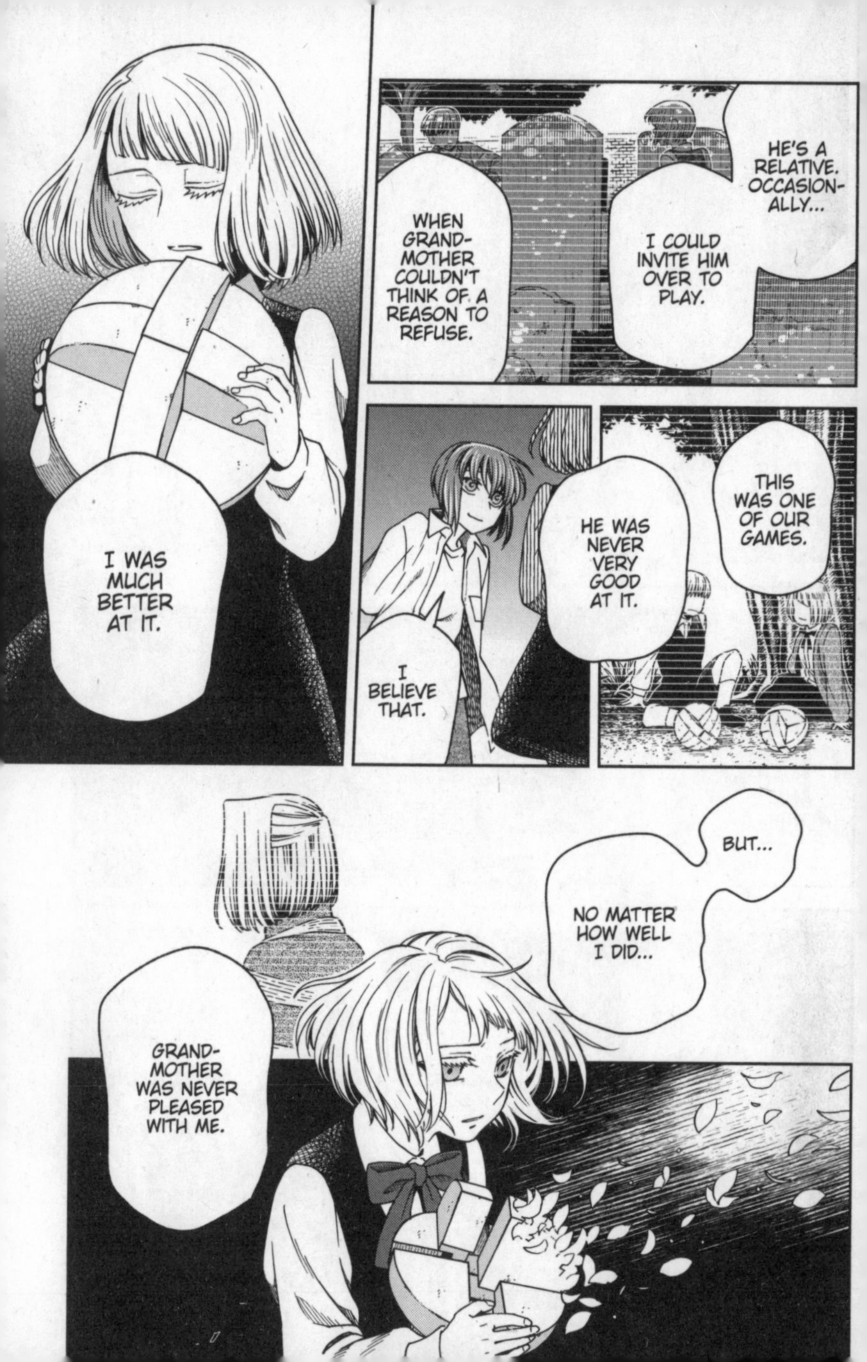
HE'S A RELATIVE. OCCASION-ALLY...
I COULD INVITE HIM OVER TO PLAY.
WHEN GRAND-MOTHER COULDN'T THINK OF A REASON TO REFUSE.
THIS WAS ONE OF OUR GAMES.
HE WAS NEVER VERY GOOD AT IT.
I BELIEVE THAT.
I WAS MUCH BETTER AT IT.
BUT...
NO MATTER HOW WELL I DID...
GRAND-MOTHER WAS NEVER PLEASED WITH ME.

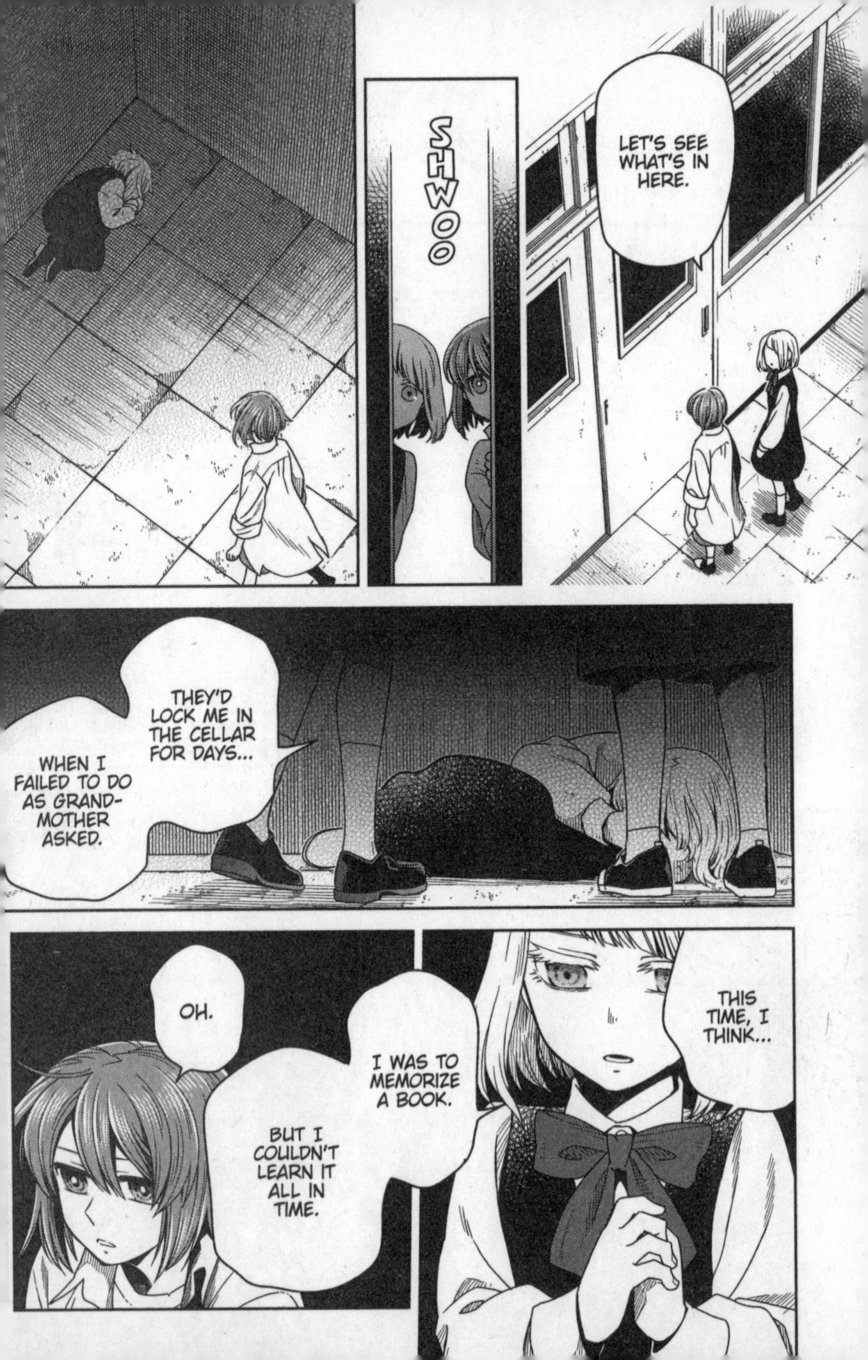
LET'S SEE WHAT'S IN HERE.
SHWOO
THEY'D LOCK ME IN THE CELLAR FOR DAYS...
WHEN I FAILED TO DO AS GRAND-MOTHER ASKED.
THIS TIME, I THINK...
I WAS TO MEMORIZE A BOOK.
BUT I COULDN'T LEARN IT ALL IN TIME.
OH.

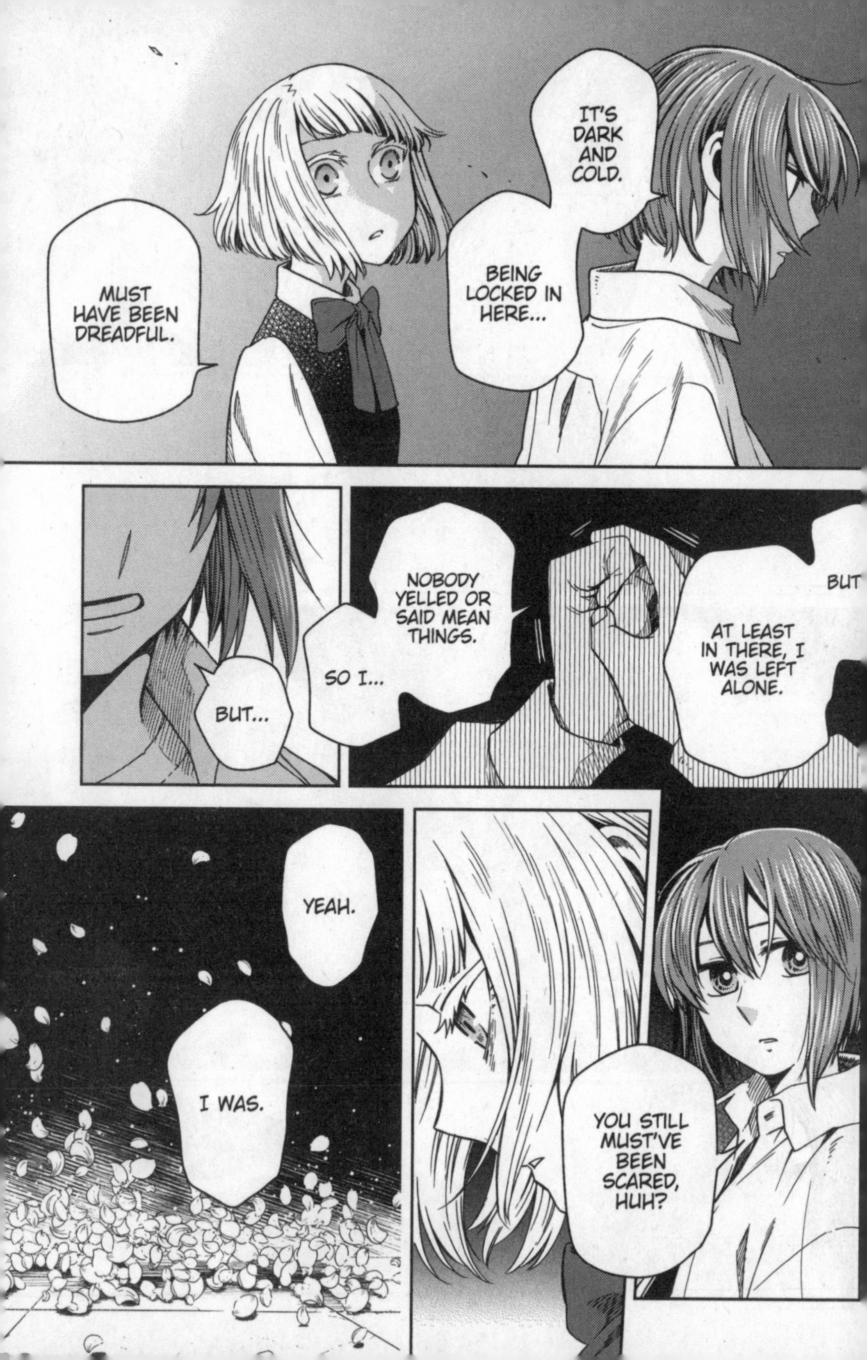
IT'S DARK AND COLD.
BEING LOCKED IN HERE...
MUST HAVE BEEN DREADFUL.
BUT
AT LEAST IN THERE, I WAS LEFT ALONE.
NOBODY YELLED OR SAID MEAN THINGS.
SO I...
BUT...
YOU STILL MUST'VE BEEN SCARED, HUH?
YEAH.
I WAS.

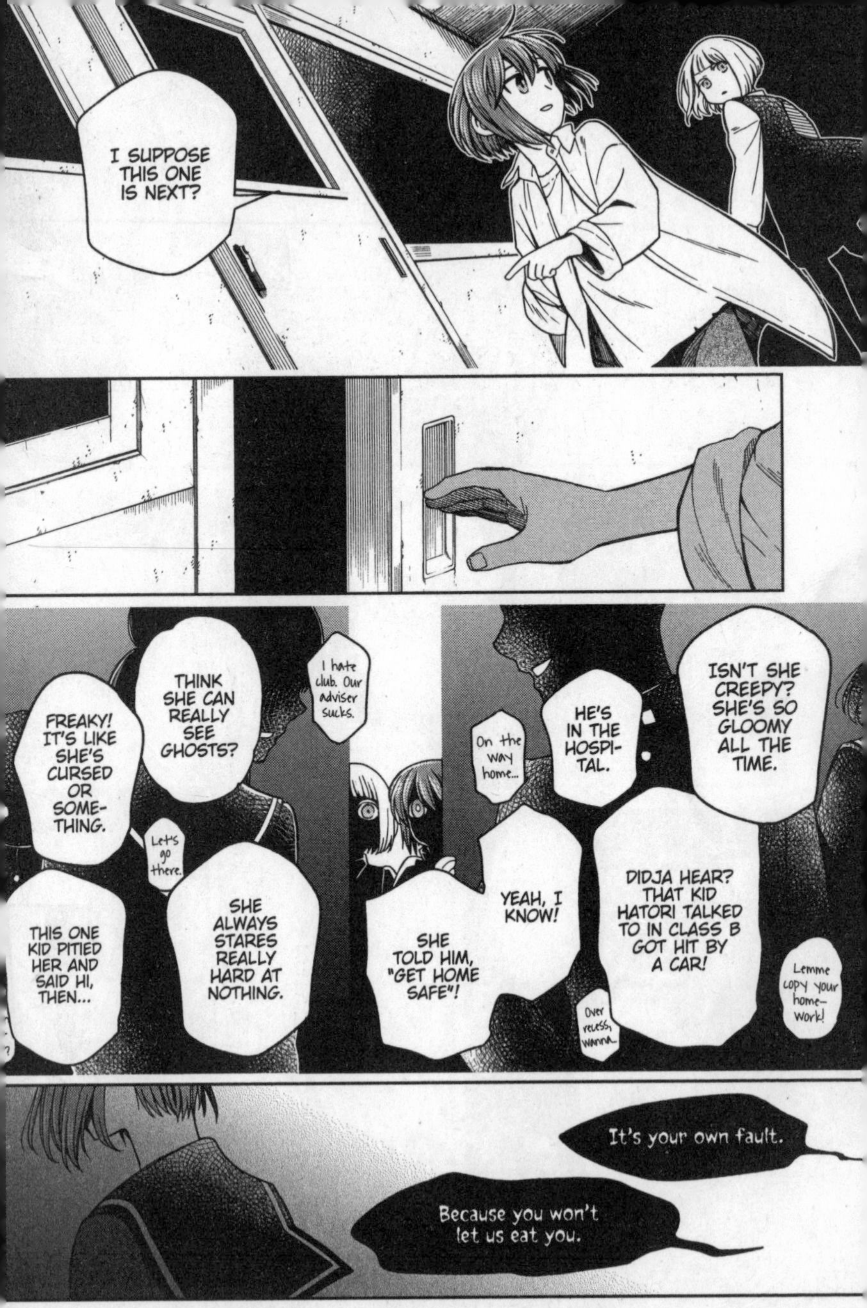
I SUPPOSE THIS ONE IS NEXT?
ISN'T SHE CREEPY? SHE'S SO GLOOMY ALL THE TIME.
HE'S IN THE HOSPITAL.
On the way home...
Lemme copy your home-work!
DIDJA HEAR? THAT KID HATORI TALKED TO IN CLASS B GOT HIT BY A CAR!
YEAH, I KNOW!
Over recess, wanna...
SHE TOLD HIM, "GET HOME SAFE"!
I hate club. Our adviser sucks.
THINK SHE CAN REALLY SEE GHOSTS?
FREAKY! IT'S LIKE SHE'S CURSED OR SOME-THING.
Let's go there.
SHE ALWAYS STARES REALLY HARD AT NOTHING.
THIS ONE KID PITIED HER AND SAID HI, THEN...
It's your own fault.
Because you won't let us eat you.

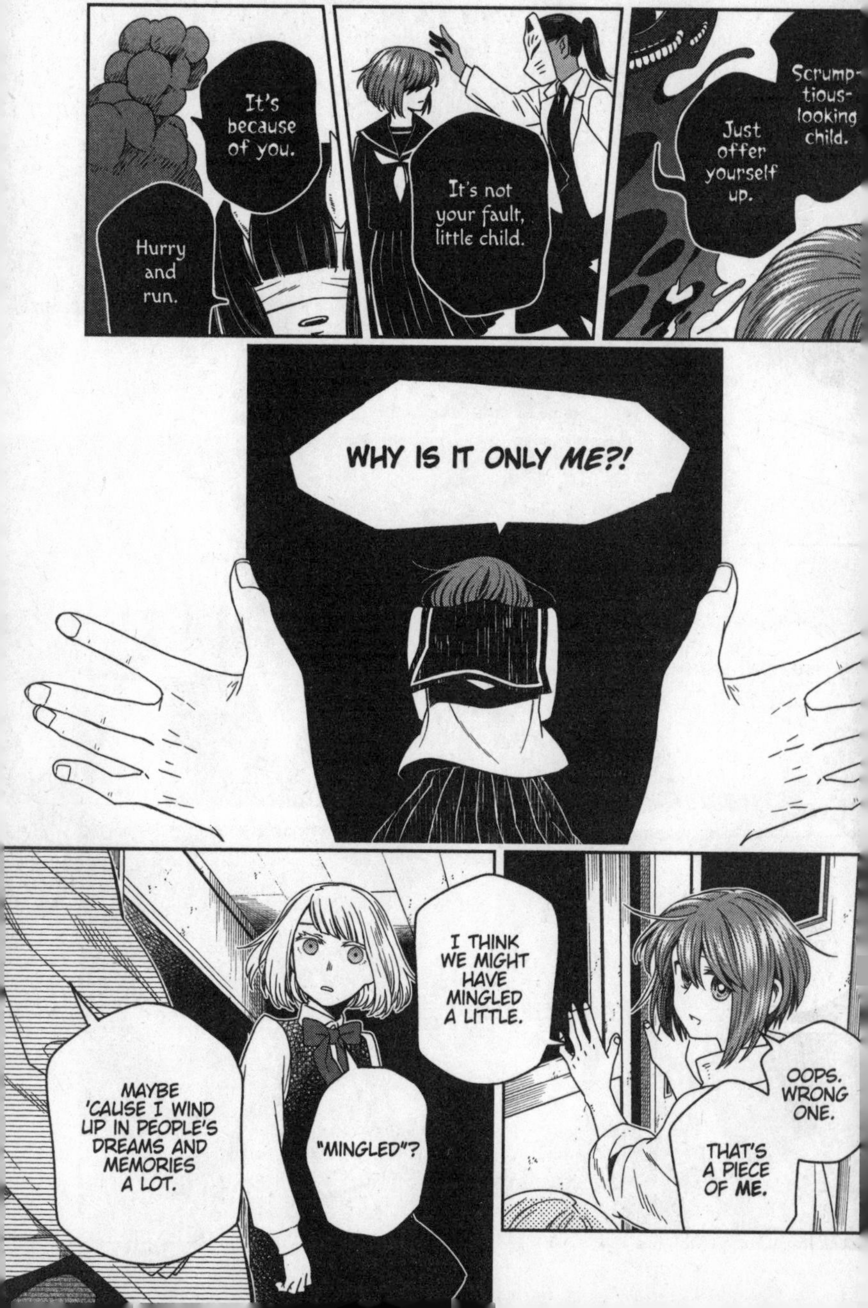
Scrump-tious-looking child.
Just offer yourself up.
It's not your fault, little child.
It's because of you.
Hurry and run.
WHY IS IT ONLY ME?!
OOPS. WRONG ONE.
THAT'S A PIECE OF ME.
I THINK WE MIGHT HAVE MINGLED A LITTLE.
"MINGLED"?
MAYBE 'CAUSE I WIND UP IN PEOPLE'S DREAMS AND MEMORIES A LOT.

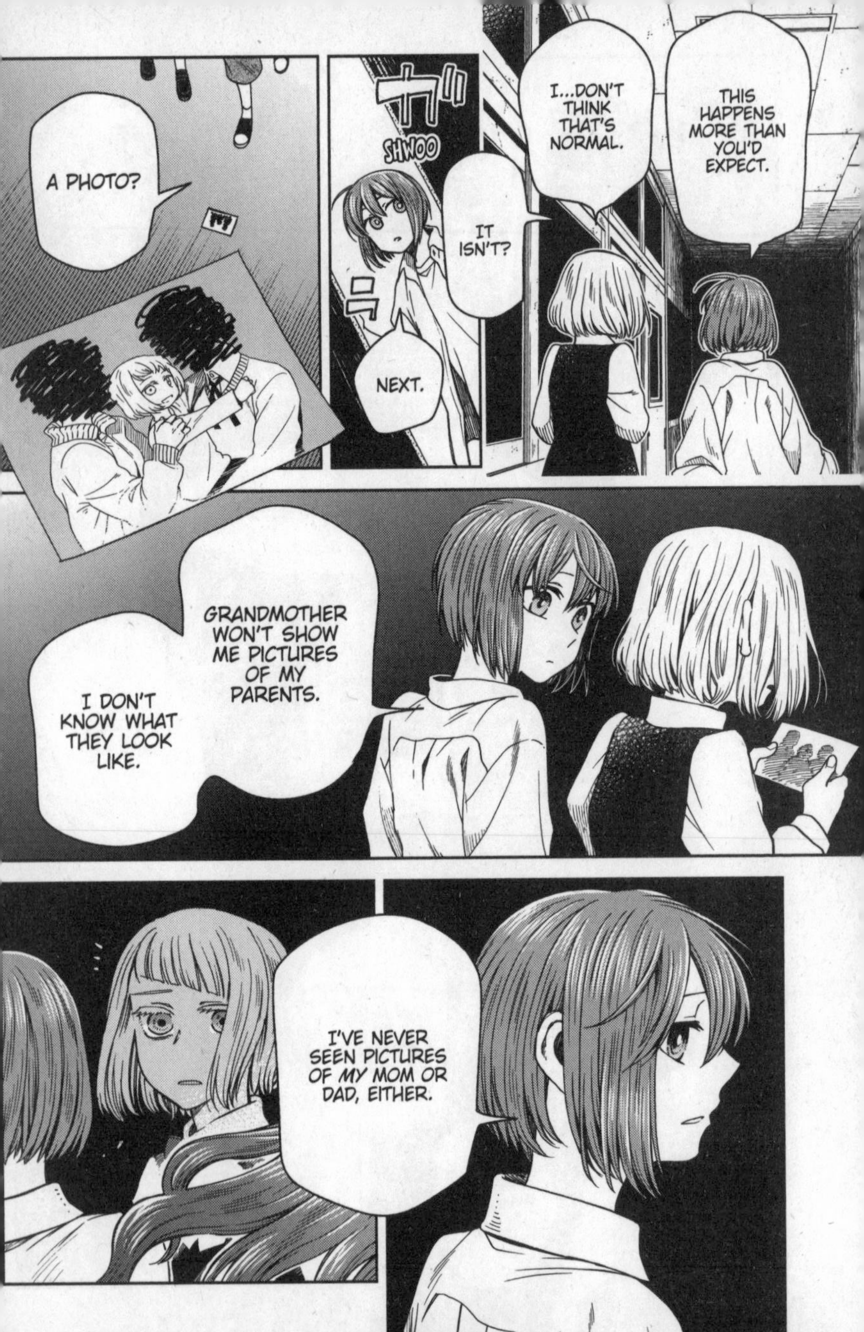
THIS HAPPENS MORE THAN YOU'D EXPECT.
I...DON'T THINK THAT'S NORMAL.
SHWOO
IT ISN'T?
NEXT.
A PHOTO?
GRANDMOTHER WON'T SHOW ME PICTURES OF MY PARENTS.
I DON'T KNOW WHAT THEY LOOK LIKE.
I'VE NEVER SEEN PICTURES OF *MY* MOM OR DAD, EITHER.

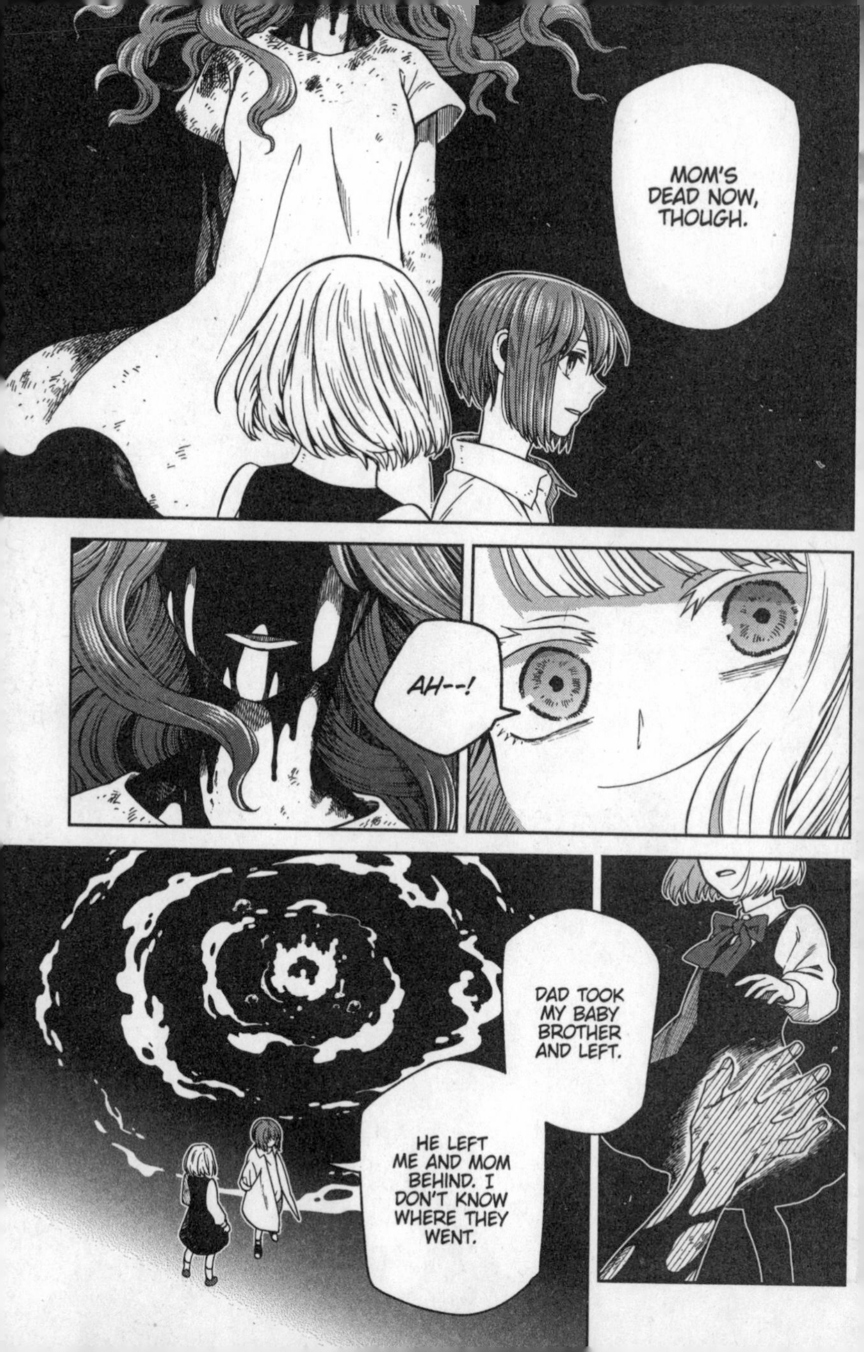
MOM'S DEAD NOW, THOUGH.
AH--!
DAD TOOK MY BABY BROTHER AND LEFT.
HE LEFT ME AND MOM BEHIND. I DON'T KNOW WHERE THEY WENT.

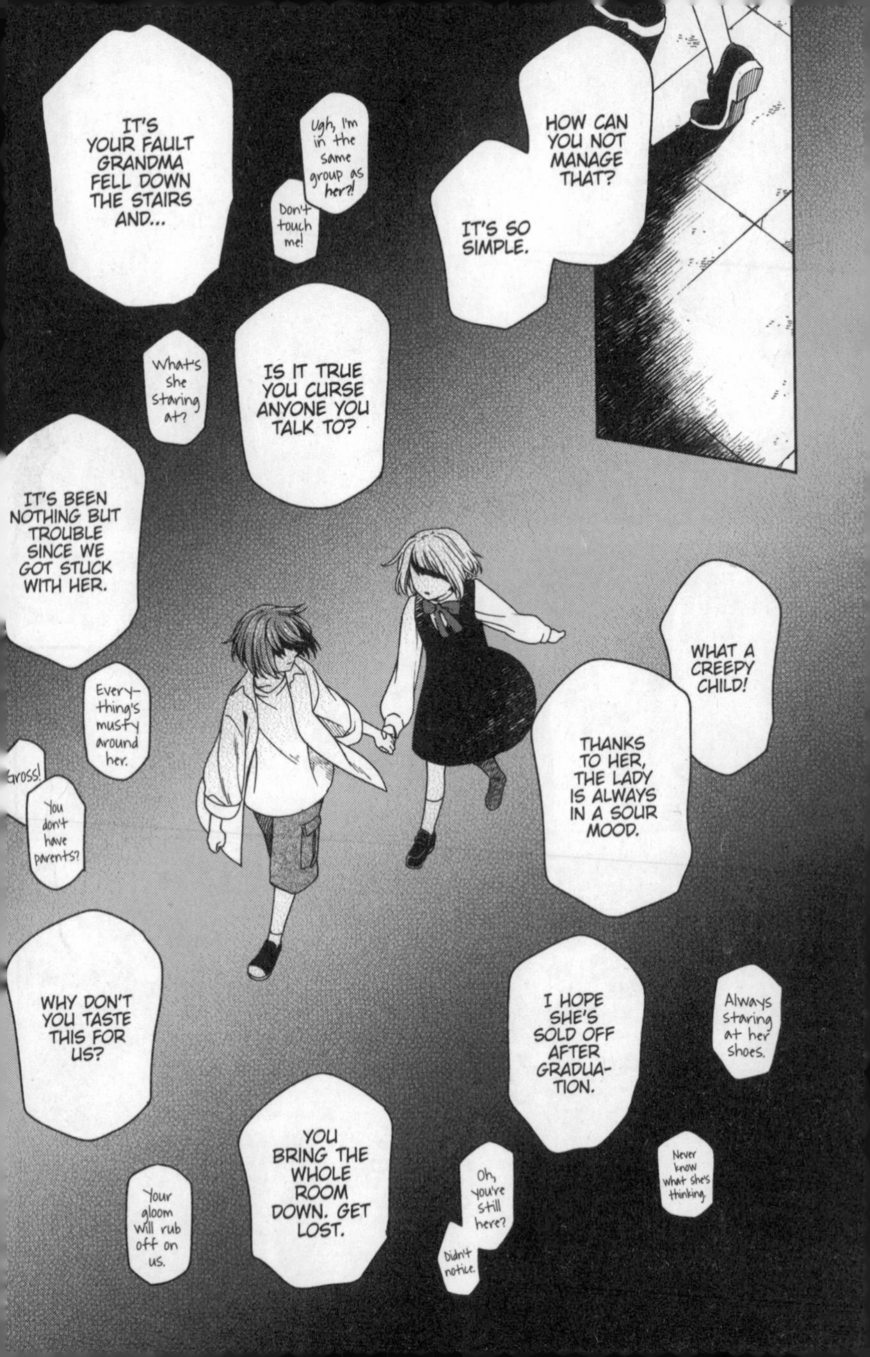
HOW CAN YOU NOT MANAGE THAT?
IT'S SO SIMPLE.
Ugh, I'm in the same group as her?!
Don't touch me!
IT'S YOUR FAULT GRANDMA FELL DOWN THE STAIRS AND...
IS IT TRUE YOU CURSE ANYONE YOU TALK TO?
What's she staring at?
IT'S BEEN NOTHING BUT TROUBLE SINCE WE GOT STUCK WITH HER.
WHAT A CREEPY CHILD!
THANKS TO HER, THE LADY IS ALWAYS IN A SOUR MOOD.
Every-thing's musty around her.
Gross!
You don't have parents?
Always staring at her shoes.
I HOPE SHE'S SOLD OFF AFTER GRADUA-TION.
WHY DON'T YOU TASTE THIS FOR US?
Never know what she's thinking.
Oh, you're still here?
Didn't notice.
YOU BRING THE WHOLE ROOM DOWN. GET LOST.
Your gloom will rub off on us.

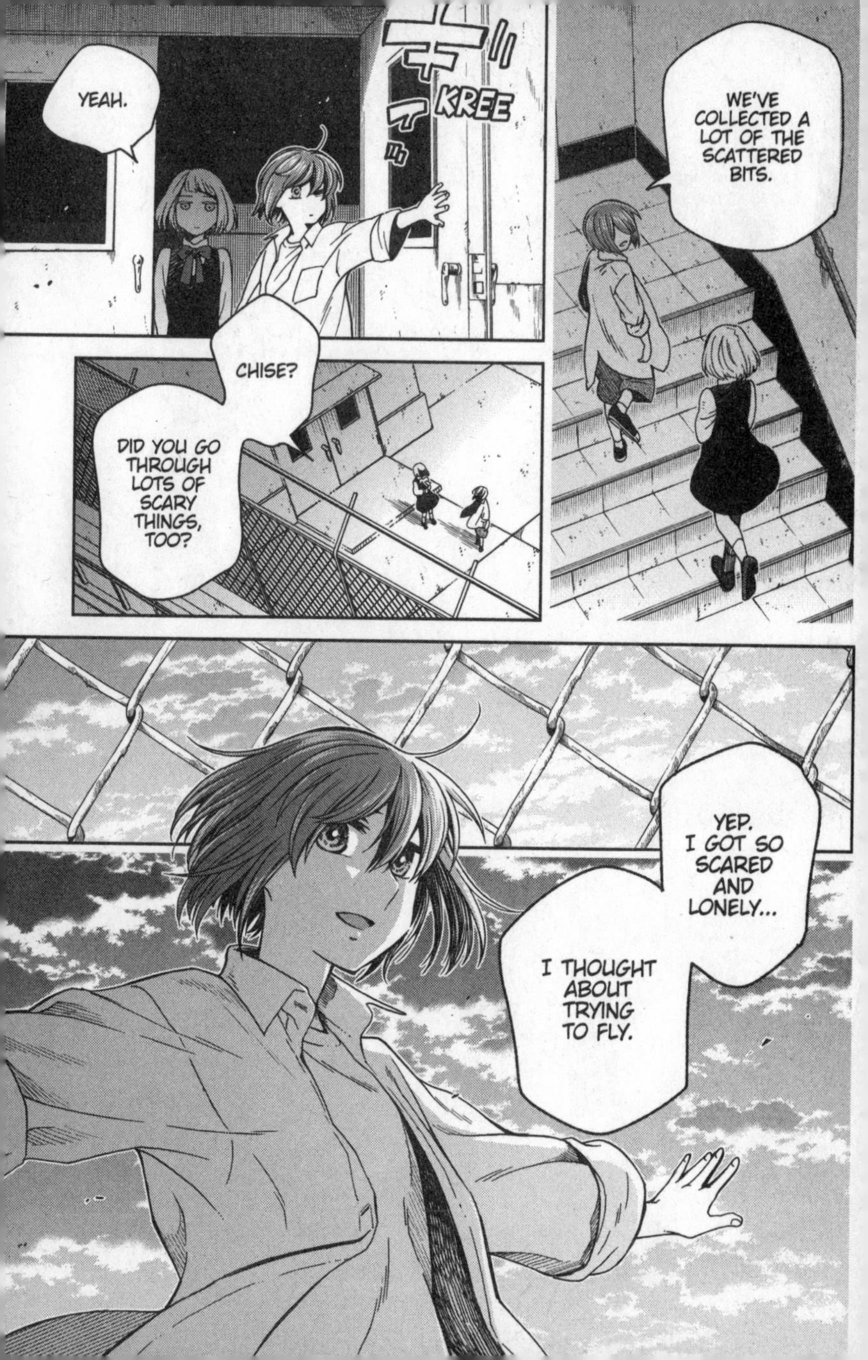
WE'VE COLLECTED A LOT OF THE SCATTERED BITS.
KREE
YEAH.
CHISE?
DID YOU GO THROUGH LOTS OF SCARY THINGS, TOO?
YEP. I GOT SO SCARED AND LONELY...
I THOUGHT ABOUT TRYING TO FLY.

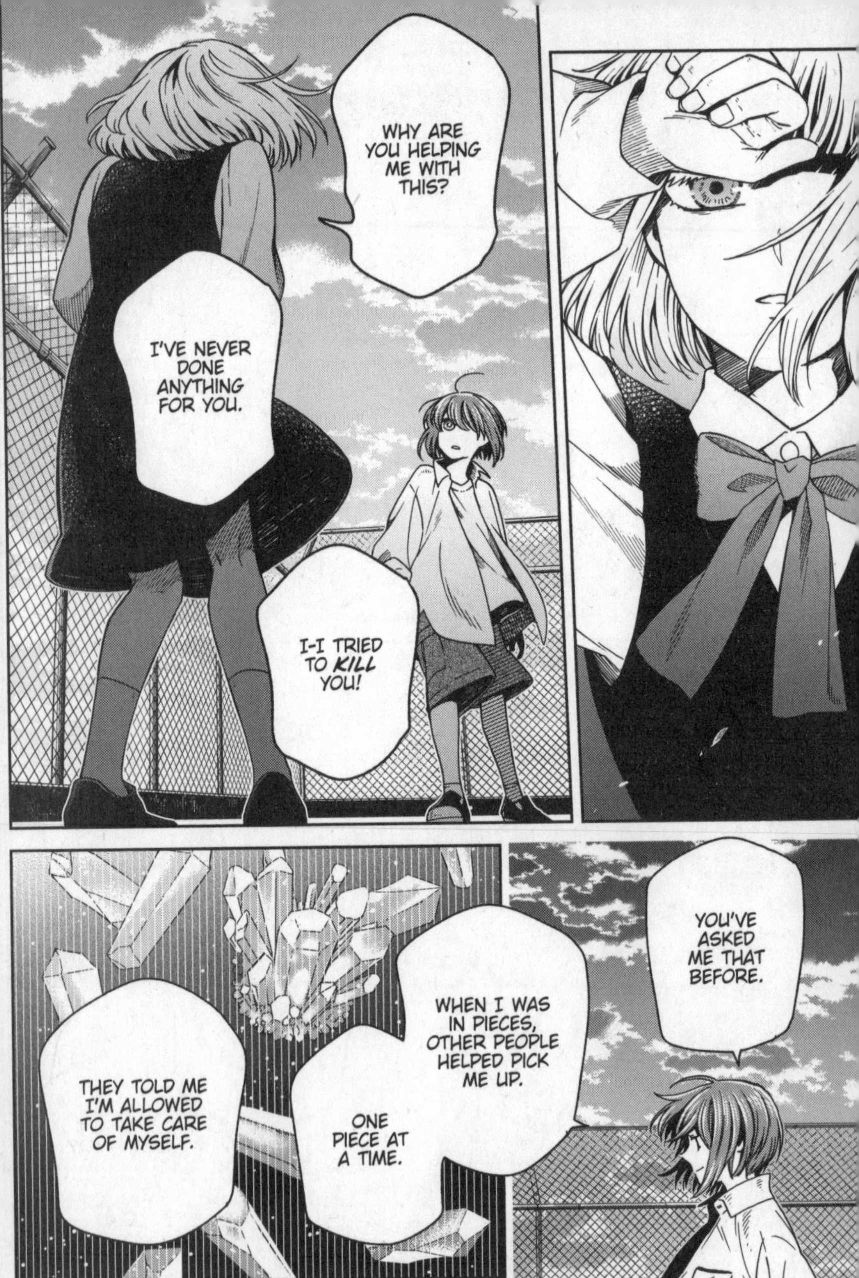
WHY ARE YOU HELPING ME WITH THIS?
I'VE NEVER DONE ANYTHING FOR YOU.
I-I TRIED TO *KILL* YOU!
YOU'VE ASKED ME THAT BEFORE.
WHEN I WAS IN PIECES, OTHER PEOPLE HELPED PICK ME UP.
ONE PIECE AT A TIME.
THEY TOLD ME I'M ALLOWED TO TAKE CARE OF MYSELF.

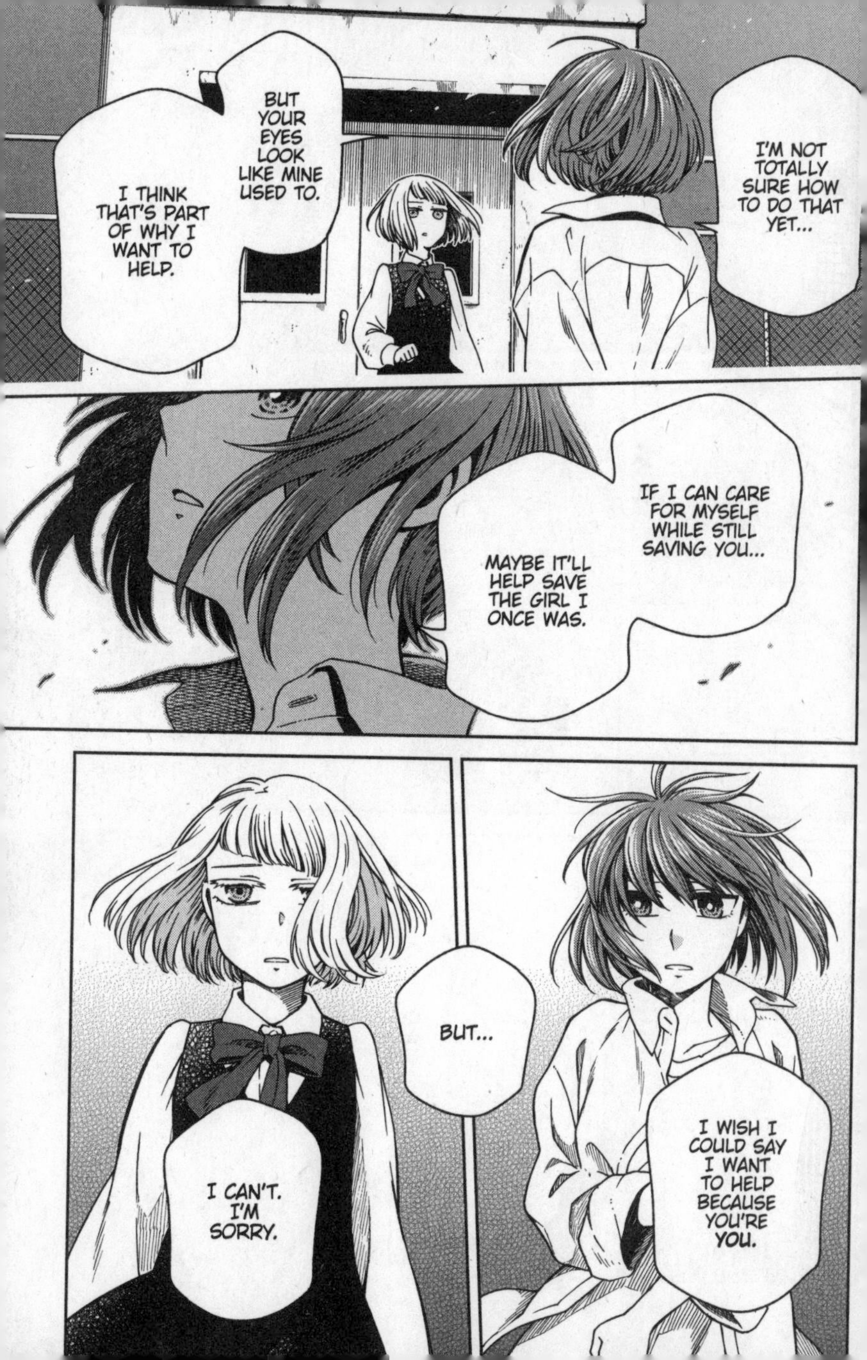
I'M NOT TOTALLY SURE HOW TO DO THAT YET...
BUT YOUR EYES LOOK LIKE MINE USED TO.
I THINK THAT'S PART OF WHY I WANT TO HELP.
IF I CAN CARE FOR MYSELF WHILE STILL SAVING YOU...
MAYBE IT'LL HELP SAVE THE GIRL I ONCE WAS.
I WISH I COULD SAY I WANT TO HELP BECAUSE YOU'RE YOU.
BUT...
I CAN'T. I'M SORRY.

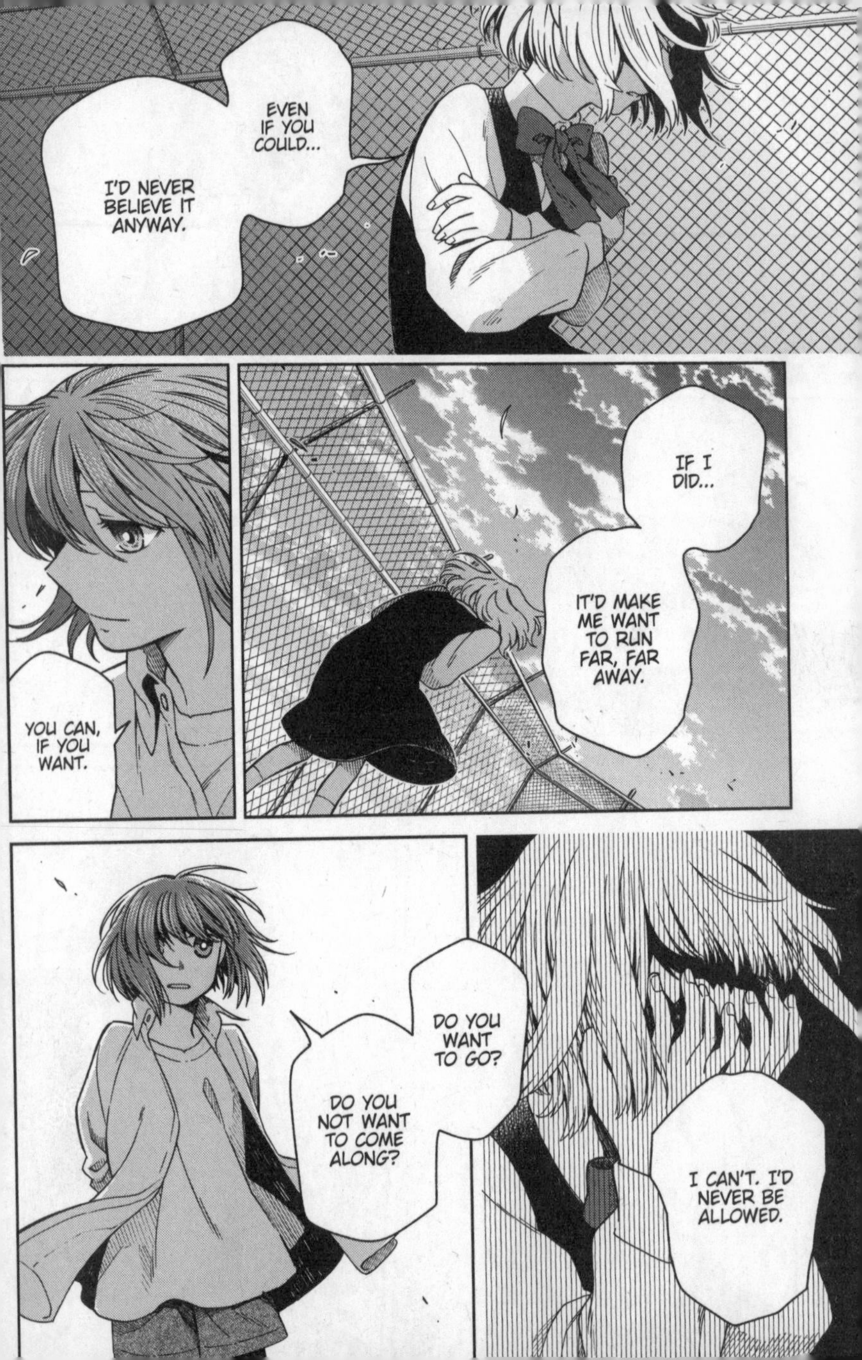
EVEN IF YOU COULD...
I'D NEVER BELIEVE IT ANYWAY.
IF I DID...
IT'D MAKE ME WANT TO RUN FAR, FAR AWAY.
YOU CAN, IF YOU WANT.
I CAN'T. I'D NEVER BE ALLOWED.
DO YOU WANT TO GO?
DO YOU NOT WANT TO COME ALONG?

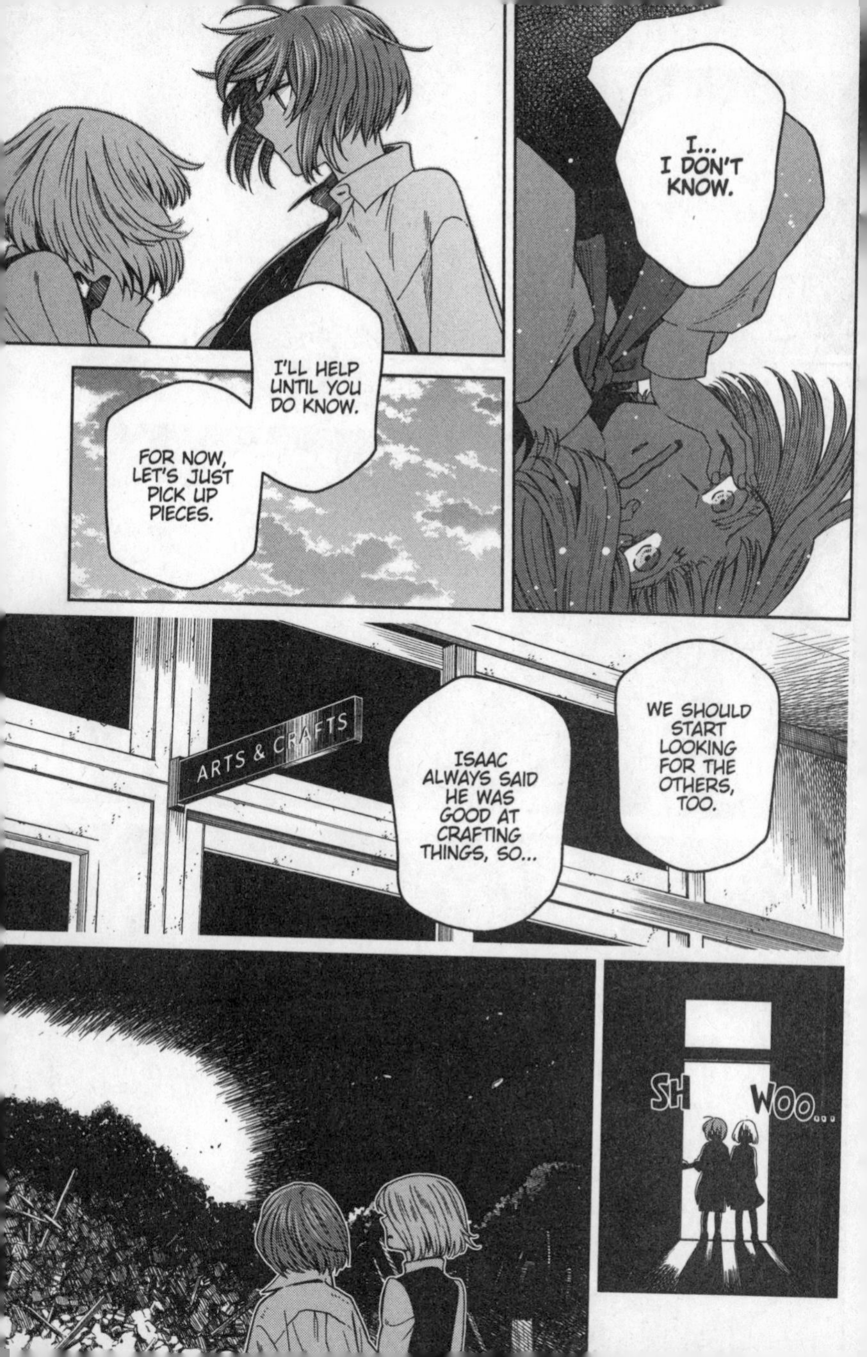
I... I DON'T KNOW.
I'LL HELP UNTIL YOU DO KNOW.
FOR NOW, LET'S JUST PICK UP PIECES.
WE SHOULD START LOOKING FOR THE OTHERS, TOO.
ISAAC ALWAYS SAID HE WAS GOOD AT CRAFTING THINGS, SO...
ARTS & CRAFTS
SH WOO...

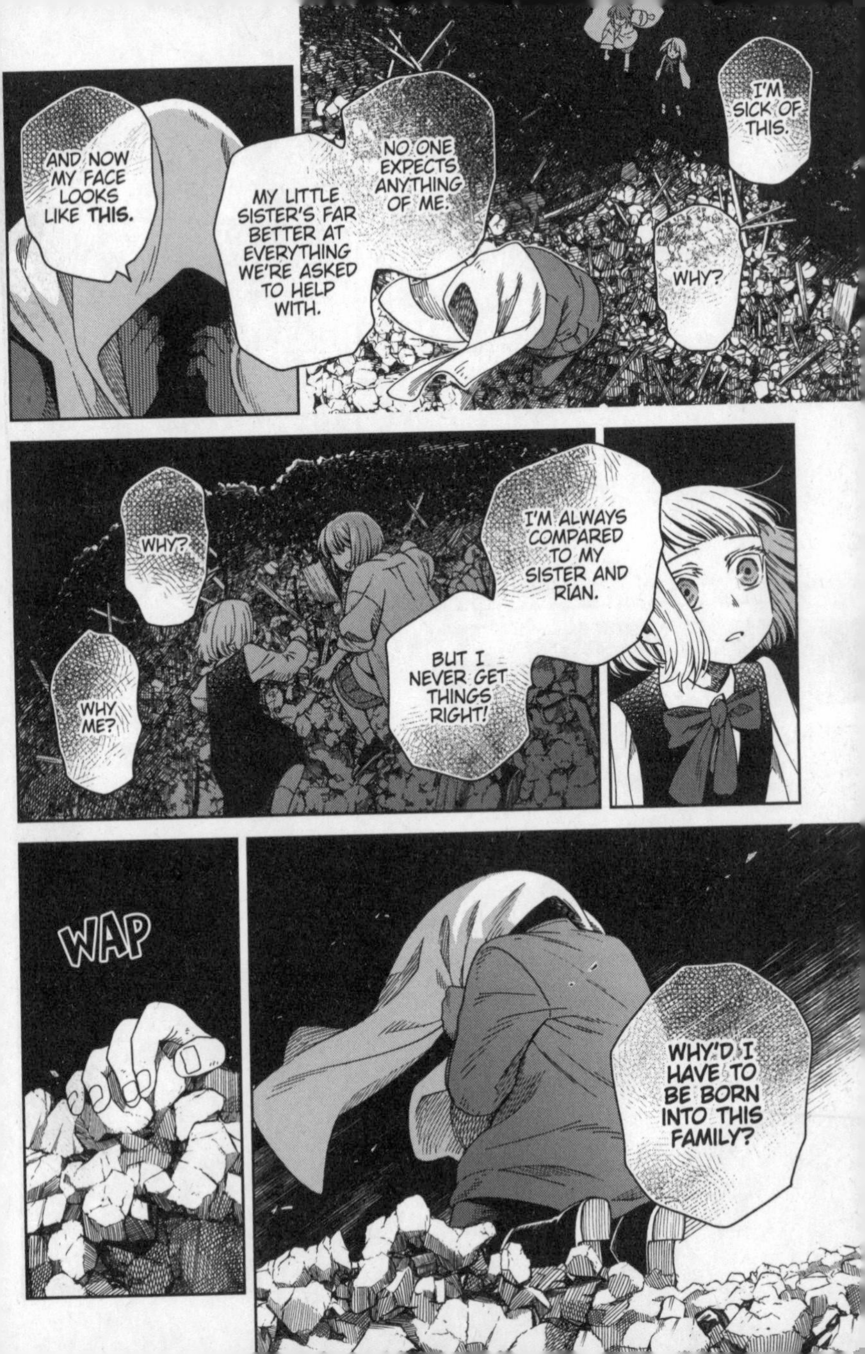
I'M SICK OF THIS.
WHY?
NO ONE EXPECTS ANYTHING OF ME.
MY LITTLE SISTER'S FAR BETTER AT EVERYTHING WE'RE ASKED TO HELP WITH.
AND NOW MY FACE LOOKS LIKE THIS.
I'M ALWAYS COMPARED TO MY SISTER AND RÍAN.
BUT I NEVER GET THINGS RIGHT!
WHY?
WHY ME?
WHY'D I HAVE TO BE BORN INTO THIS FAMILY?
WAP

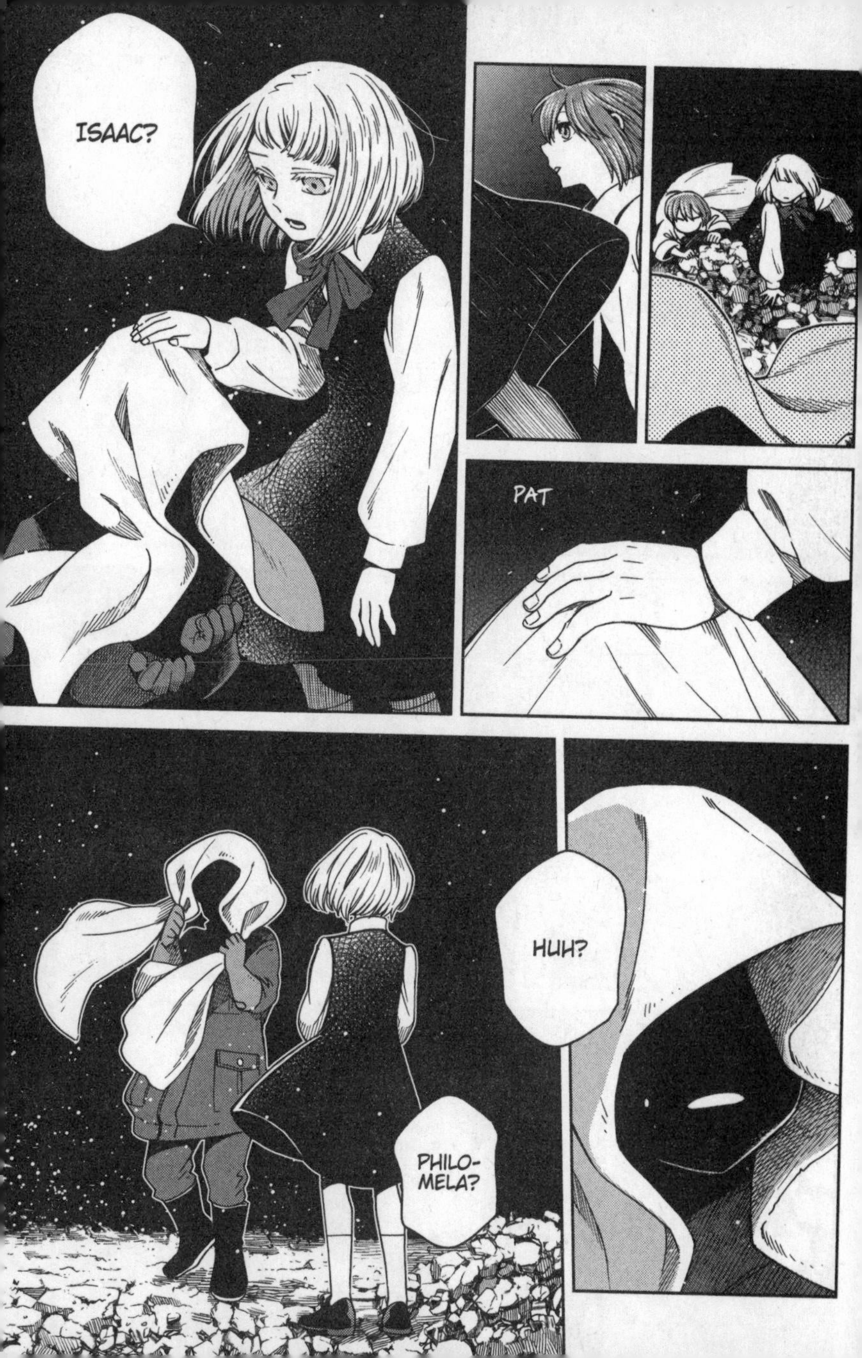
PAT
ISAAC?
HUH?
PHILO-
MELA?

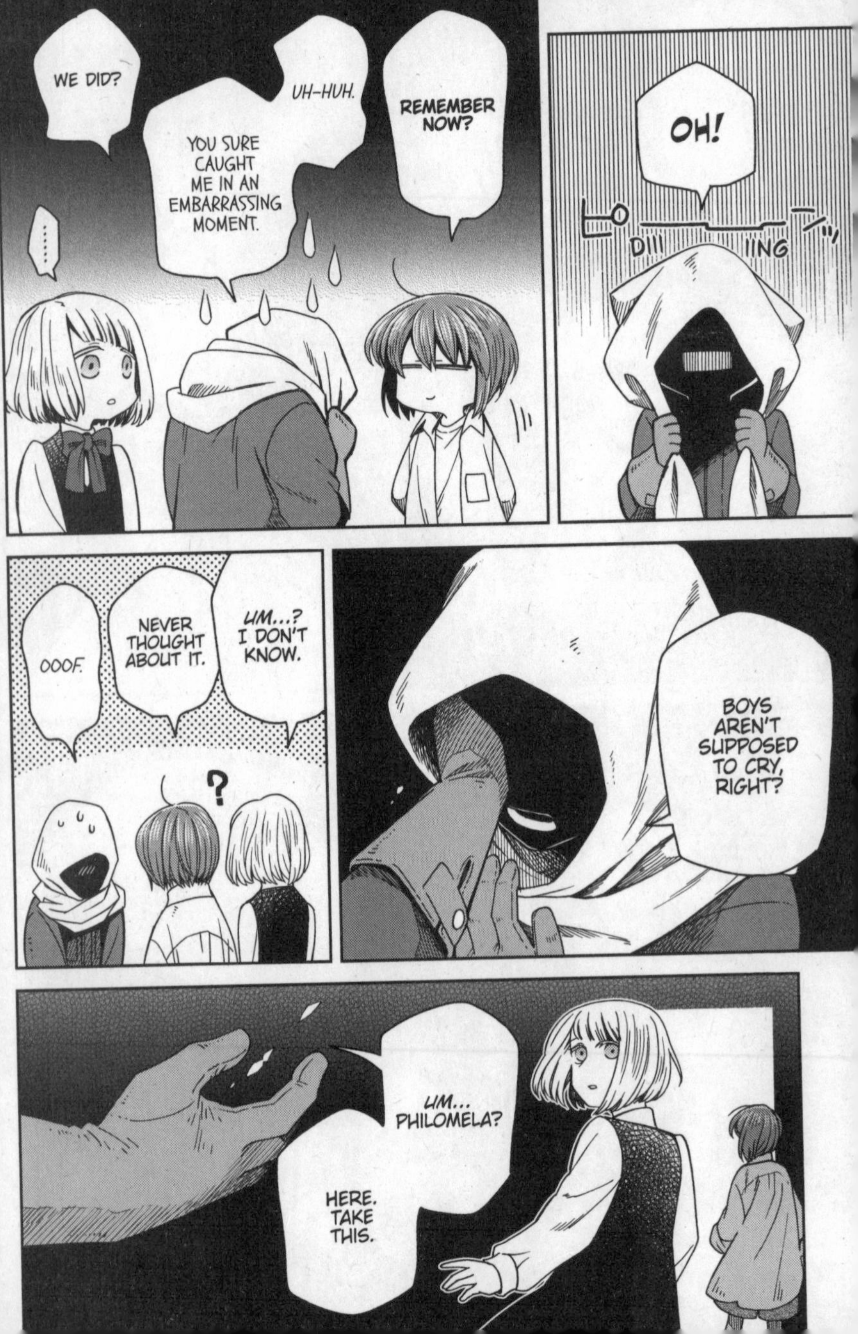
OH!
DIII IING
REMEMBER NOW?
UH-HUH.
YOU SURE CAUGHT ME IN AN EMBARRASSING MOMENT.
WE DID?
......
BOYS AREN'T SUPPOSED TO CRY, RIGHT?
UM...? I DON'T KNOW.
NEVER THOUGHT ABOUT IT.
OOOF.
?
UM... PHILOMELA?
HERE. TAKE THIS.

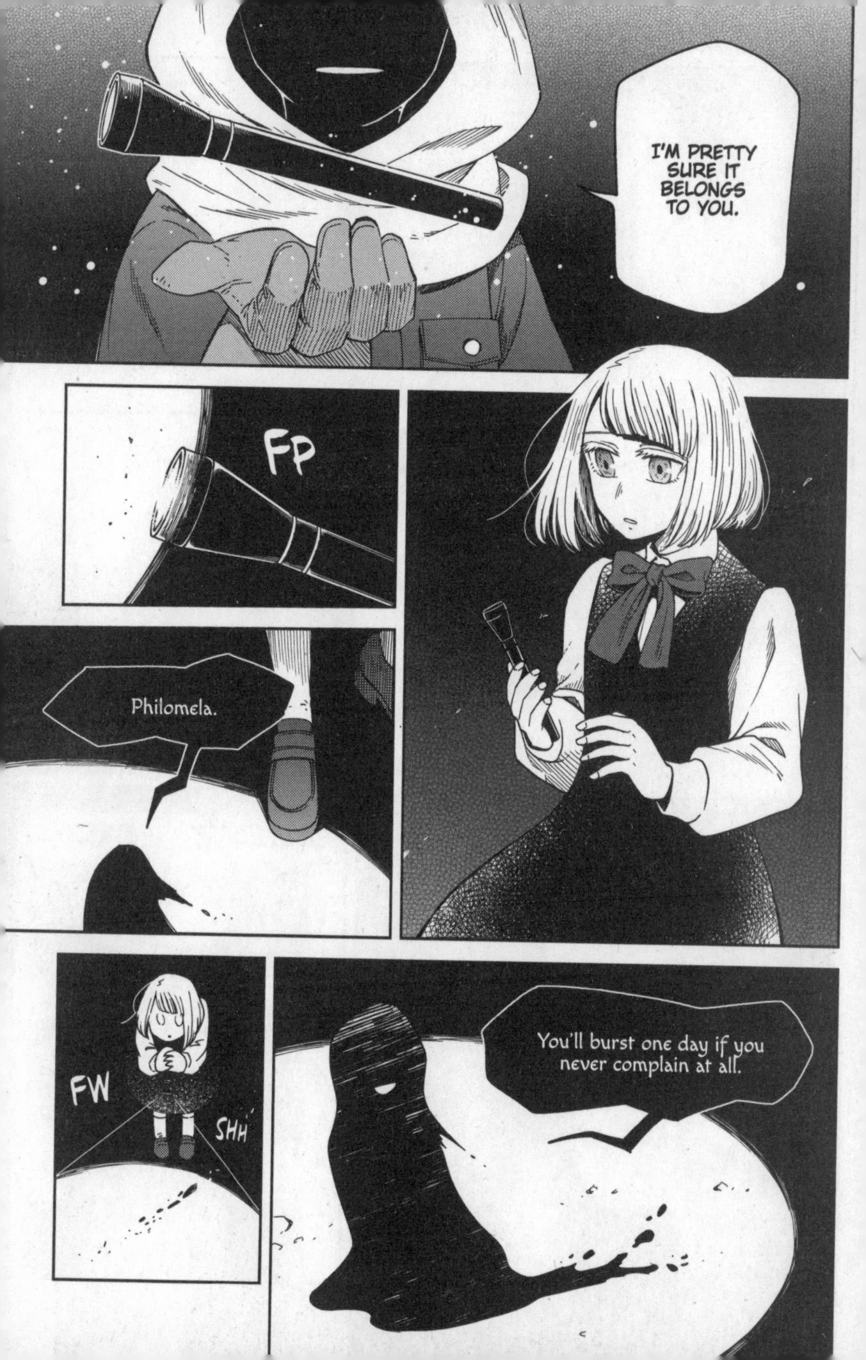
I'M PRETTY SURE IT BELONGS TO YOU.
FP
Philomela.
You'll burst one day if you never complain at all.
FW
SHH

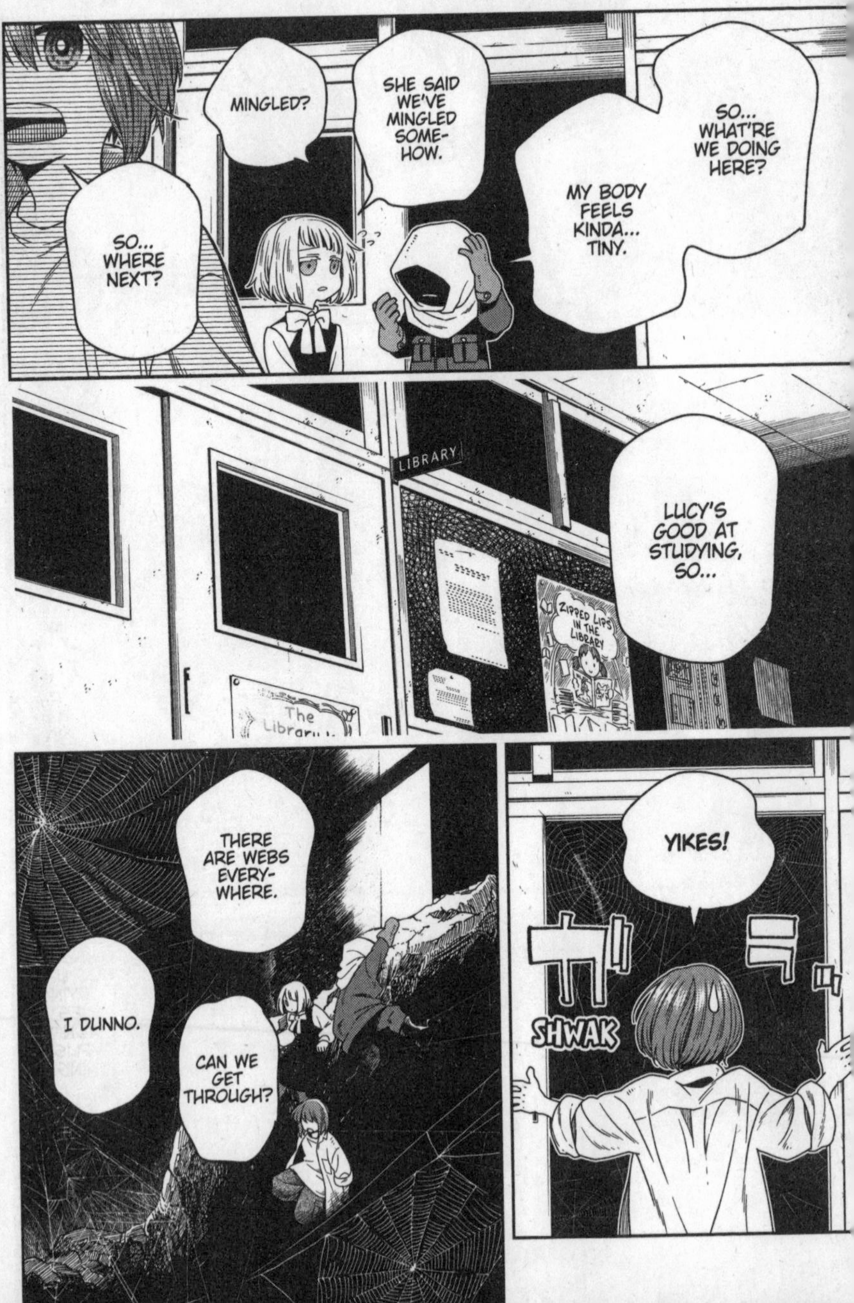
SO... WHAT'RE WE DOING HERE?
MY BODY FEELS KINDA... TINY.
SHE SAID WE'VE MINGLED SOME-HOW.
MINGLED?
SO... WHERE NEXT?
LIBRARY
LUCY'S GOOD AT STUDYING, SO...
ZIPPED LIPS IN THE LIBRARY
YIKES!
SHWAK
THERE ARE WEBS EVERY-WHERE.
CAN WE GET THROUGH?
I DUNNO.

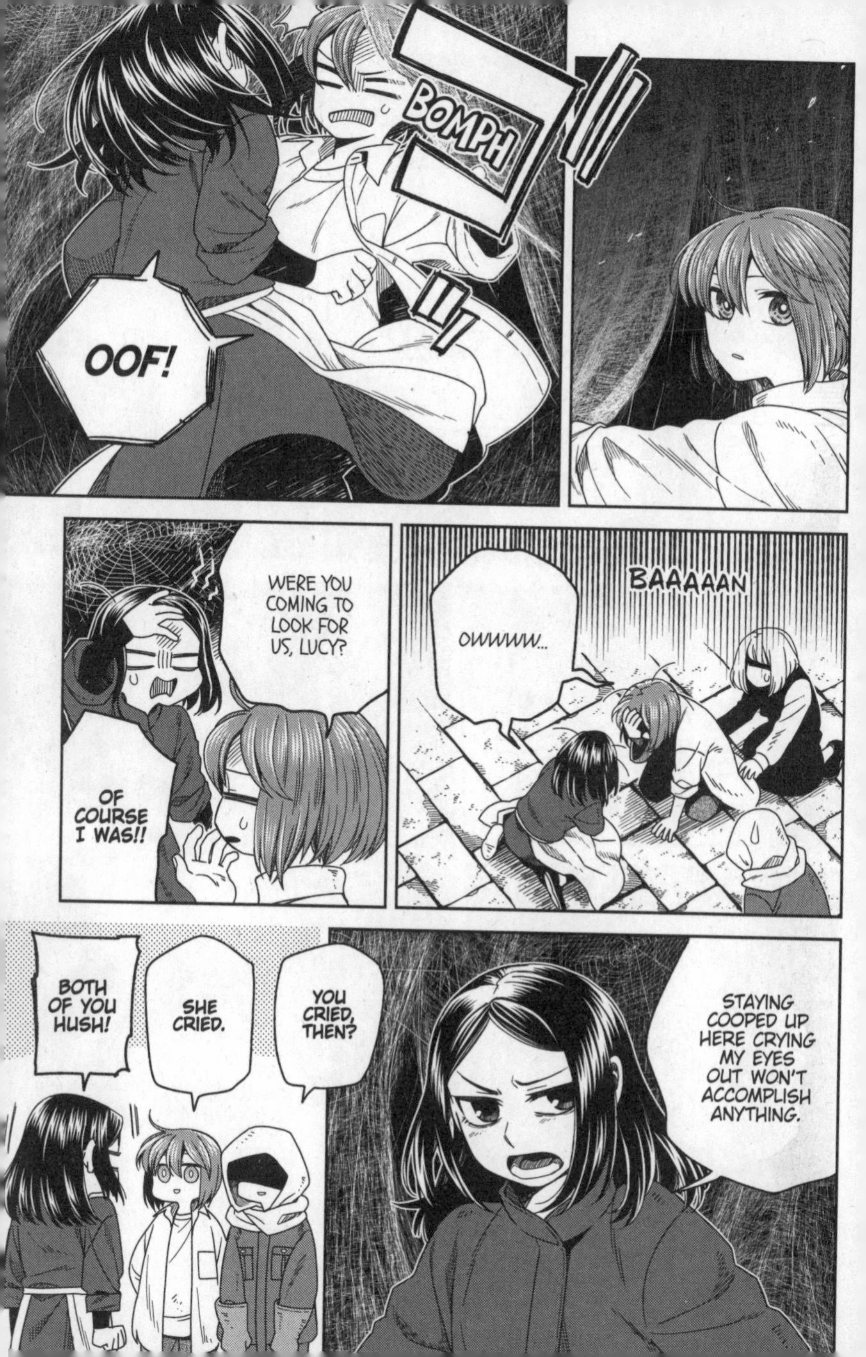
BOMPH
OOF!
BAAAAAN
OWWWW...
WERE YOU COMING TO LOOK FOR US, LUCY?
OF COURSE I WAS!!
STAYING COOPED UP HERE CRYING MY EYES OUT WON'T ACCOMPLISH ANYTHING.
YOU CRIED, THEN?
SHE CRIED.
BOTH OF YOU HUSH!

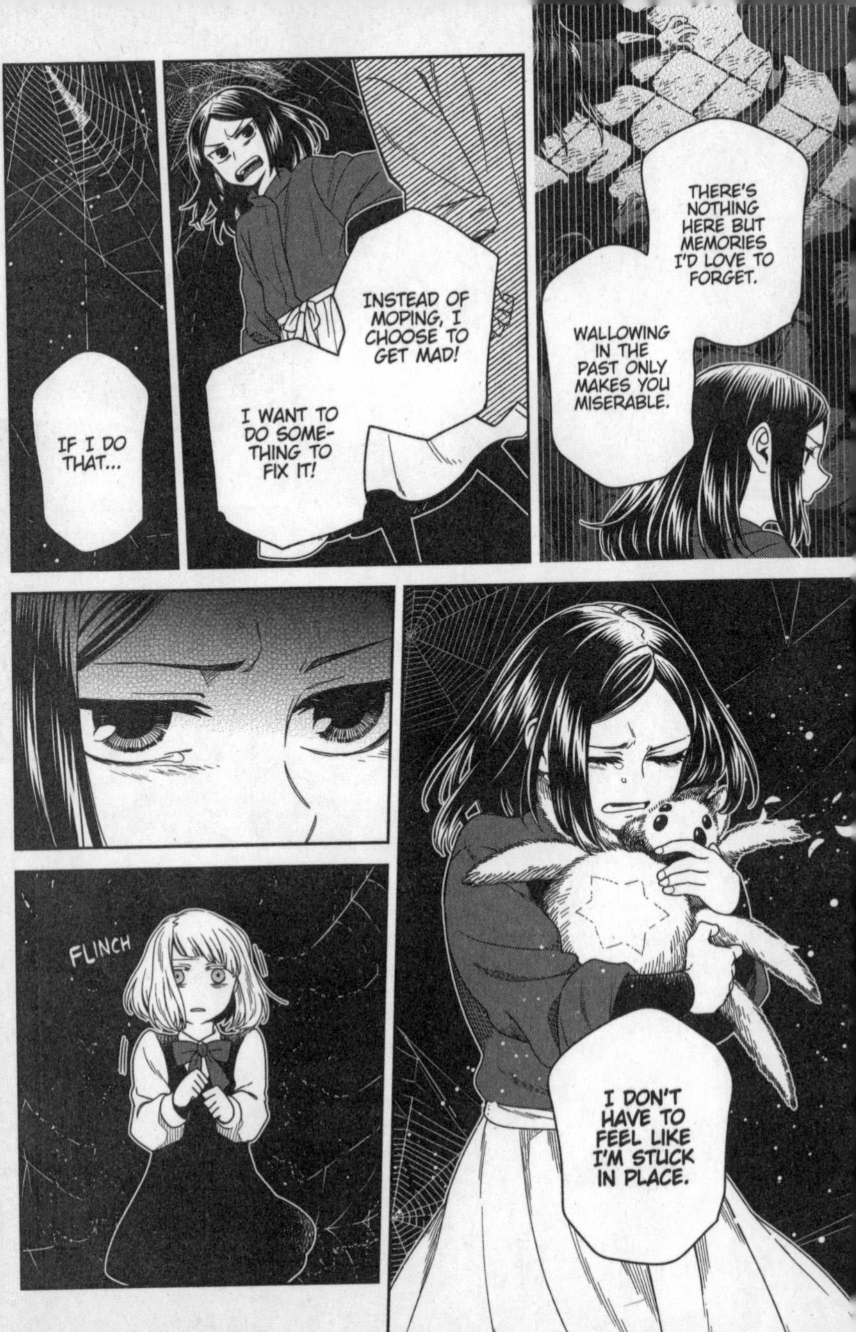
THERE'S NOTHING HERE BUT MEMORIES I'D LOVE TO FORGET.
WALLOWING IN THE PAST ONLY MAKES YOU MISERABLE.
INSTEAD OF MOPING, I CHOOSE TO GET MAD!
I WANT TO DO SOME-THING TO FIX IT!
IF I DO THAT...
I DON'T HAVE TO FEEL LIKE I'M STUCK IN PLACE.
FLINCH

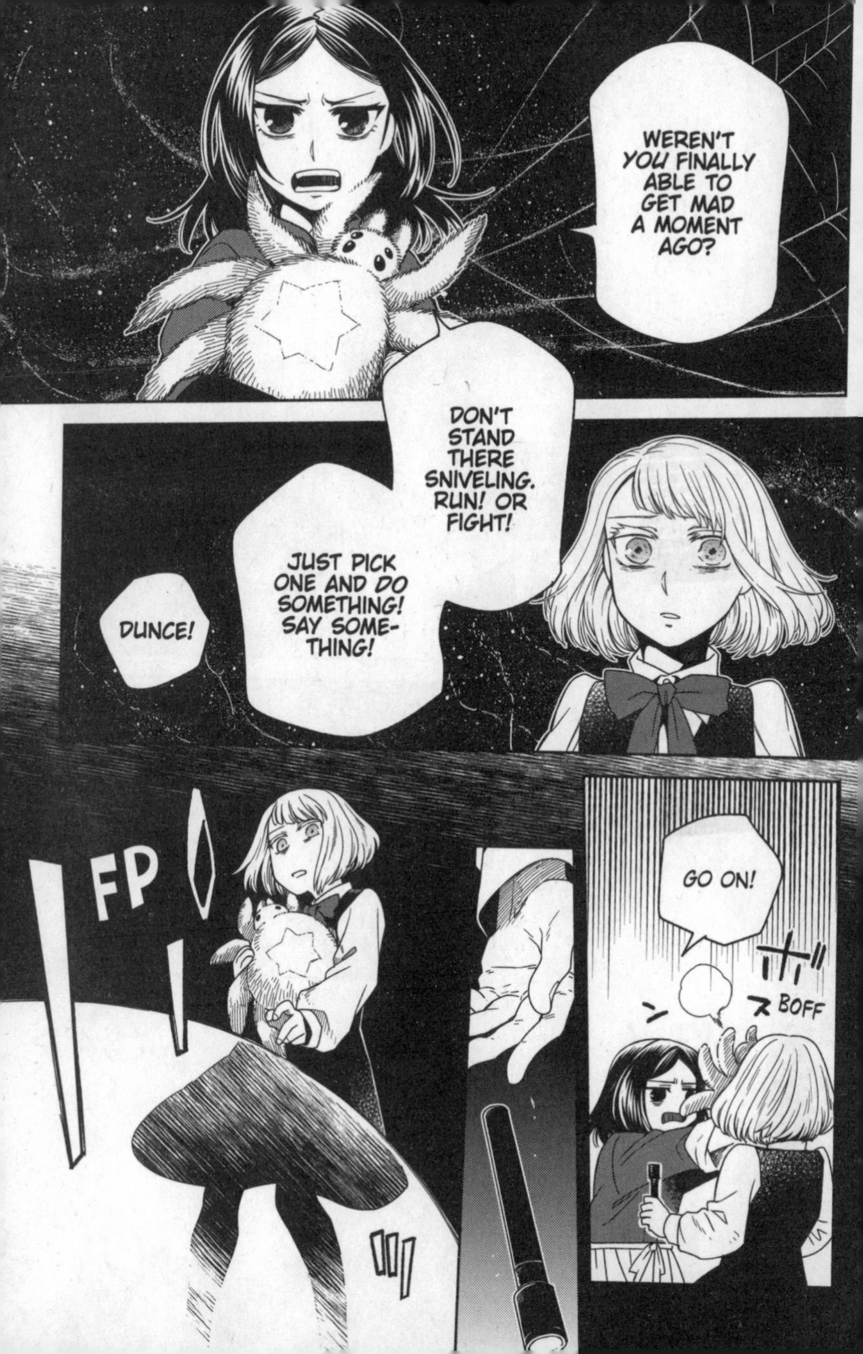
WEREN'T *YOU* FINALLY ABLE TO GET MAD A MOMENT AGO?
DON'T STAND THERE SNIVELING. RUN! OR FIGHT!
JUST PICK ONE AND *DO* SOMETHING! SAY SOME-THING!
DUNCE!
GO ON!
BOFF
FP

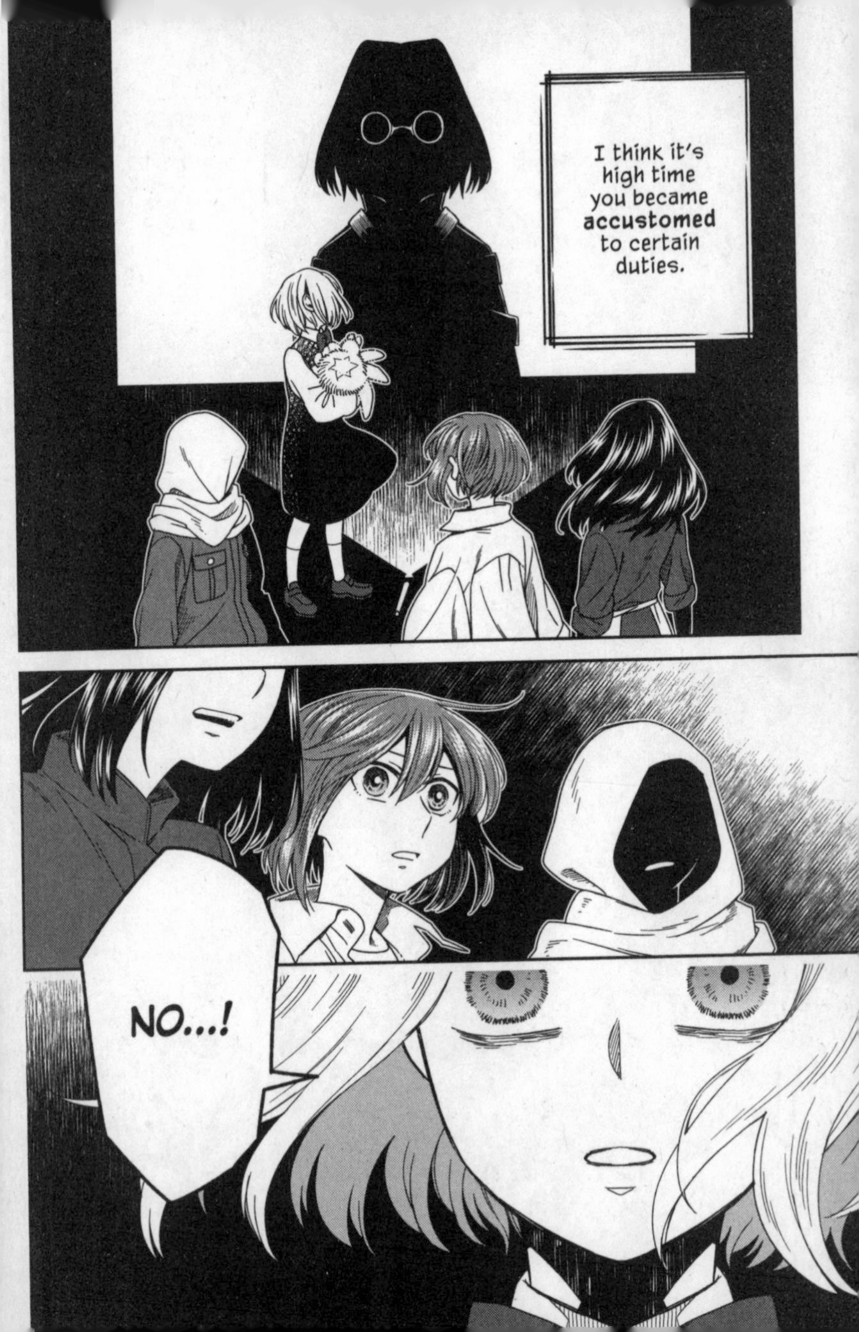
I think it's high time you became **accustomed** to certain duties.
NO...!

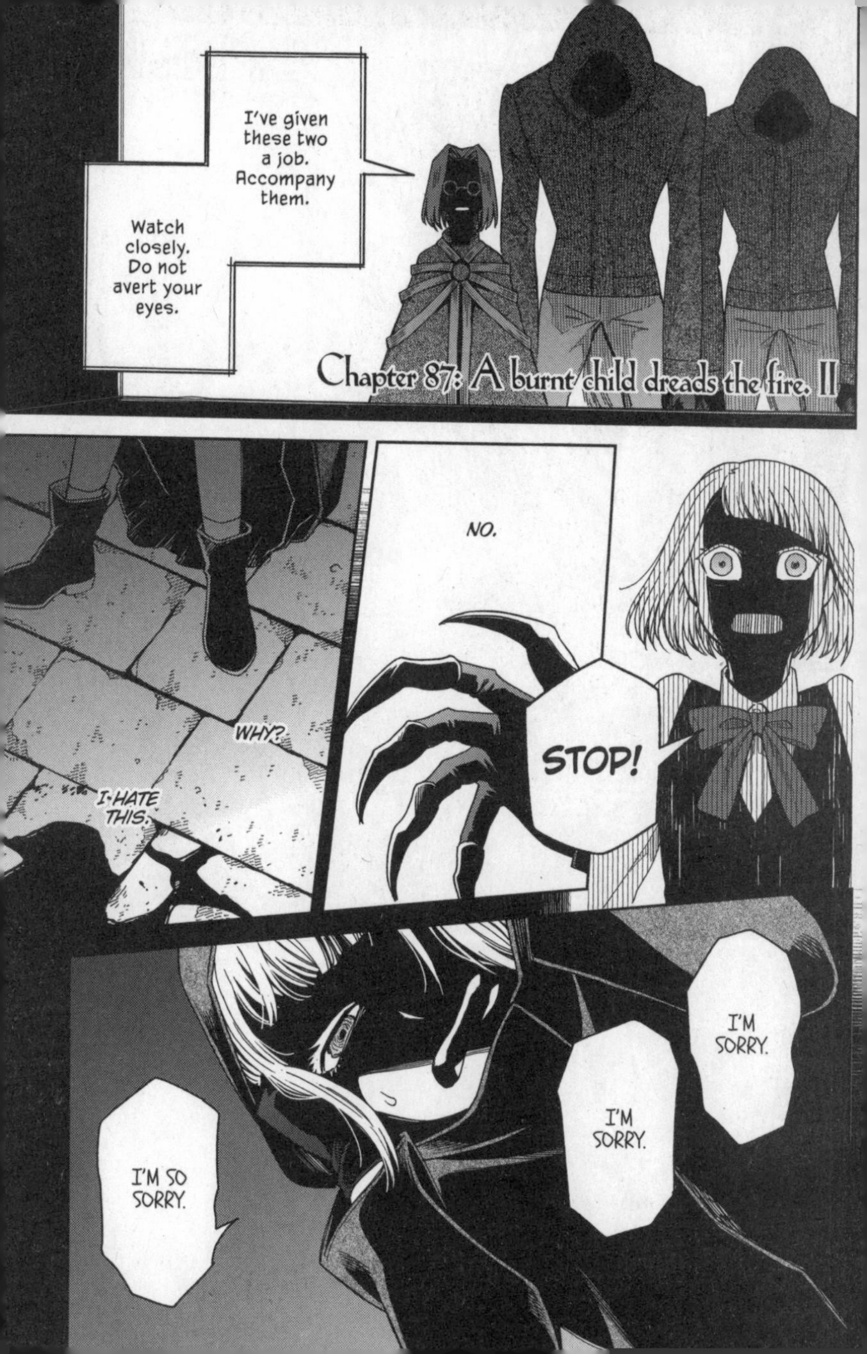
I've given these two a job. Accompany them.
Watch closely. Do not avert your eyes.
Chapter 87: A burnt child dreads the fire. II
STOP!
NO.
WHY?
I HATE THIS.
I'M SORRY.
I'M SORRY.
I'M SO SORRY.

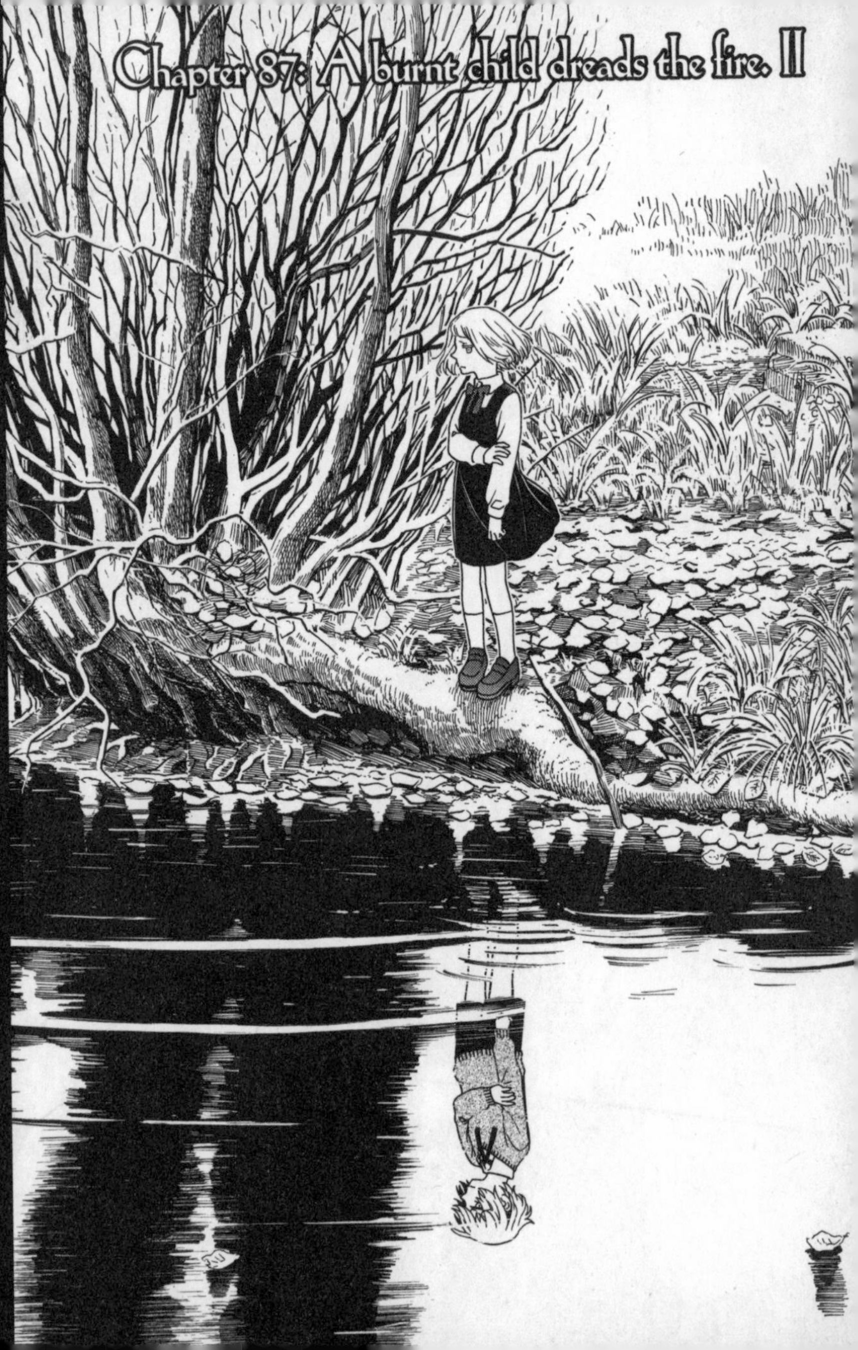
Chapter 87: A burnt child dreads the fire. II

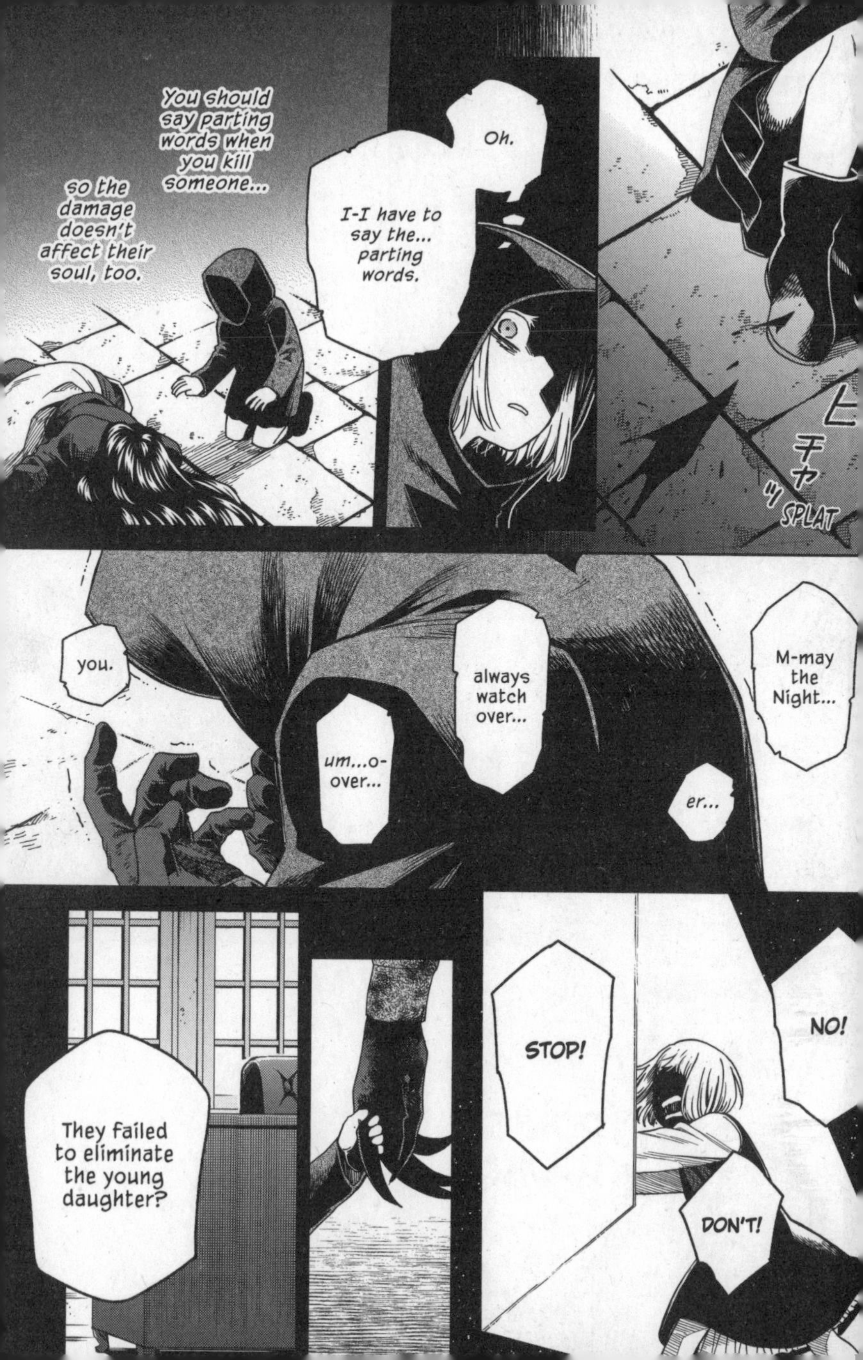
ピチャッ
SPLAT
Oh.
I-I have to say the... parting words.
You should say parting words when you kill someone...
so the damage doesn't affect their soul, too.
M-may the Night...
er...
always watch over...
um...o-over...
you.
NO!
STOP!
DON'T!
They failed to eliminate the young daughter?

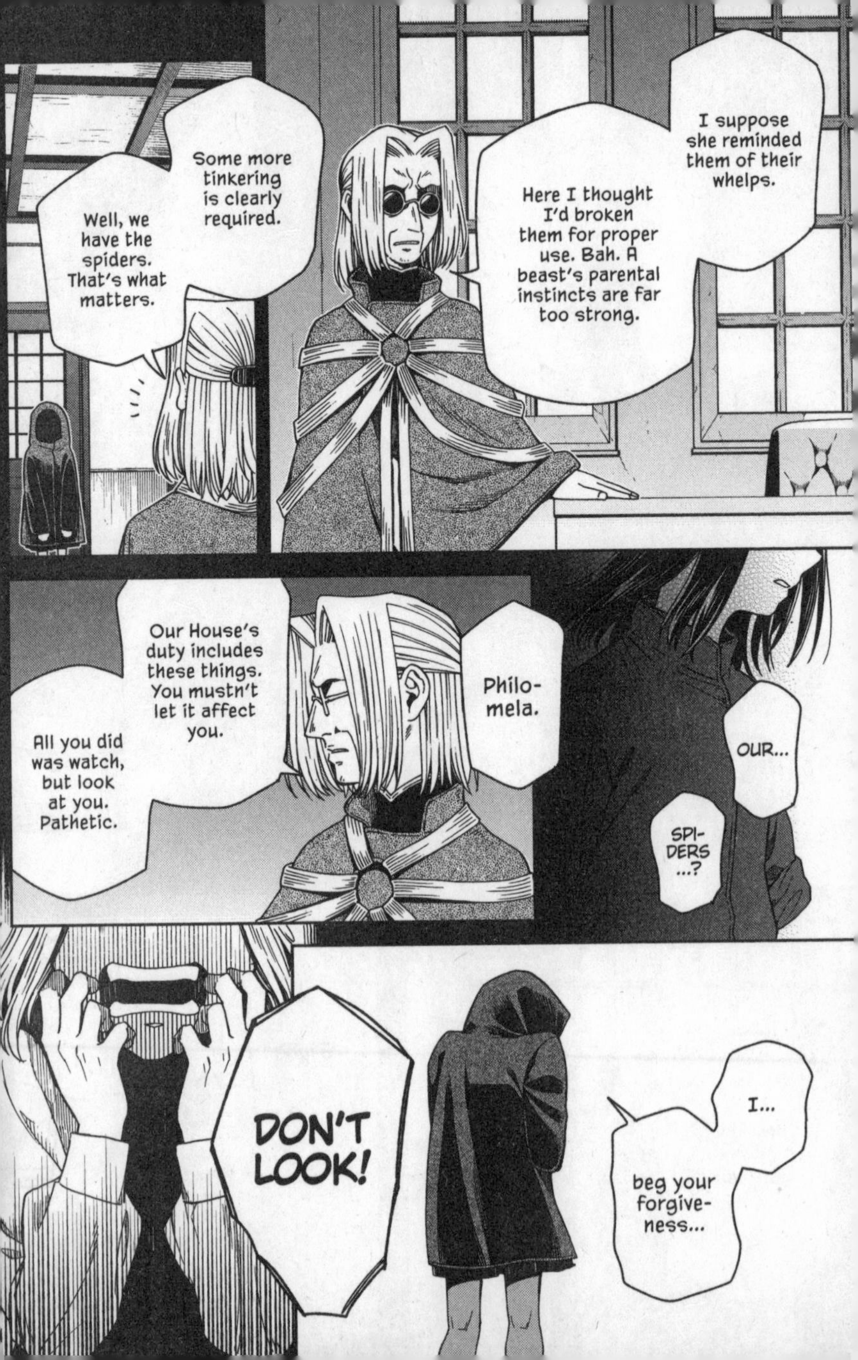
I suppose she reminded them of their whelps.
Here I thought I'd broken them for proper use. Bah. A beast's parental instincts are far too strong.
Some more tinkering is clearly required.
Well, we have the spiders. That's what matters.
OUR...
SPI-DERS ...?
Philo-mela.
Our House's duty includes these things. You mustn't let it affect you.
All you did was watch, but look at you. Pathetic.
I...
beg your forgive-ness...
DON'T LOOK!

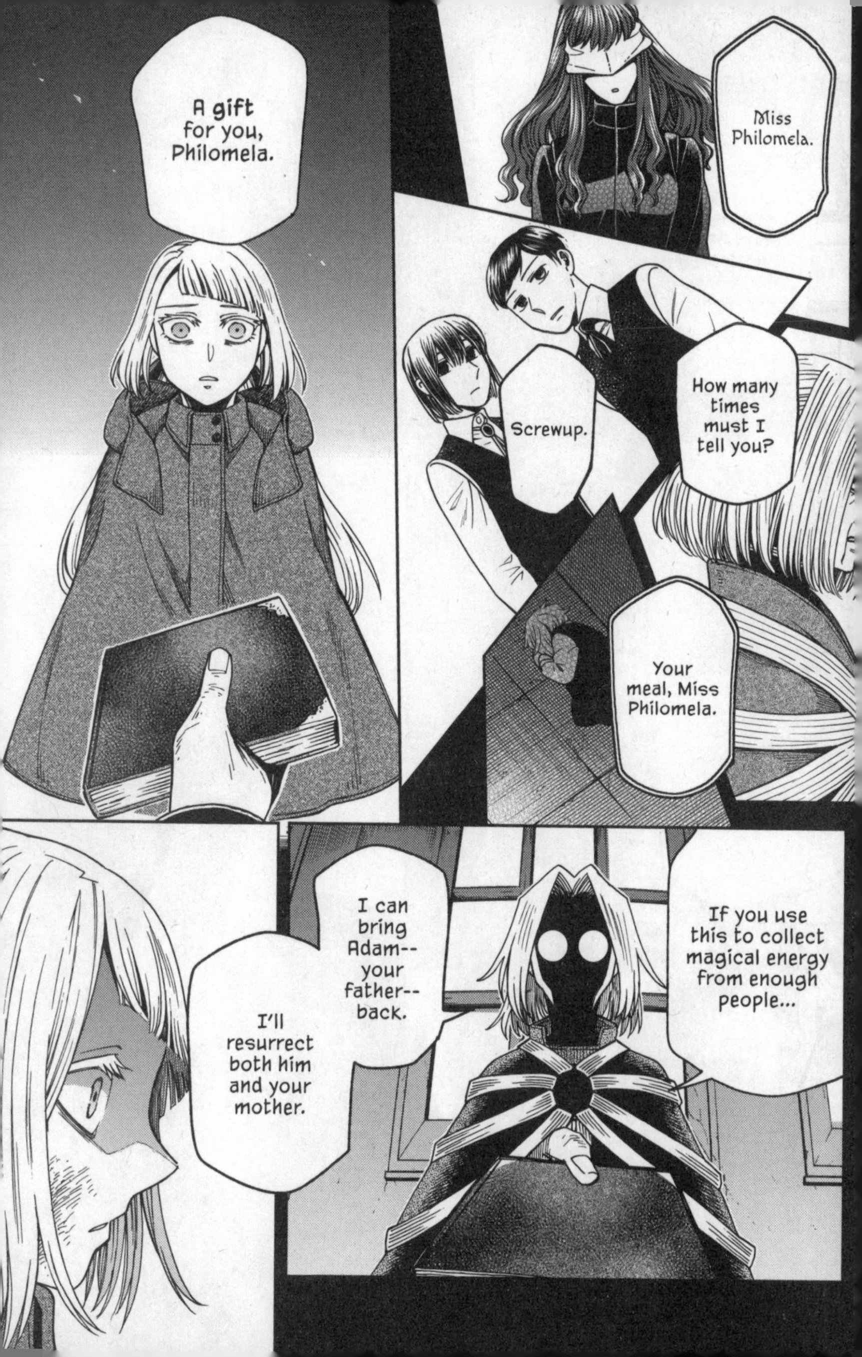
Miss Philomela.
How many times must I tell you?
Screwup.
Your meal, Miss Philomela.
A gift for you, Philomela.
If you use this to collect magical energy from enough people...
I can bring Adam-- your father-- back.
I'll resurrect both him and your mother.

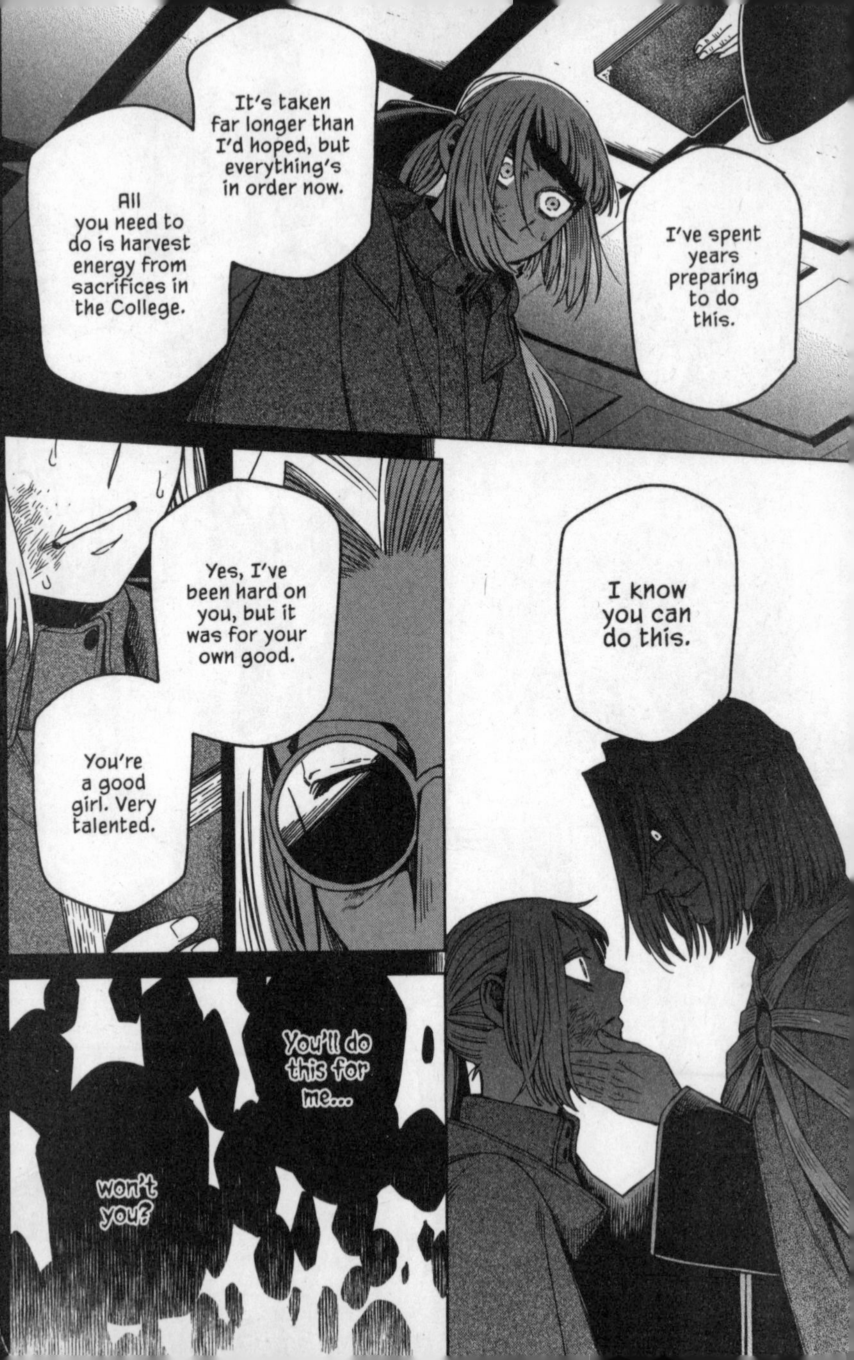
I've spent years preparing to do this.
It's taken far longer than I'd hoped, but everything's in order now.
All you need to do is harvest energy from sacrifices in the College.
I know you can do this.
Yes, I've been hard on you, but it was for your own good.
You're a good girl. Very talented.
You'll do this for me...
won't you?

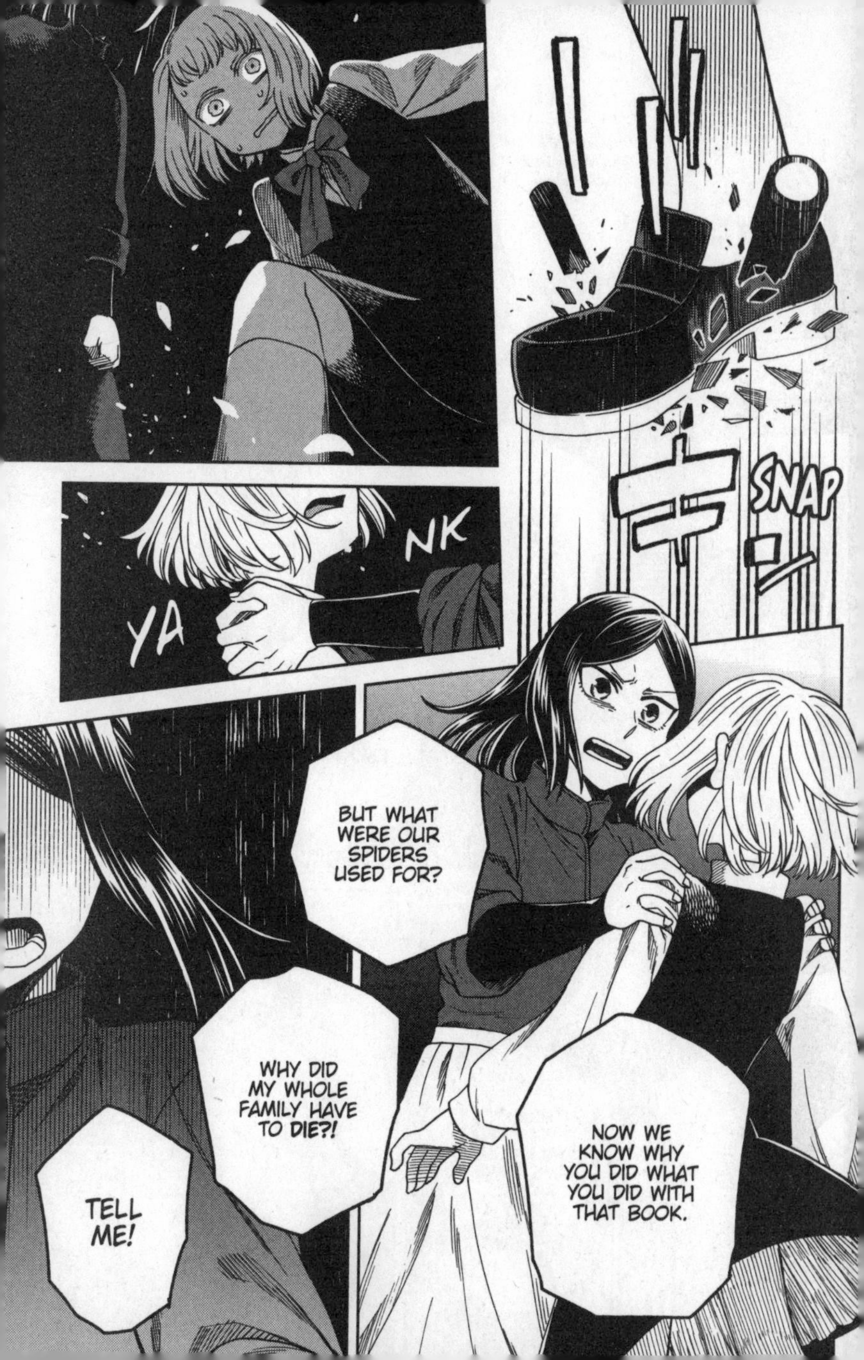
SNAP
YANK
NOW WE KNOW WHY YOU DID WHAT YOU DID WITH THAT BOOK.
BUT WHAT WERE OUR SPIDERS USED FOR?
WHY DID MY WHOLE FAMILY HAVE TO DIE?!
TELL ME!

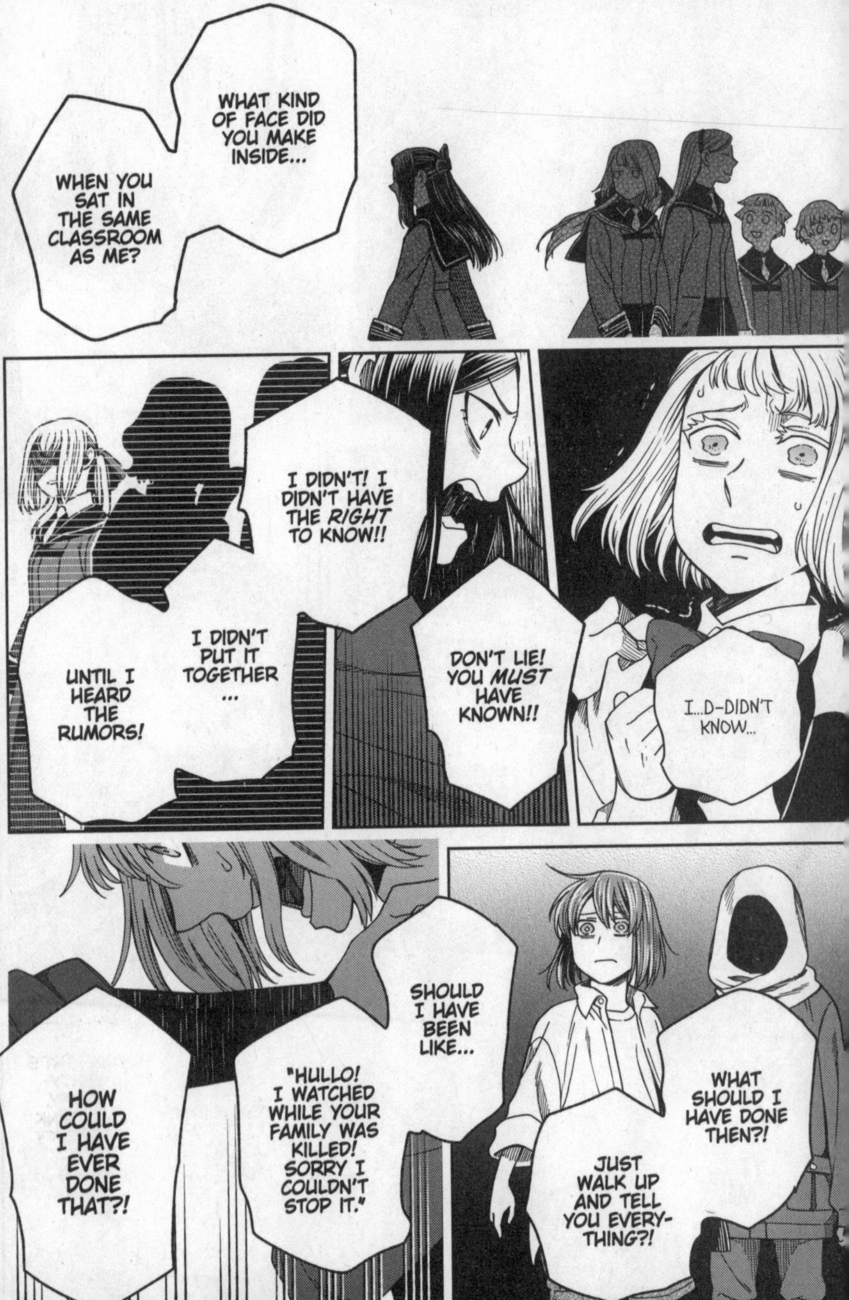
WHAT KIND OF FACE DID YOU MAKE INSIDE...
WHEN YOU SAT IN THE SAME CLASSROOM AS ME?
I...D-DIDN'T KNOW...
DON'T LIE! YOU *MUST* HAVE KNOWN!!
I DIDN'T! I DIDN'T HAVE THE *RIGHT* TO KNOW!!
I DIDN'T PUT IT TOGETHER...
UNTIL I HEARD THE RUMORS!
WHAT SHOULD I HAVE DONE THEN?!
JUST WALK UP AND TELL YOU EVERYTHING?!
SHOULD I HAVE BEEN LIKE...
"HULLO! I WATCHED WHILE YOUR FAMILY WAS KILLED! SORRY I COULDN'T STOP IT."
HOW COULD I HAVE EVER DONE THAT?!

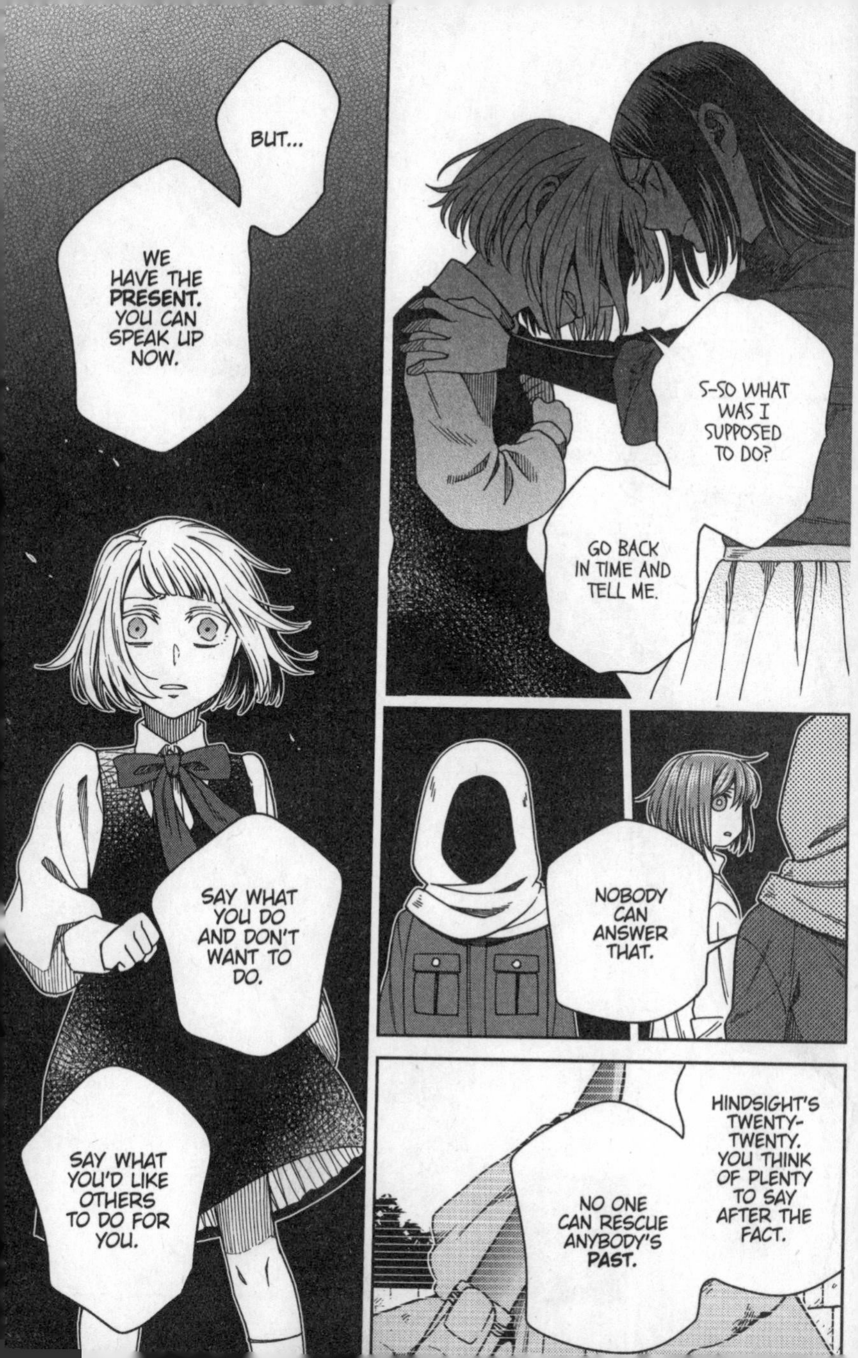
S-SO WHAT WAS I SUPPOSED TO DO?
GO BACK IN TIME AND TELL ME.
NOBODY CAN ANSWER THAT.
HINDSIGHT'S TWENTY-TWENTY. YOU THINK OF PLENTY TO SAY AFTER THE FACT.
NO ONE CAN RESCUE ANYBODY'S PAST.
BUT...
WE HAVE THE PRESENT. YOU CAN SPEAK UP NOW.
SAY WHAT YOU DO AND DON'T WANT TO DO.
SAY WHAT YOU'D LIKE OTHERS TO DO FOR YOU.

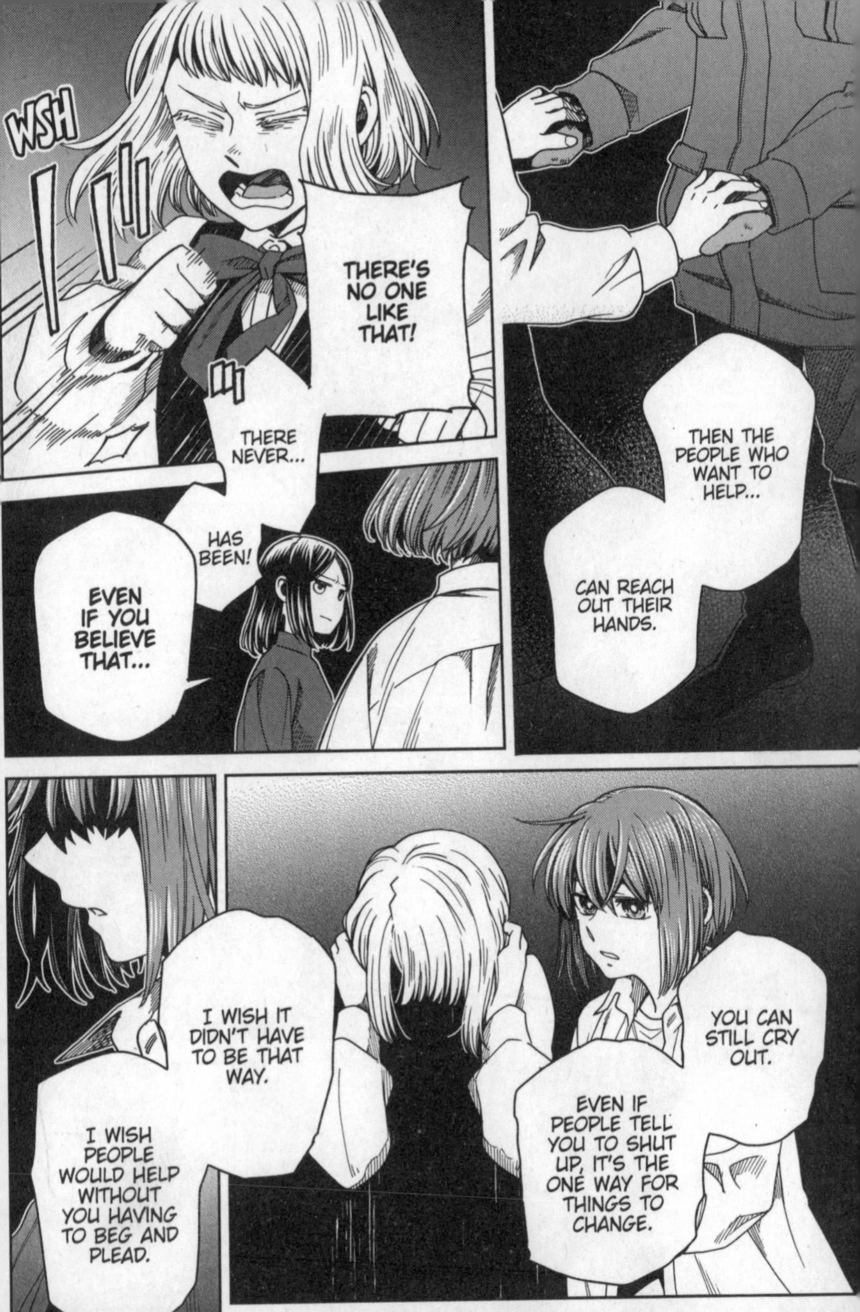
THEN THE PEOPLE WHO WANT TO HELP...
CAN REACH OUT THEIR HANDS.
WSH
THERE'S NO ONE LIKE THAT!
THERE NEVER...
HAS BEEN!
EVEN IF YOU BELIEVE THAT...
YOU CAN STILL CRY OUT.
EVEN IF PEOPLE TELL YOU TO SHUT UP, IT'S THE ONE WAY FOR THINGS TO CHANGE.
I WISH IT DIDN'T HAVE TO BE THAT WAY.
I WISH PEOPLE WOULD HELP WITHOUT YOU HAVING TO BEG AND PLEAD.

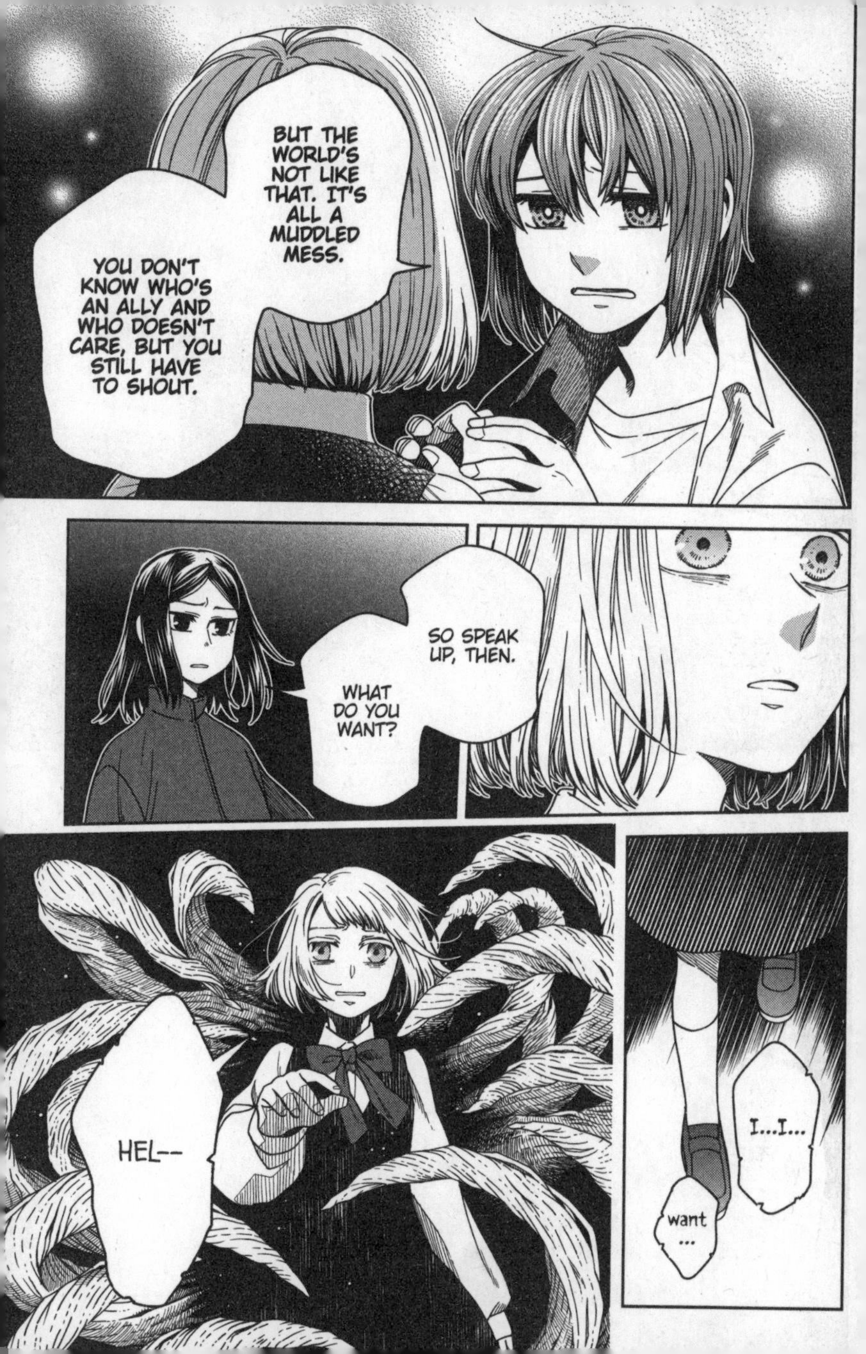
BUT THE WORLD'S NOT LIKE THAT. IT'S ALL A MUDDLED MESS.
YOU DON'T KNOW WHO'S AN ALLY AND WHO DOESN'T CARE, BUT YOU STILL HAVE TO SHOUT.
SO SPEAK UP, THEN.
WHAT DO YOU WANT?
I...I...
want ...
HEL--

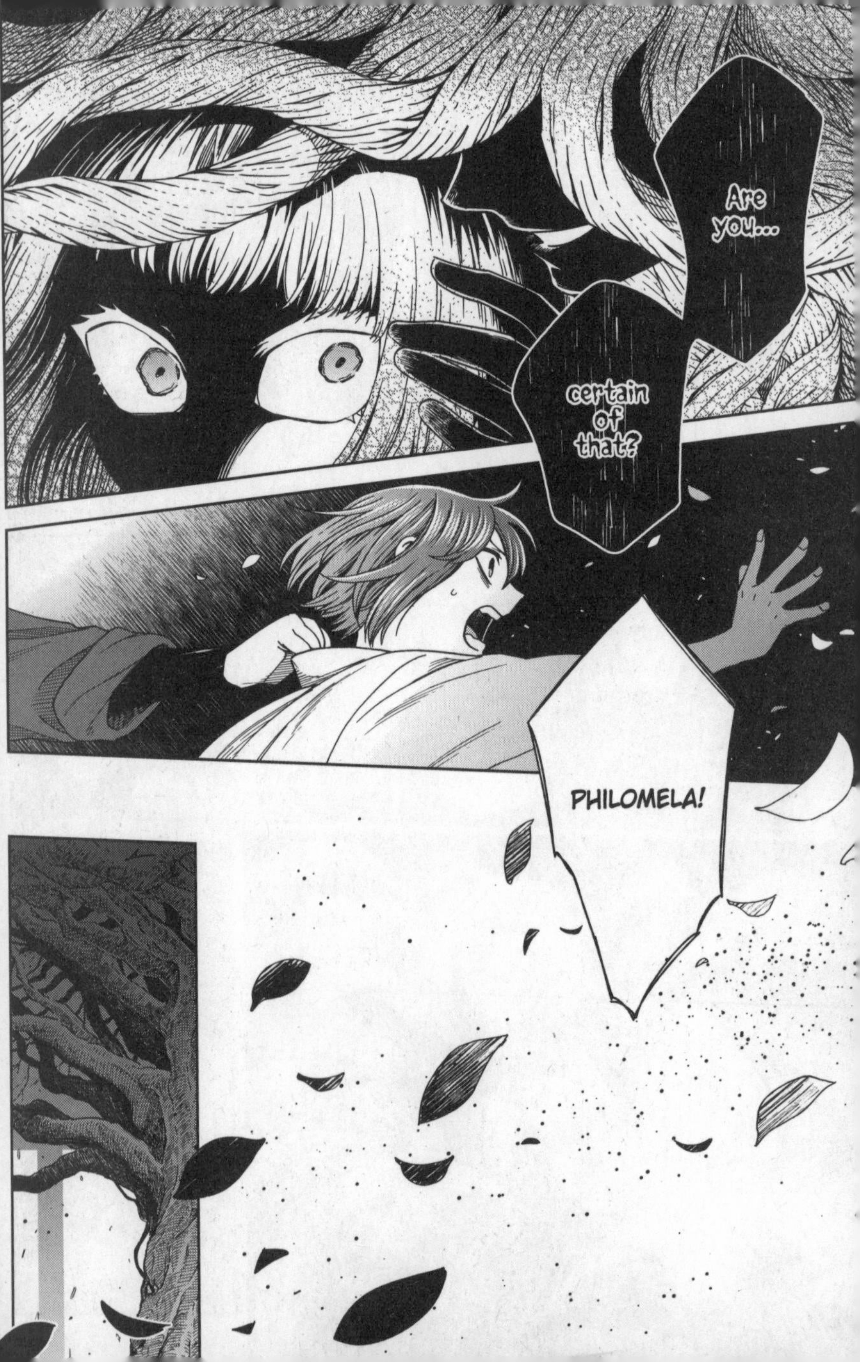
Are you...
certain of that?
PHILOMELA!

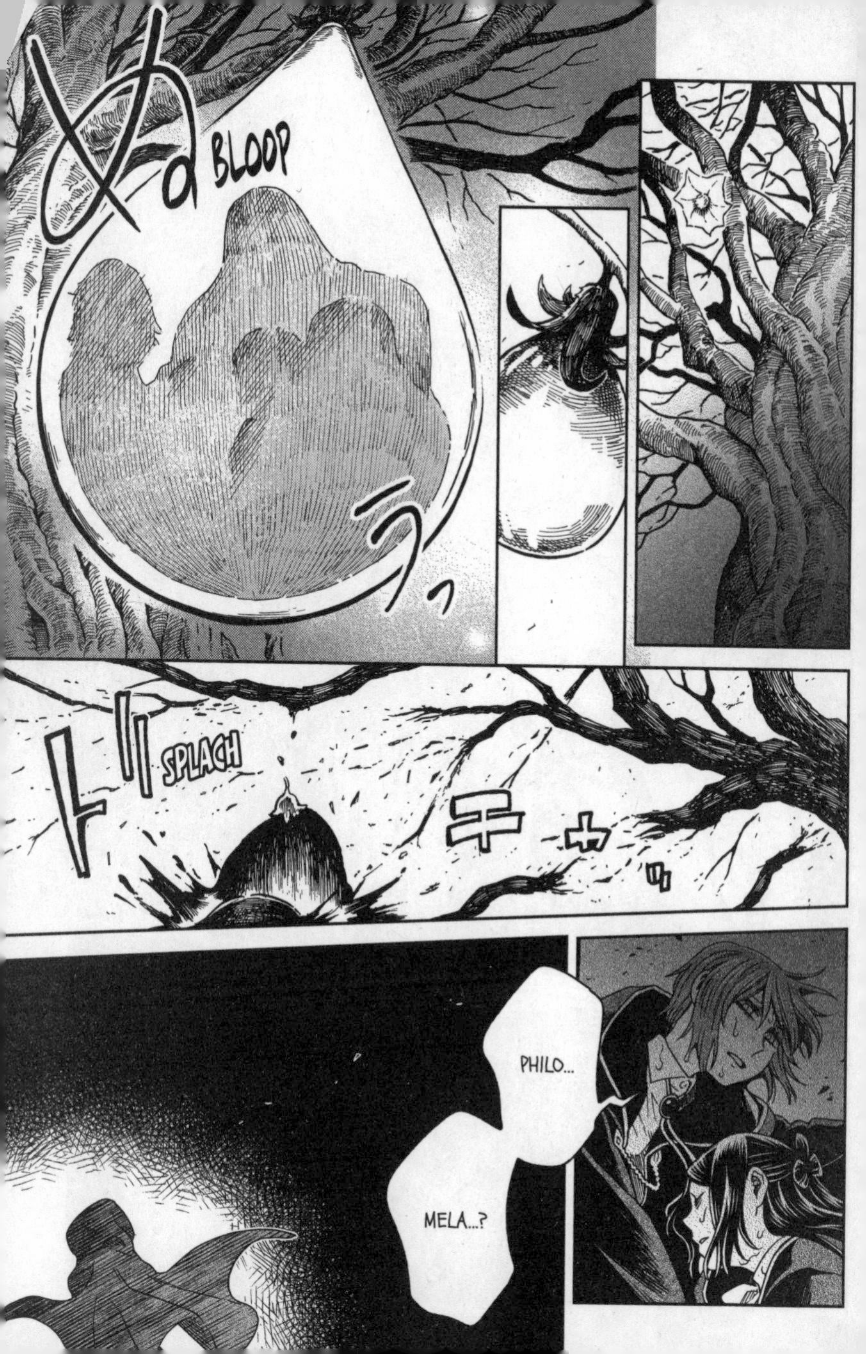
BLOOP
SPLACH
PHILO...
MELA...?

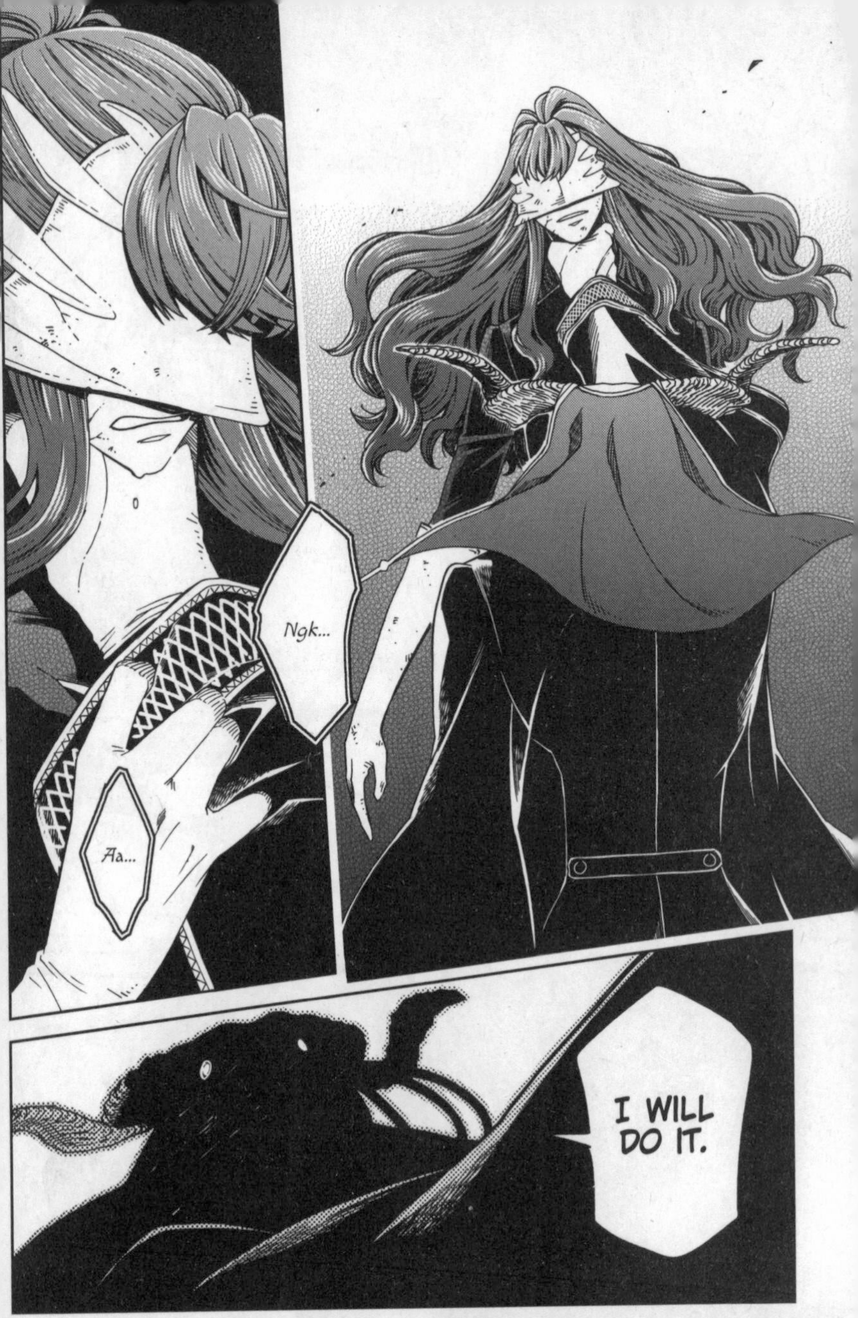
Ngk...
Aa...
I WILL DO IT.

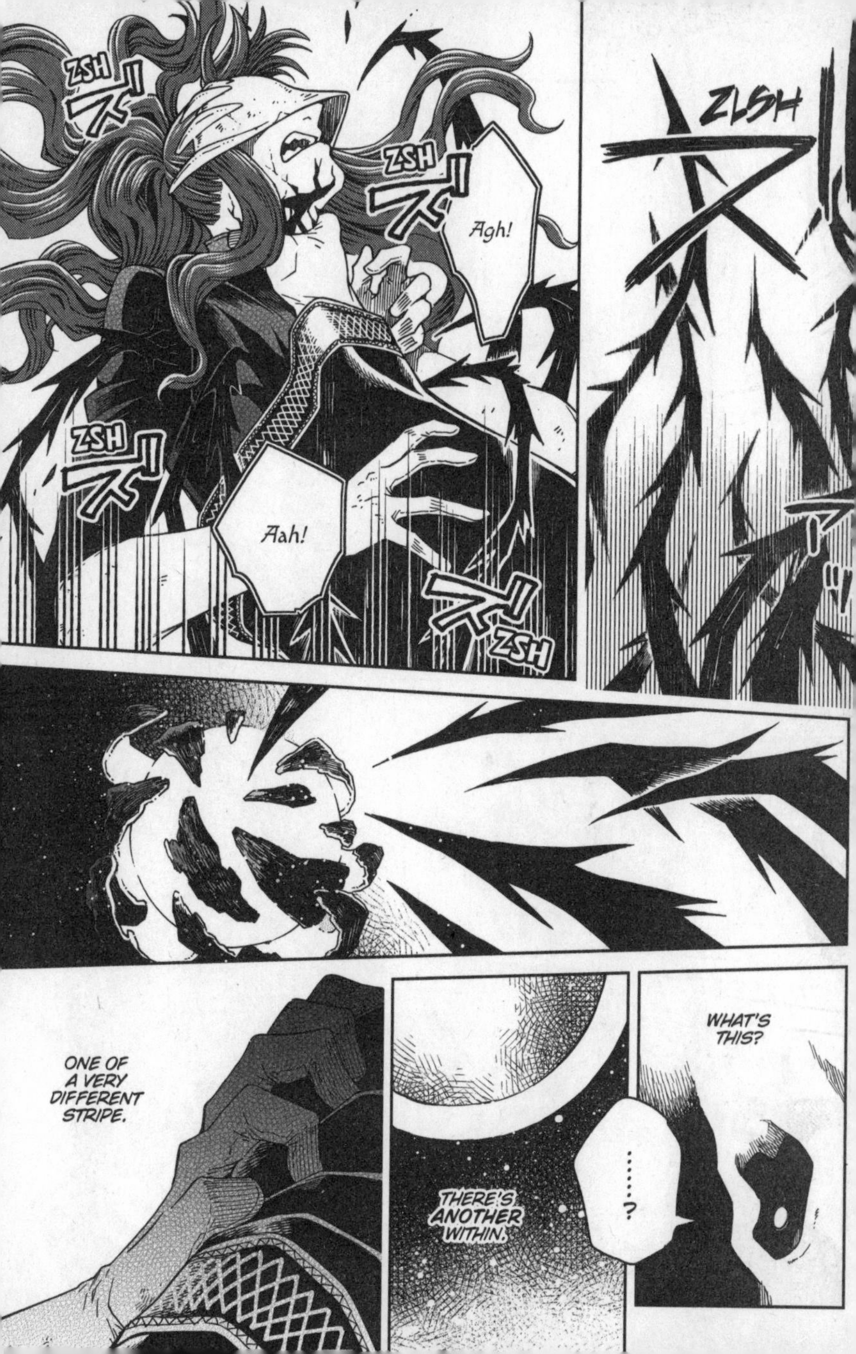
ZLSH
Agh!
ZSH
ZSH
ZSH
Aah!
ZSH
WHAT'S THIS?
......?
THERE'S ANOTHER WITHIN.
ONE OF A VERY DIFFERENT STRIPE.

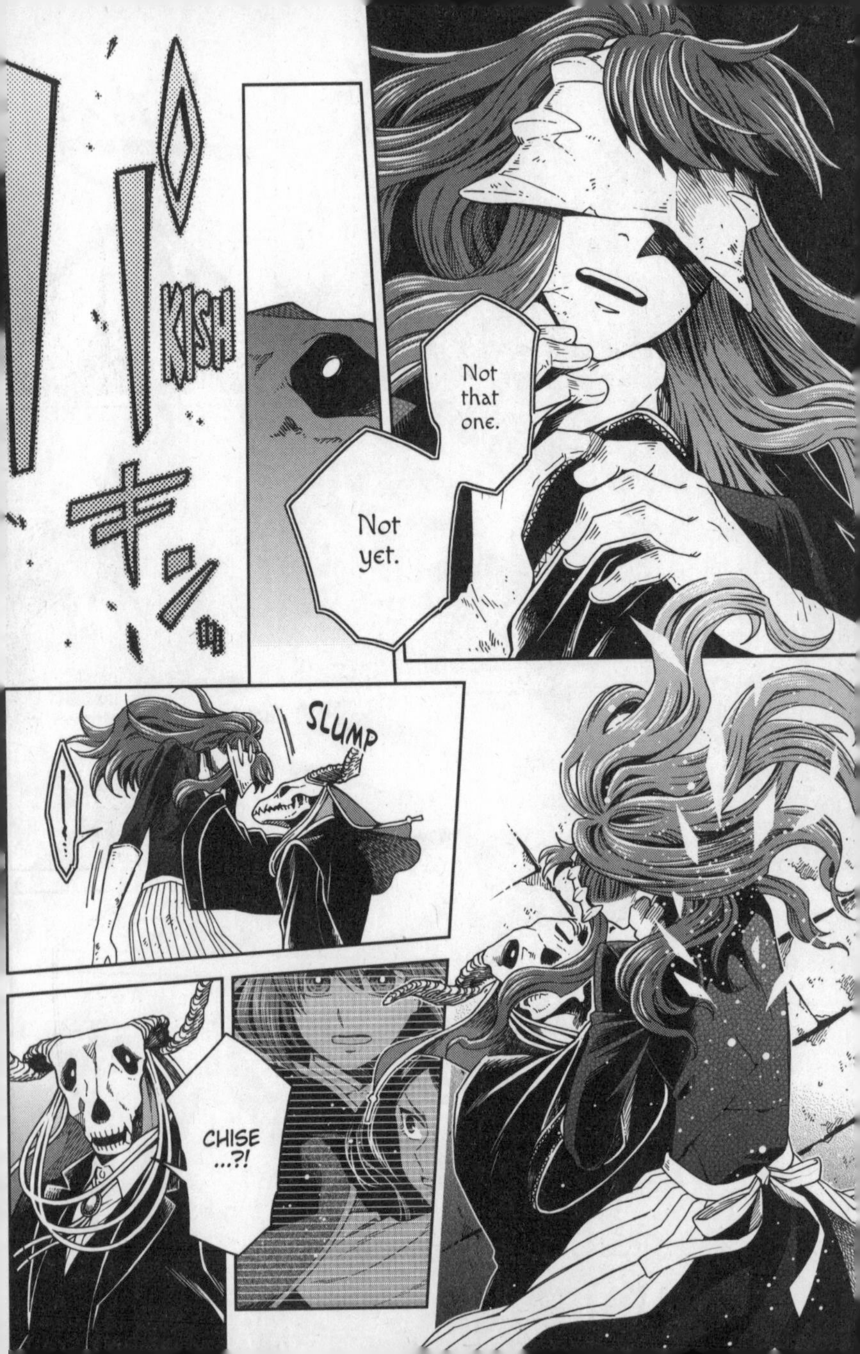
Not that one.
Not yet.
KISH
キン
SLUMP
CHISE ...?!

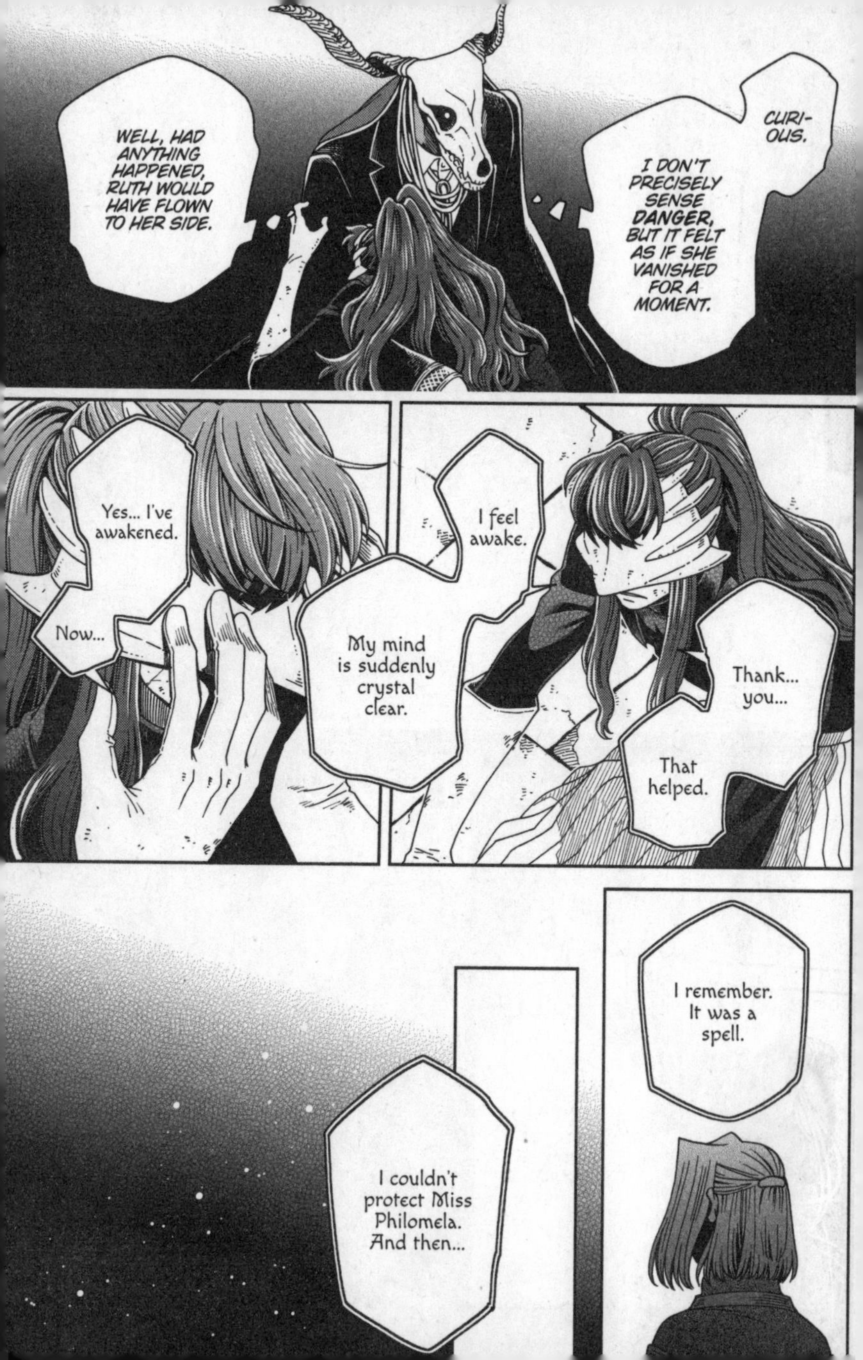
CURI-OUS.
I DON'T PRECISELY SENSE DANGER, BUT IT FELT AS IF SHE VANISHED FOR A MOMENT.
WELL, HAD ANYTHING HAPPENED, RUTH WOULD HAVE FLOWN TO HER SIDE.
I feel awake.
My mind is suddenly crystal clear.
Thank... you...
That helped.
Yes... I've awakened.
Now...
I remember. It was a spell.
I couldn't protect Miss Philomela. And then...

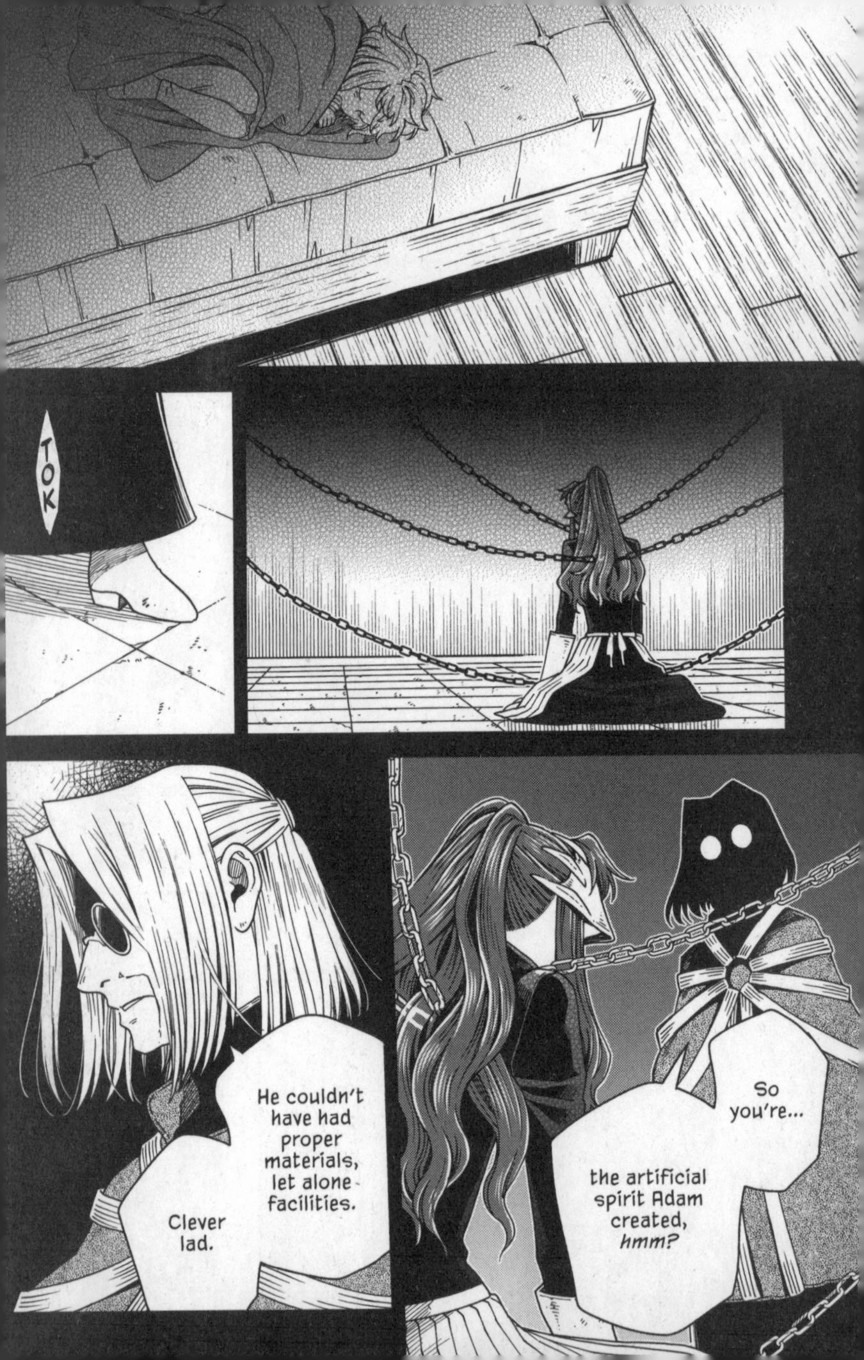
TOK
So you're...
the artificial spirit Adam created, *hmm?*
He couldn't have had proper materials, let alone facilities.
Clever lad.

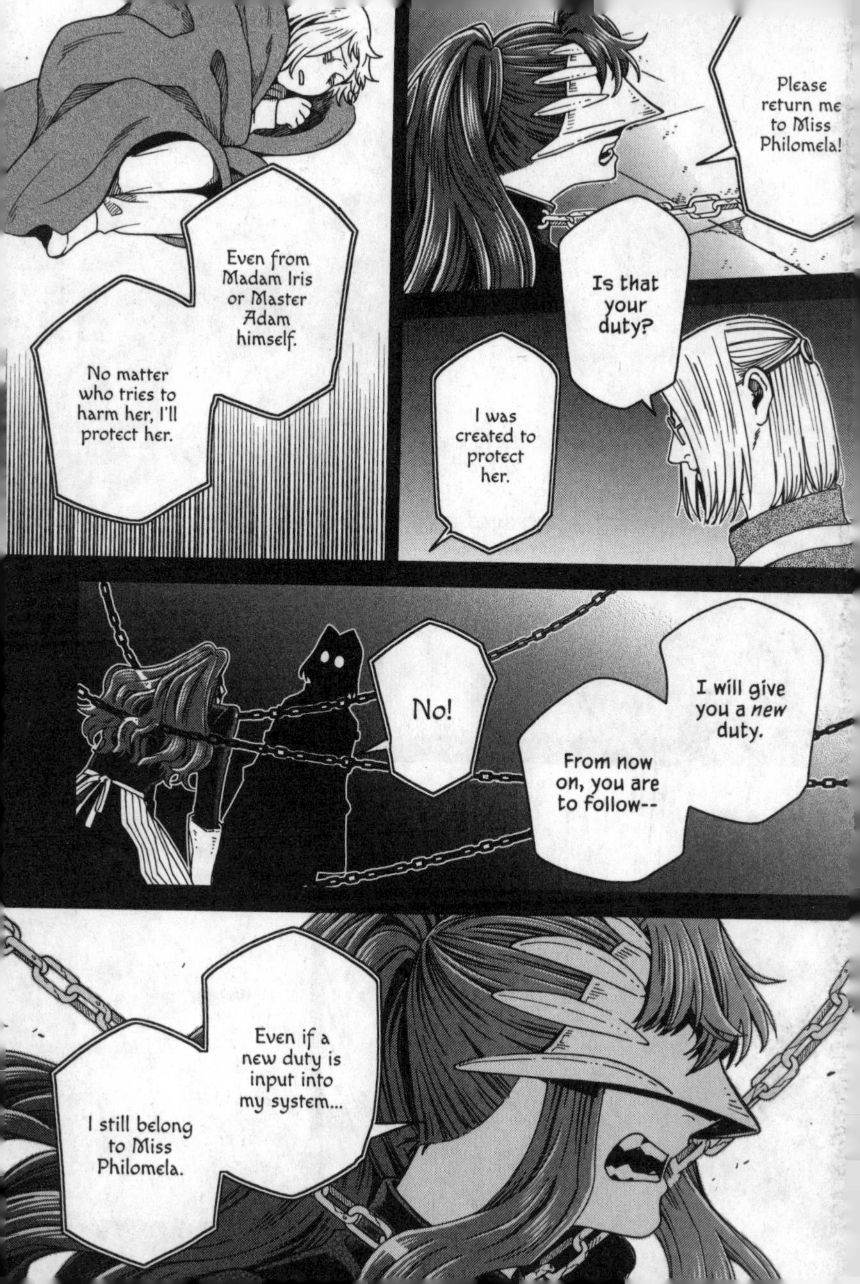
Please return me to Miss Philomela!
Is that your duty?
I was created to protect her.
Even from Madam Iris or Master Adam himself.
No matter who tries to harm her, I'll protect her.
I will give you a *new* duty.
From now on, you are to follow--
No!
Even if a new duty is input into my system...
I still belong to Miss Philomela.

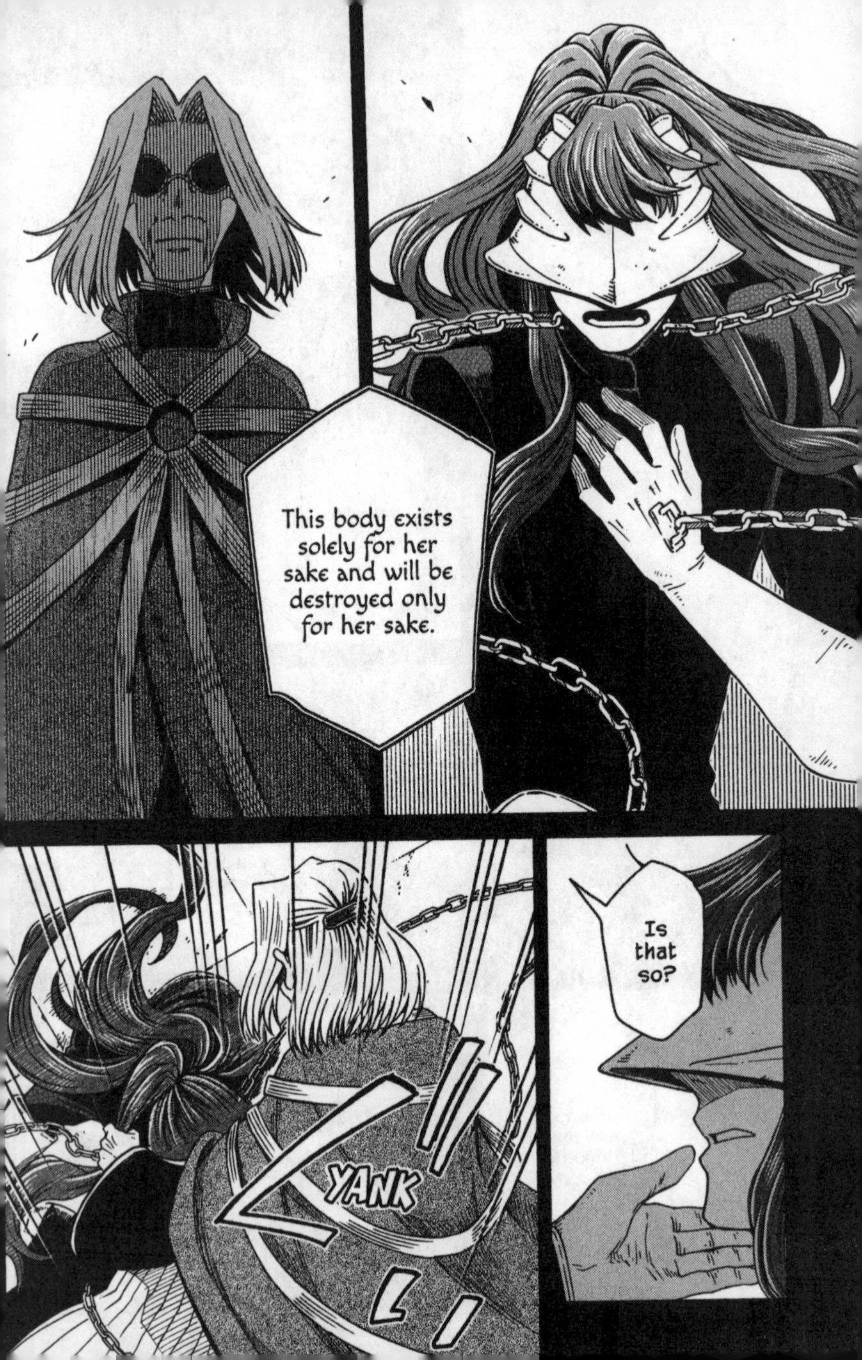
This body exists solely for her sake and will be destroyed only for her sake.
Is that so?
YANK

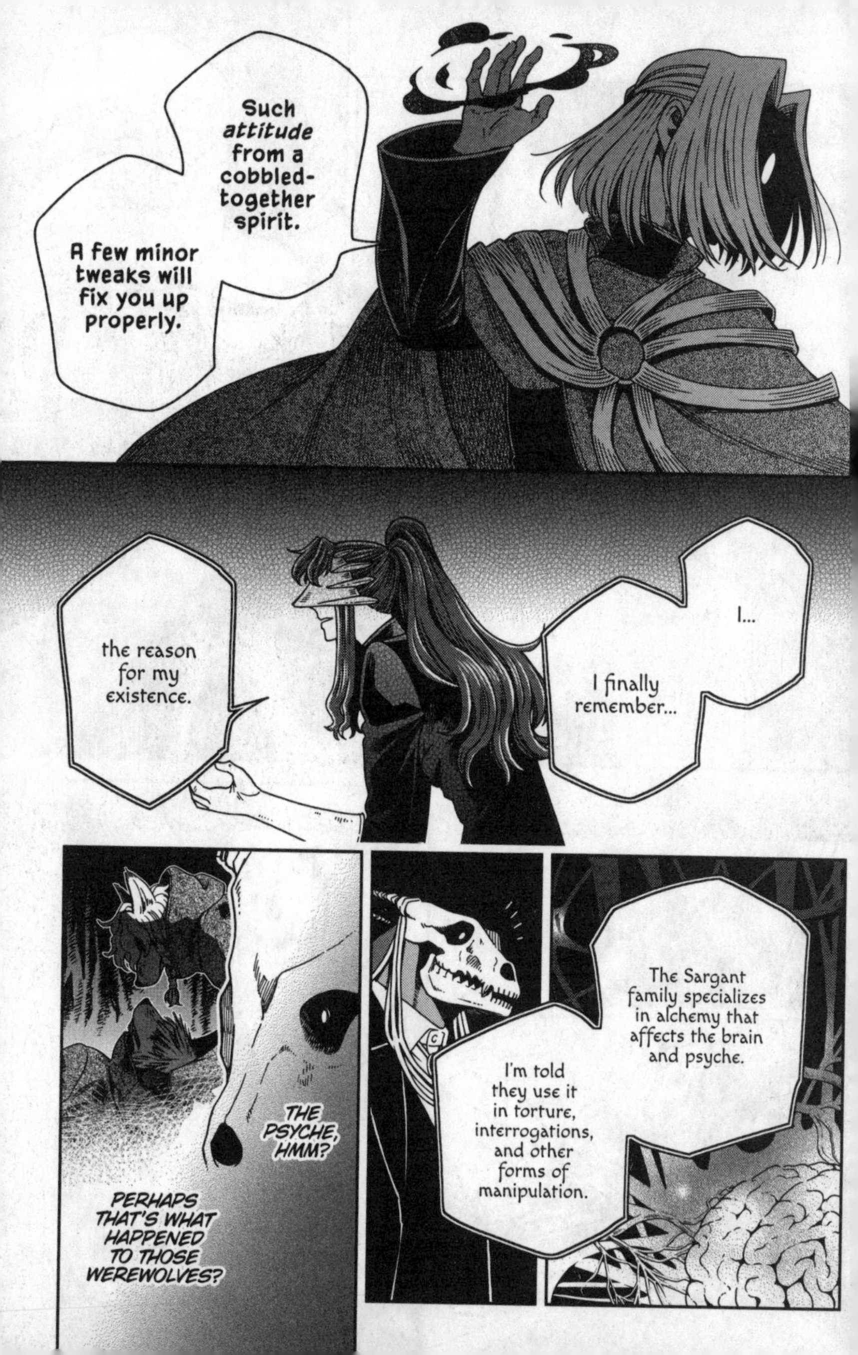
Such *attitude* from a cobbled-together spirit.
A few minor tweaks will fix you up properly.
I...
I finally remember...
the reason for my existence.
The Sargant family specializes in alchemy that affects the brain and psyche.
I'm told they use it in torture, interrogations, and other forms of manipulation.
THE PSYCHE, HMM?
PERHAPS THAT'S WHAT HAPPENED TO THOSE WEREWOLVES?

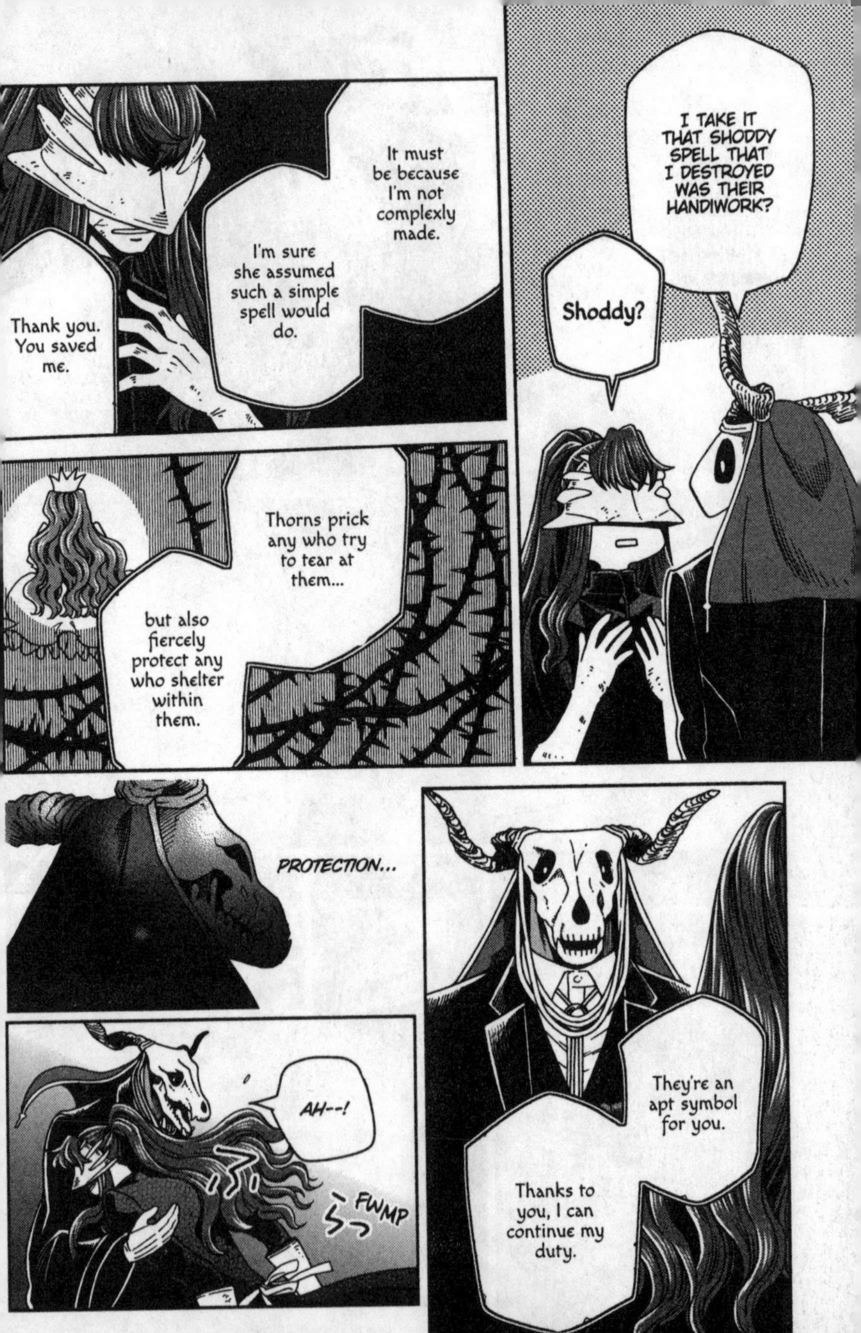
I TAKE IT THAT SHODDY SPELL THAT I DESTROYED WAS THEIR HANDIWORK?
Shoddy?
It must be because I'm not complexly made.
I'm sure she assumed such a simple spell would do.
Thank you. You saved me.
Thorns prick any who try to tear at them...
but also fiercely protect any who shelter within them.
They're an apt symbol for you.
Thanks to you, I can continue my duty.
PROTECTION...
AH--!
FWMP

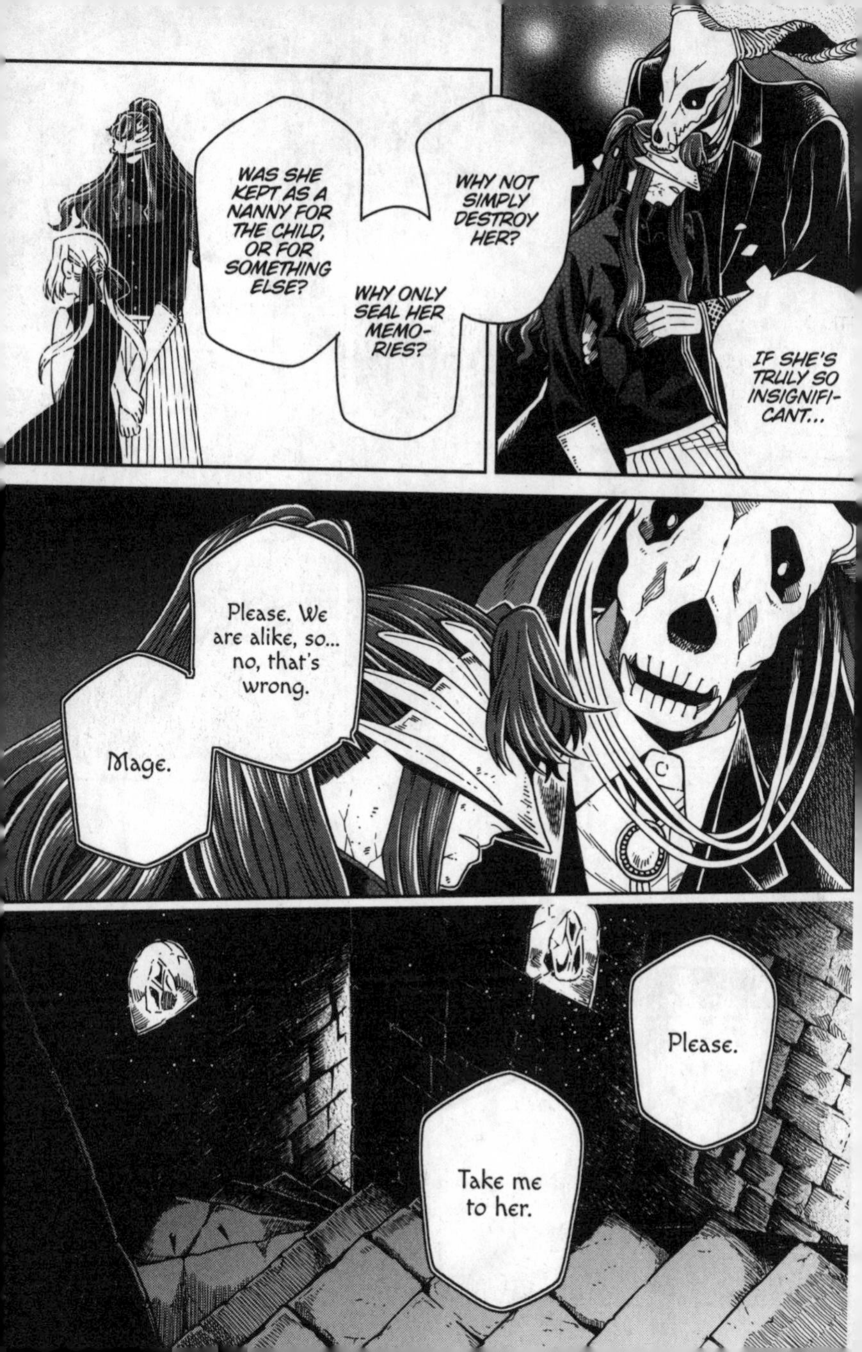
IF SHE'S TRULY SO INSIGNIFICANT...
WHY NOT SIMPLY DESTROY HER?
WHY ONLY SEAL HER MEMORIES?
WAS SHE KEPT AS A NANNY FOR THE CHILD, OR FOR SOMETHING ELSE?
Please. We are alike, so... no, that's wrong.
Mage.
Please.
Take me to her.

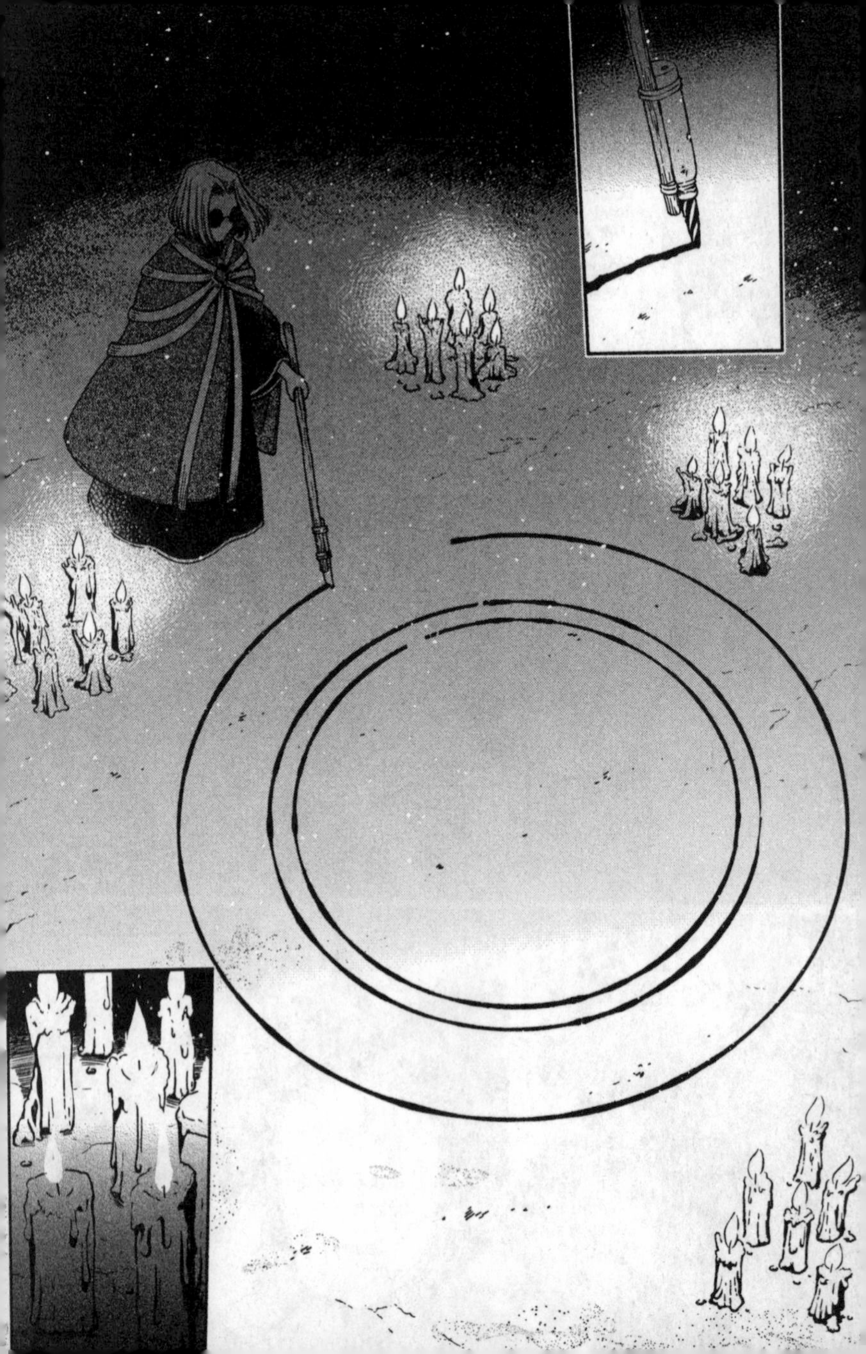

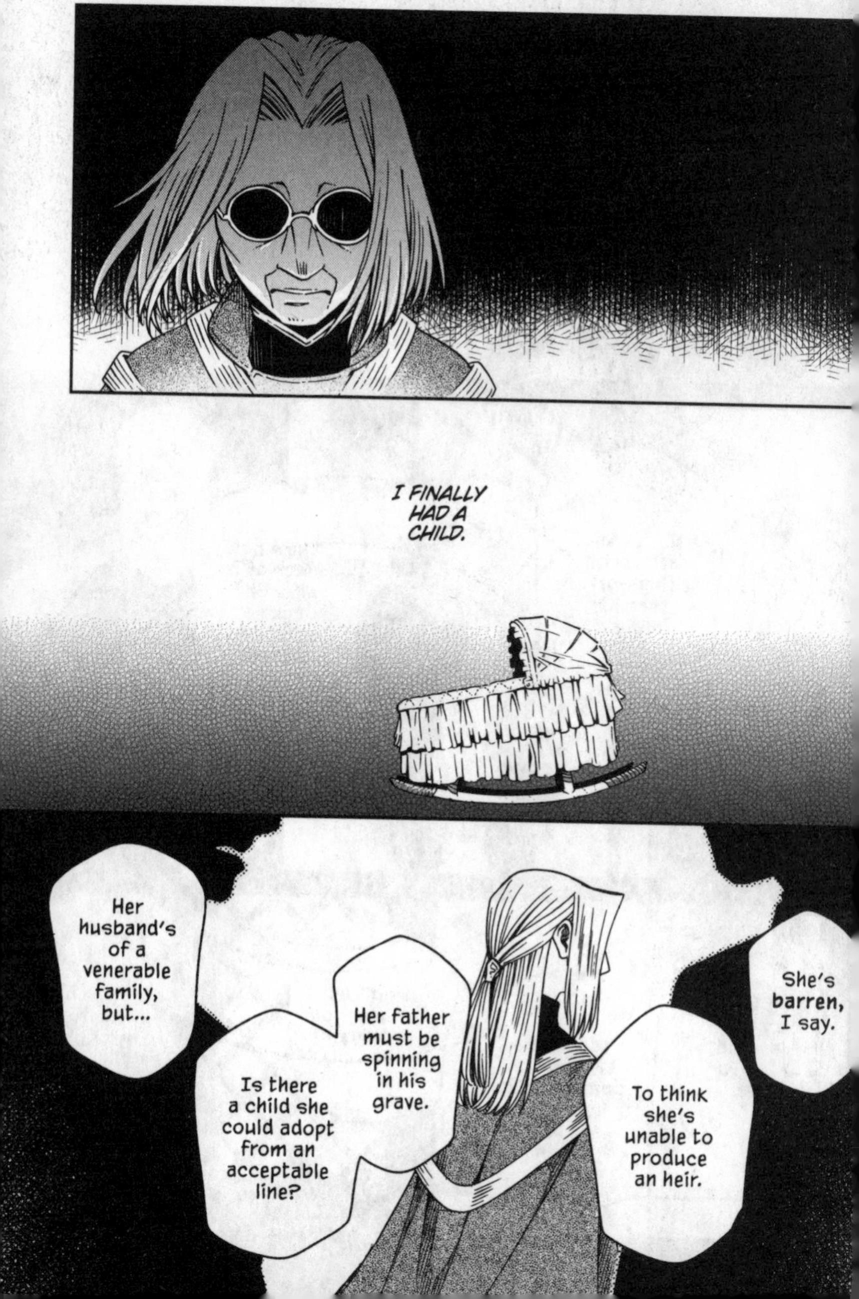
I FINALLY HAD A CHILD.
She's barren, I say.
To think she's unable to produce an heir.
Her father must be spinning in his grave.
Her husband's of a venerable family, but...
Is there a child she could adopt from an acceptable line?

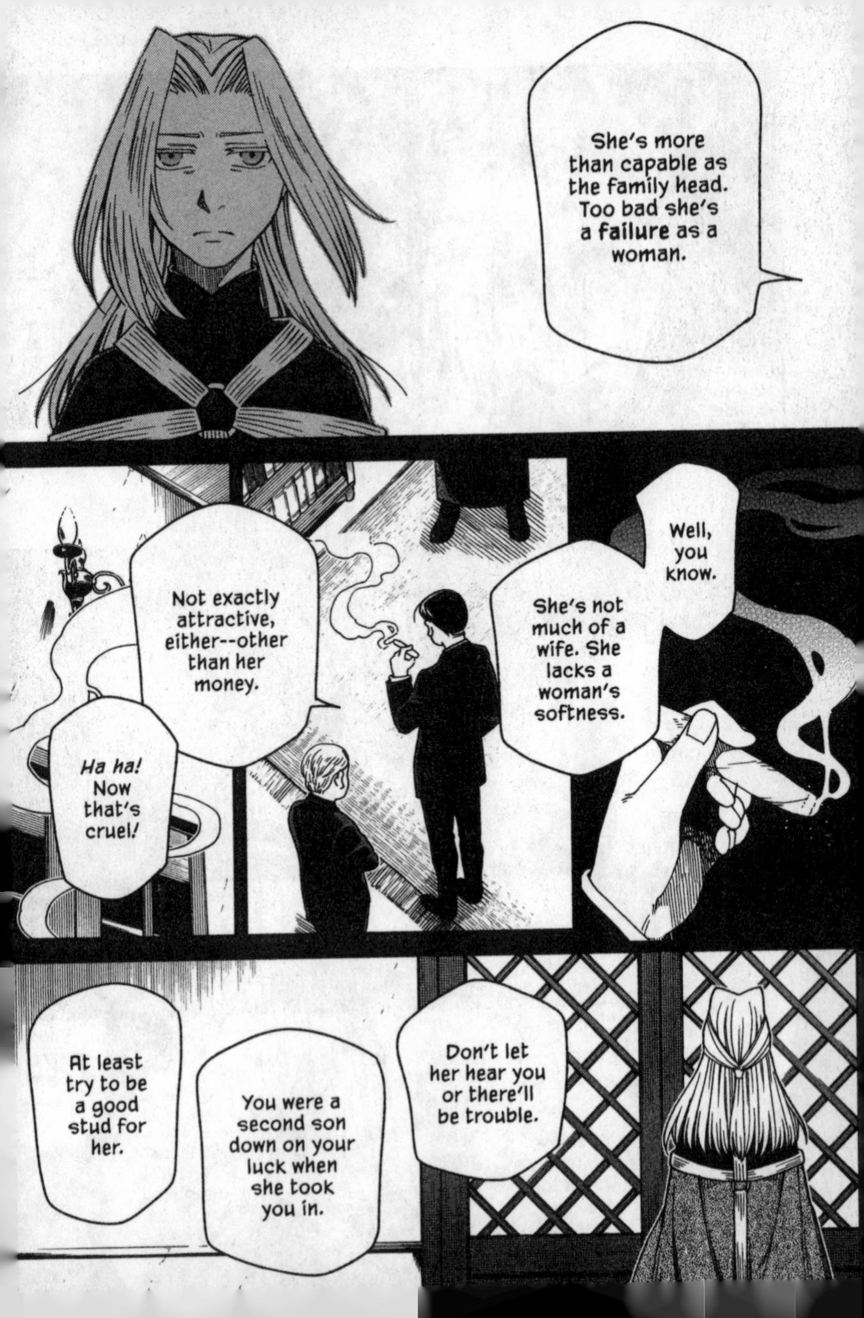
She's more than capable as the family head. Too bad she's a **failure** as a woman.
Well, you know.
She's not much of a wife. She lacks a woman's softness.
Not exactly attractive, either--other than her money.
Ha ha! Now that's cruel!
Don't let her hear you or there'll be trouble.
You were a second son down on your luck when she took you in.
At least try to be a good stud for her.

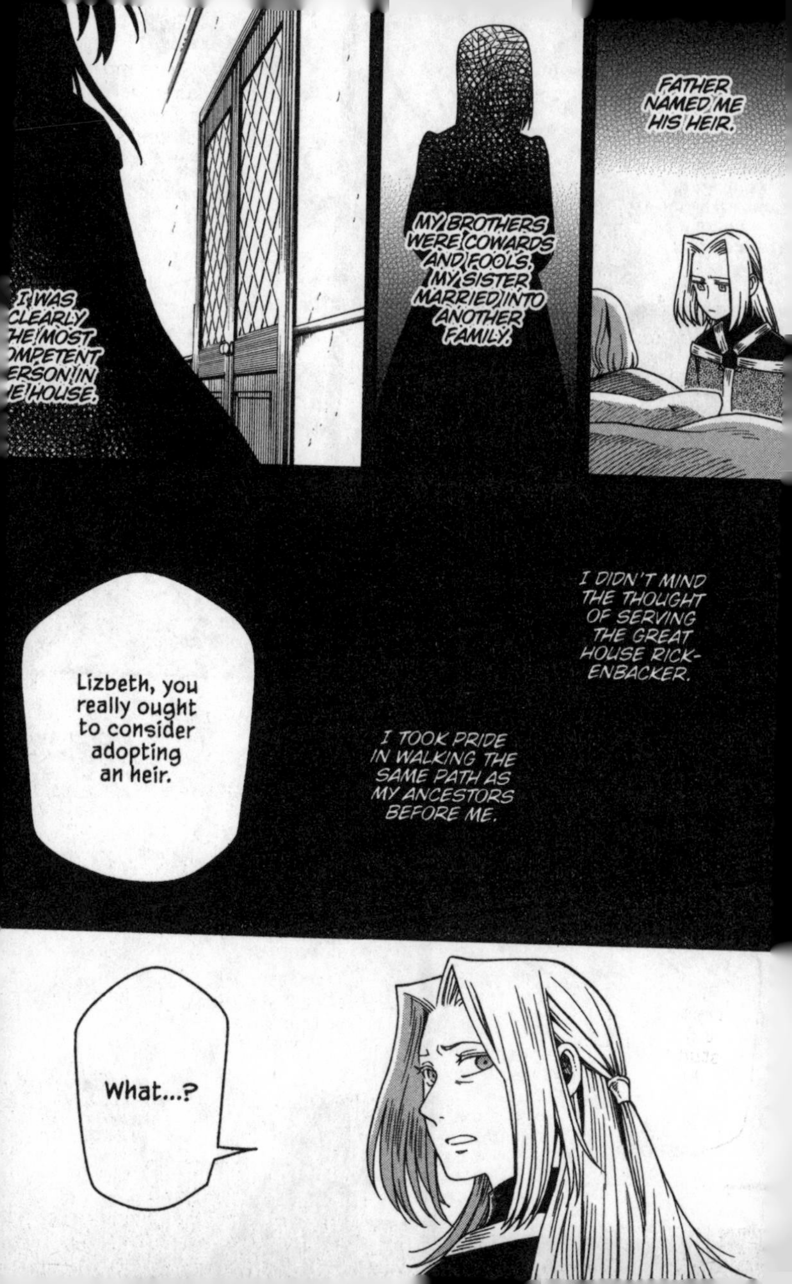
FATHER NAMED ME HIS HEIR.
MY BROTHERS WERE COWARDS AND FOOLS. MY SISTER MARRIED INTO ANOTHER FAMILY.
I WAS CLEARLY HE MOST OMPETENT ERSON IN E HOUSE.
I DIDN'T MIND THE THOUGHT OF SERVING THE GREAT HOUSE RICK-ENBACKER.
I TOOK PRIDE IN WALKING THE SAME PATH AS MY ANCESTORS BEFORE ME.
Lizbeth, you really ought to consider adopting an heir.
What...?

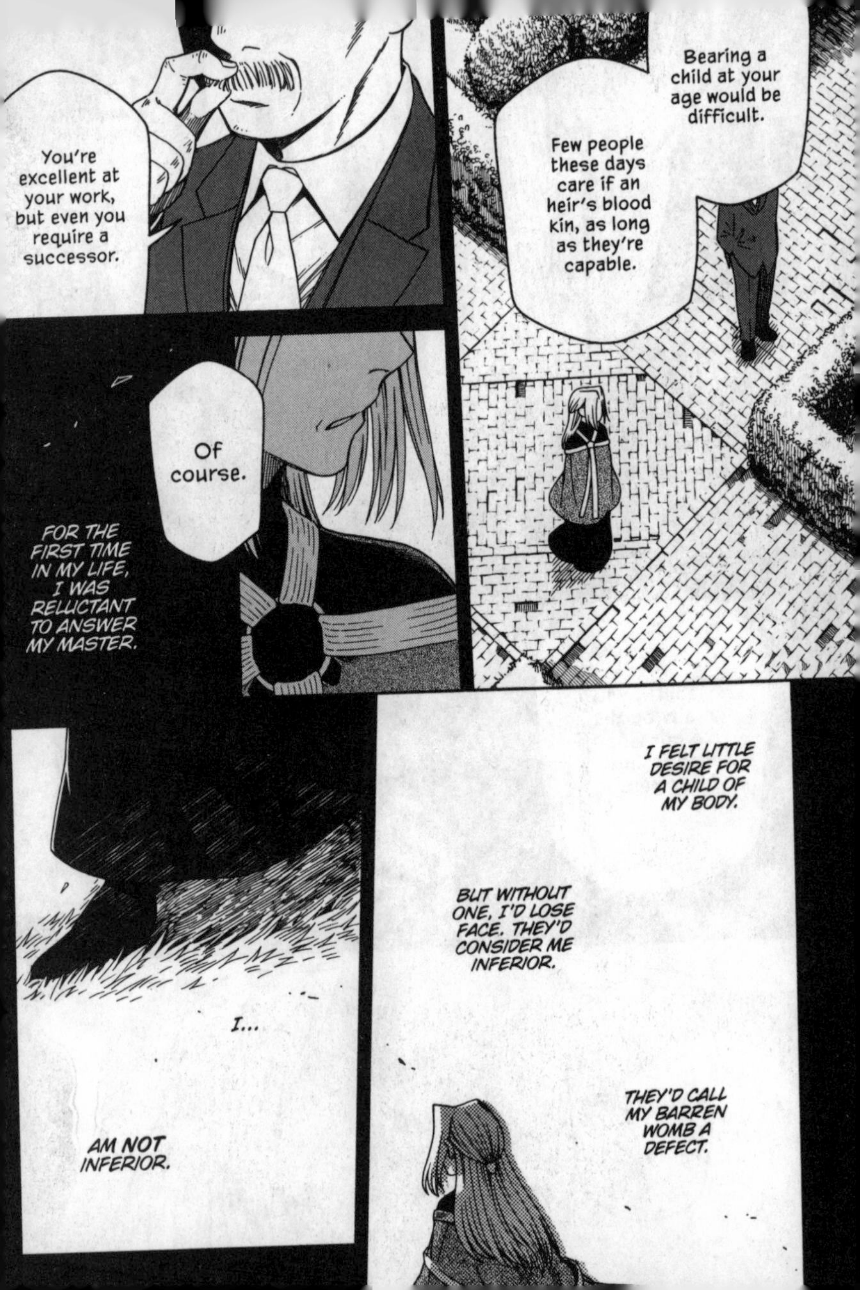
Bearing a child at your age would be difficult.
Few people these days care if an heir's blood kin, as long as they're capable.
You're excellent at your work, but even you require a successor.
Of course.
FOR THE FIRST TIME IN MY LIFE, I WAS RELUCTANT TO ANSWER MY MASTER.
I FELT LITTLE DESIRE FOR A CHILD OF MY BODY.
BUT WITHOUT ONE, I'D LOSE FACE. THEY'D CONSIDER ME INFERIOR.
THEY'D CALL MY BARREN WOMB A DEFECT.
I...
AM NOT INFERIOR.

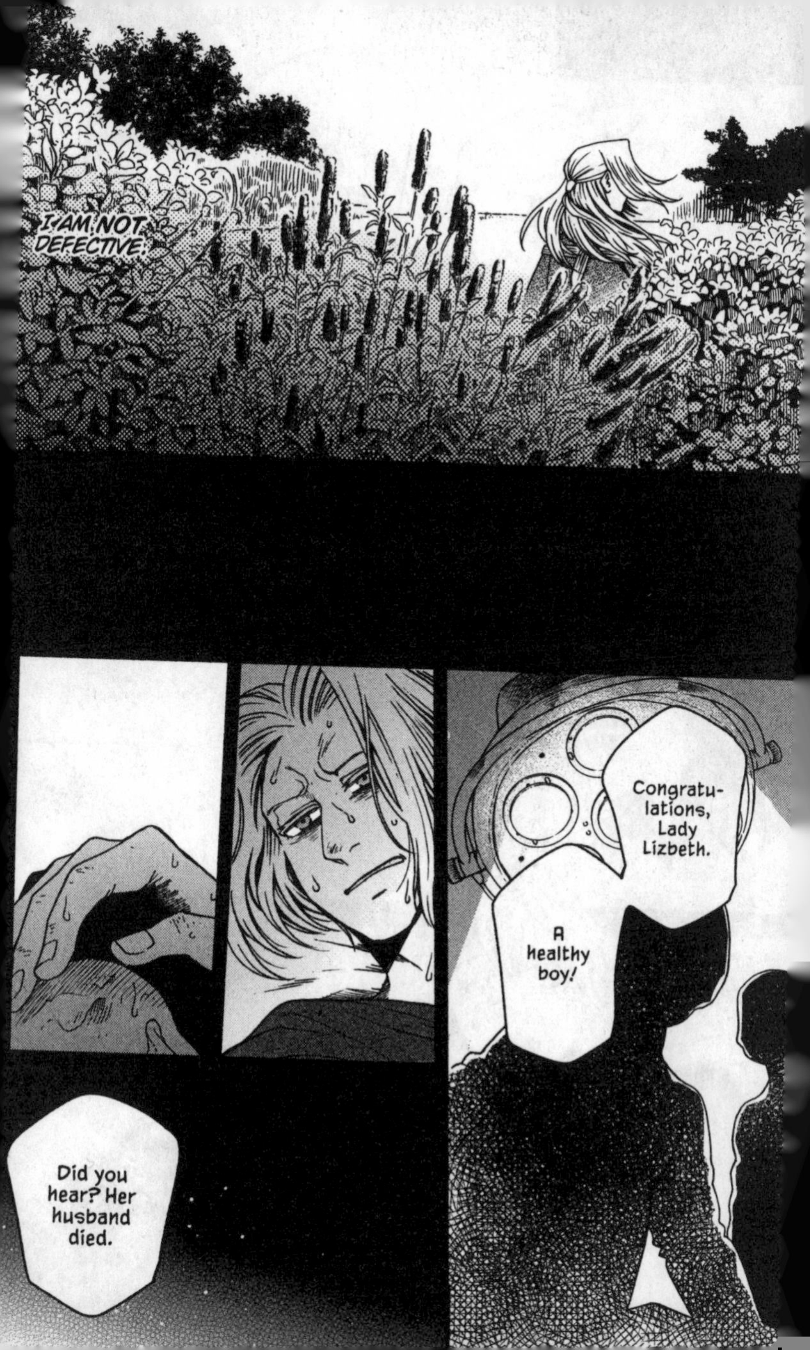
I AM NOT DEFECTIVE.
Congratulations, Lady Lizbeth.
A healthy boy!
Did you hear? Her husband died.

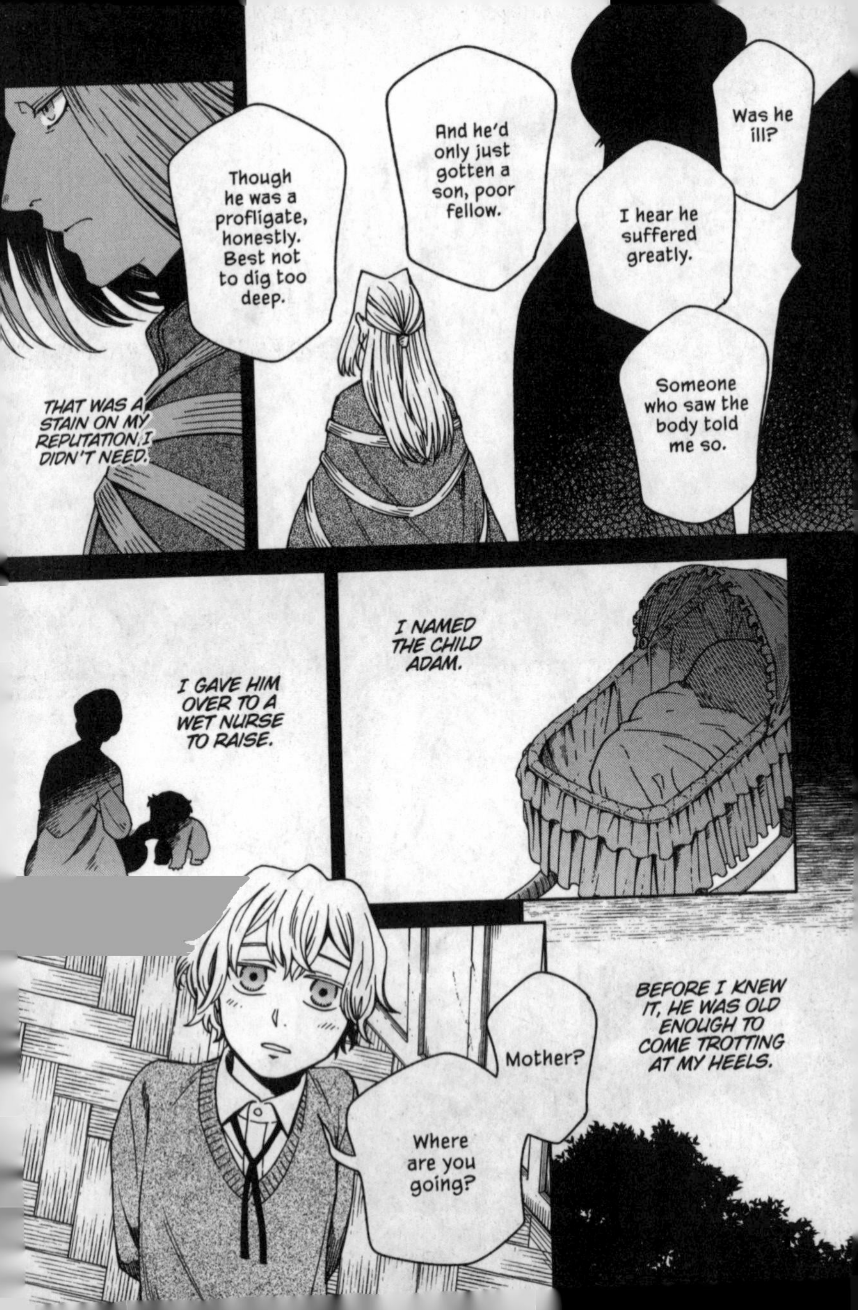
Was he ill?
I hear he suffered greatly.
Someone who saw the body told me so.
And he'd only just gotten a son, poor fellow.
Though he was a profligate, honestly. Best not to dig too deep.
THAT WAS A STAIN ON MY REPUTATION I DIDN'T NEED.
I NAMED THE CHILD ADAM.
I GAVE HIM OVER TO A WET NURSE TO RAISE.
BEFORE I KNEW IT, HE WAS OLD ENOUGH TO COME TROTTING AT MY HEELS.
Mother?
Where are you going?

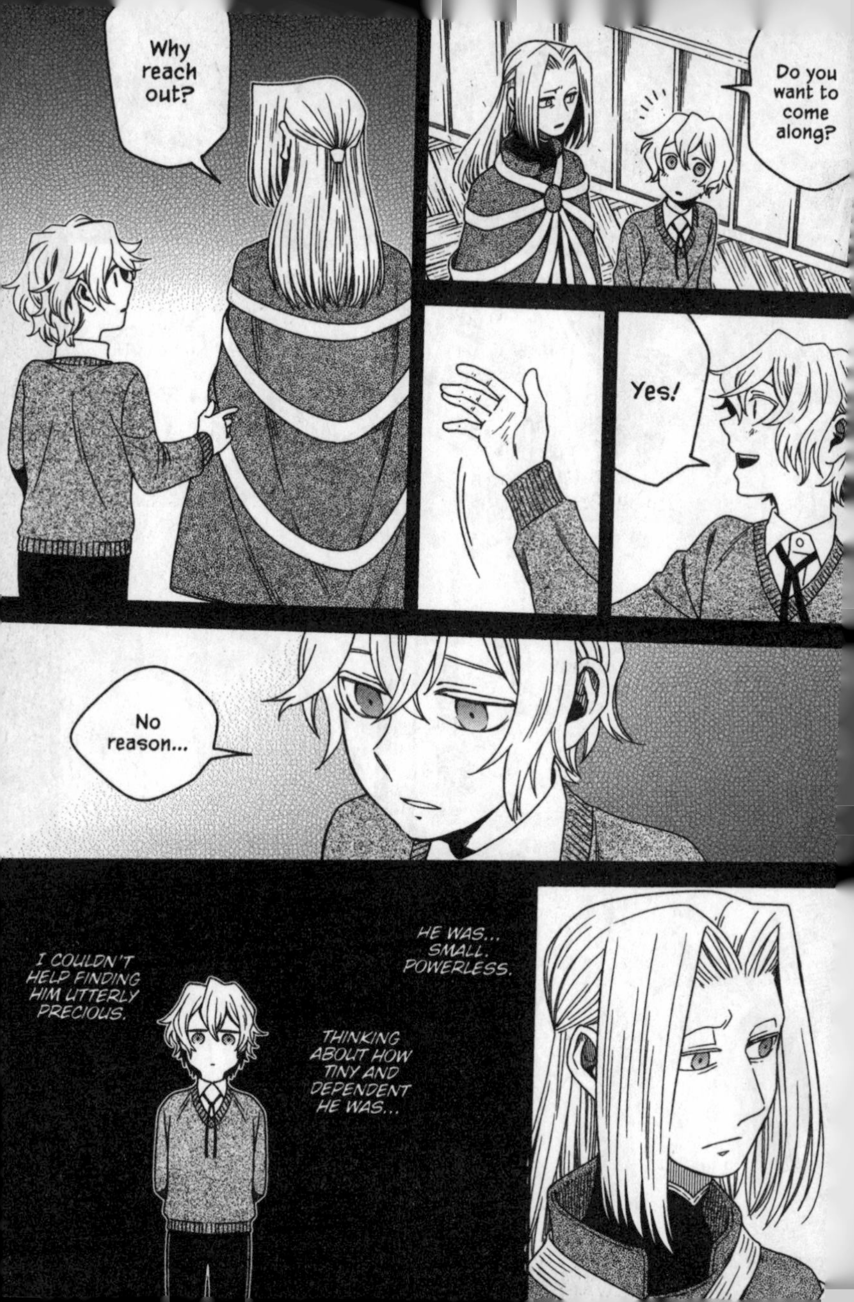
Do you want to come along?
Yes!
Why reach out?
No reason...
HE WAS... SMALL. POWERLESS.
THINKING ABOUT HOW TINY AND DEPENDENT HE WAS...
I COULDN'T HELP FINDING HIM UTTERLY PRECIOUS.

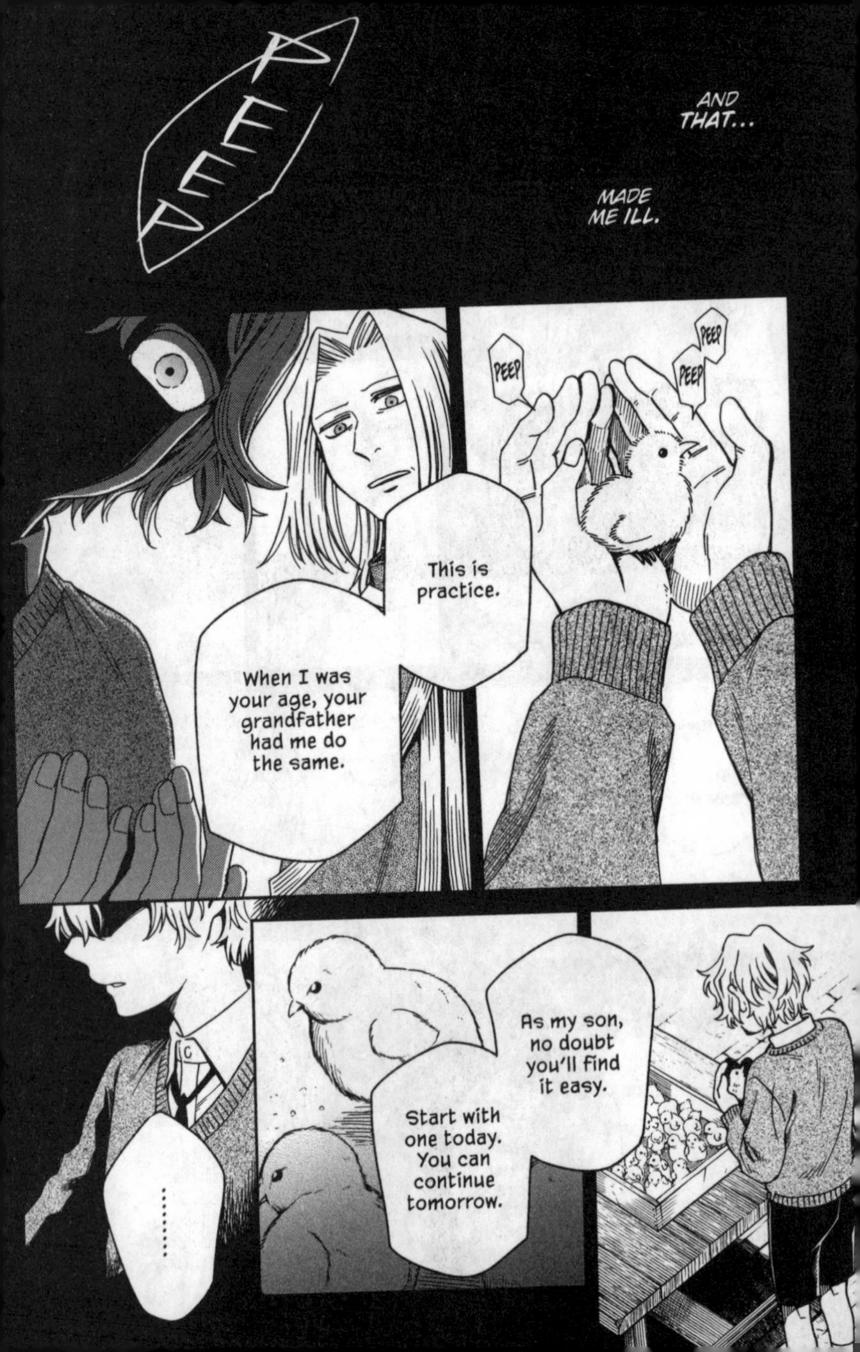
AND THAT...
MADE ME ILL.
PEEP
PEEP
PEEP
PEEP
This is practice.
When I was your age, your grandfather had me do the same.
As my son, no doubt you'll find it easy.
Start with one today. You can continue tomorrow.
....

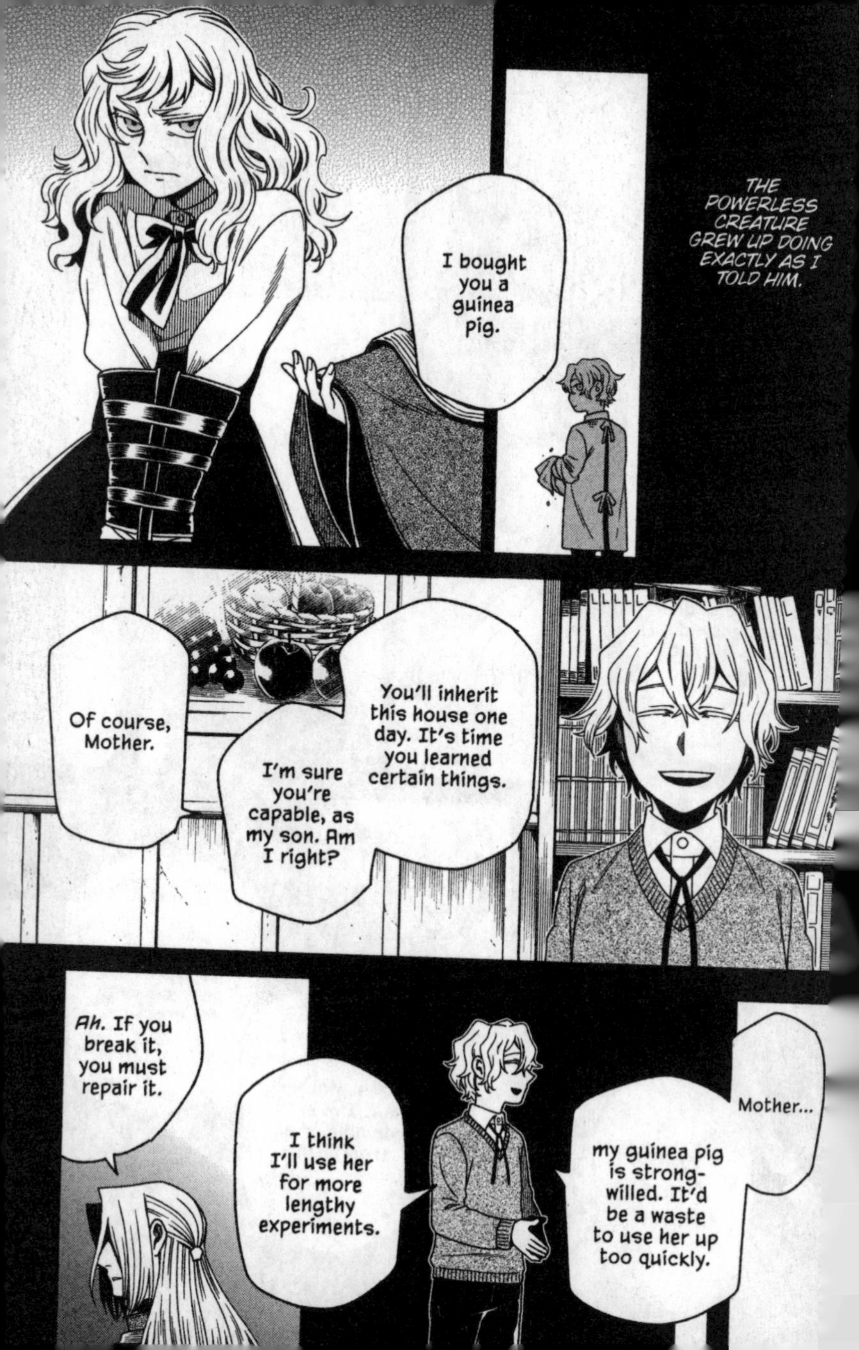
THE POWERLESS CREATURE GREW UP DOING EXACTLY AS I TOLD HIM.
I bought you a guinea pig.
You'll inherit this house one day. It's time you learned certain things.
I'm sure you're capable, as my son. Am I right?
Of course, Mother.
Mother...
my guinea pig is strong-willed. It'd be a waste to use her up too quickly.
I think I'll use her for more lengthy experiments.
Ah. If you break it, you must repair it.

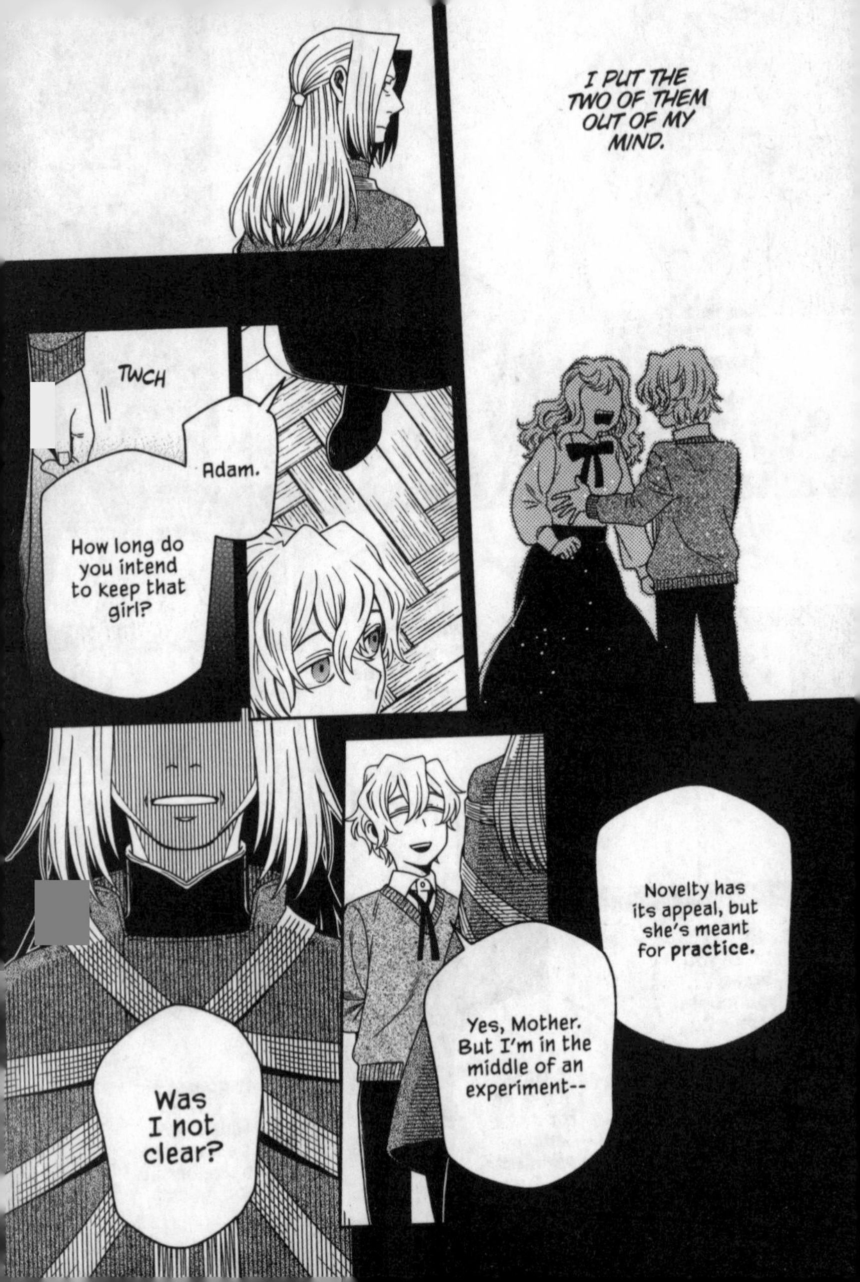
I PUT THE TWO OF THEM OUT OF MY MIND.
TWCH
Adam.
How long do you intend to keep that girl?
Novelty has its appeal, but she's meant for practice.
Yes, Mother. But I'm in the middle of an experiment--
Was I not clear?

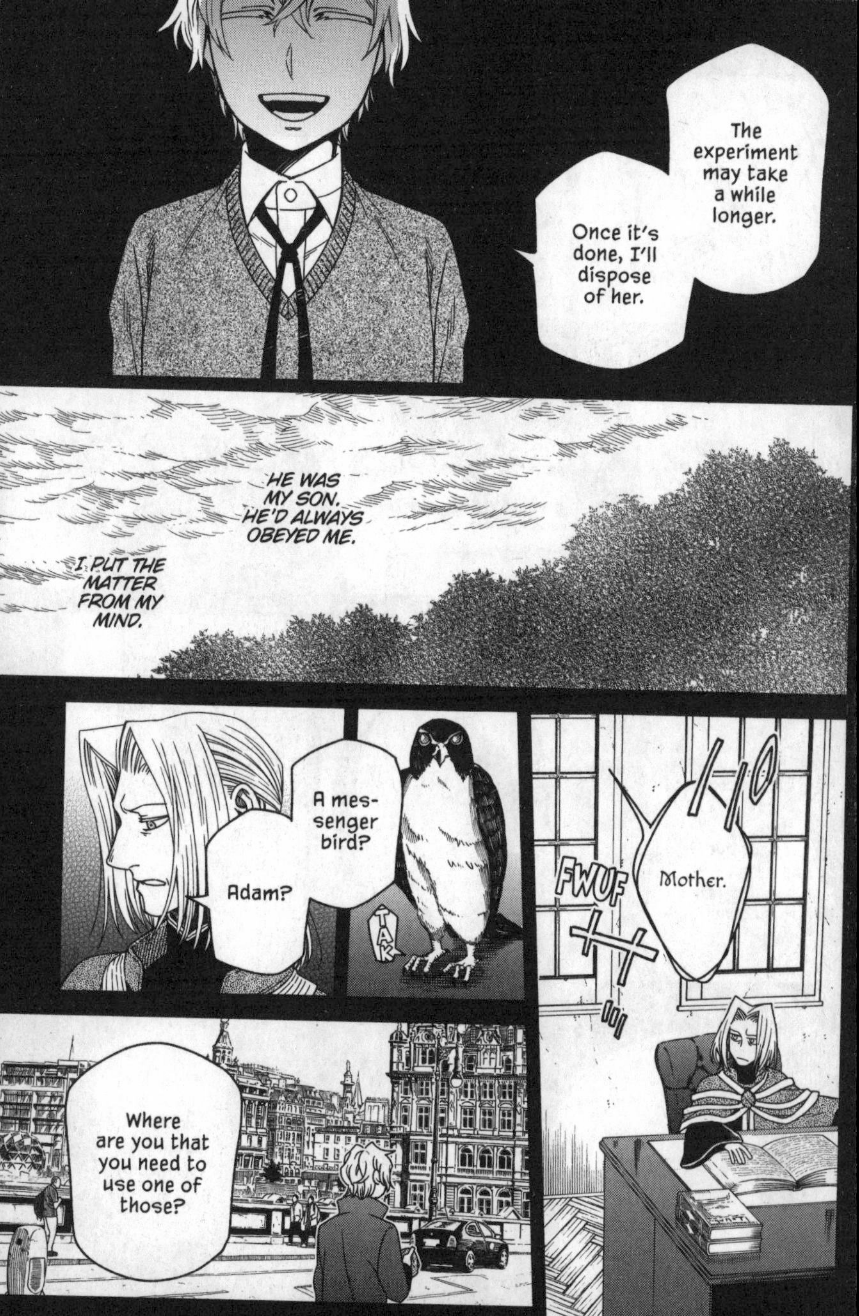
The experiment may take a while longer.
Once it's done, I'll dispose of her.
HE WAS MY SON. HE'D ALWAYS OBEYED ME.
I PUT THE MATTER FROM MY MIND.
FWUF
Mother.
TAK
A messenger bird?
Adam?
Where are you that you need to use one of those?

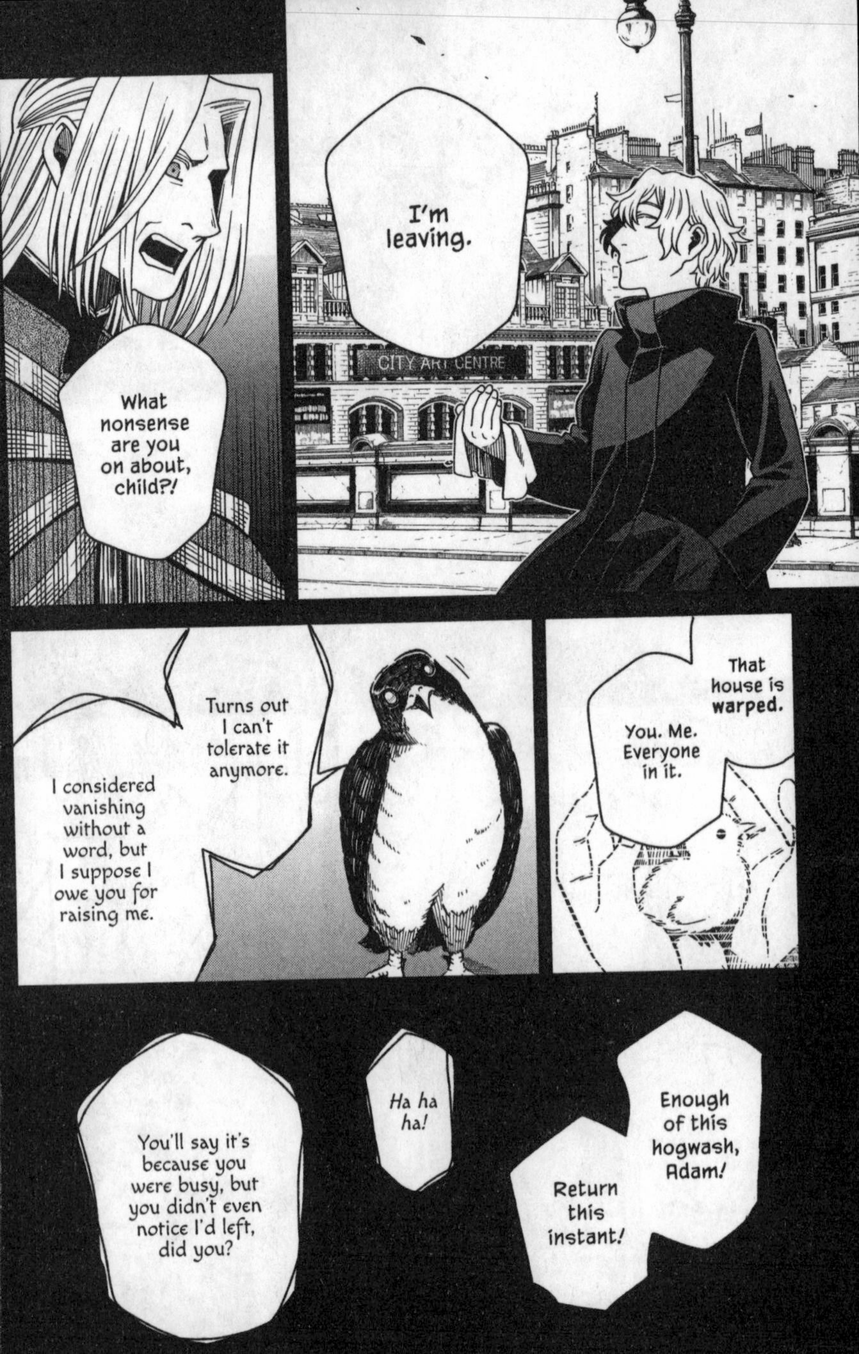
I'm leaving.
CITY ART CENTRE
What nonsense are you on about, child?!
That house is warped.
You. Me. Everyone in it.
Turns out I can't tolerate it anymore.
I considered vanishing without a word, but I suppose I owe you for raising me.
Enough of this hogwash, Adam!
Return this instant!
Ha ha ha!
You'll say it's because you were busy, but you didn't even notice I'd left, did you?

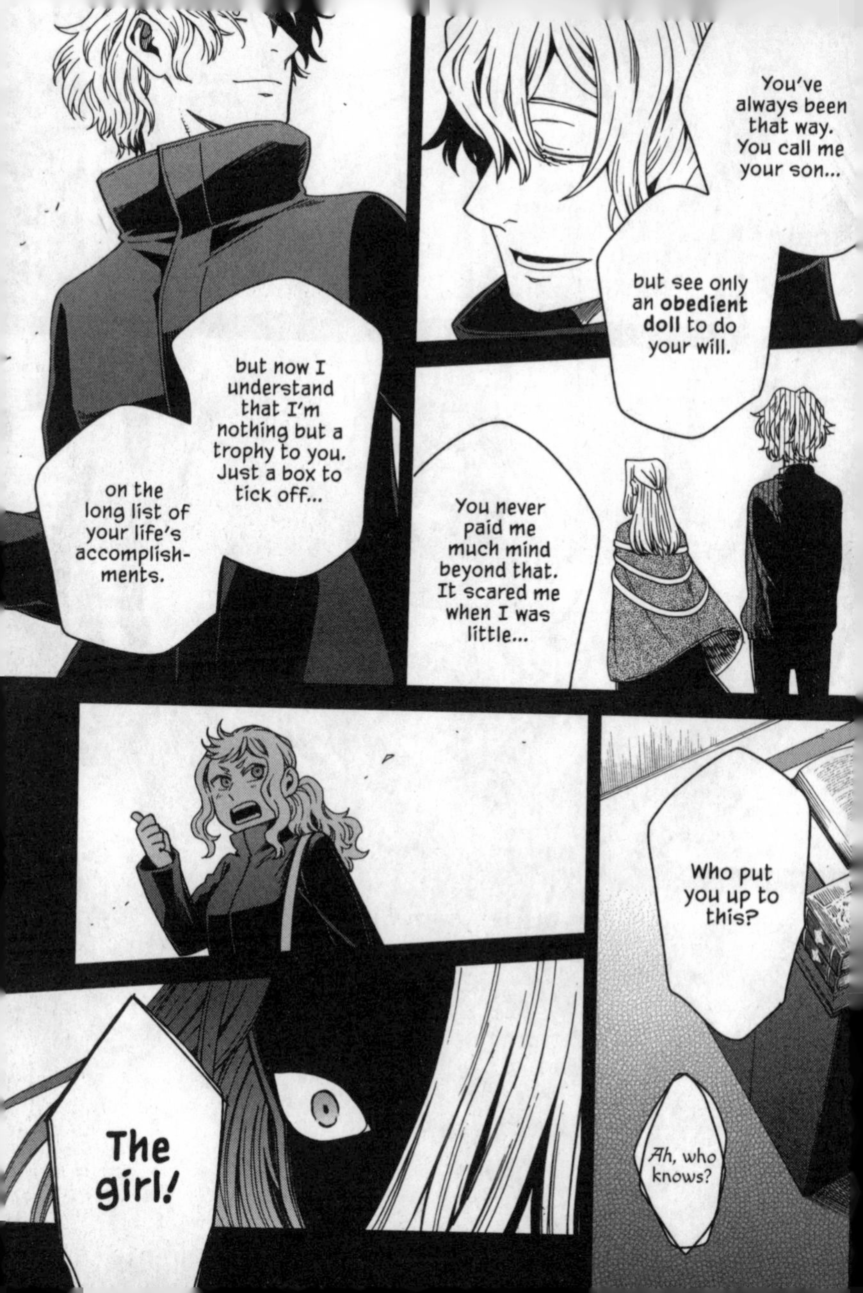
You've always been that way. You call me your son...
but see only an **obedient doll** to do your will.
You never paid me much mind beyond that. It scared me when I was little...
but now I understand that I'm nothing but a trophy to you. Just a box to tick off...
on the long list of your life's accomplish-ments.
Who put you up to this?
Ah, who knows?
The girl!

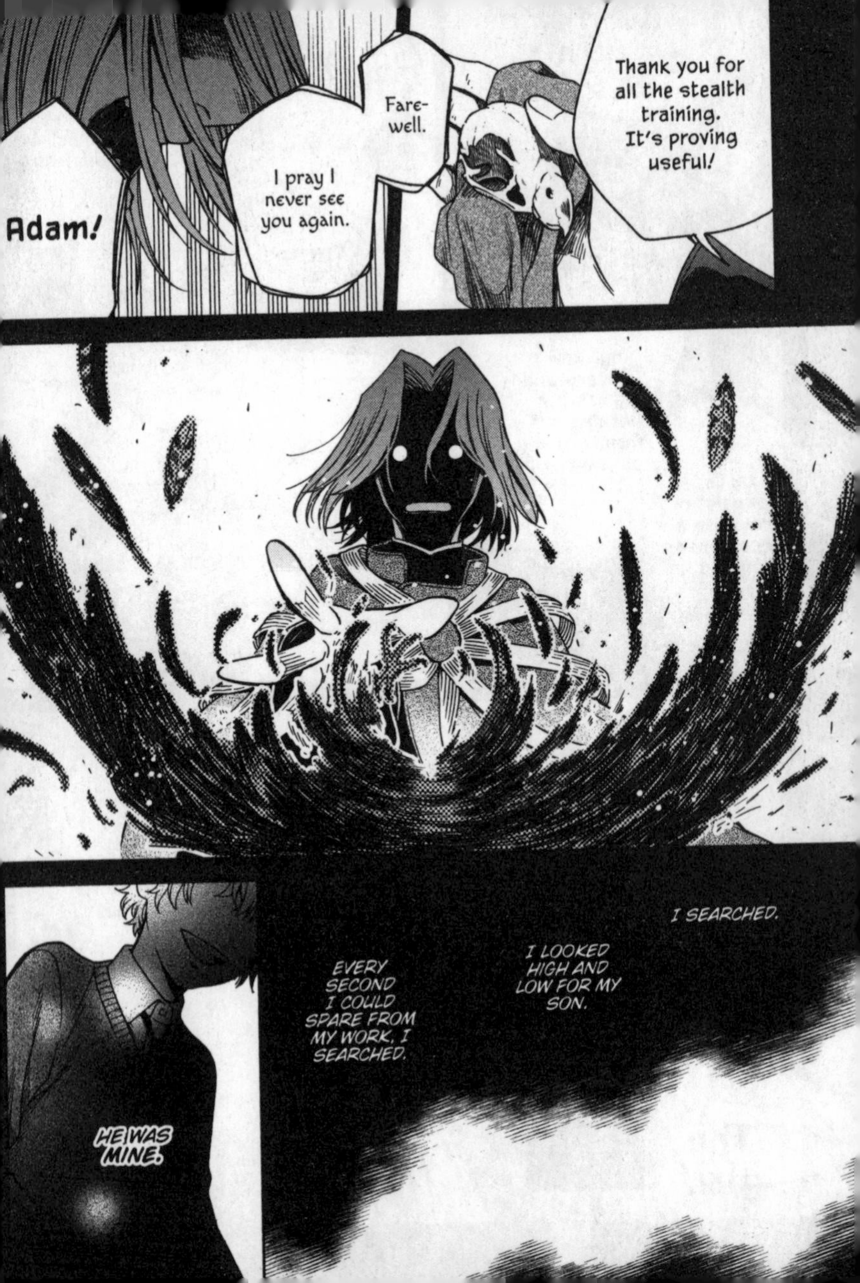
Thank you for all the stealth training. It's proving useful!
Fare-well.
I pray I never see you again.
Adam!
I SEARCHED.
I LOOKED HIGH AND LOW FOR MY SON.
EVERY SECOND I COULD SPARE FROM MY WORK, I SEARCHED.
HE WAS MINE.

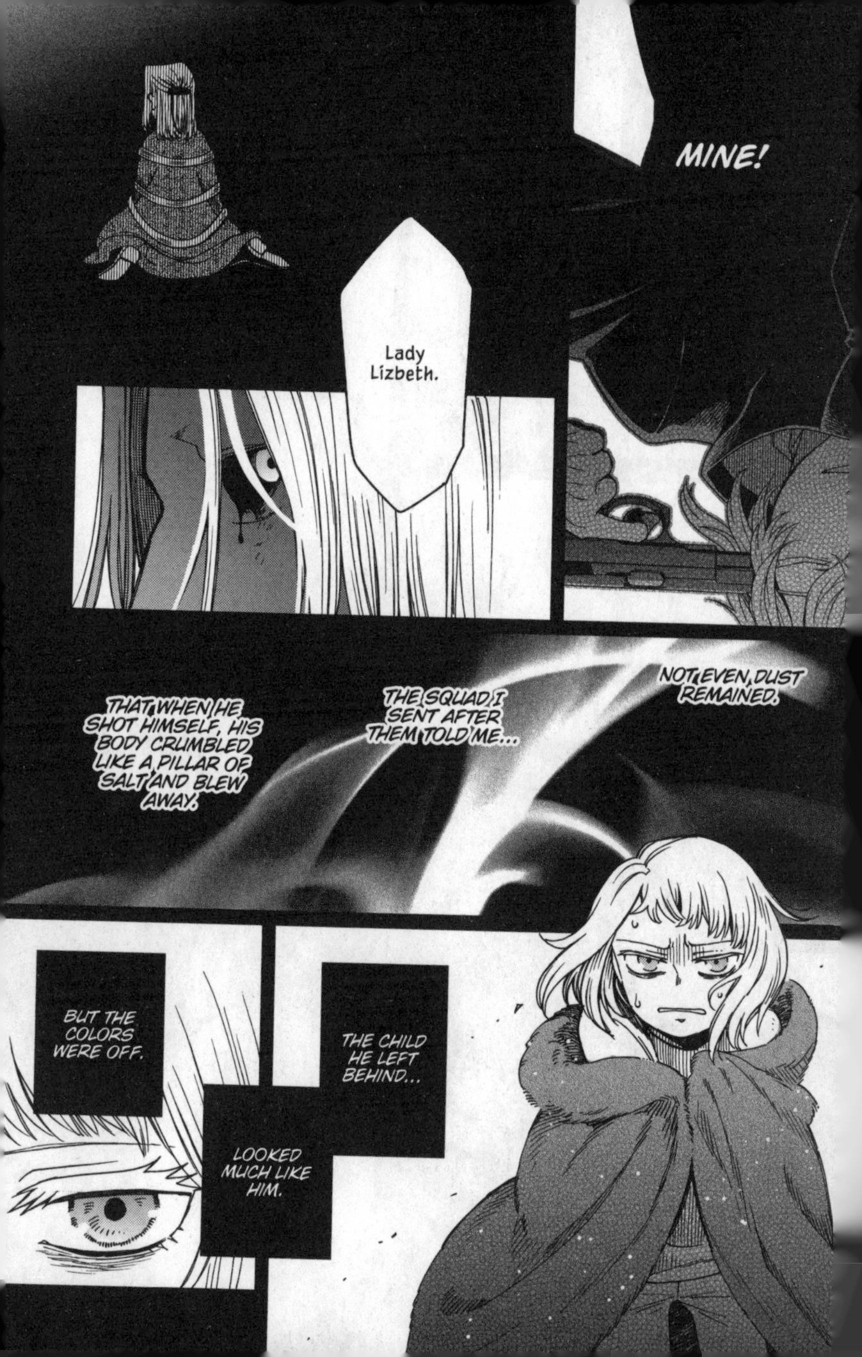

MINE!
Lady Lizbeth.
NOT EVEN DUST REMAINED.
THE SQUAD I SENT AFTER THEM TOLD ME...
THAT WHEN HE SHOT HIMSELF, HIS BODY CRUMBLED LIKE A PILLAR OF SALT AND BLEW AWAY.
THE CHILD HE LEFT BEHIND...
LOOKED MUCH LIKE HIM.
BUT THE COLORS WERE OFF.

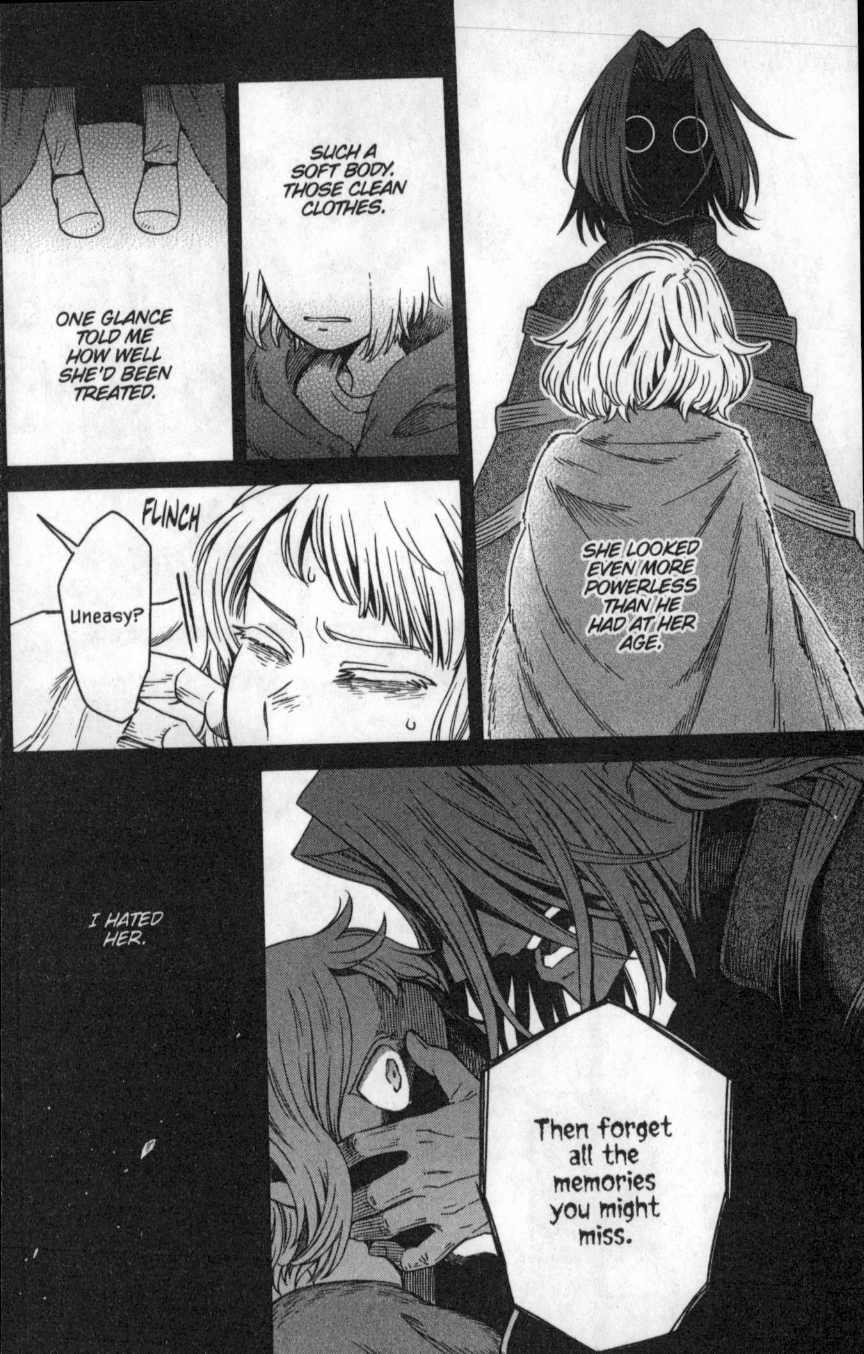
SHE LOOKED EVEN MORE POWERLESS THAN HE HAD AT HER AGE.
SUCH A SOFT BODY. THOSE CLEAN CLOTHES.
ONE GLANCE TOLD ME HOW WELL SHE'D BEEN TREATED.
FLINCH
Uneasy?
Then forget all the memories you might miss.
I HATED HER.

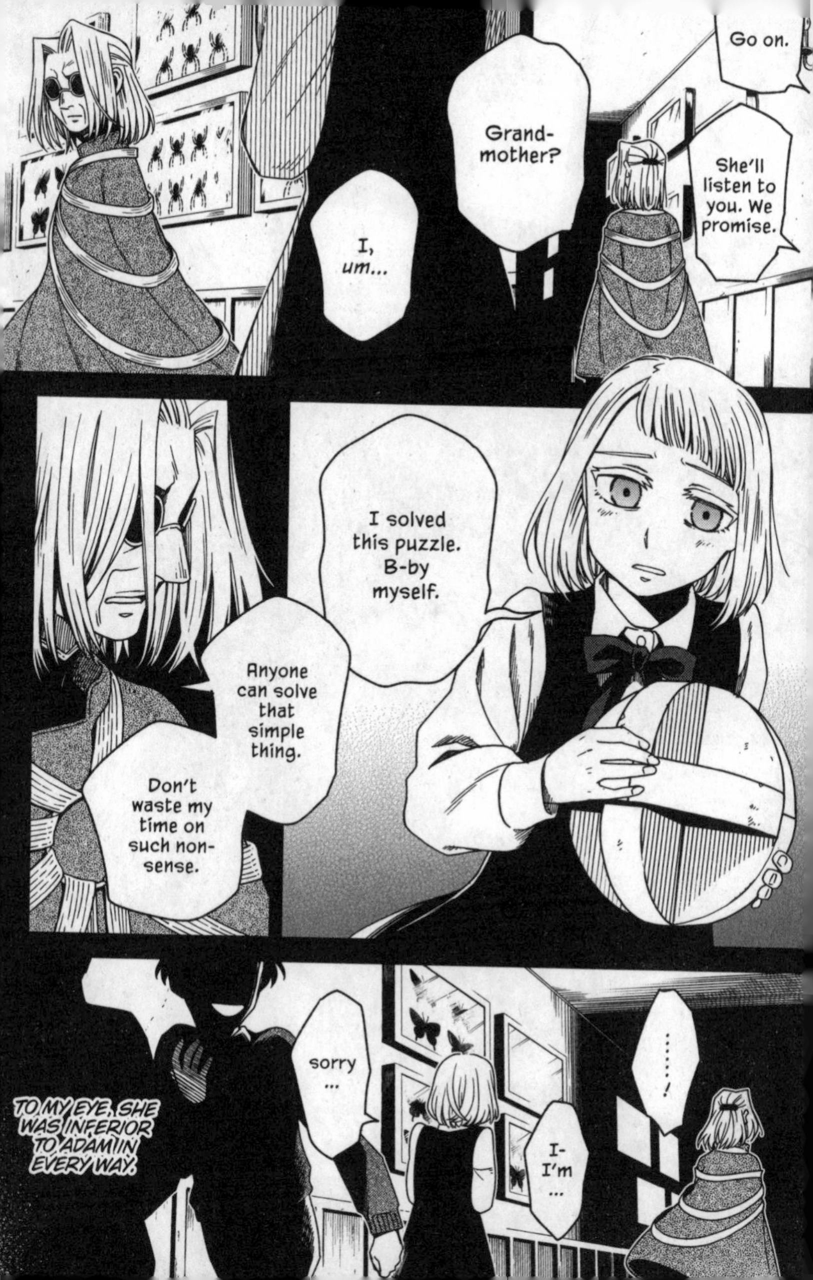
Go on.
She'll listen to you. We promise.
Grand-mother?
I, um...
I solved this puzzle. B-by myself.
Anyone can solve that simple thing.
Don't waste my time on such non-sense.
......!
I- I'm ...
sorry ...
TO MY EYE, SHE WAS INFERIOR TO ADAM IN EVERY WAY.

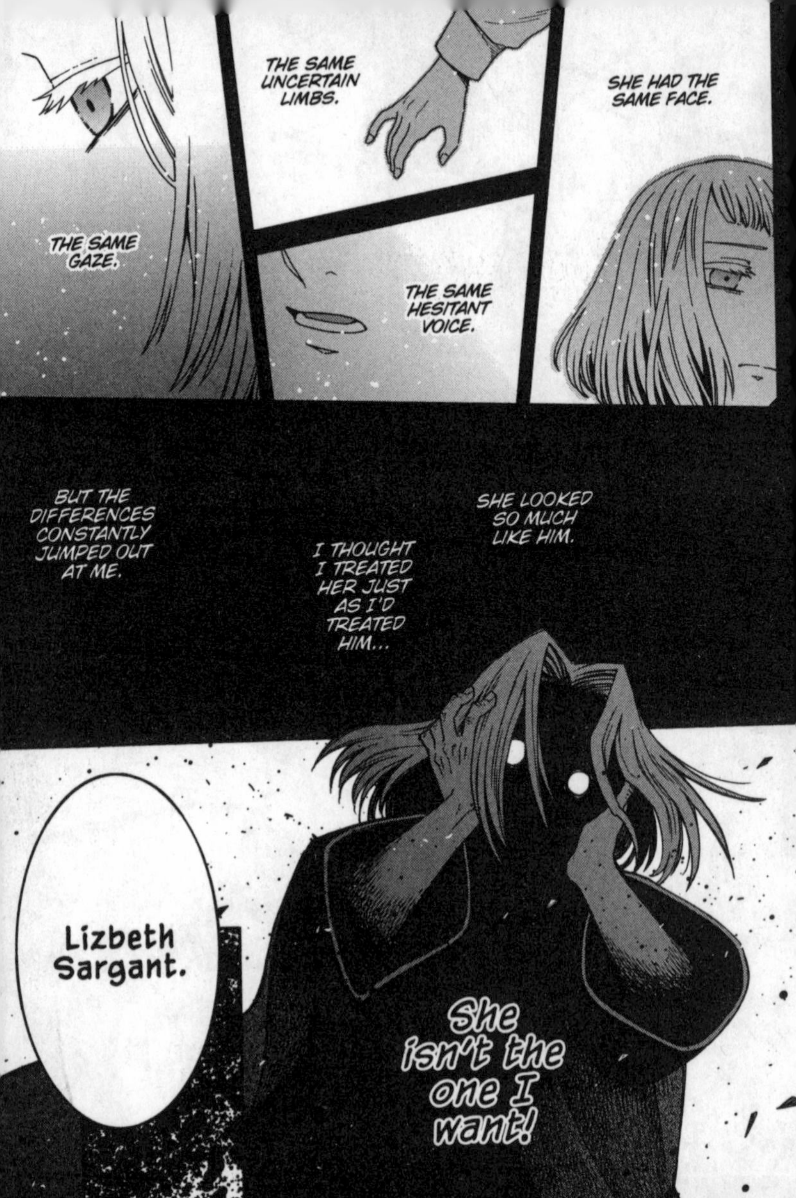
SHE HAD THE SAME FACE.
THE SAME UNCERTAIN LIMBS.
THE SAME HESITANT VOICE.
THE SAME GAZE.
SHE LOOKED SO MUCH LIKE HIM.
I THOUGHT I TREATED HER JUST AS I'D TREATED HIM...
BUT THE DIFFERENCES CONSTANTLY JUMPED OUT AT ME.
She isn't the one I want!
Lizbeth Sargant.

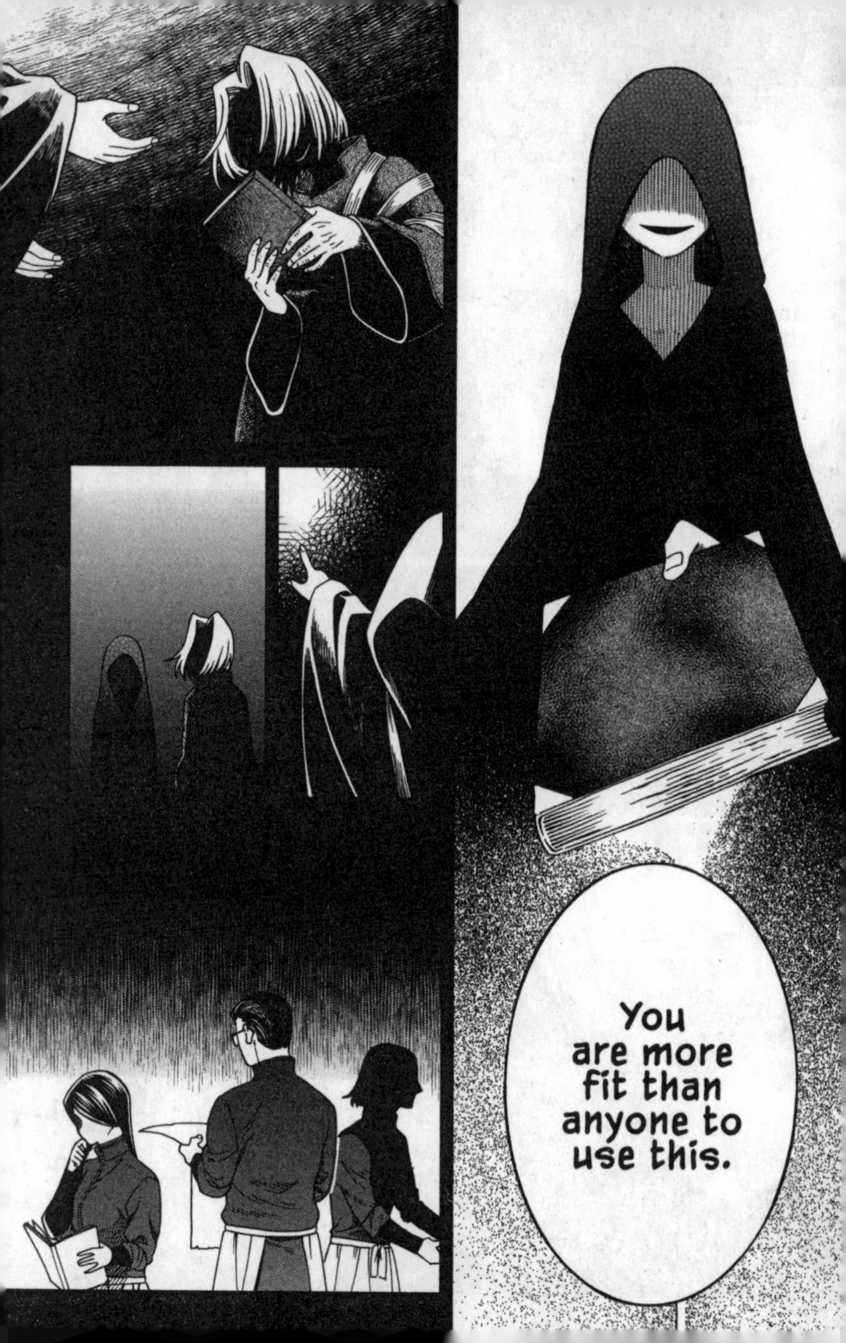
You are more fit than anyone to use this.

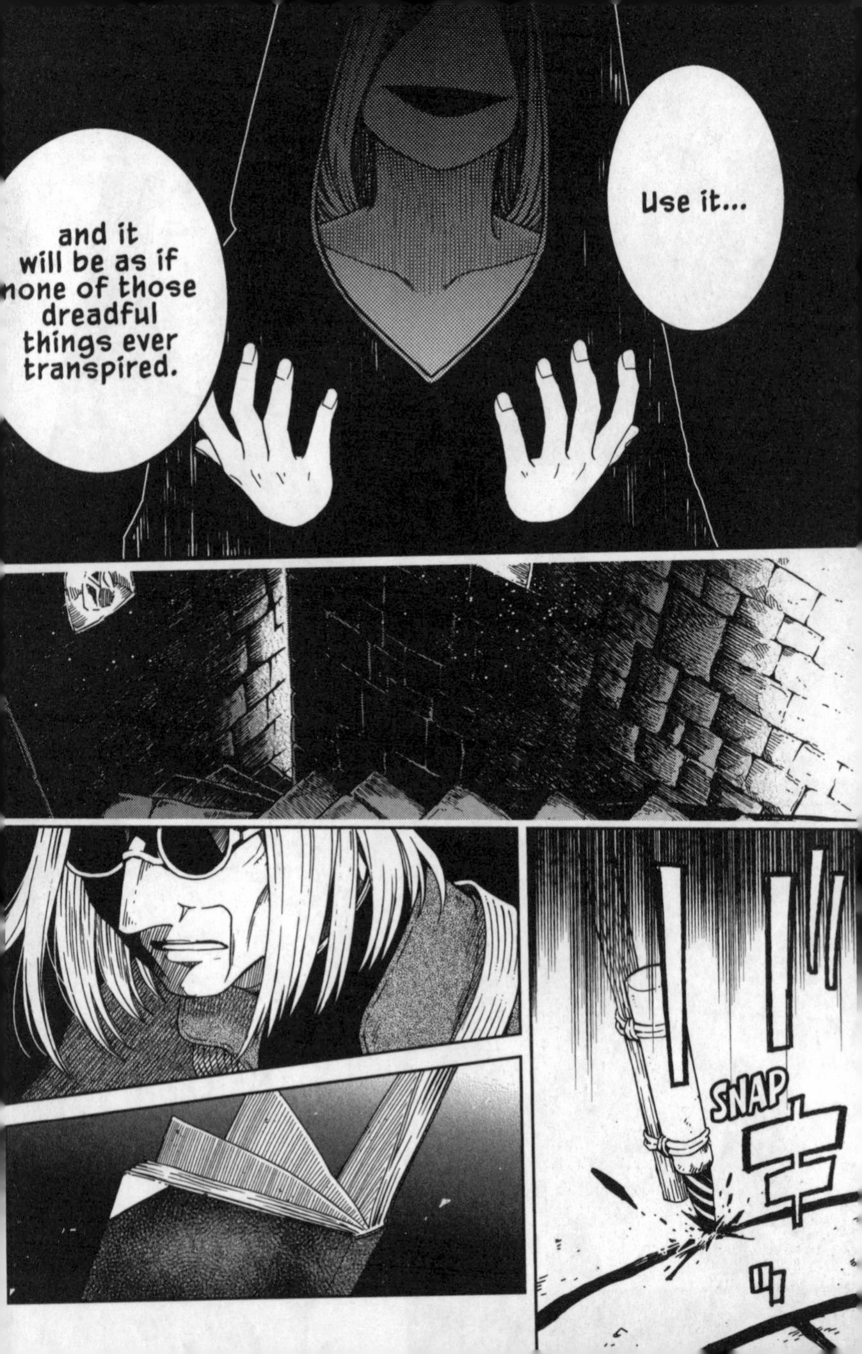
Use it...
and it will be as if none of those dreadful things ever transpired.
SNAP

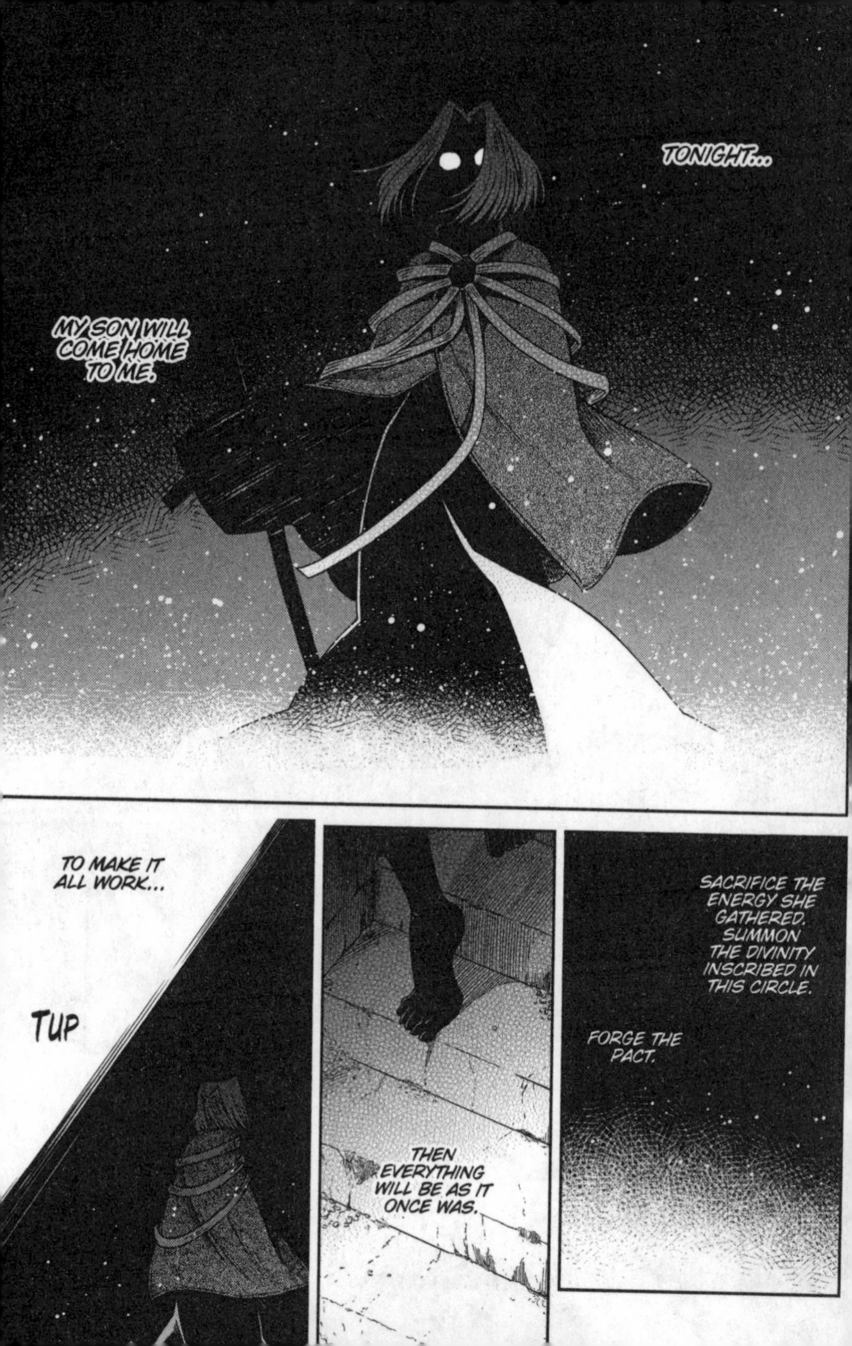
TONIGHT...
MY SON WILL COME HOME TO ME.
SACRIFICE THE ENERGY SHE GATHERED. SUMMON THE DIVINITY INSCRIBED IN THIS CIRCLE.
FORGE THE PACT.
THEN EVERYTHING WILL BE AS IT ONCE WAS.
TO MAKE IT ALL WORK...
TUP

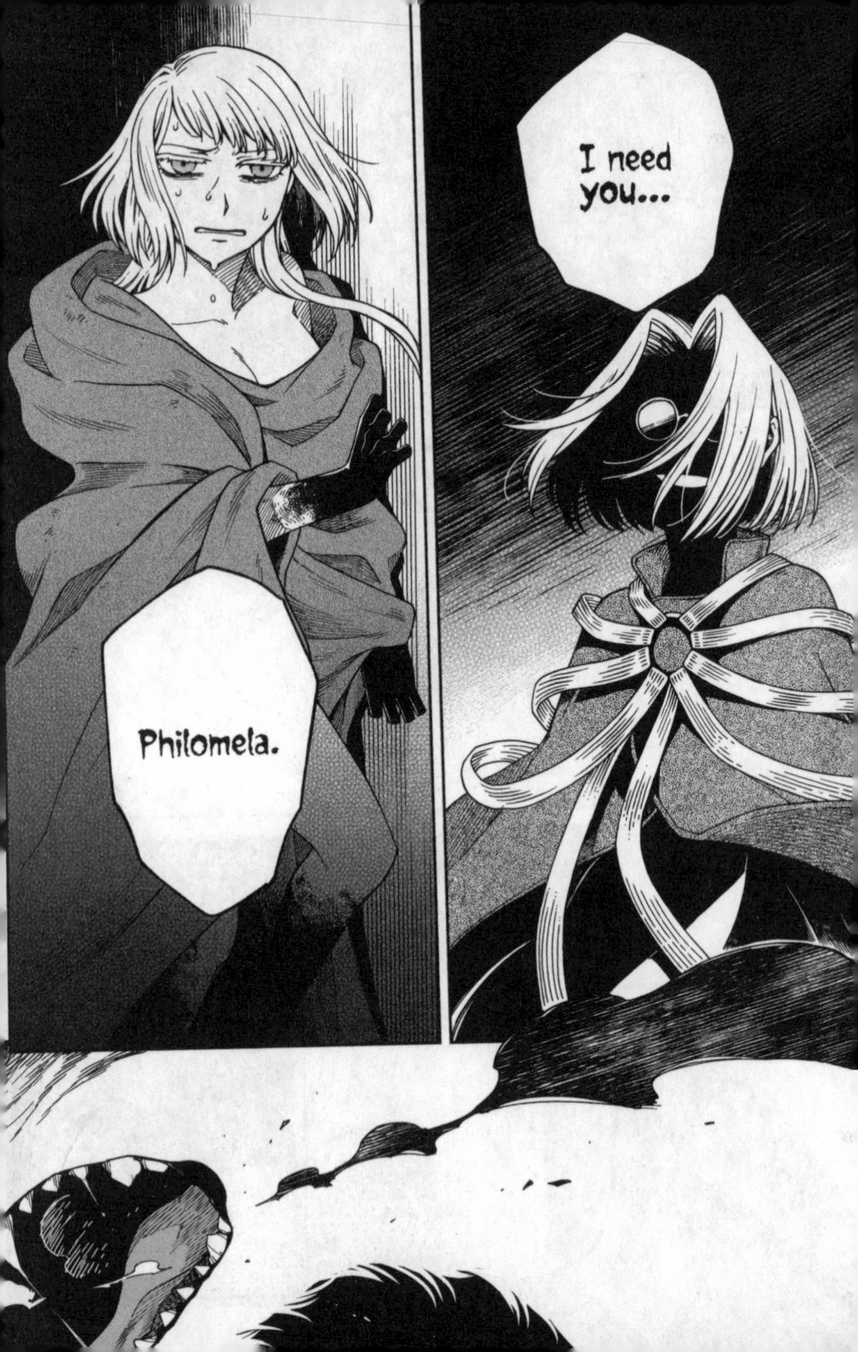
I need you...
Philomela.

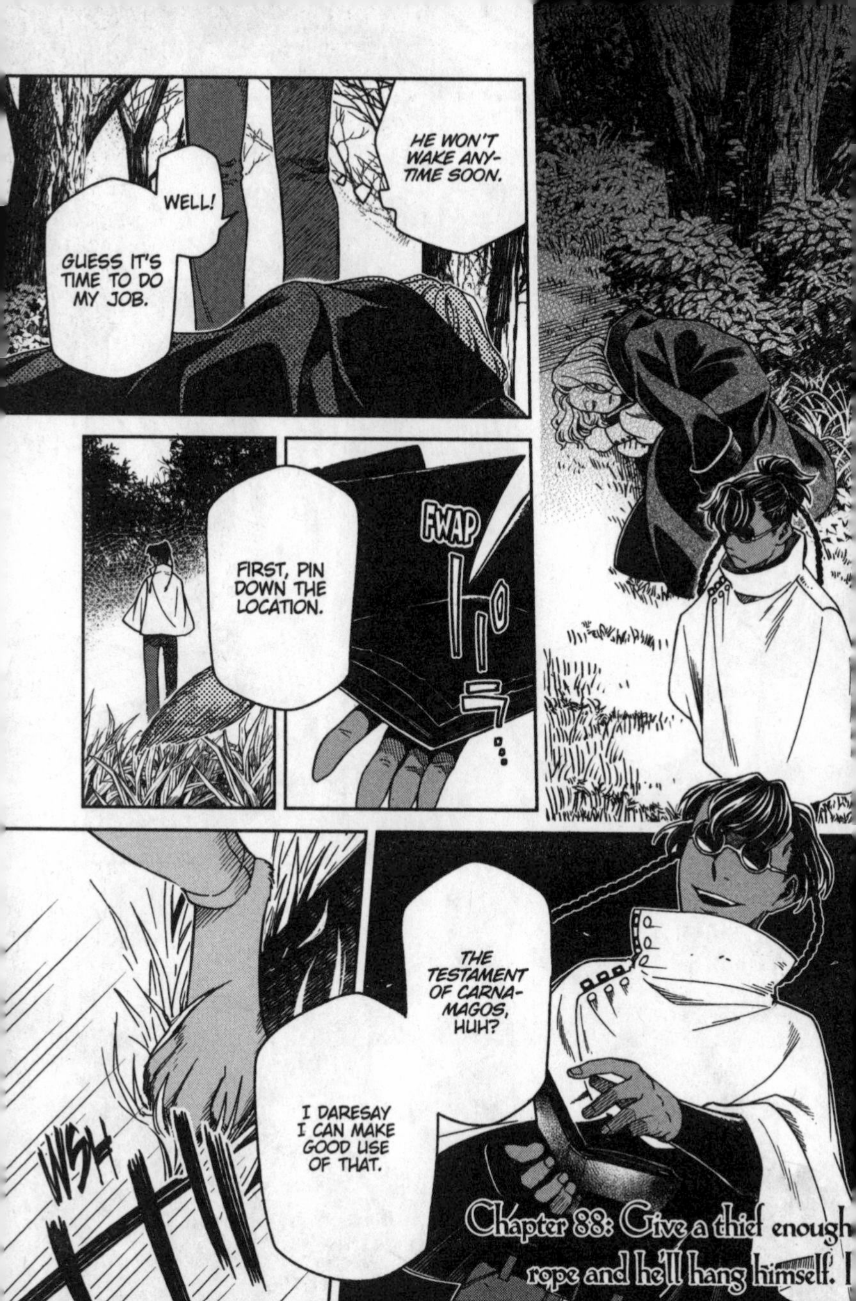
HE WON'T WAKE ANY-TIME SOON.
WELL!
GUESS IT'S TIME TO DO MY JOB.
FWAP
FIRST, PIN DOWN THE LOCATION.
THE TESTAMENT OF CARNA-MAGOS, HUH?
I DARESAY I CAN MAKE GOOD USE OF THAT.
Chapter 88: Give a thief enough rope and he'll hang himself. I
WSH

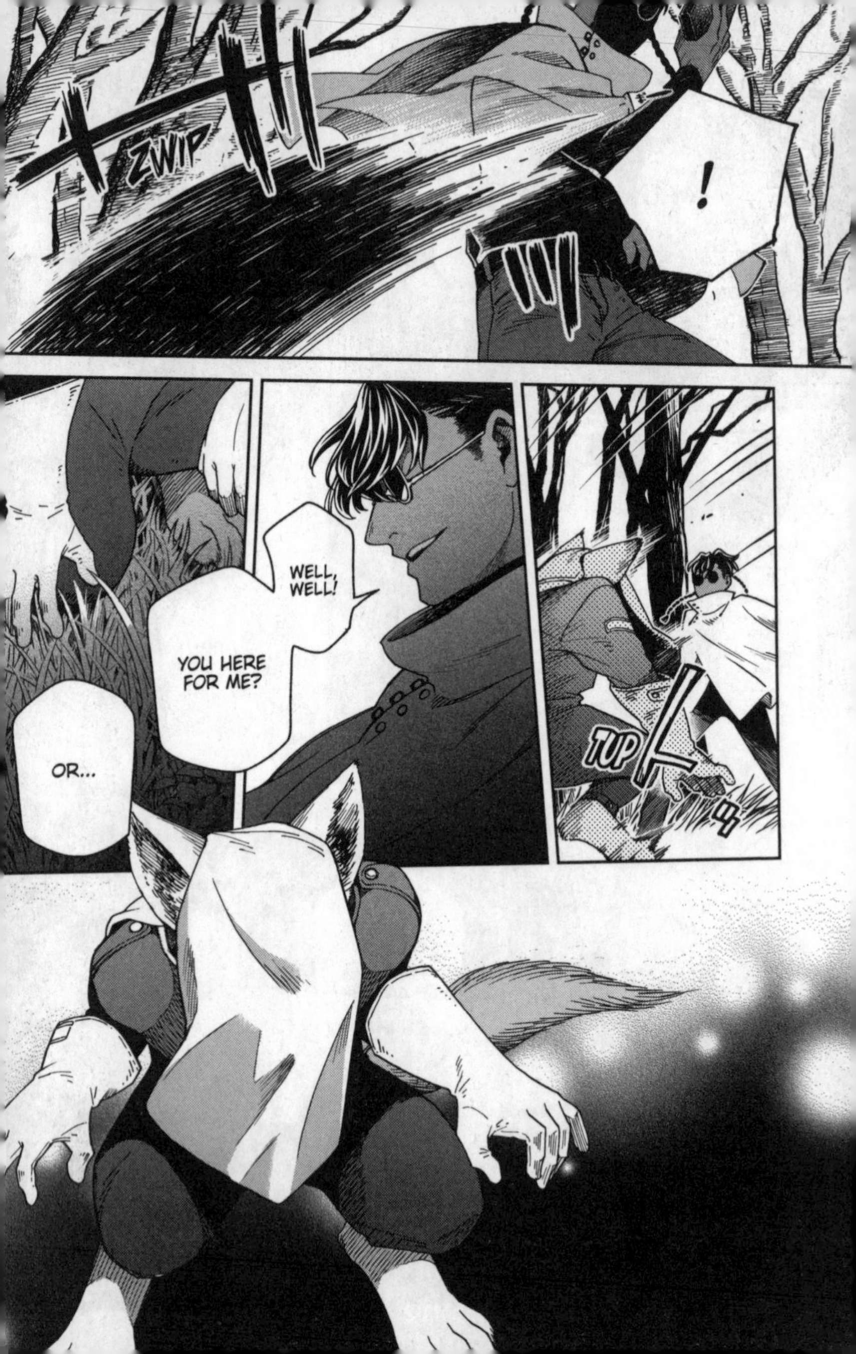
!
ZWIP
TUP
WELL, WELL!
YOU HERE FOR ME?
OR...

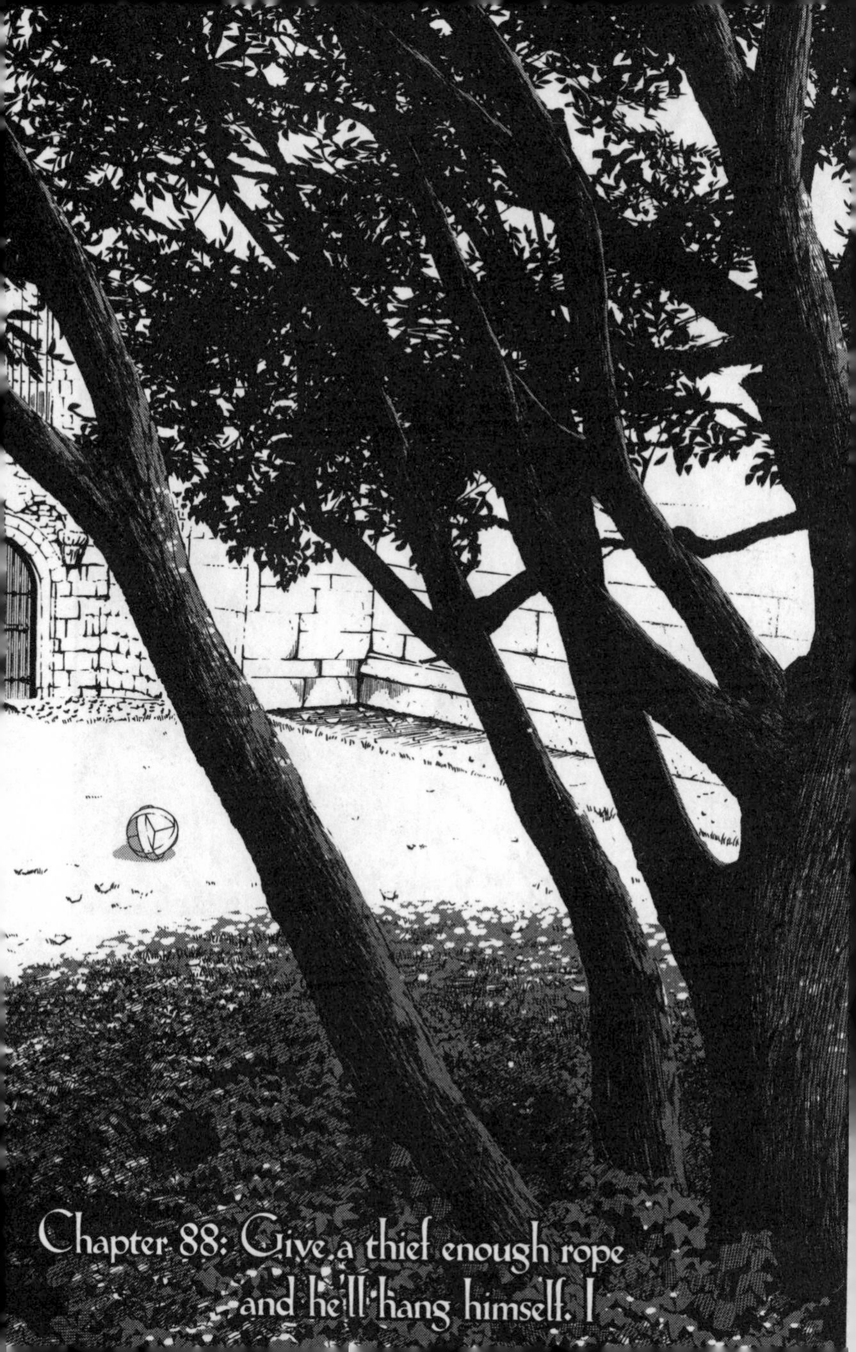
Chapter 88: Give a thief enough rope
and he'll hang himself. I

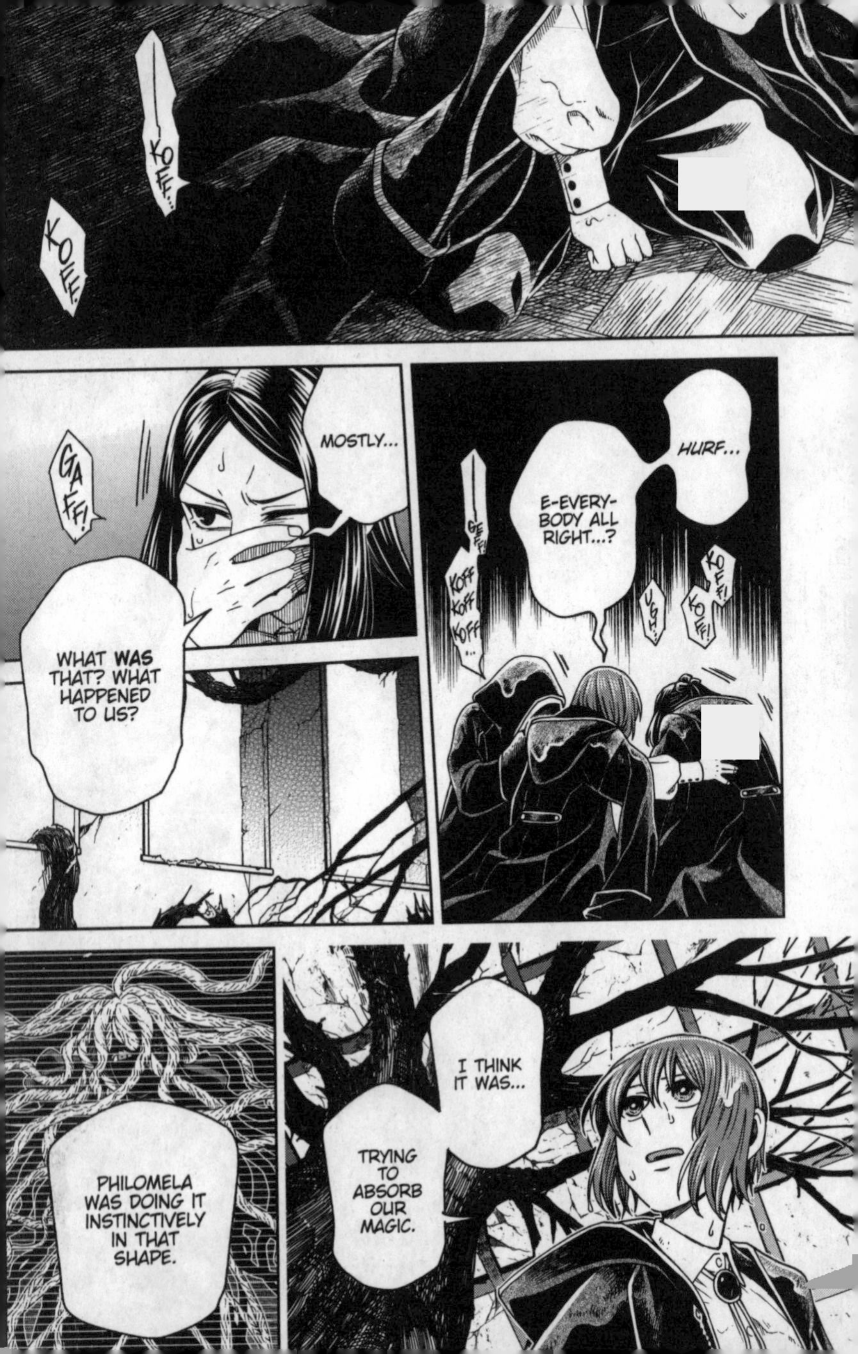

KOFF...
KOFF.
HURF...
E-EVERYBODY ALL RIGHT...?
KOFF!
KOFF!
UGH!
GEFF!
KOFF KOFF KOFF...
MOSTLY...
GAFF!
WHAT WAS THAT? WHAT HAPPENED TO US?
I THINK IT WAS...
TRYING TO ABSORB OUR MAGIC.
PHILOMELA WAS DOING IT INSTINCTIVELY IN THAT SHAPE.

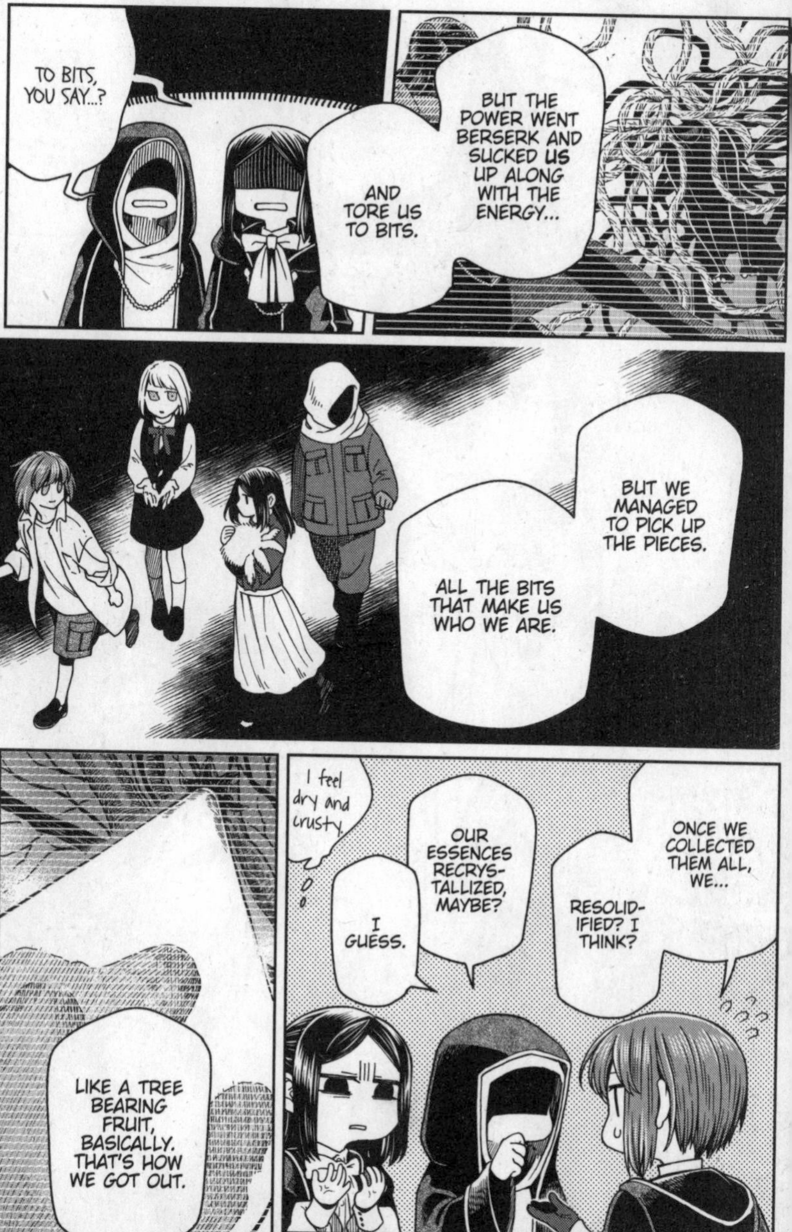
BUT THE POWER WENT BERSERK AND SUCKED US UP ALONG WITH THE ENERGY...
AND TORE US TO BITS.
TO BITS, YOU SAY...?
BUT WE MANAGED TO PICK UP THE PIECES.
ALL THE BITS THAT MAKE US WHO WE ARE.
ONCE WE COLLECTED THEM ALL, WE...
RESOLID-IFIED? I THINK?
OUR ESSENCES RECRYS-TALLIZED, MAYBE?
I GUESS.
I feel dry and crusty.
LIKE A TREE BEARING FRUIT, BASICALLY. THAT'S HOW WE GOT OUT.

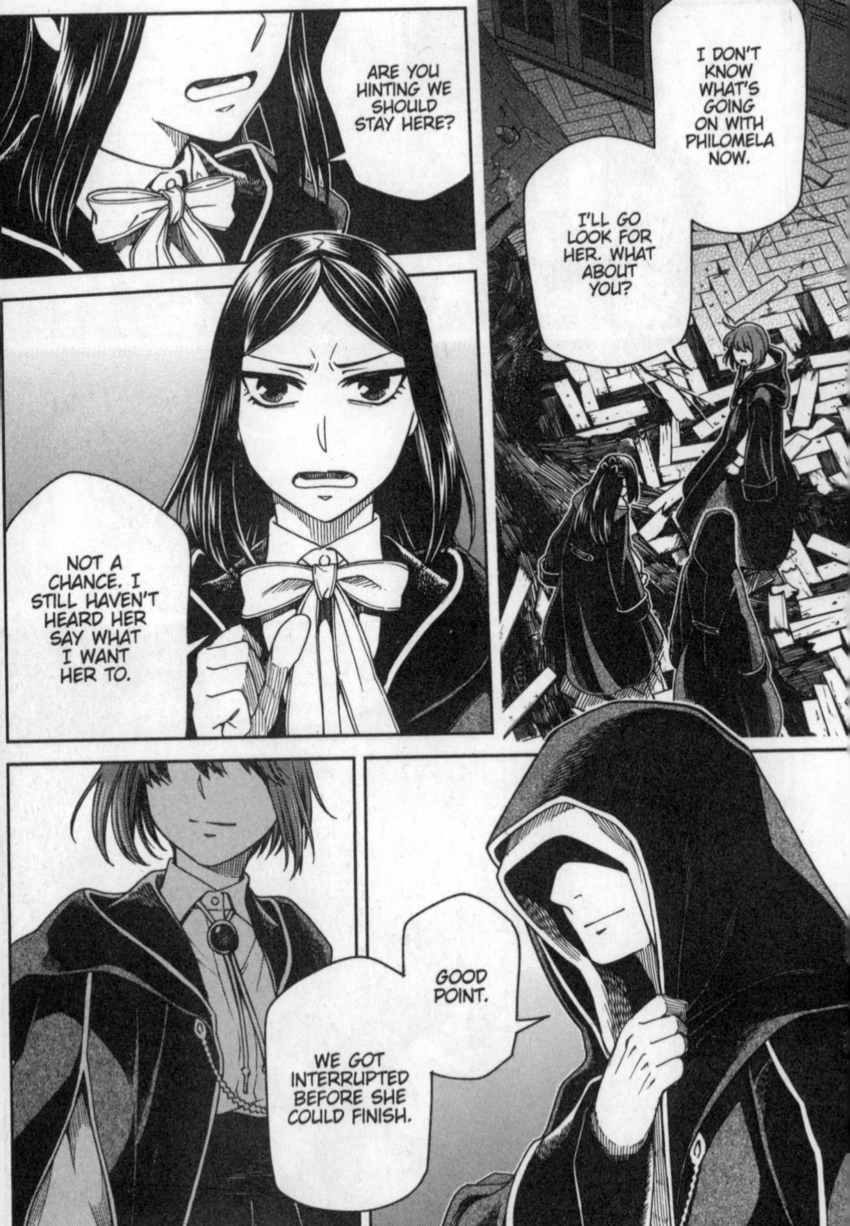
I DON'T KNOW WHAT'S GOING ON WITH PHILOMELA NOW.
I'LL GO LOOK FOR HER. WHAT ABOUT YOU?
ARE YOU HINTING WE SHOULD STAY HERE?
NOT A CHANCE. I STILL HAVEN'T HEARD HER SAY WHAT I WANT HER TO.
GOOD POINT.
WE GOT INTERRUPTED BEFORE SHE COULD FINISH.

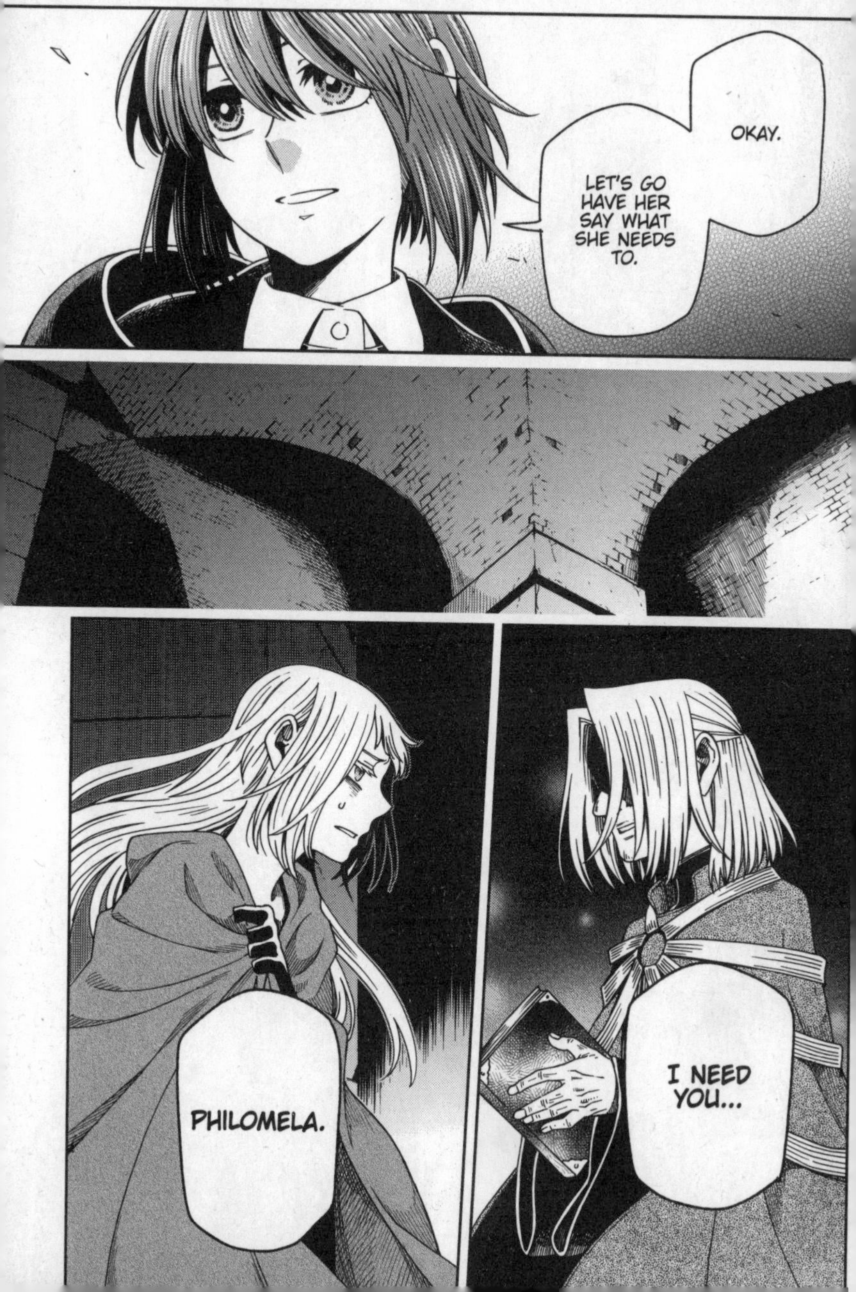
OKAY.
LET'S GO HAVE HER SAY WHAT SHE NEEDS TO.
I NEED YOU...
PHILOMELA.

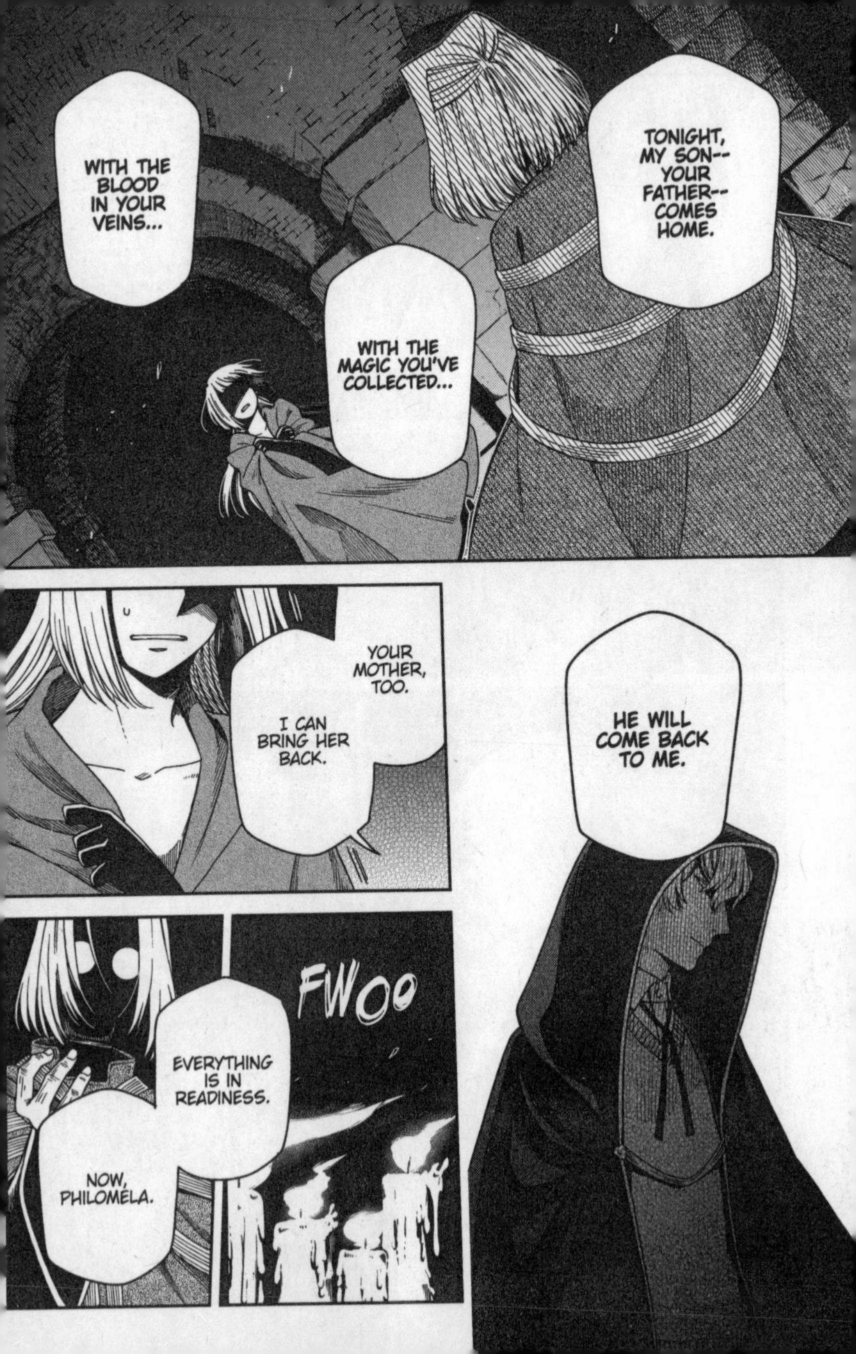
TONIGHT, MY SON-- YOUR FATHER-- COMES HOME.
WITH THE BLOOD IN YOUR VEINS...
WITH THE MAGIC YOU'VE COLLECTED...
HE WILL COME BACK TO ME.
YOUR MOTHER, TOO.
I CAN BRING HER BACK.
FWOO
EVERYTHING IS IN READINESS.
NOW, PHILOMELA.

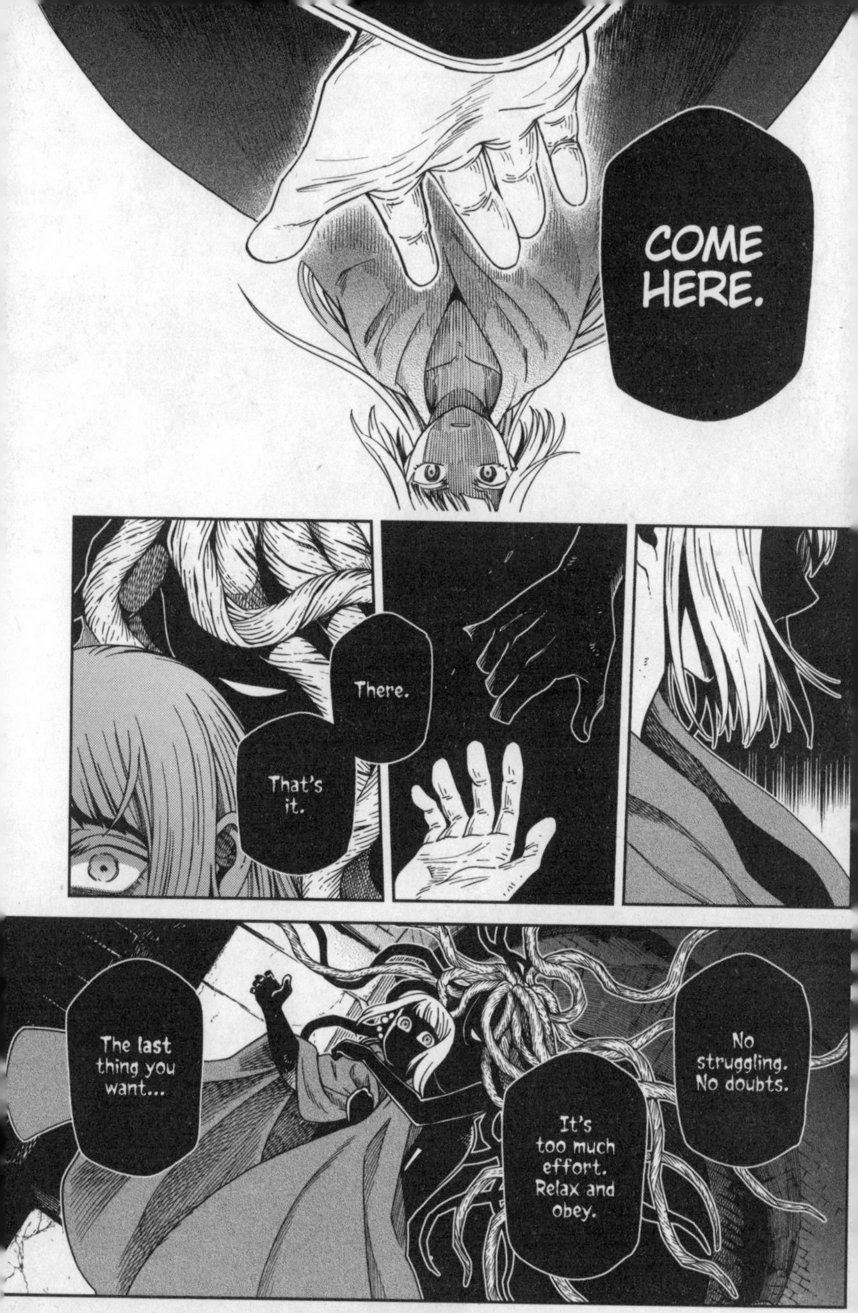
COME HERE.
There.
That's it.
No struggling. No doubts.
It's too much effort. Relax and obey.
The last thing you want...

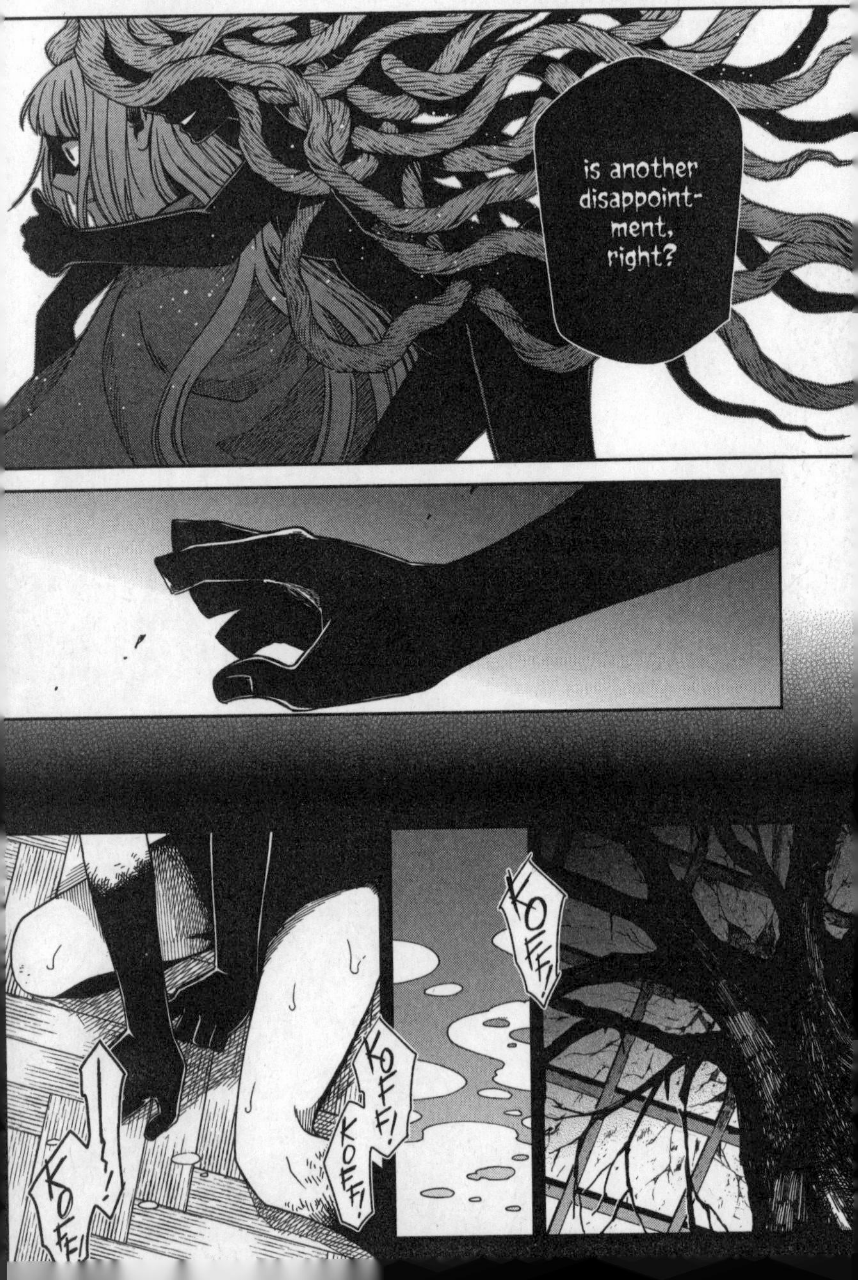
is another disappointment, right?
KOFF!
KOFF!
KOFF!
!
KOFF!

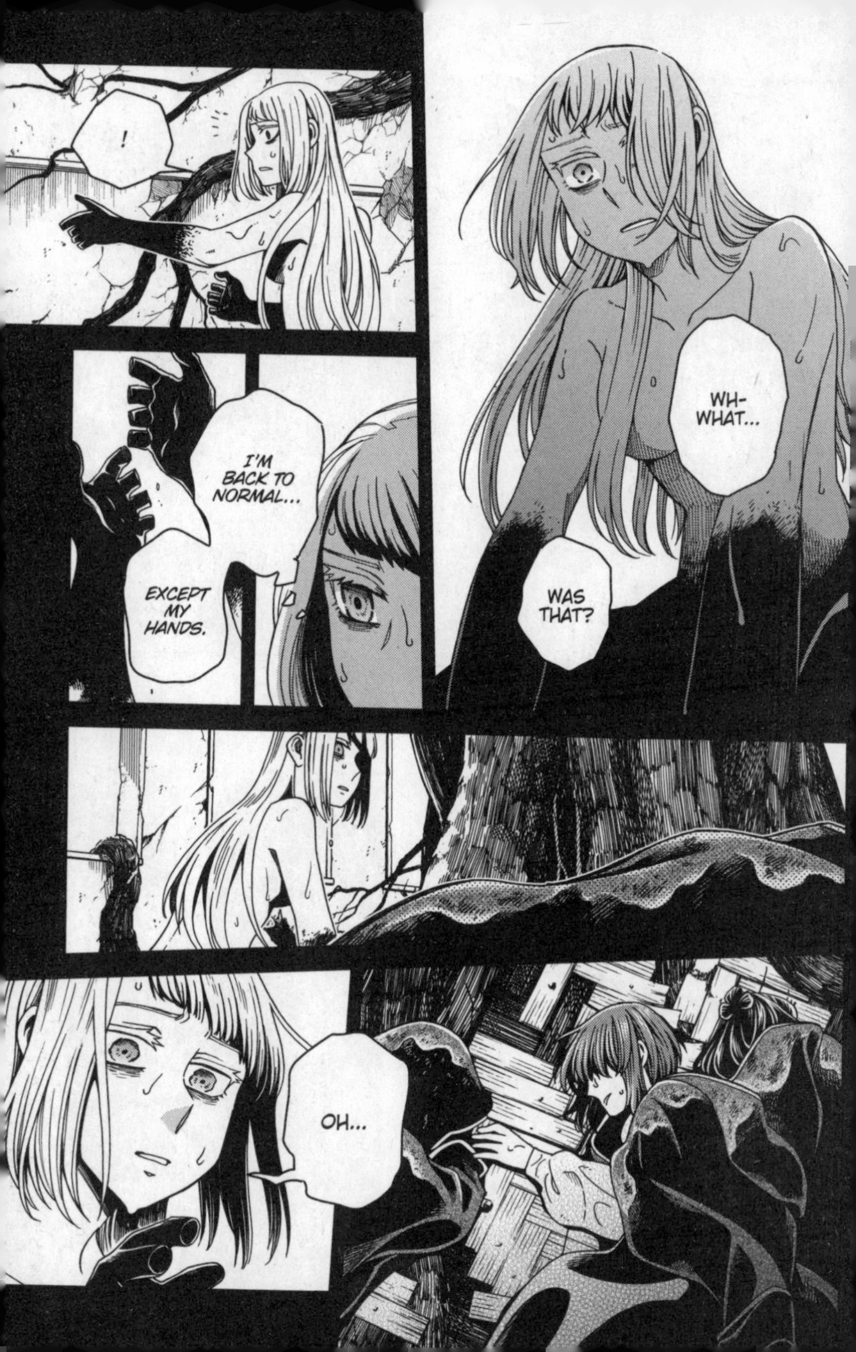
WH-WHAT...
WAS THAT?
!
I'M BACK TO NORMAL...
EXCEPT MY HANDS.
OH...

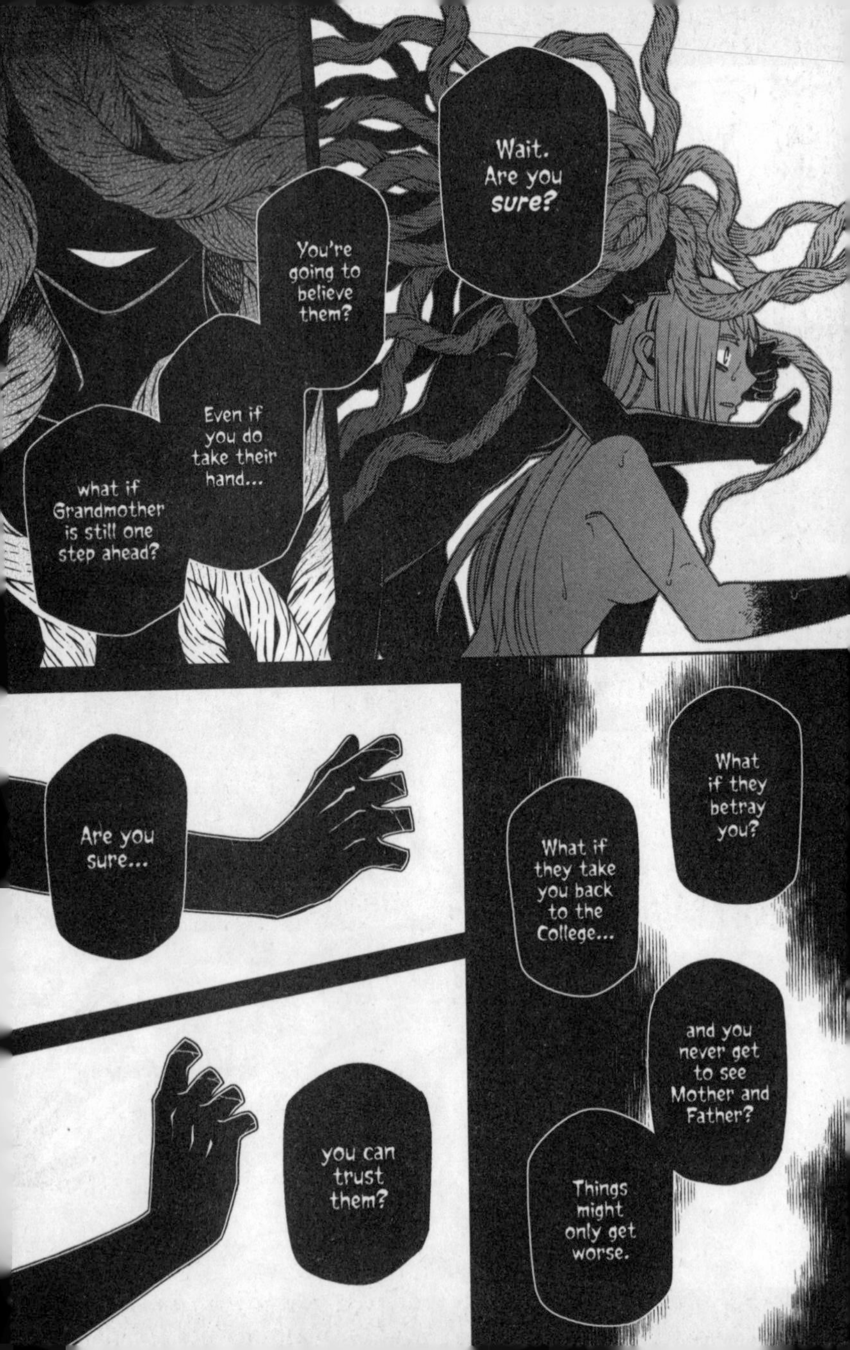
Wait. Are you *sure?*
You're going to believe them?
Even if you do take their hand...
what if Grandmother is still one step ahead?
What if they betray you?
What if they take you back to the College...
and you never get to see Mother and Father?
Things might only get worse.
Are you sure...
you can trust them?

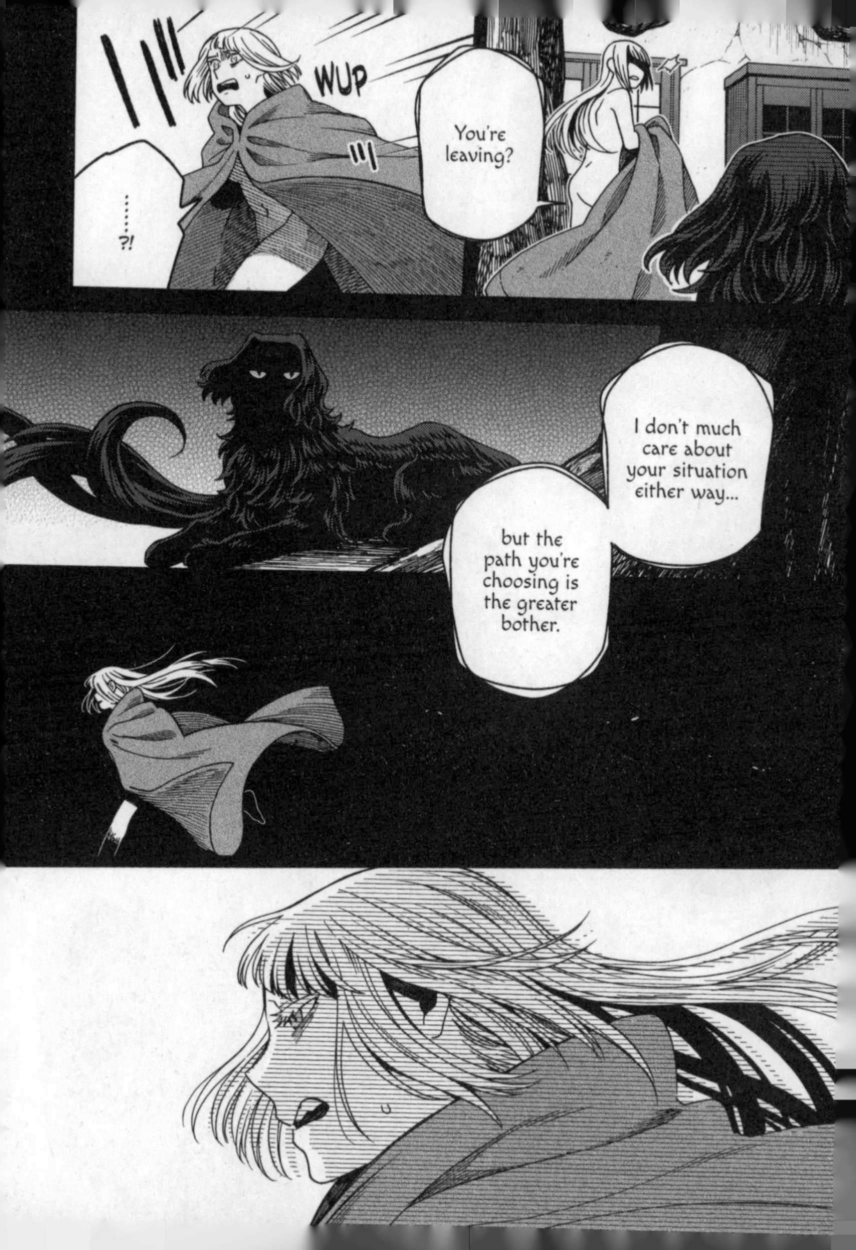
You're leaving?
WUP
......?!
I don't much care about your situation either way...
but the path you're choosing is the greater bother.

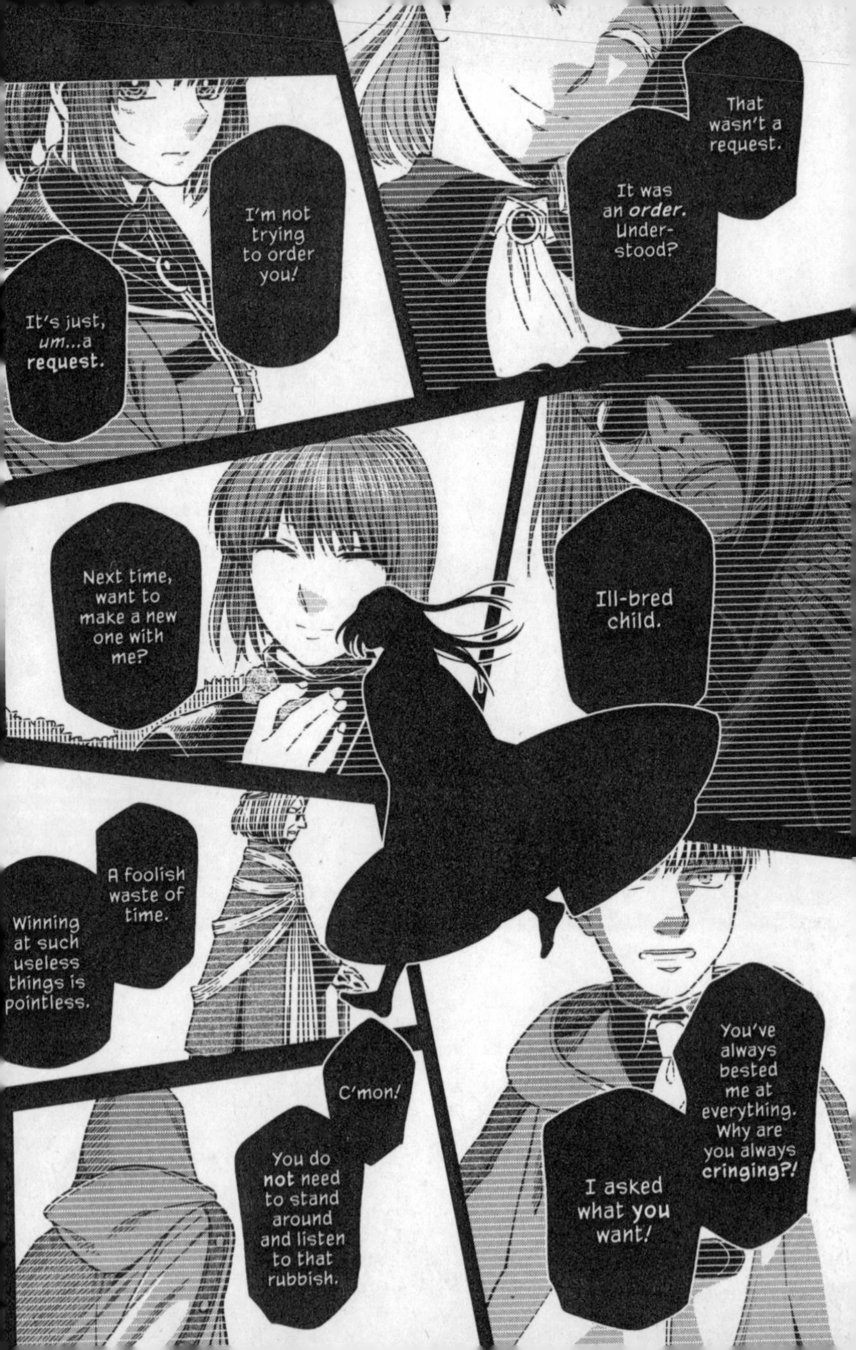
That wasn't a request.
It was an *order*. Understood?
I'm not trying to order you!
It's just, *um*...a **request**.
Ill-bred child.
Next time, want to make a new one with me?
You've always bested me at everything. Why are you always **cringing?!**
I asked what **you** want!
A foolish waste of time.
Winning at such useless things is pointless.
C'mon!
You do **not** need to stand around and listen to that rubbish.

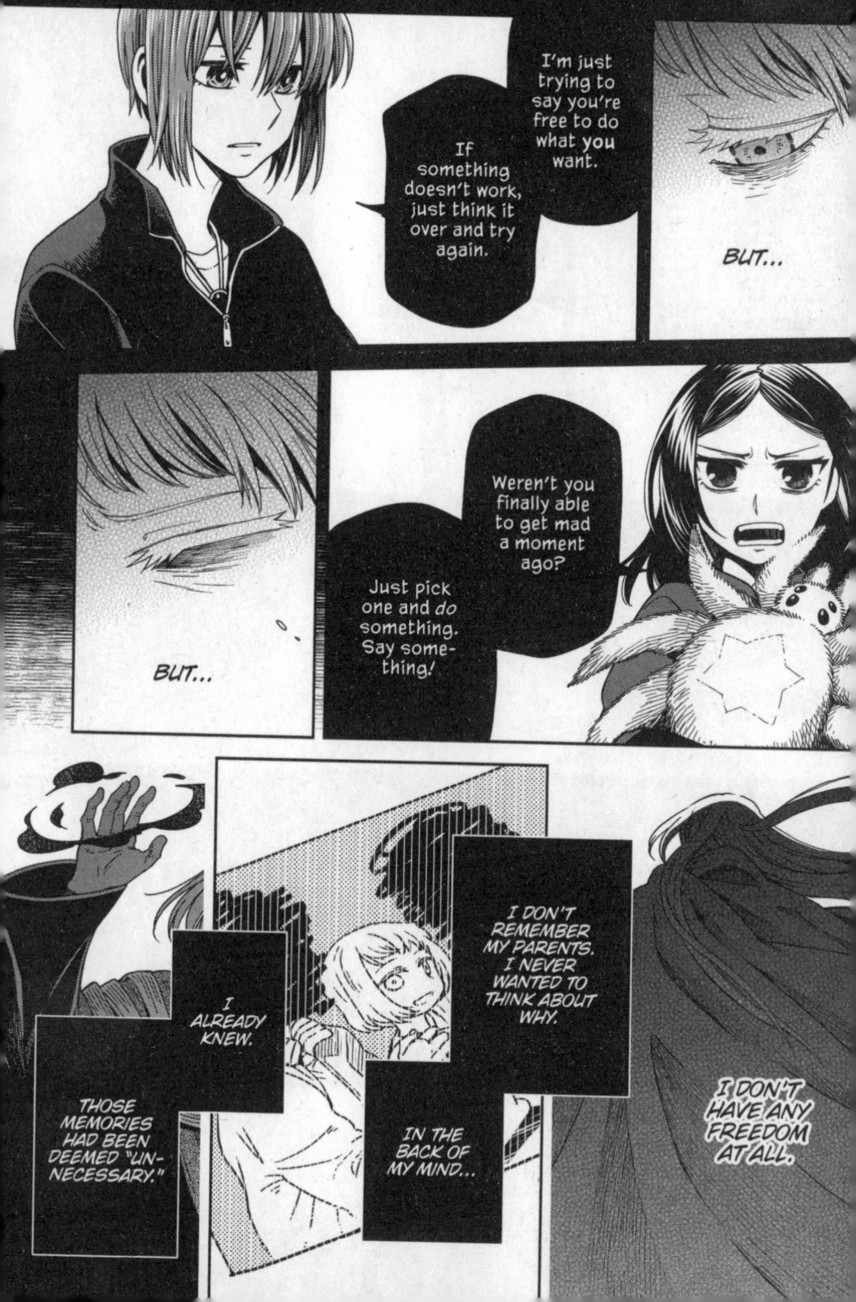
BUT...
I'm just trying to say you're free to do what you want.
If something doesn't work, just think it over and try again.
Weren't you finally able to get mad a moment ago?
Just pick one and do something. Say something!
BUT...
I DON'T HAVE ANY FREEDOM AT ALL.
I DON'T REMEMBER MY PARENTS. I NEVER WANTED TO THINK ABOUT WHY.
IN THE BACK OF MY MIND...
I ALREADY KNEW.
THOSE MEMORIES HAD BEEN DEEMED "UN-NECESSARY."

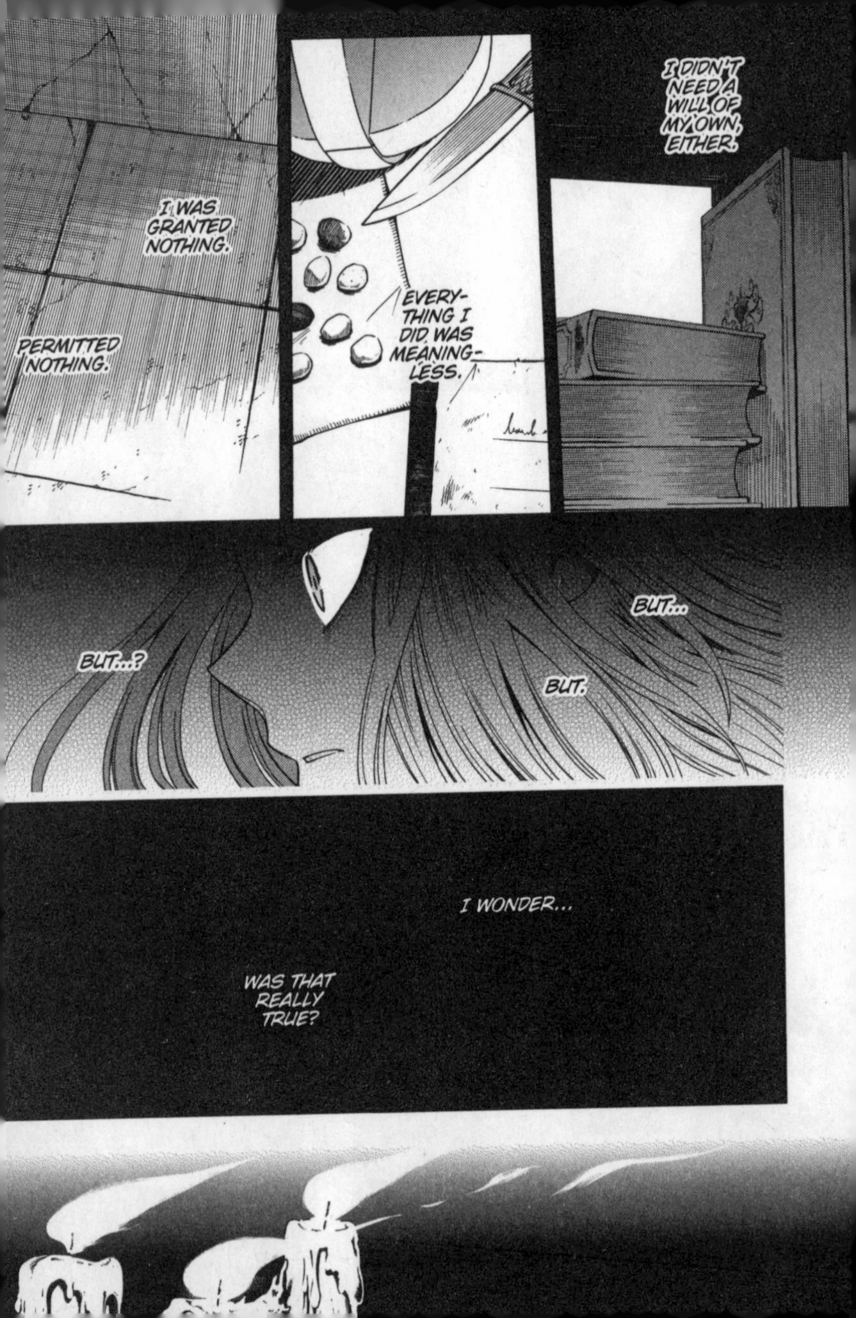
I DIDN'T NEED A WILL OF MY OWN, EITHER.
EVERY-THING I DID WAS MEANING-LESS.
I WAS GRANTED NOTHING.
PERMITTED NOTHING.
BUT...
BUT.
BUT...?
I WONDER...
WAS THAT REALLY TRUE?

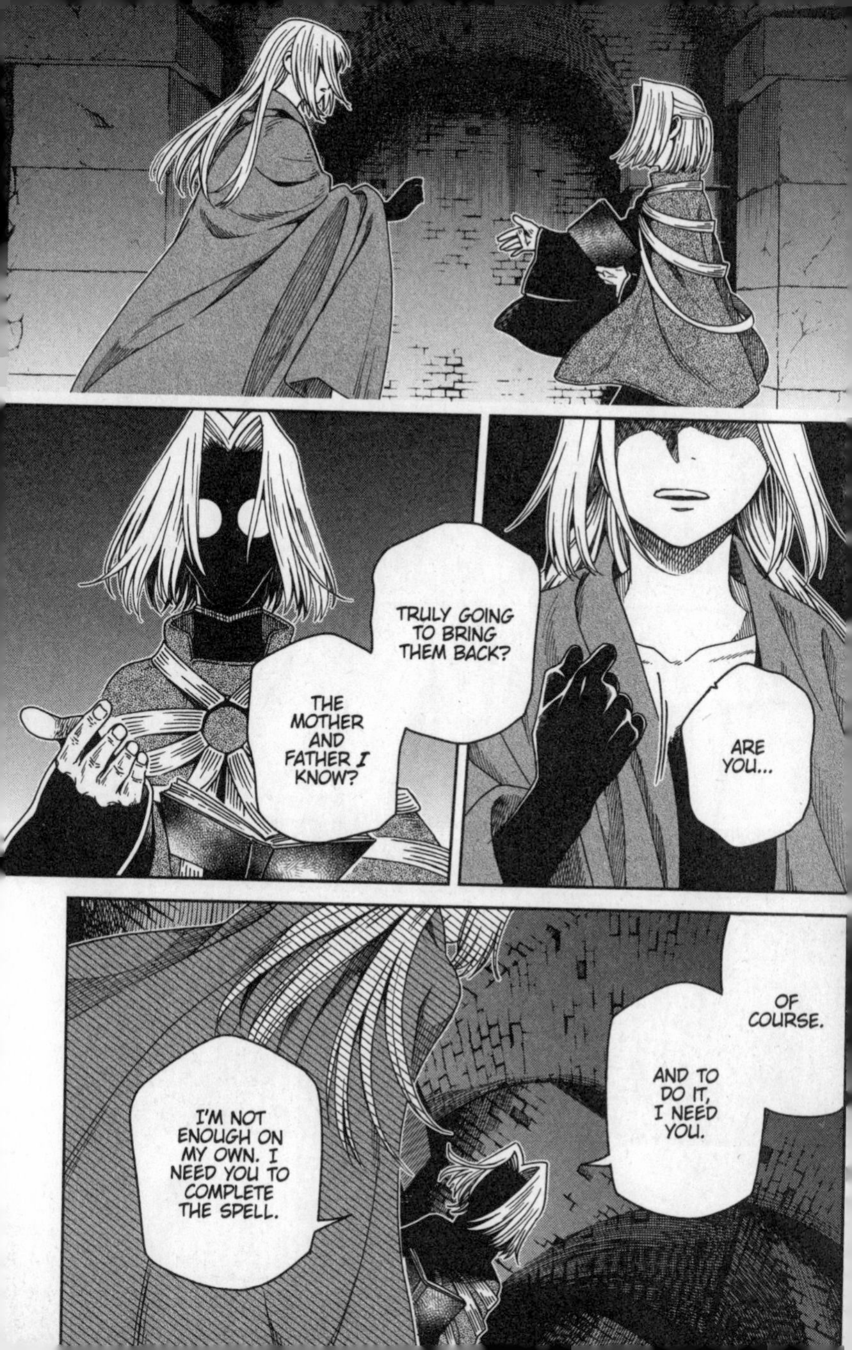
ARE YOU...
TRULY GOING TO BRING THEM BACK?
THE MOTHER AND FATHER I KNOW?
OF COURSE.
AND TO DO IT, I NEED YOU.
I'M NOT ENOUGH ON MY OWN. I NEED YOU TO COMPLETE THE SPELL.

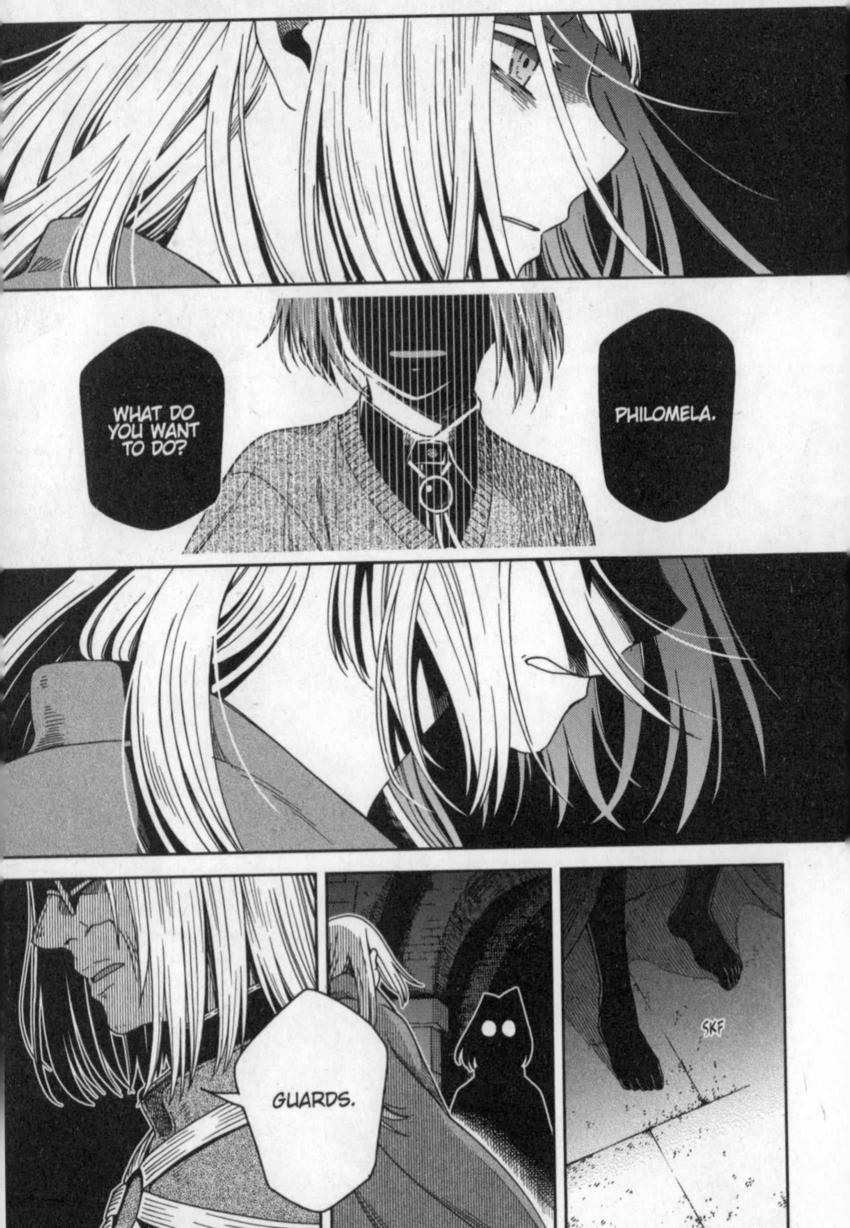
PHILOMELA.
WHAT DO YOU WANT TO DO?
SKF
GUARDS.

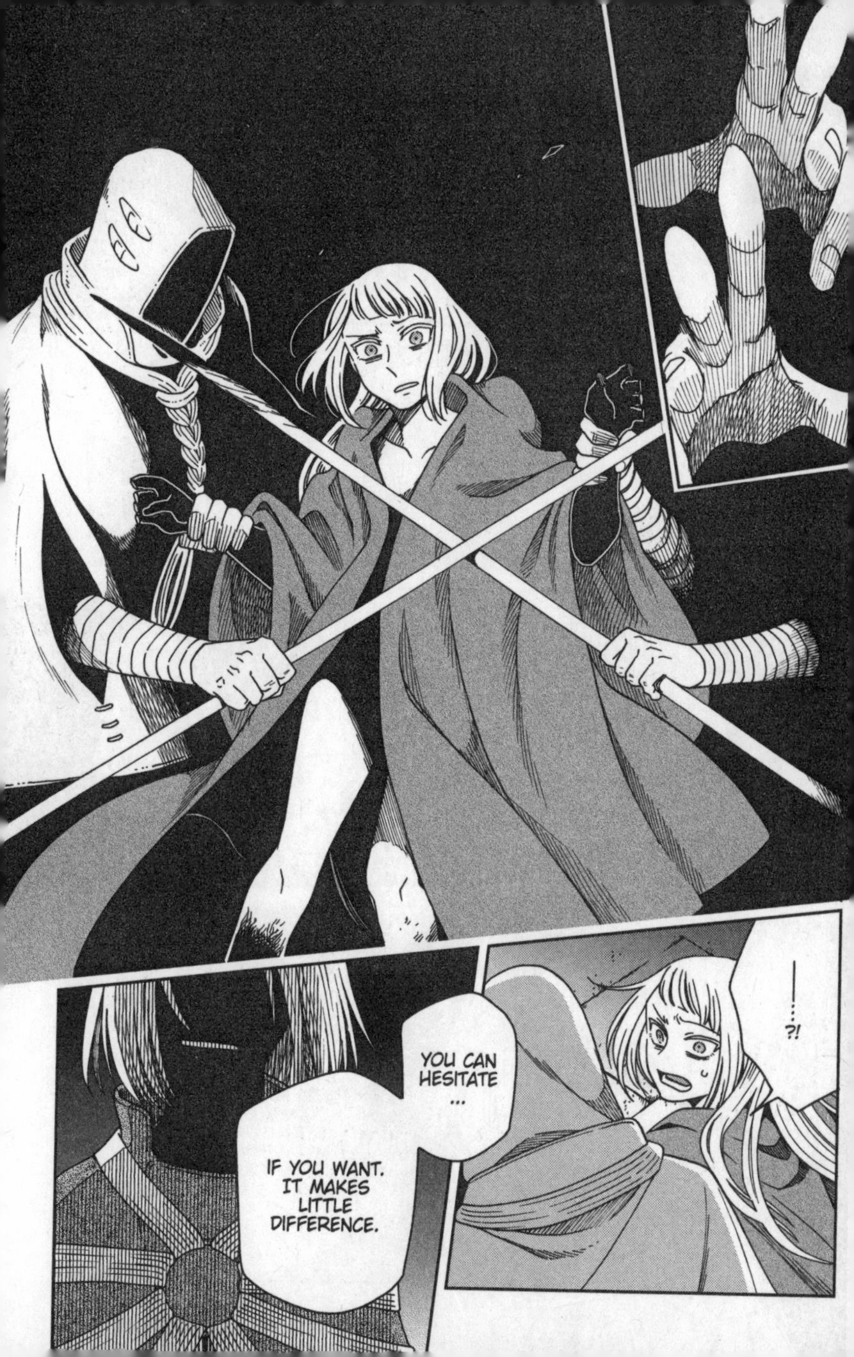
......?!
YOU CAN HESITATE...
IF YOU WANT. IT MAKES LITTLE DIFFERENCE.

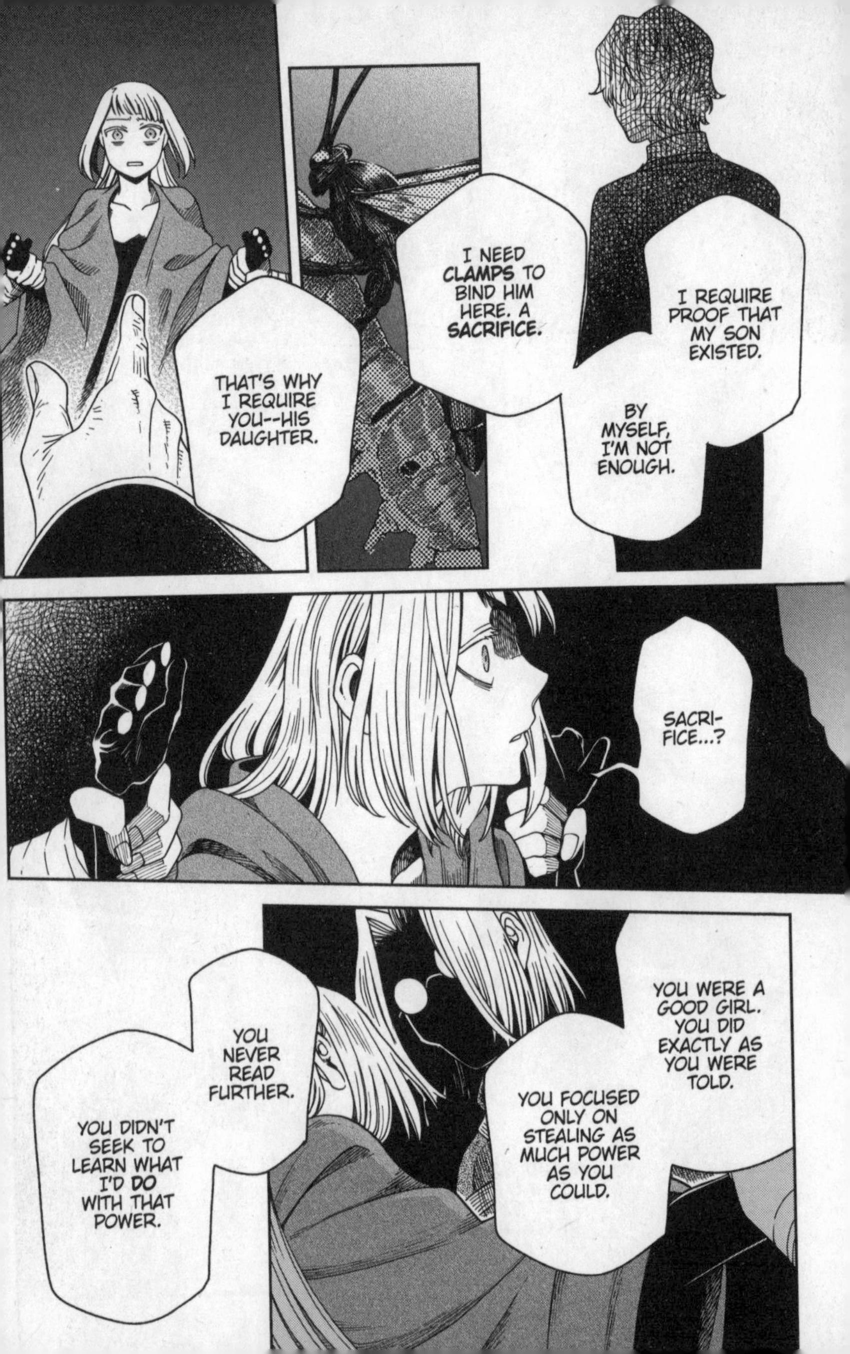
I REQUIRE PROOF THAT MY SON EXISTED.
BY MYSELF, I'M NOT ENOUGH.
I NEED CLAMPS TO BIND HIM HERE. A SACRIFICE.
THAT'S WHY I REQUIRE YOU--HIS DAUGHTER.
SACRI-FICE...?
YOU WERE A GOOD GIRL. YOU DID EXACTLY AS YOU WERE TOLD.
YOU FOCUSED ONLY ON STEALING AS MUCH POWER AS YOU COULD.
YOU NEVER READ FURTHER.
YOU DIDN'T SEEK TO LEARN WHAT I'D DO WITH THAT POWER.

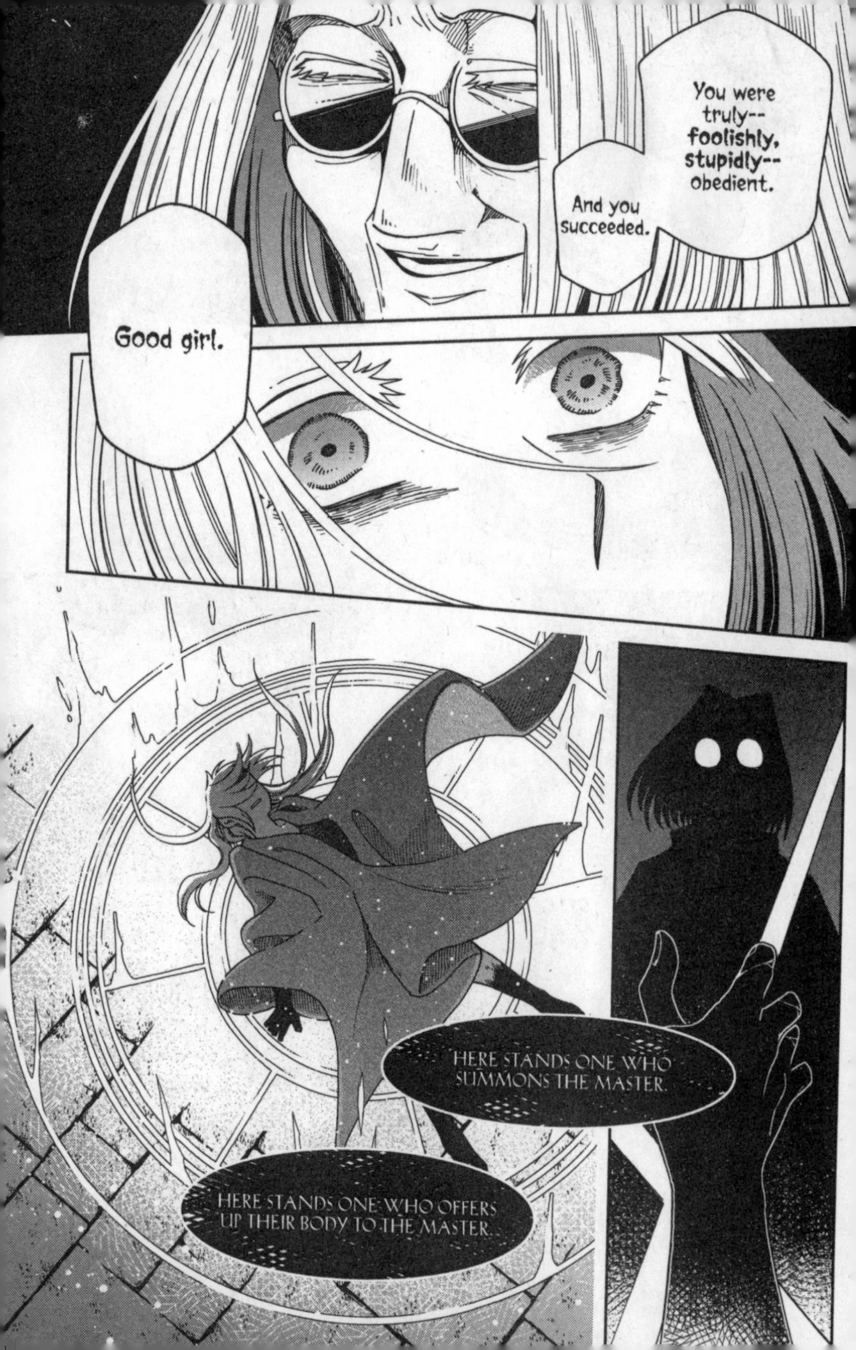
You were truly-- foolishly, stupidly-- obedient.
And you succeeded.
Good girl.
HERE STANDS ONE WHO SUMMONS THE MASTER.
HERE STANDS ONE WHO OFFERS UP THEIR BODY TO THE MASTER.

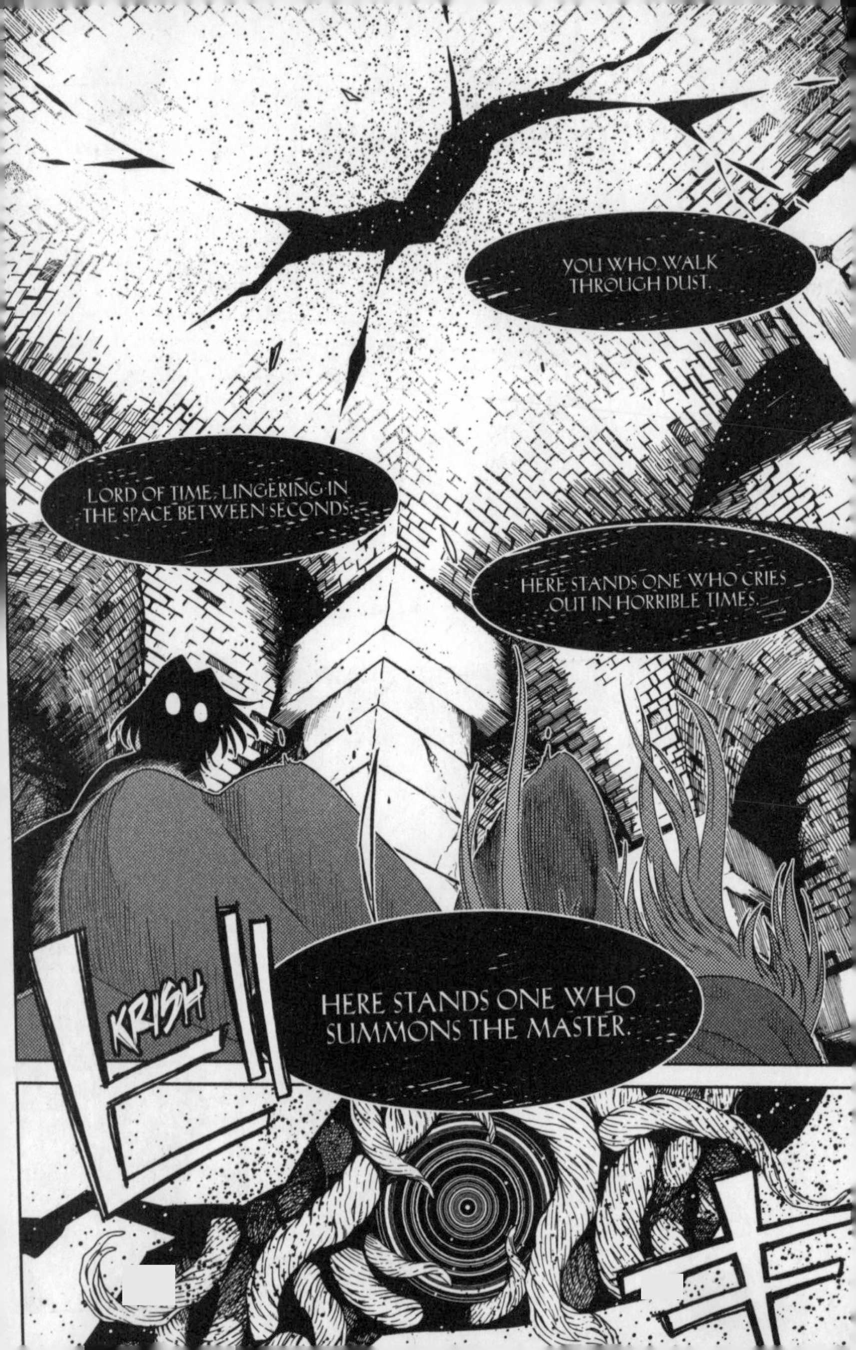
YOU WHO WALK THROUGH DUST.
LORD OF TIME, LINGERING IN THE SPACE BETWEEN SECONDS.
HERE STANDS ONE WHO CRIES OUT IN HORRIBLE TIMES.
HERE STANDS ONE WHO SUMMONS THE MASTER.
KRISH

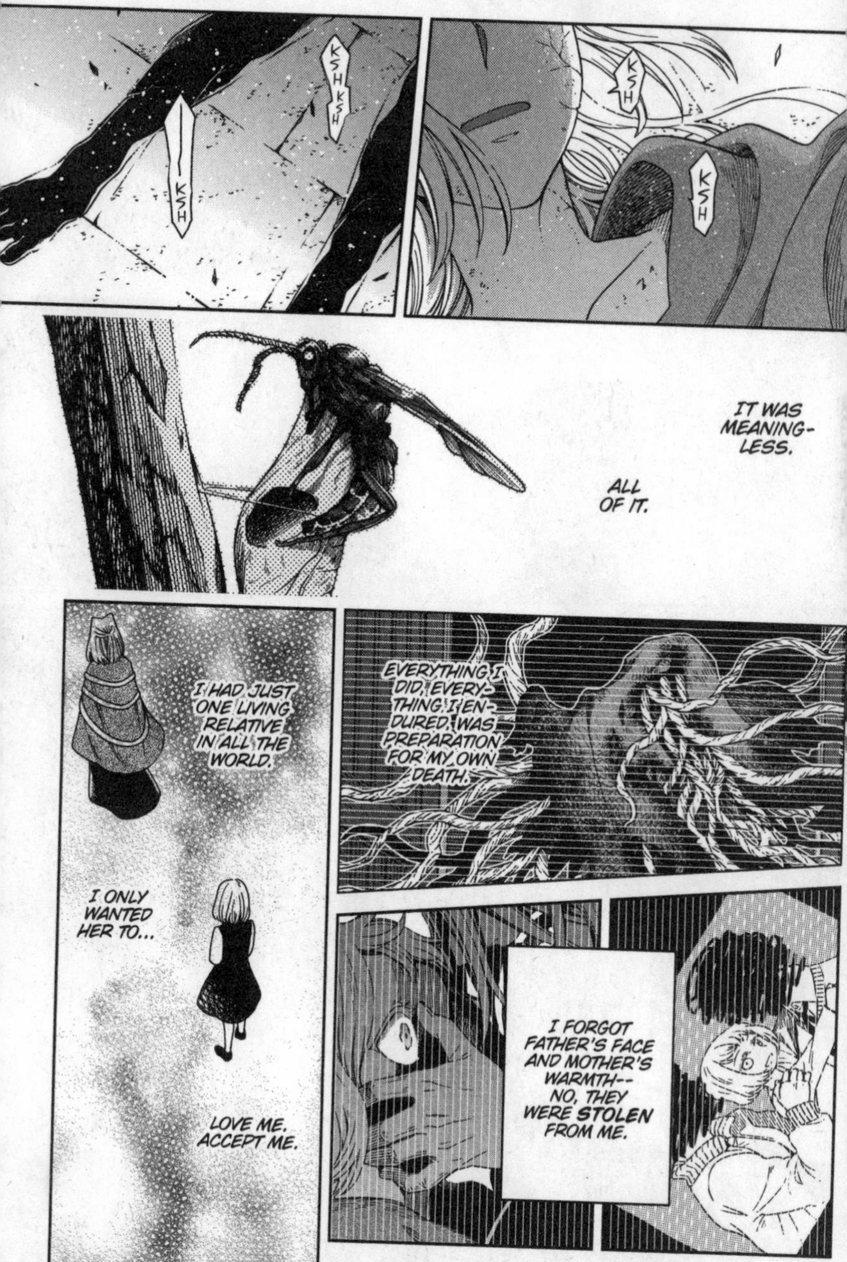
KSH
KSH
KSH KSH
KSH
IT WAS MEANING-LESS.
ALL OF IT.
EVERYTHING I DID, EVERYTHING I ENDURED, WAS PREPARATION FOR MY OWN DEATH.
I FORGOT FATHER'S FACE AND MOTHER'S WARMTH-- NO, THEY WERE **STOLEN** FROM ME.
I HAD JUST ONE LIVING RELATIVE IN ALL THE WORLD.
I ONLY WANTED HER TO...
LOVE ME. ACCEPT ME.

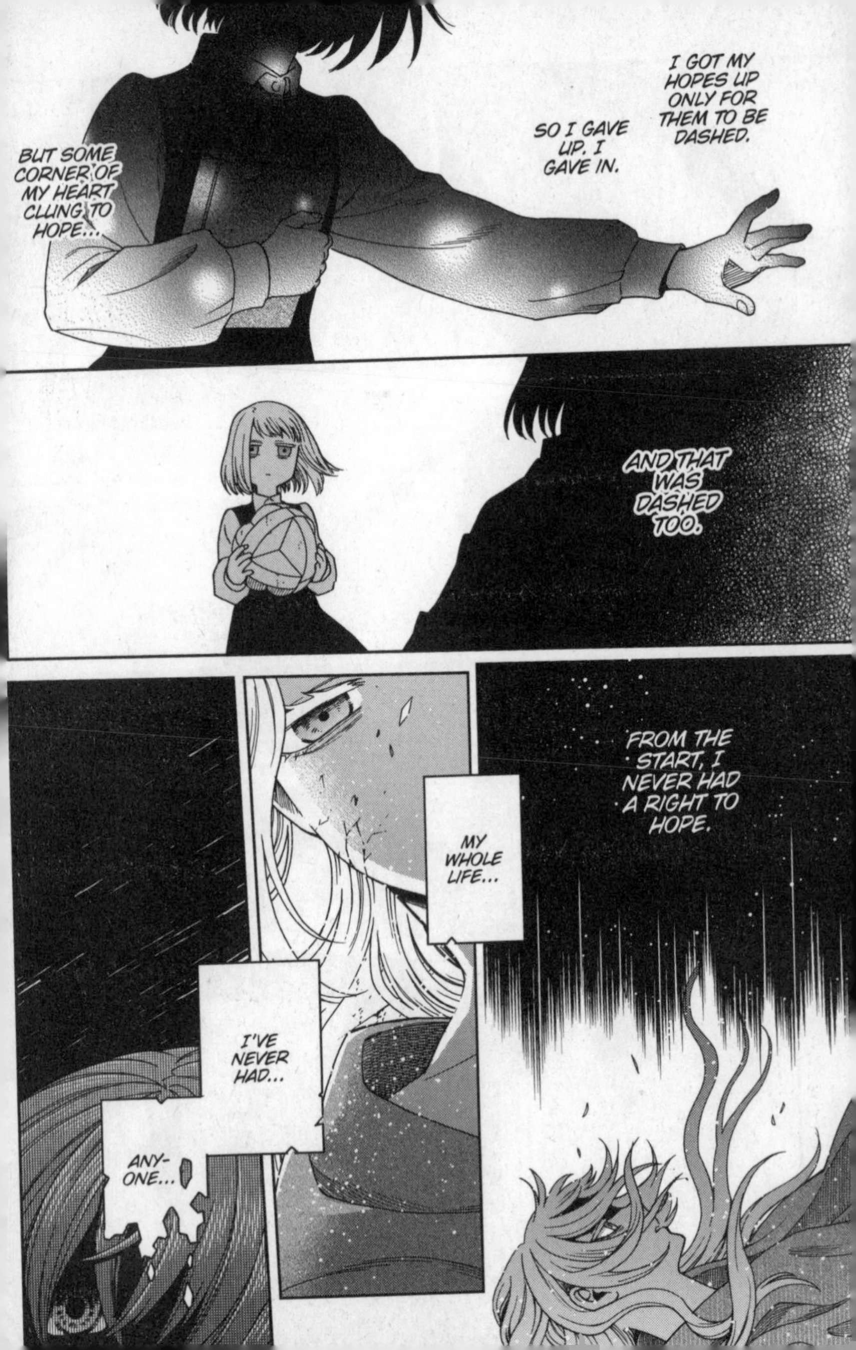
I GOT MY HOPES UP ONLY FOR THEM TO BE DASHED.
SO I GAVE UP. I GAVE IN.
BUT SOME CORNER OF MY HEART CLUNG TO HOPE...
AND THAT WAS DASHED TOO.
FROM THE START, I NEVER HAD A RIGHT TO HOPE.
MY WHOLE LIFE...
I'VE NEVER HAD...
ANY-ONE...

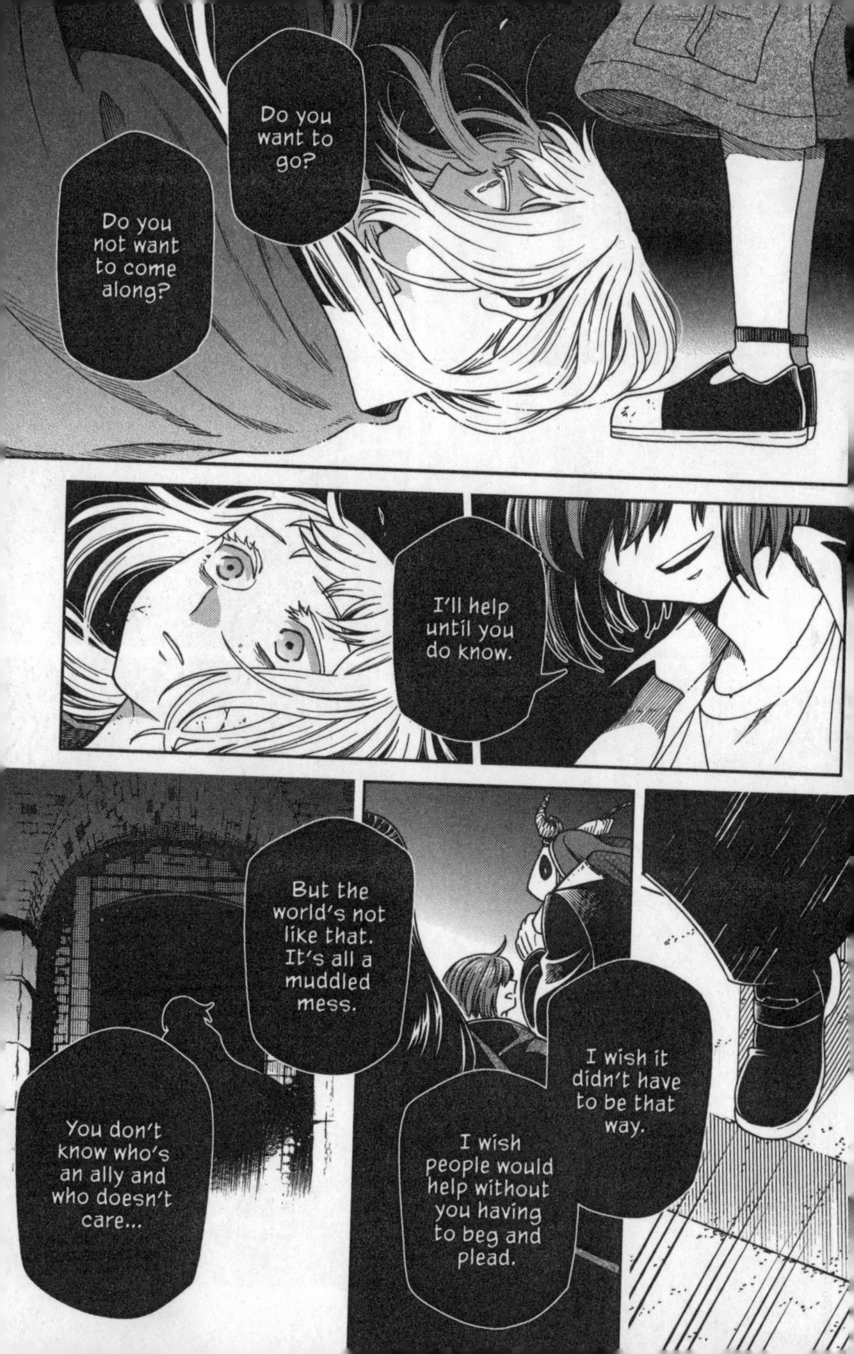
Do you want to go?
Do you not want to come along?
I'll help until you do know.
But the world's not like that. It's all a muddled mess.
You don't know who's an ally and who doesn't care...
I wish it didn't have to be that way.
I wish people would help without you having to beg and plead.

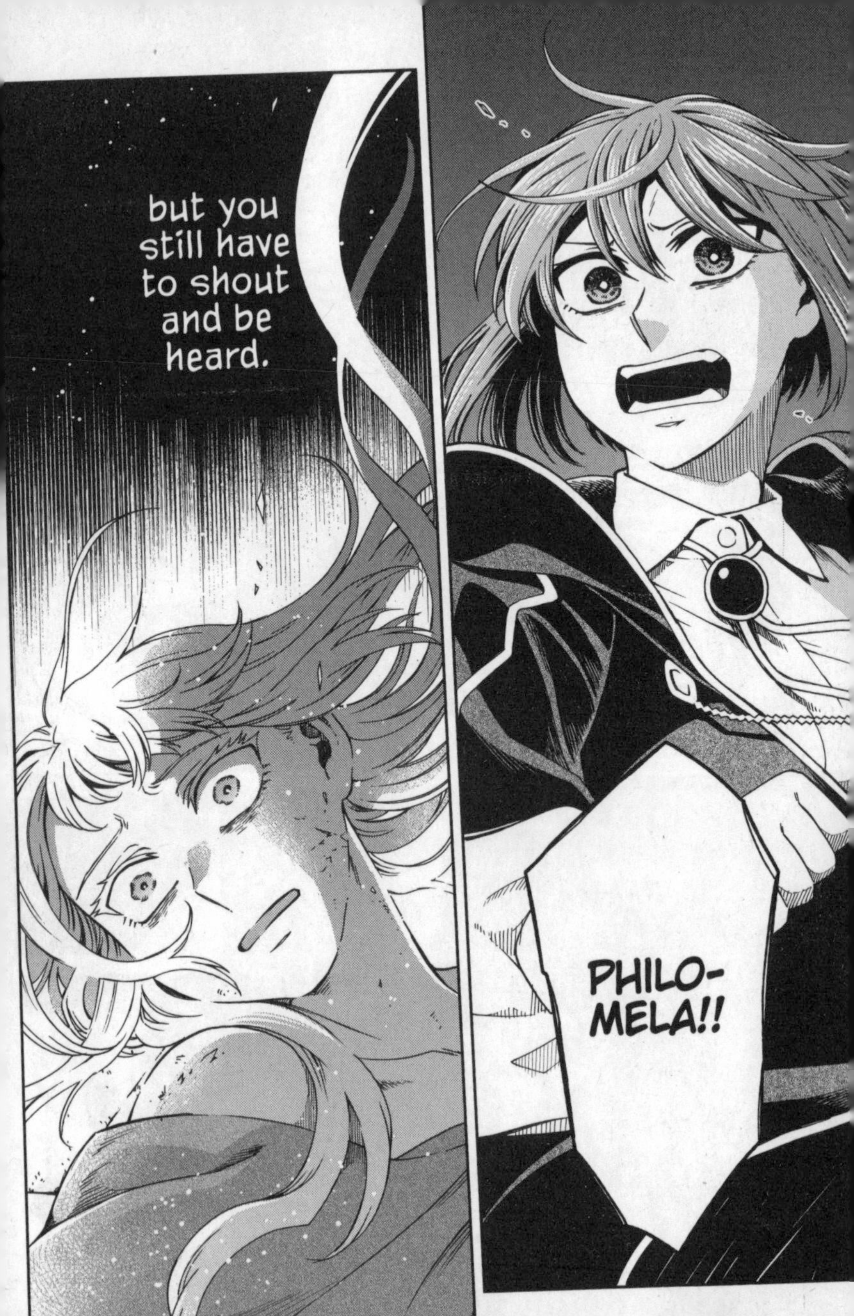
PHILO-MELA!!
but you still have to shout and be heard.

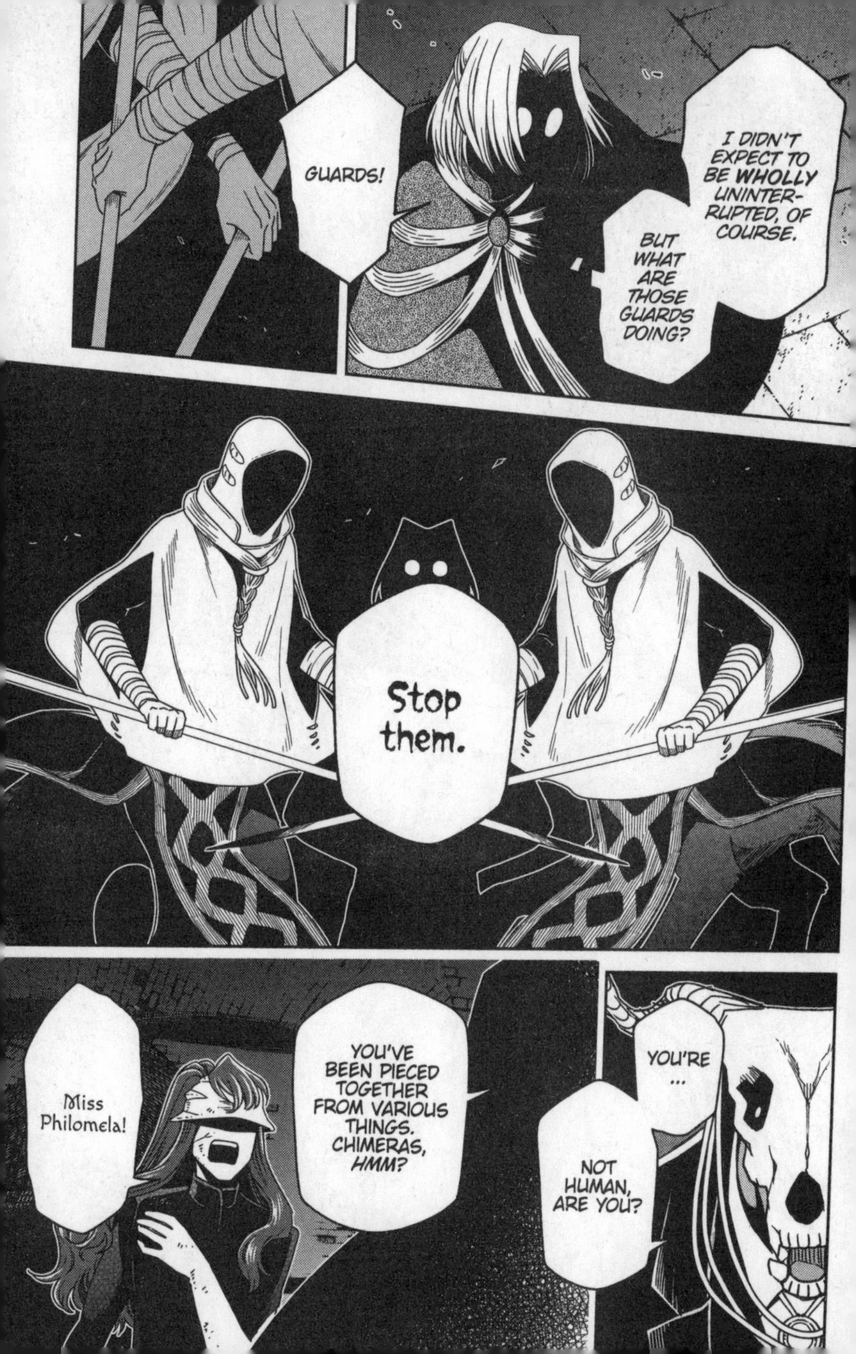

I DIDN'T EXPECT TO BE WHOLLY UNINTER-RUPTED, OF COURSE.
BUT WHAT ARE THOSE GUARDS DOING?
GUARDS!
Stop them.
YOU'RE ...
NOT HUMAN, ARE YOU?
YOU'VE BEEN PIECED TOGETHER FROM VARIOUS THINGS. CHIMERAS, HMM?
Miss Philomela!

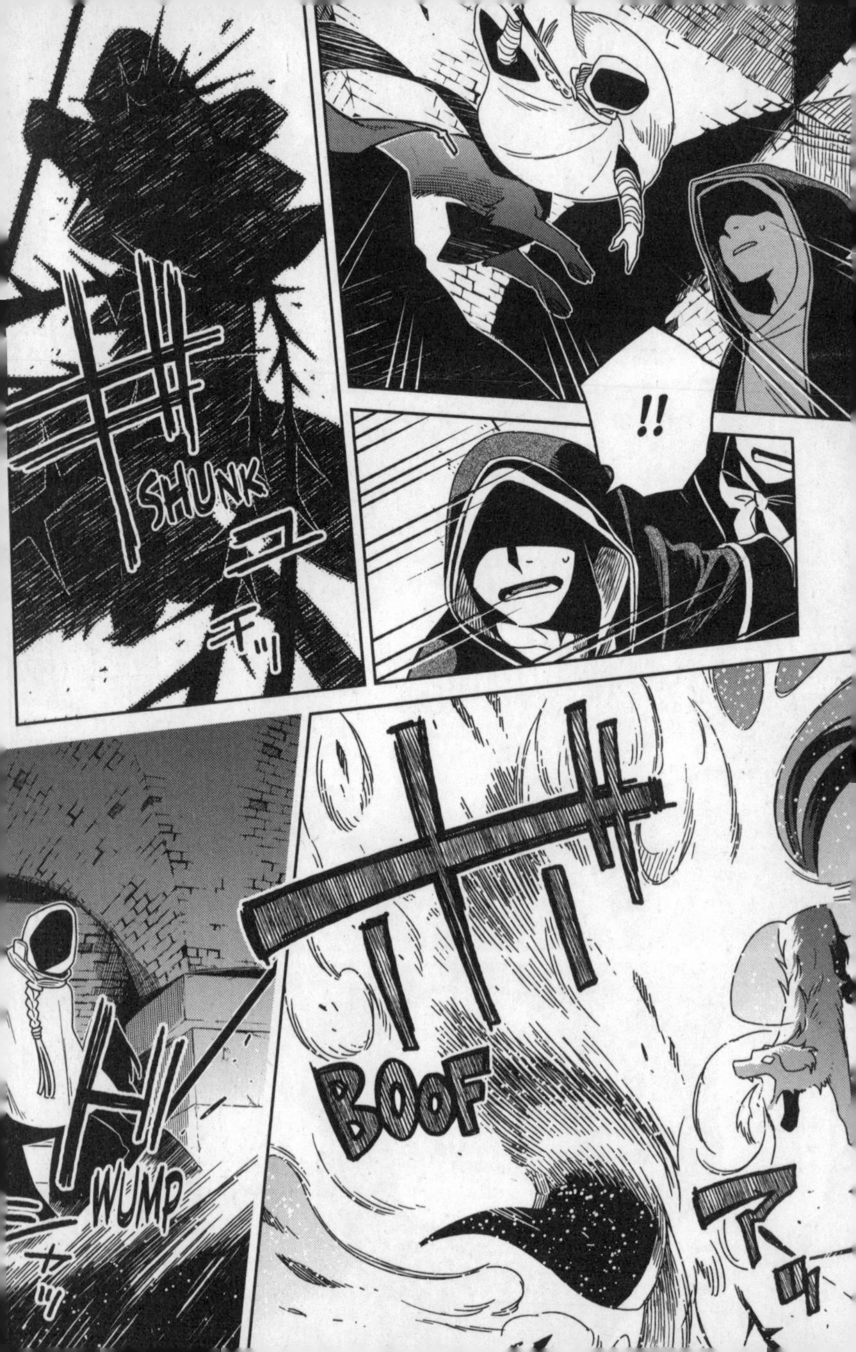
!!
SHUNK
BOOF
WUMP

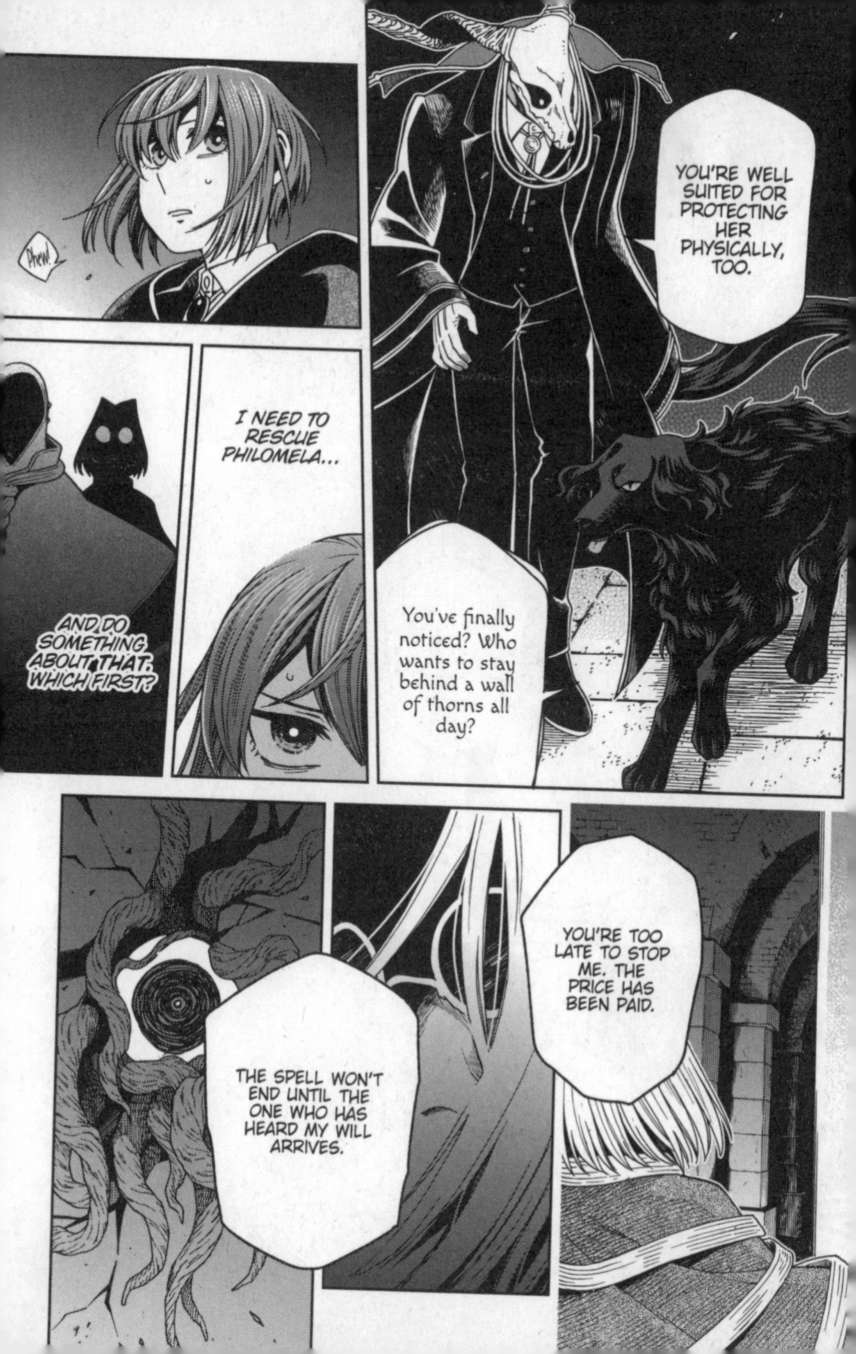
YOU'RE WELL SUITED FOR PROTECTING HER PHYSICALLY, TOO.
You've finally noticed? Who wants to stay behind a wall of thorns all day?
Phew!
I NEED TO RESCUE PHILOMELA...
AND DO SOMETHING ABOUT THAT. WHICH FIRST?
YOU'RE TOO LATE TO STOP ME. THE PRICE HAS BEEN PAID.
THE SPELL WON'T END UNTIL THE ONE WHO HAS HEARD MY WILL ARRIVES.

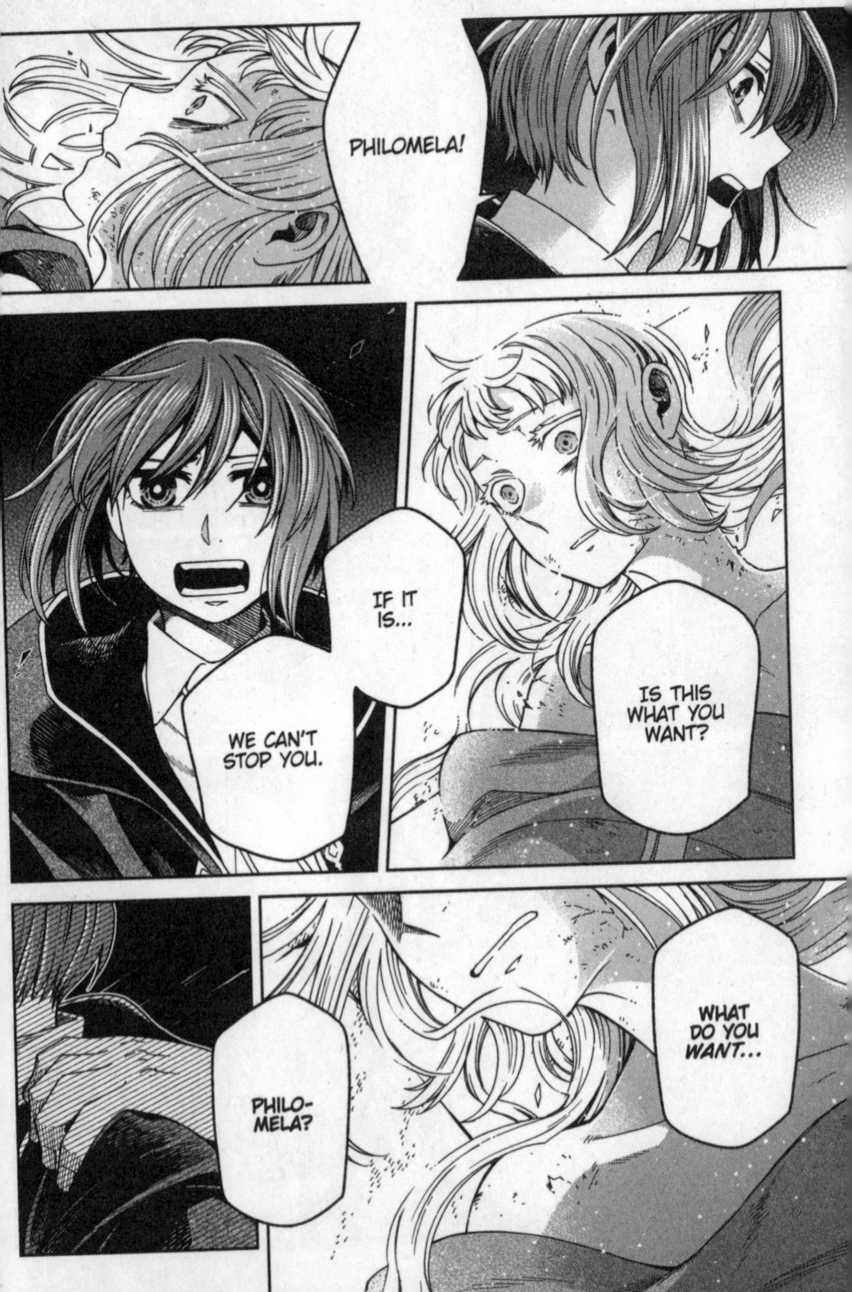
PHILOMELA!
IS THIS WHAT YOU WANT?
IF IT IS...
WE CAN'T STOP YOU.
WHAT DO YOU WANT...
PHILO-MELA?

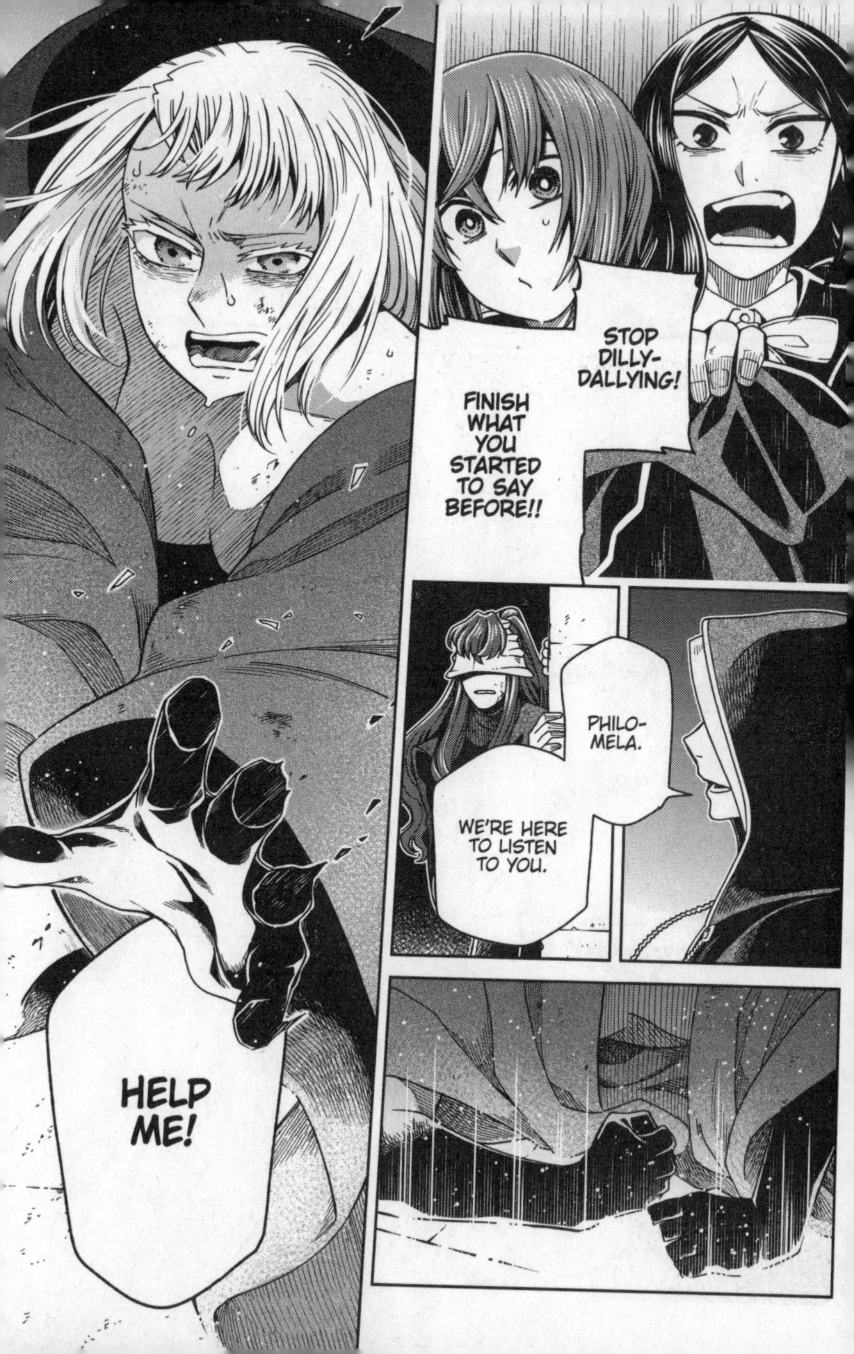
STOP DILLY-DALLYING!
FINISH WHAT YOU STARTED TO SAY BEFORE!!
PHILO-MELA.
WE'RE HERE TO LISTEN TO YOU.
HELP ME!

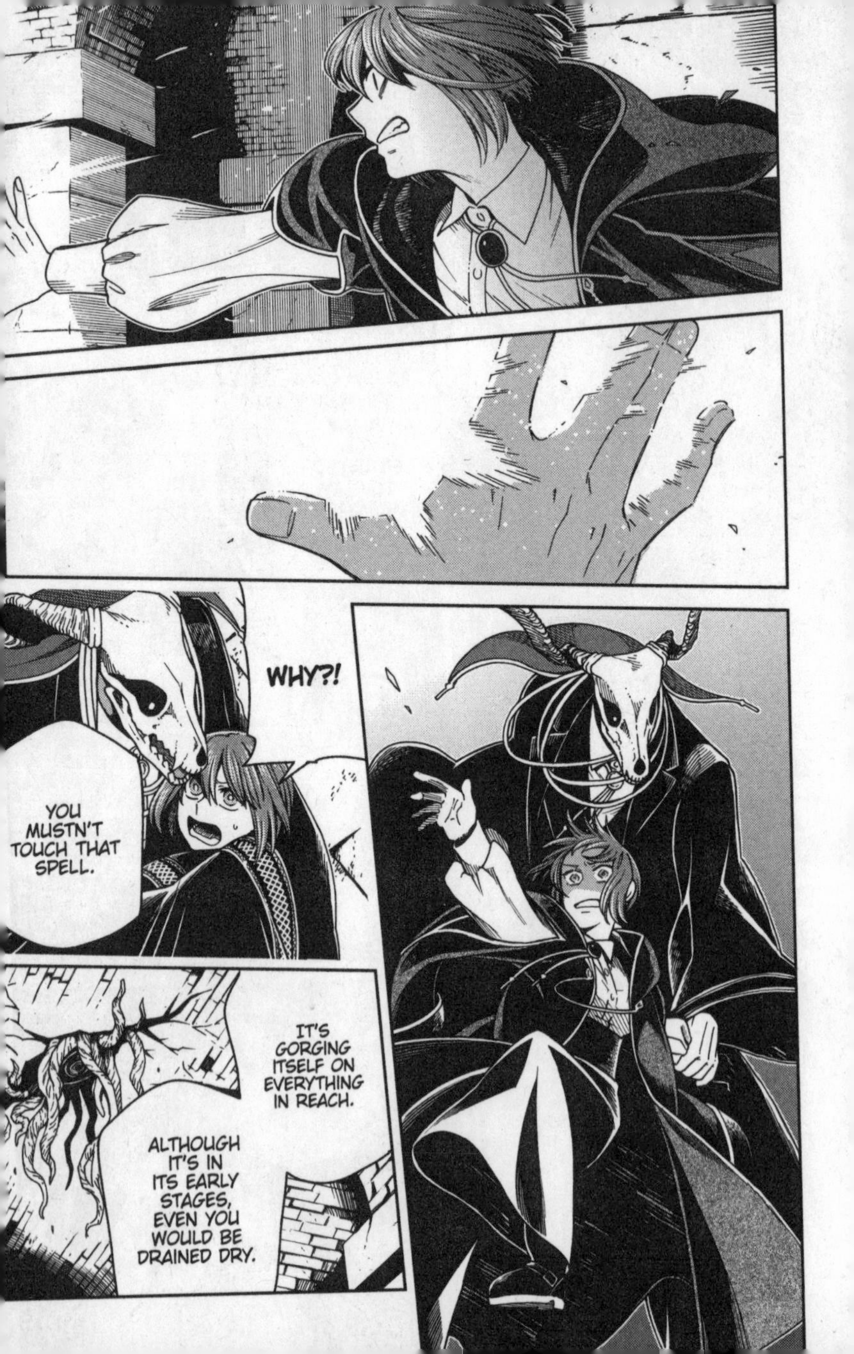
WHY?!
YOU MUSTN'T TOUCH THAT SPELL.
IT'S GORGING ITSELF ON EVERYTHING IN REACH.
ALTHOUGH IT'S IN ITS EARLY STAGES, EVEN YOU WOULD BE DRAINED DRY.

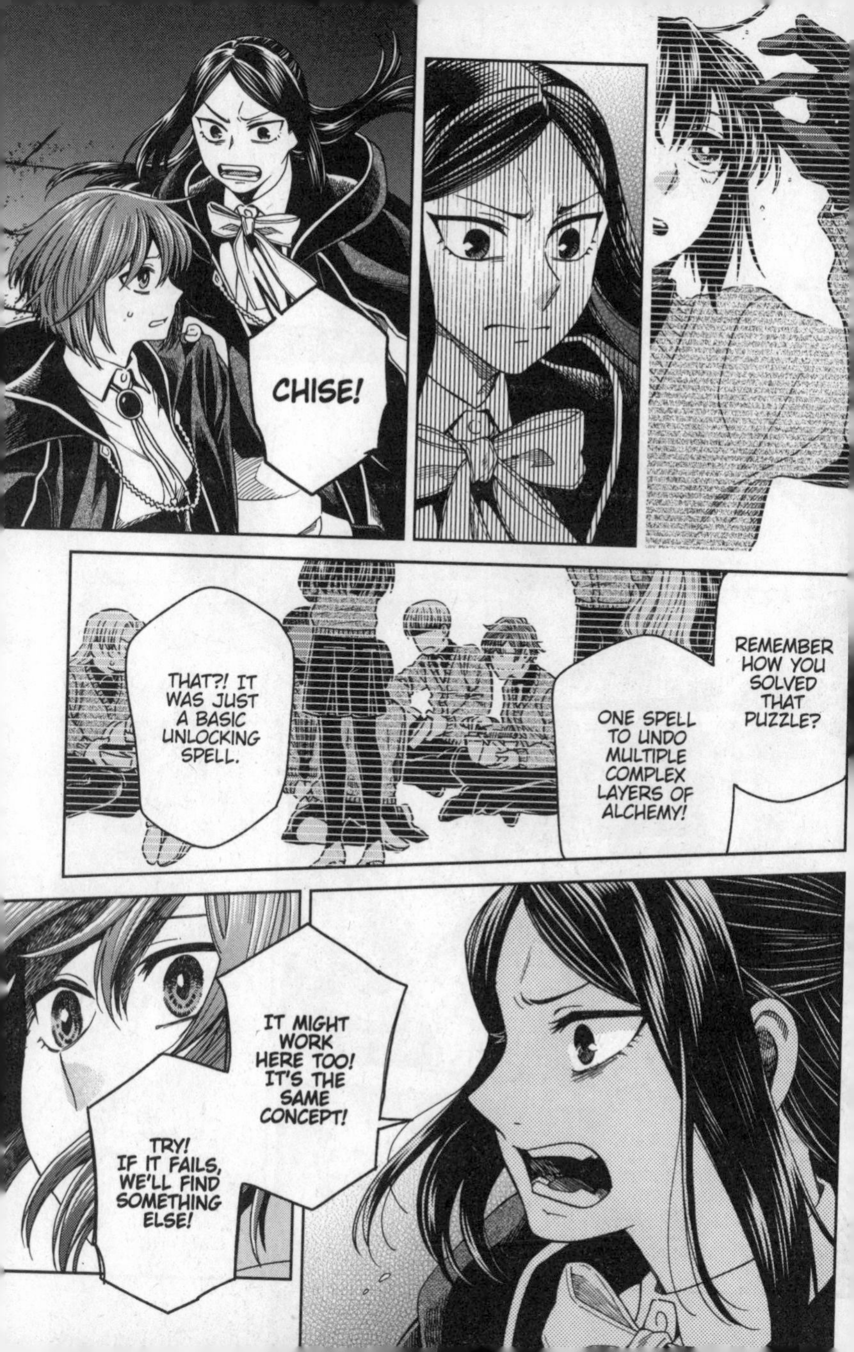
CHISE!
REMEMBER HOW YOU SOLVED THAT PUZZLE?
ONE SPELL TO UNDO MULTIPLE COMPLEX LAYERS OF ALCHEMY!
THAT?! IT WAS JUST A BASIC UNLOCKING SPELL.
IT MIGHT WORK HERE TOO! IT'S THE SAME CONCEPT!
TRY! IF IT FAILS, WE'LL FIND SOMETHING ELSE!

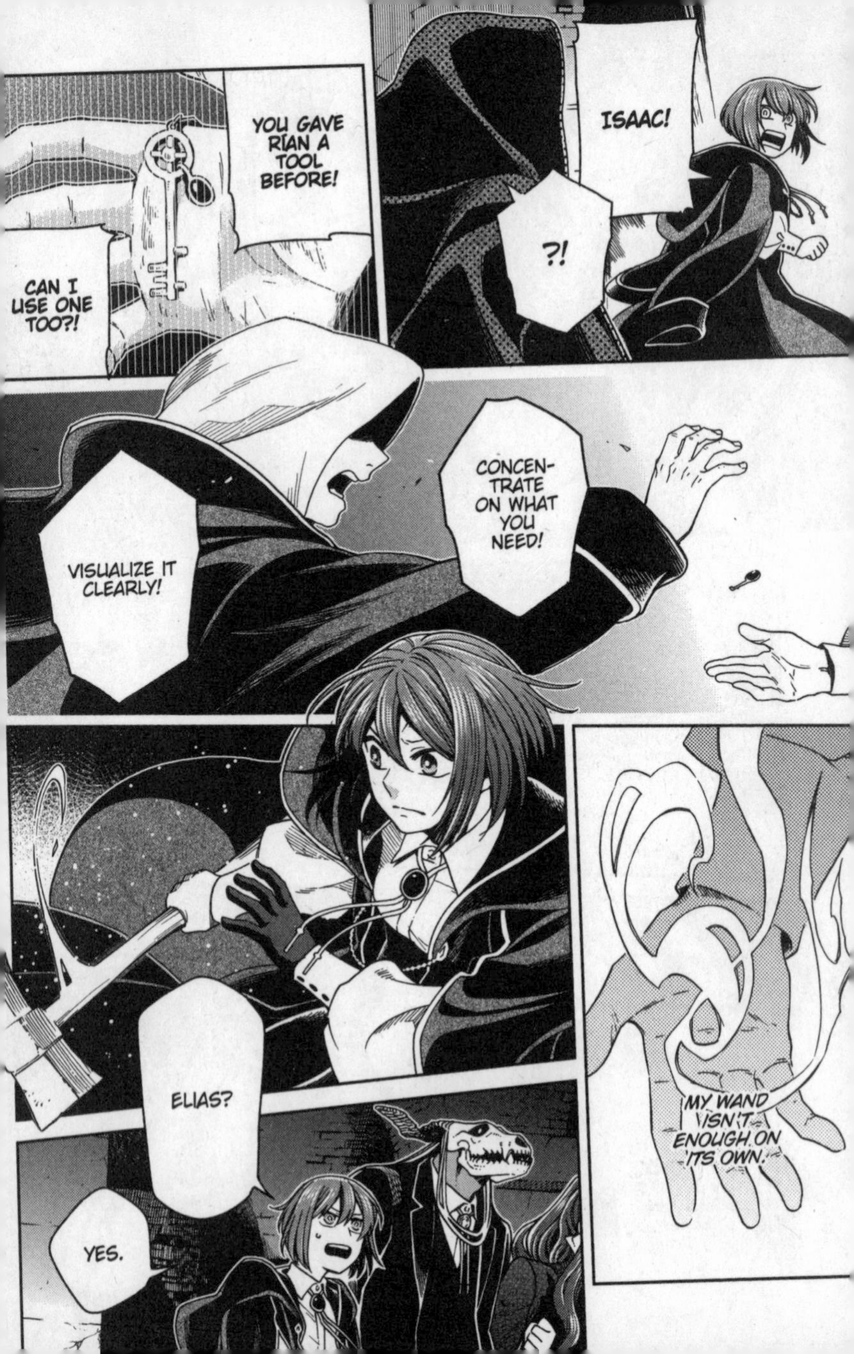
ISAAC!
?!
YOU GAVE RÍAN A TOOL BEFORE!
CAN I USE ONE TOO?!
CONCEN-TRATE ON WHAT YOU NEED!
VISUALIZE IT CLEARLY!
MY WAND ISN'T ENOUGH ON ITS OWN.
ELIAS?
YES.

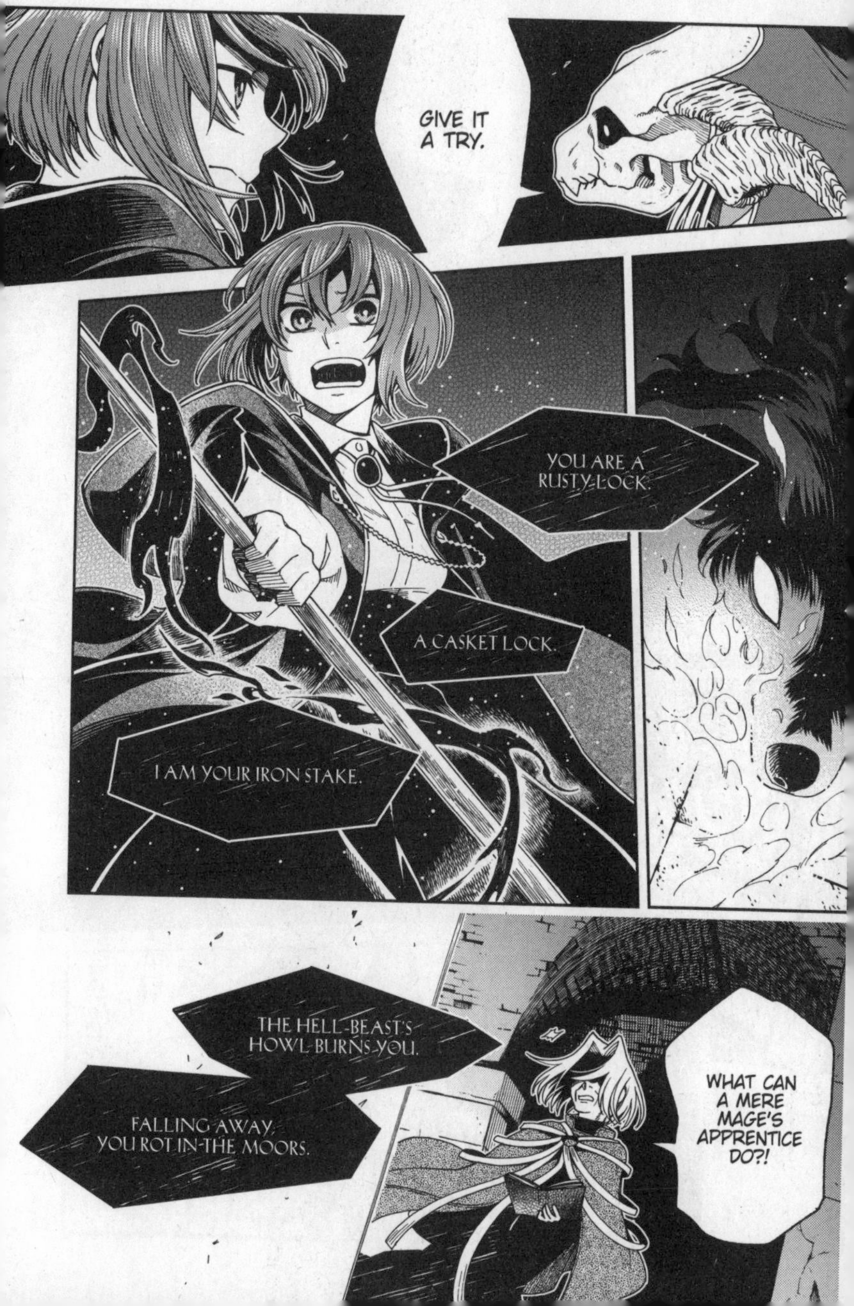
GIVE IT A TRY.
YOU ARE A RUSTY LOCK.
A CASKET LOCK.
I AM YOUR IRON STAKE.
WHAT CAN A MERE MAGE'S APPRENTICE DO?!
THE HELL-BEAST'S HOWL BURNS YOU.
FALLING AWAY, YOU ROT IN THE MOORS.

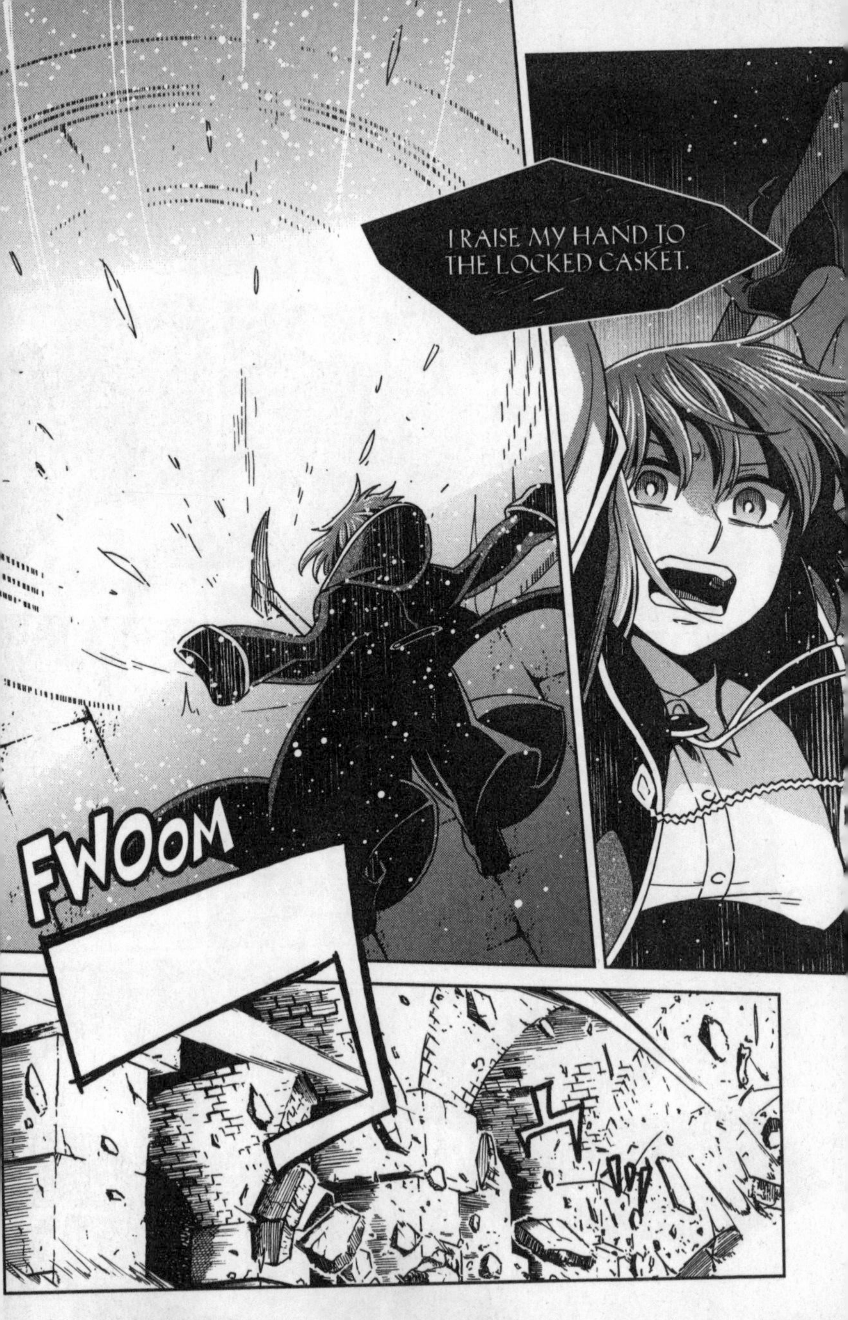
I RAISE MY HAND TO THE LOCKED CASKET.
FWOOM

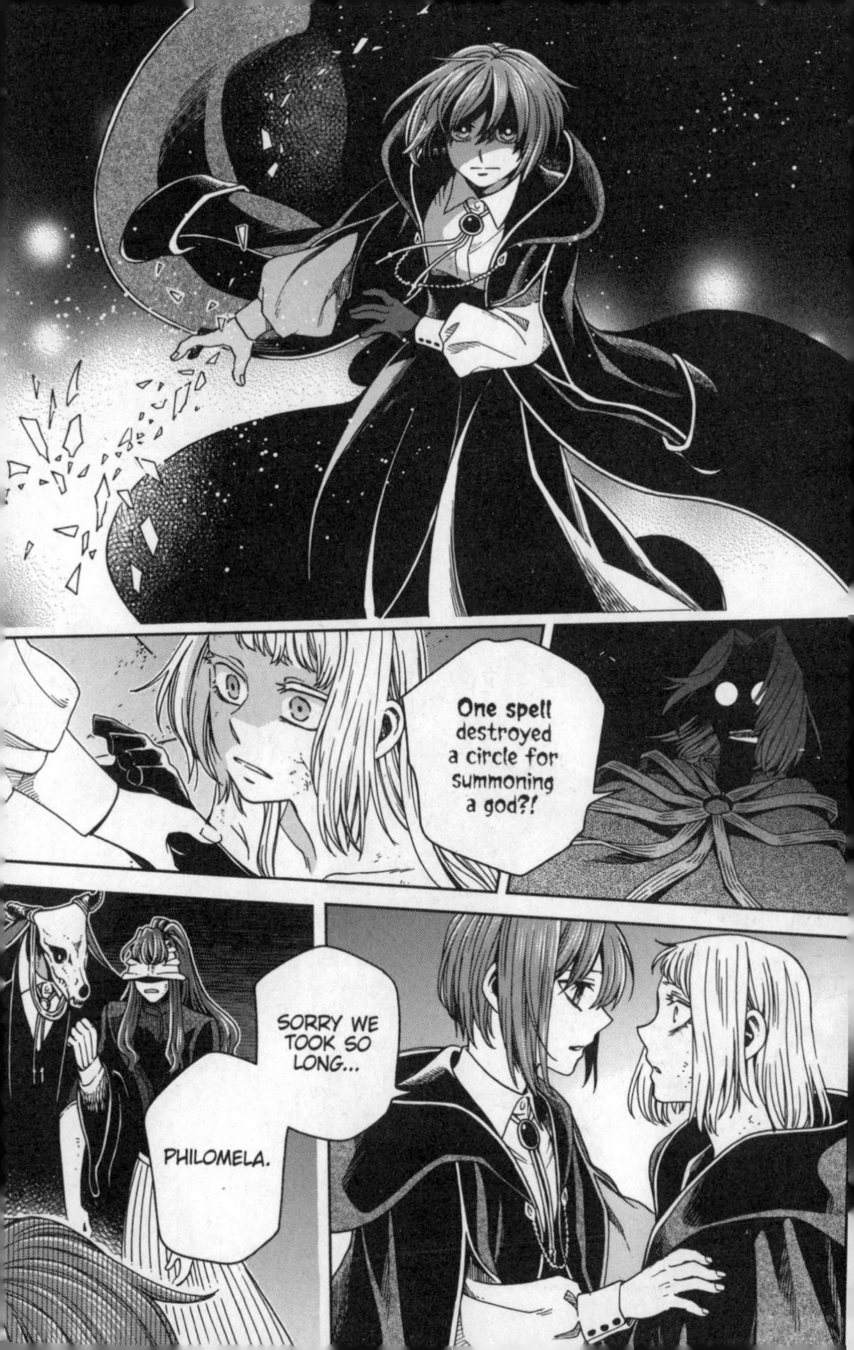
One spell destroyed a circle for summoning a god?!
SORRY WE TOOK SO LONG...
PHILOMELA.

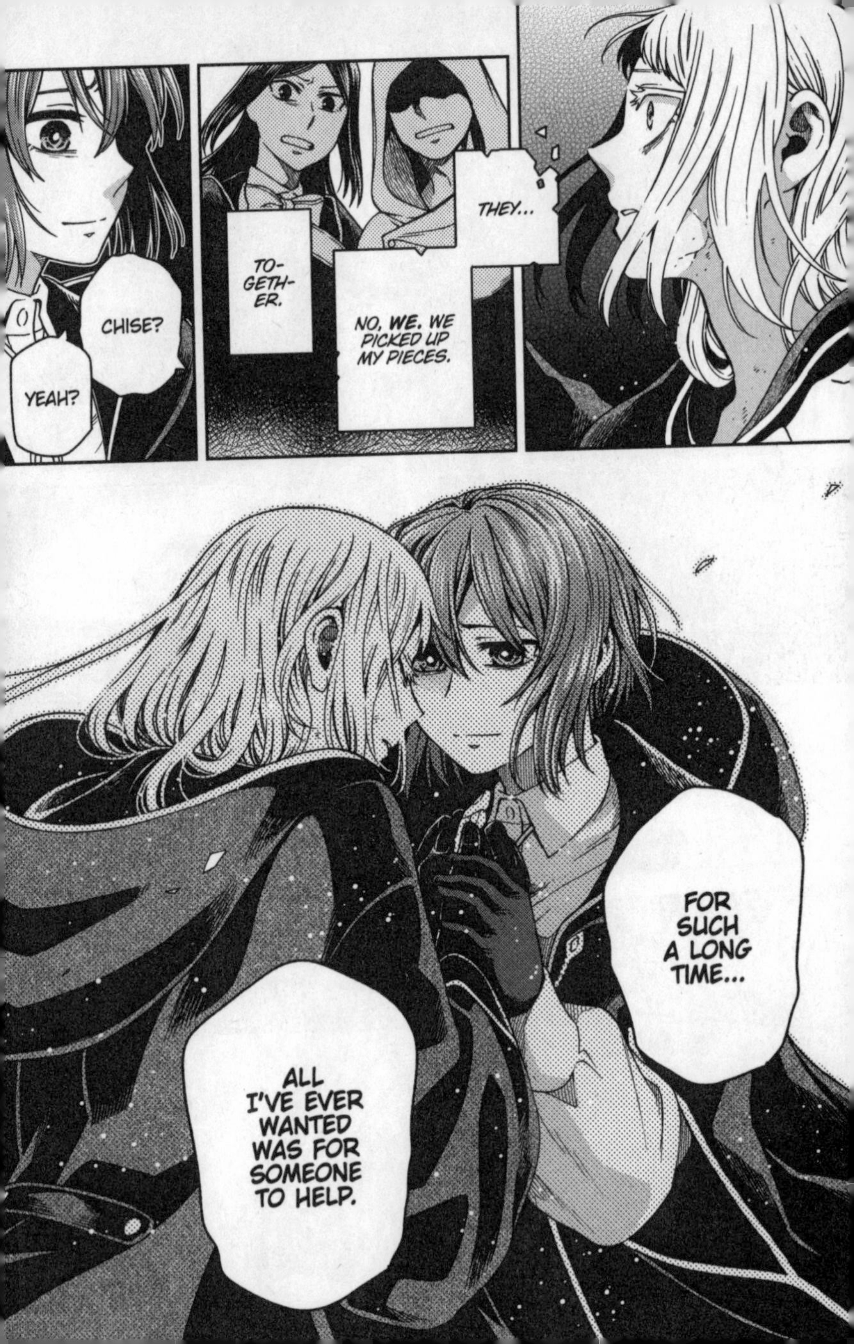
THEY...
NO, WE. WE PICKED UP MY PIECES.
TO-GETH-ER.
CHISE?
YEAH?
FOR SUCH A LONG TIME...
ALL I'VE EVER WANTED WAS FOR SOMEONE TO HELP.

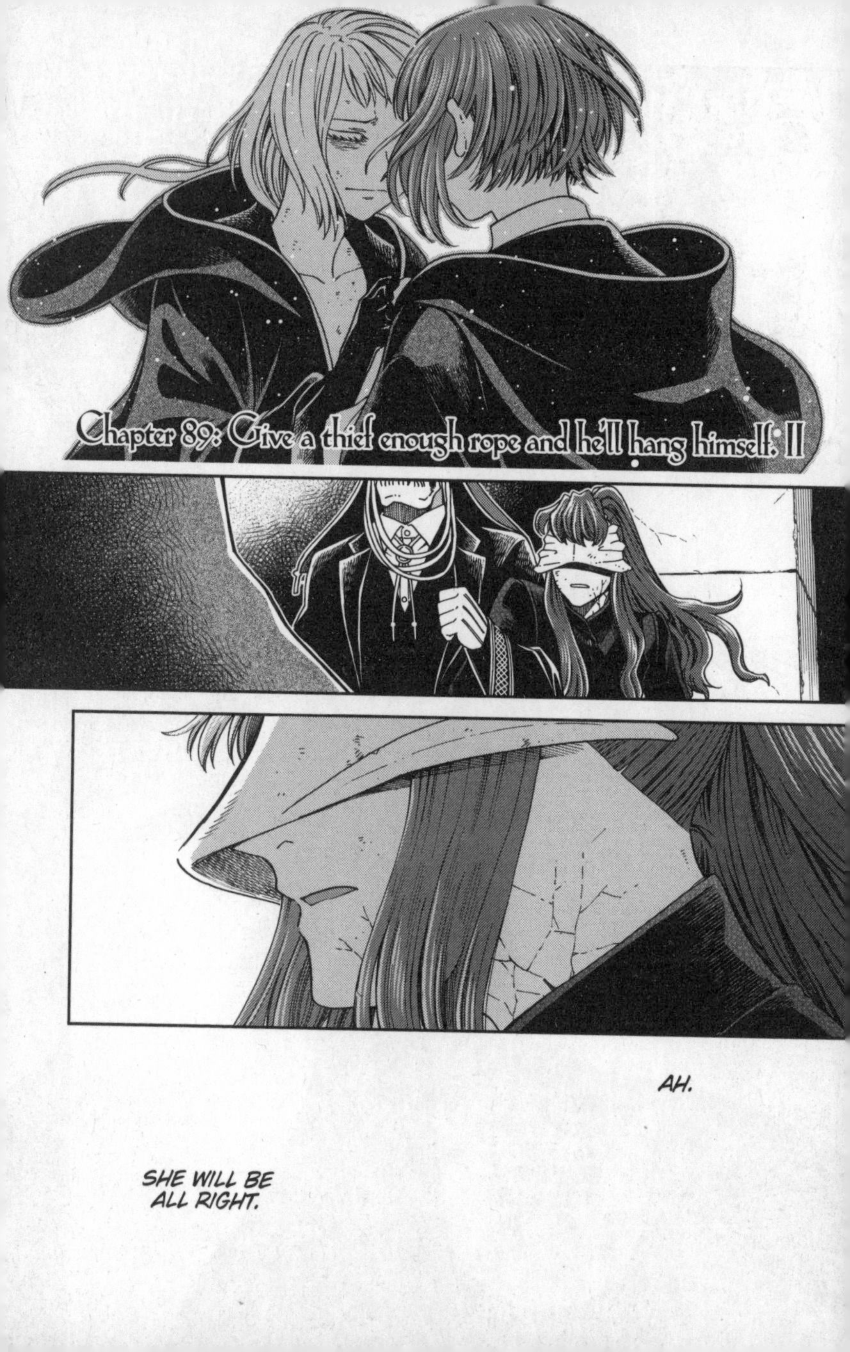
Chapter 89: Give a thief enough rope and he'll hang himself: II
AH.
SHE WILL BE ALL RIGHT.

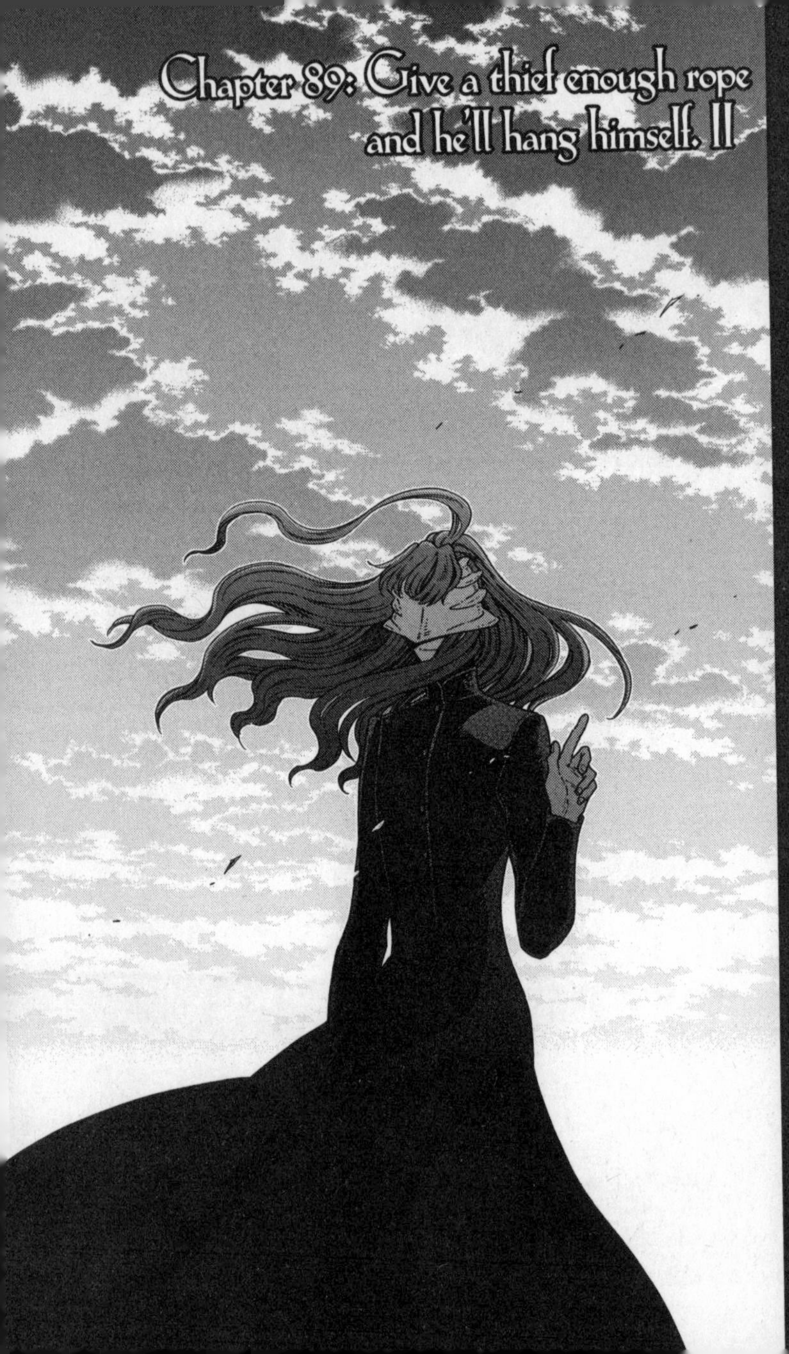
Chapter 89: Give a thief enough rope
and he'll hang himself. II

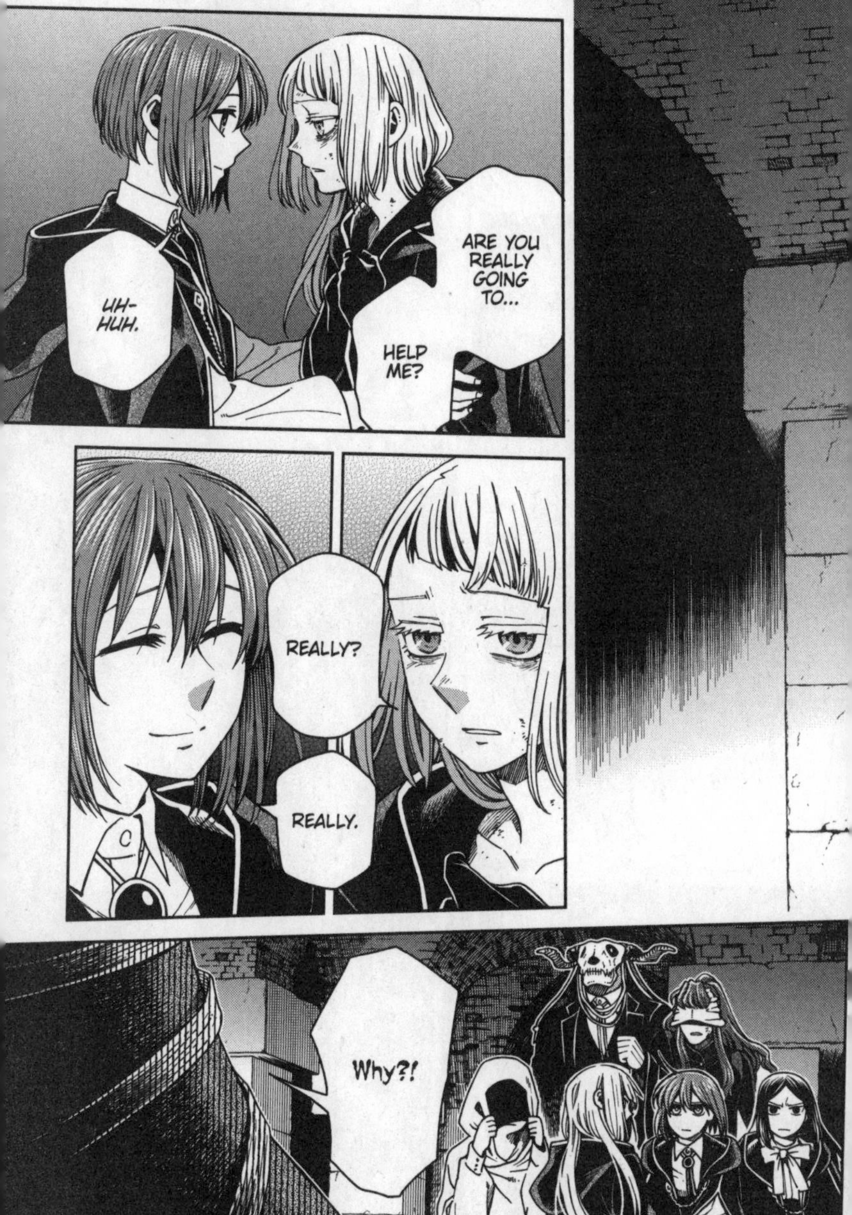
ARE YOU REALLY GOING TO...
HELP ME?
UH-HUH.
REALLY?
REALLY.
Why?!

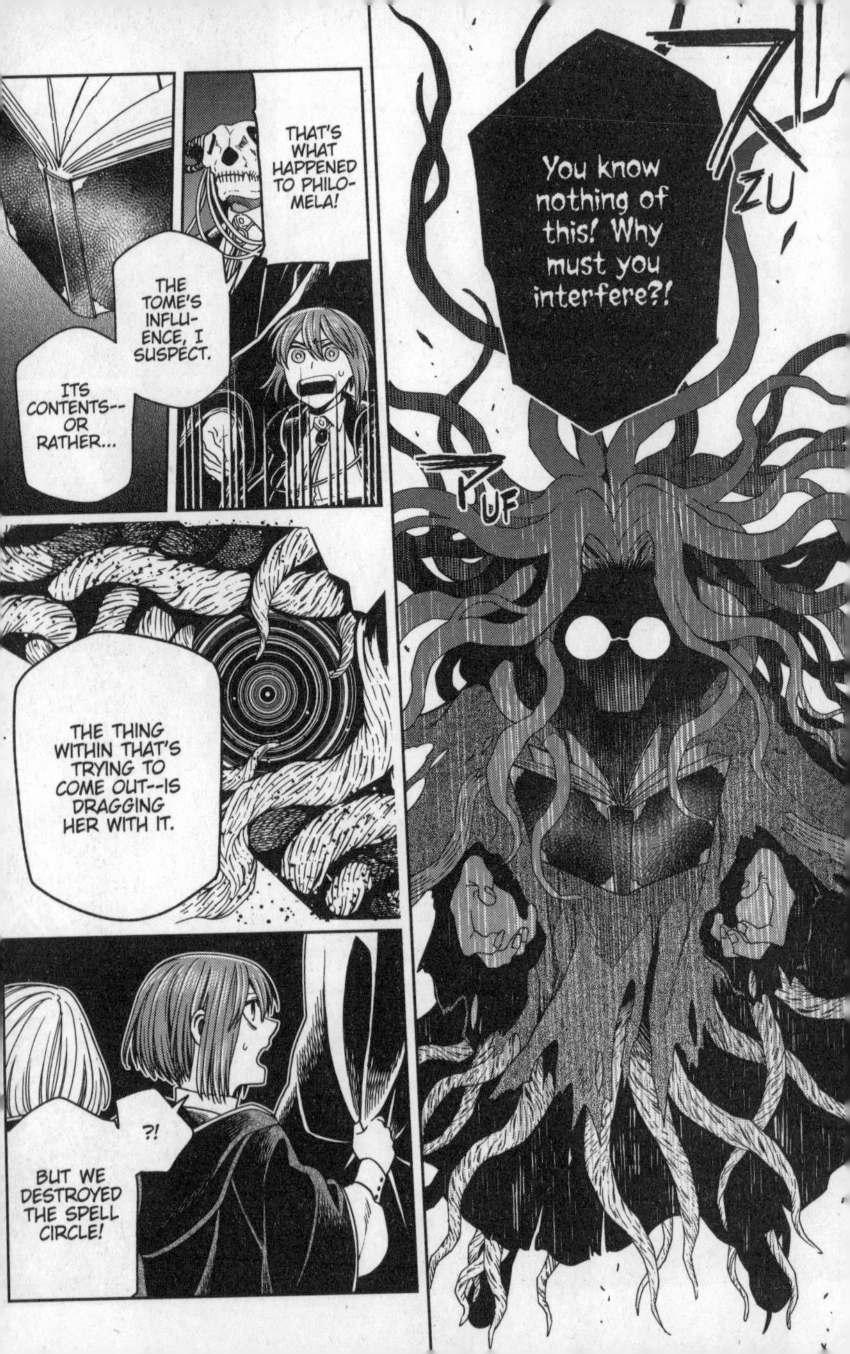
ZU
You know nothing of this! Why must you interfere?!
PUF
THAT'S WHAT HAPPENED TO PHILOMELA!
THE TOME'S INFLUENCE, I SUSPECT.
ITS CONTENTS--OR RATHER...
THE THING WITHIN THAT'S TRYING TO COME OUT--IS DRAGGING HER WITH IT.
?!
BUT WE DESTROYED THE SPELL CIRCLE!

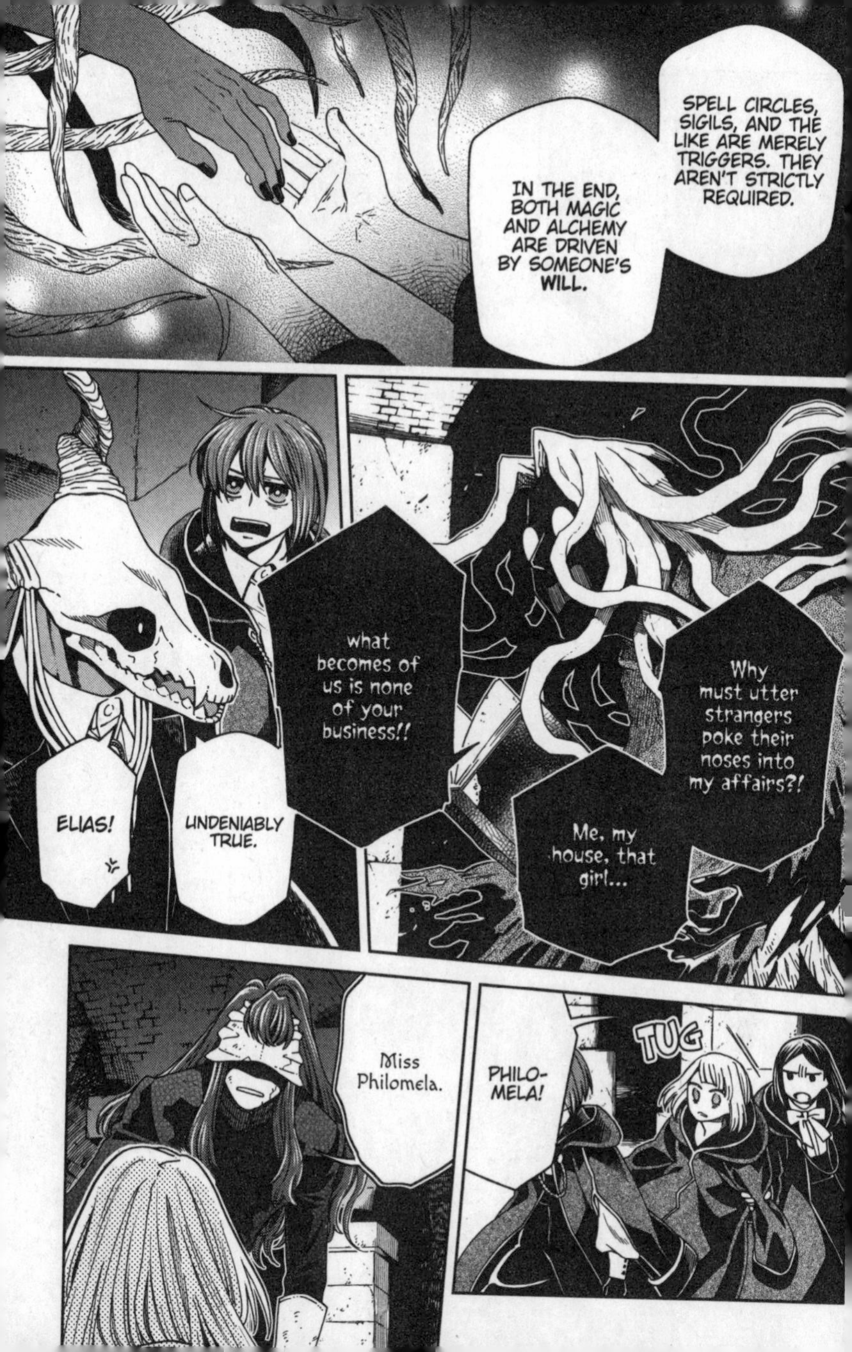
SPELL CIRCLES, SIGILS, AND THE LIKE ARE MERELY TRIGGERS. THEY AREN'T STRICTLY REQUIRED.
IN THE END, BOTH MAGIC AND ALCHEMY ARE DRIVEN BY SOMEONE'S WILL.
Why must utter strangers poke their noses into my affairs?!
Me, my house, that girl...
what becomes of us is none of your business!!
UNDENIABLY TRUE.
ELIAS!
TUG
PHILO-MELA!
Miss Philomela.

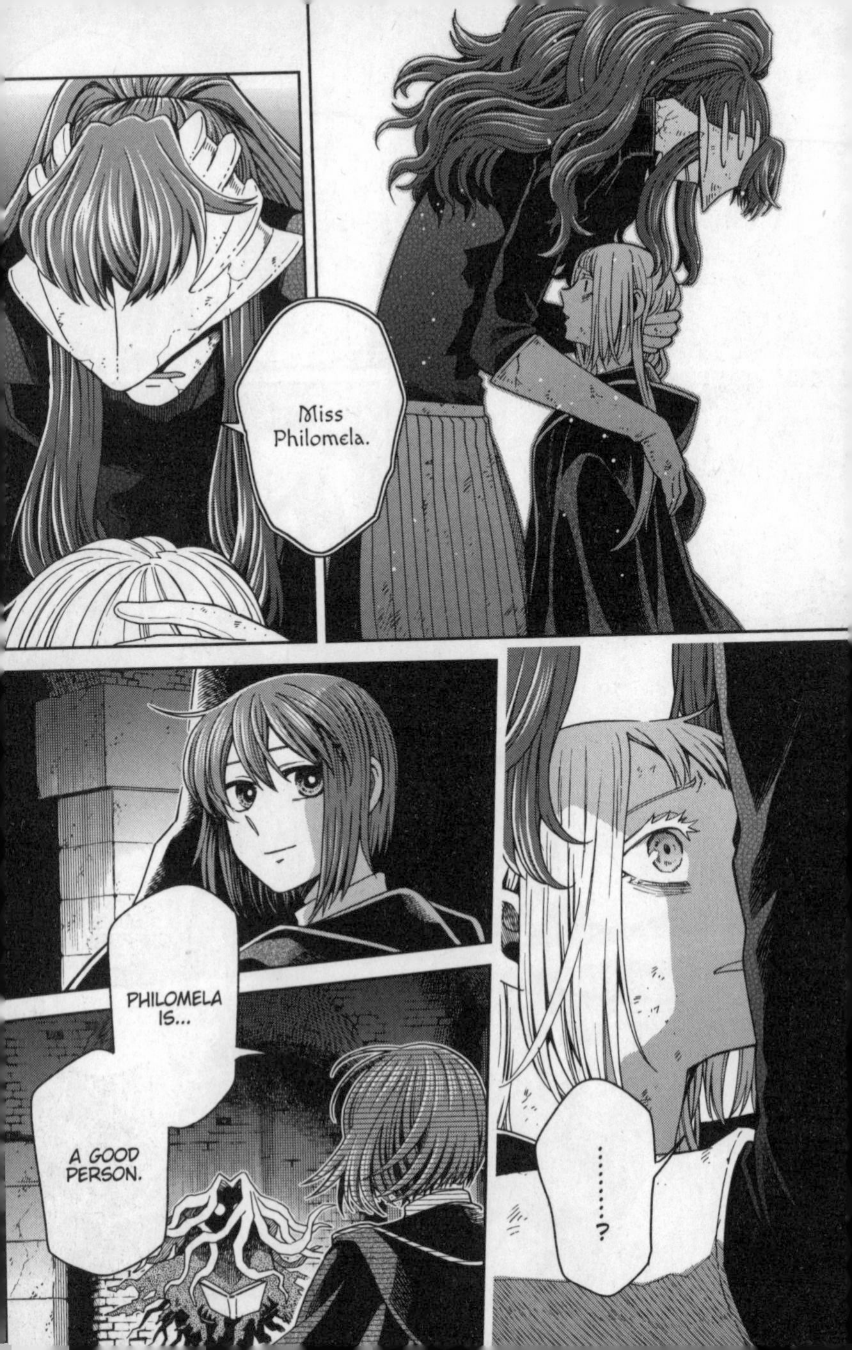
Miss Philomela.
……?
PHILOMELA IS...
A GOOD PERSON.

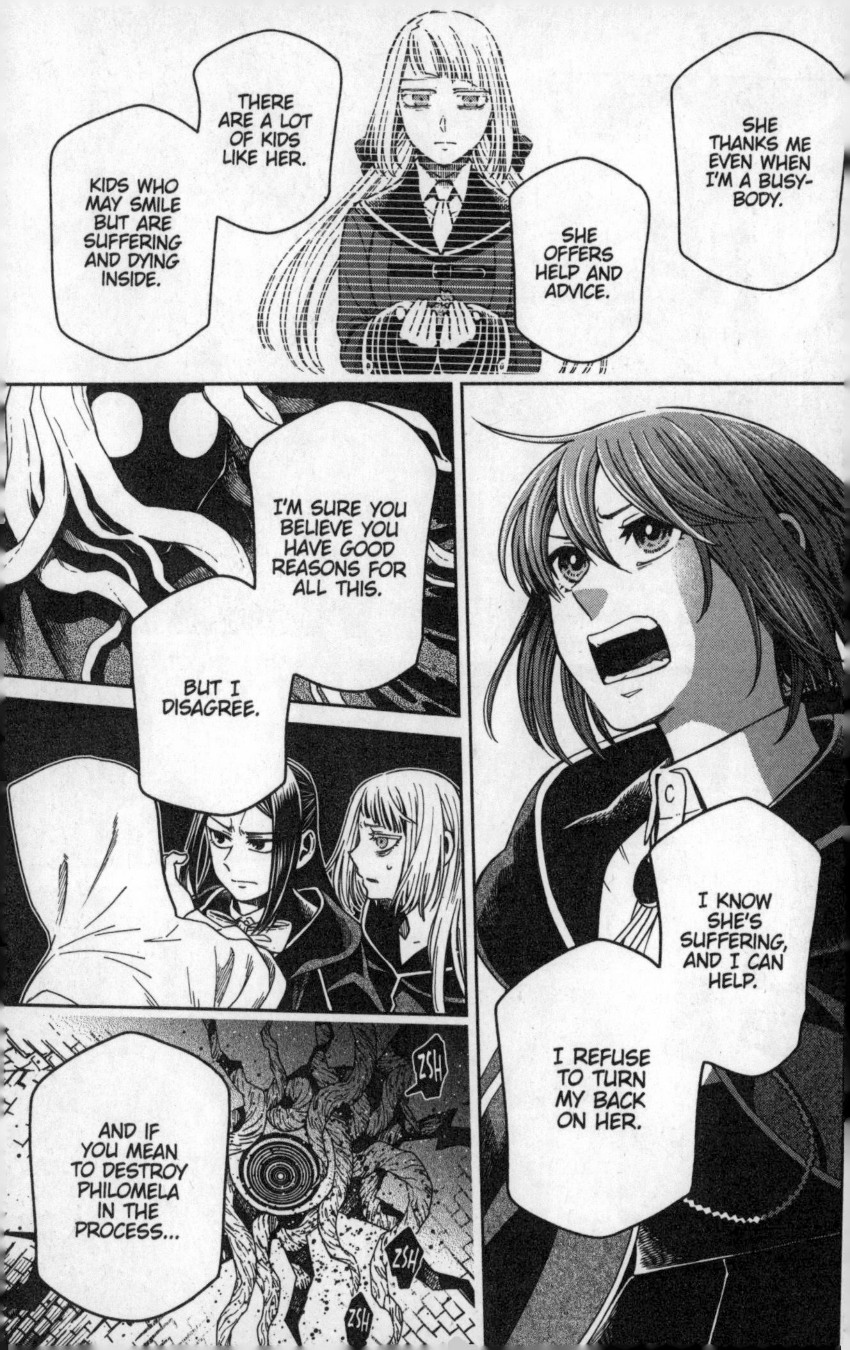
SHE THANKS ME EVEN WHEN I'M A BUSY-BODY.
SHE OFFERS HELP AND ADVICE.
THERE ARE A LOT OF KIDS LIKE HER.
KIDS WHO MAY SMILE BUT ARE SUFFERING AND DYING INSIDE.
I KNOW SHE'S SUFFERING, AND I CAN HELP.
I REFUSE TO TURN MY BACK ON HER.
I'M SURE YOU BELIEVE YOU HAVE GOOD REASONS FOR ALL THIS.
BUT I DISAGREE.
ZSH
AND IF YOU MEAN TO DESTROY PHILOMELA IN THE PROCESS...
ZSH
ZSH

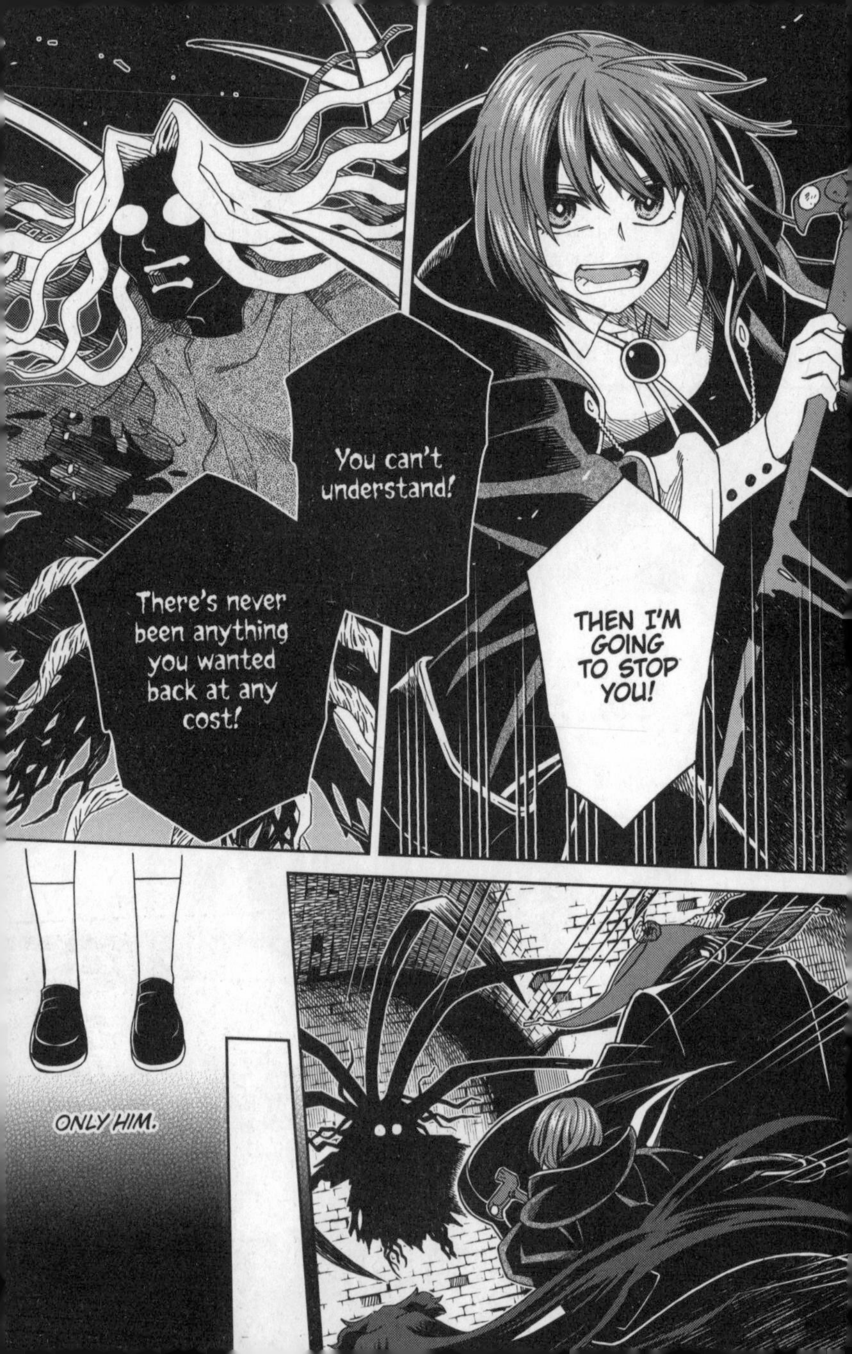
THEN I'M GOING TO STOP YOU!
You can't understand!
There's never been anything you wanted back at any cost!
ONLY HIM.

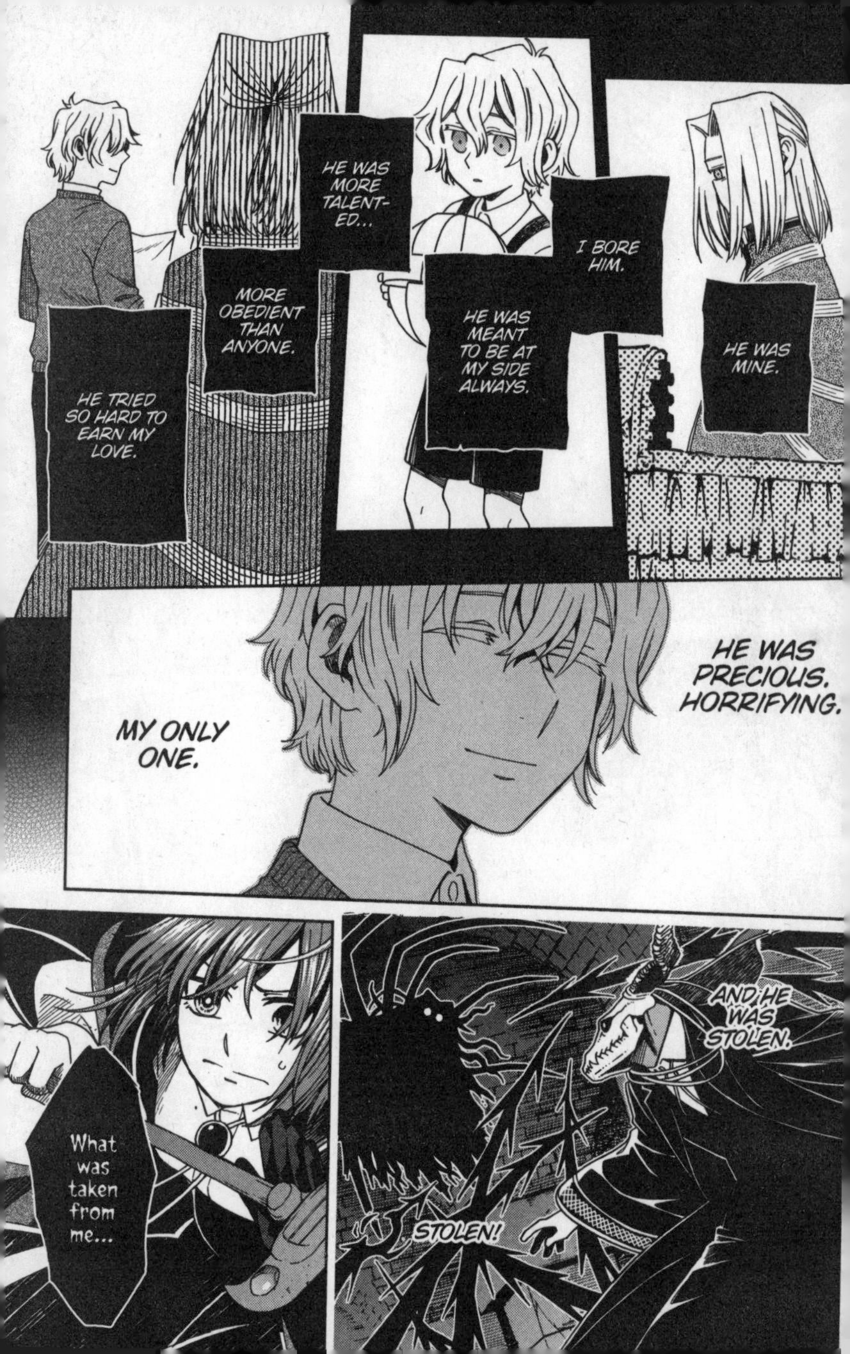
I BORE HIM.
HE WAS MINE.
HE WAS MEANT TO BE AT MY SIDE ALWAYS.
HE WAS MORE TALENT-ED...
MORE OBEDIENT THAN ANYONE.
HE TRIED SO HARD TO EARN MY LOVE.
HE WAS PRECIOUS. HORRIFYING.
MY ONLY ONE.
AND HE WAS STOLEN.
STOLEN!
What was taken from me...

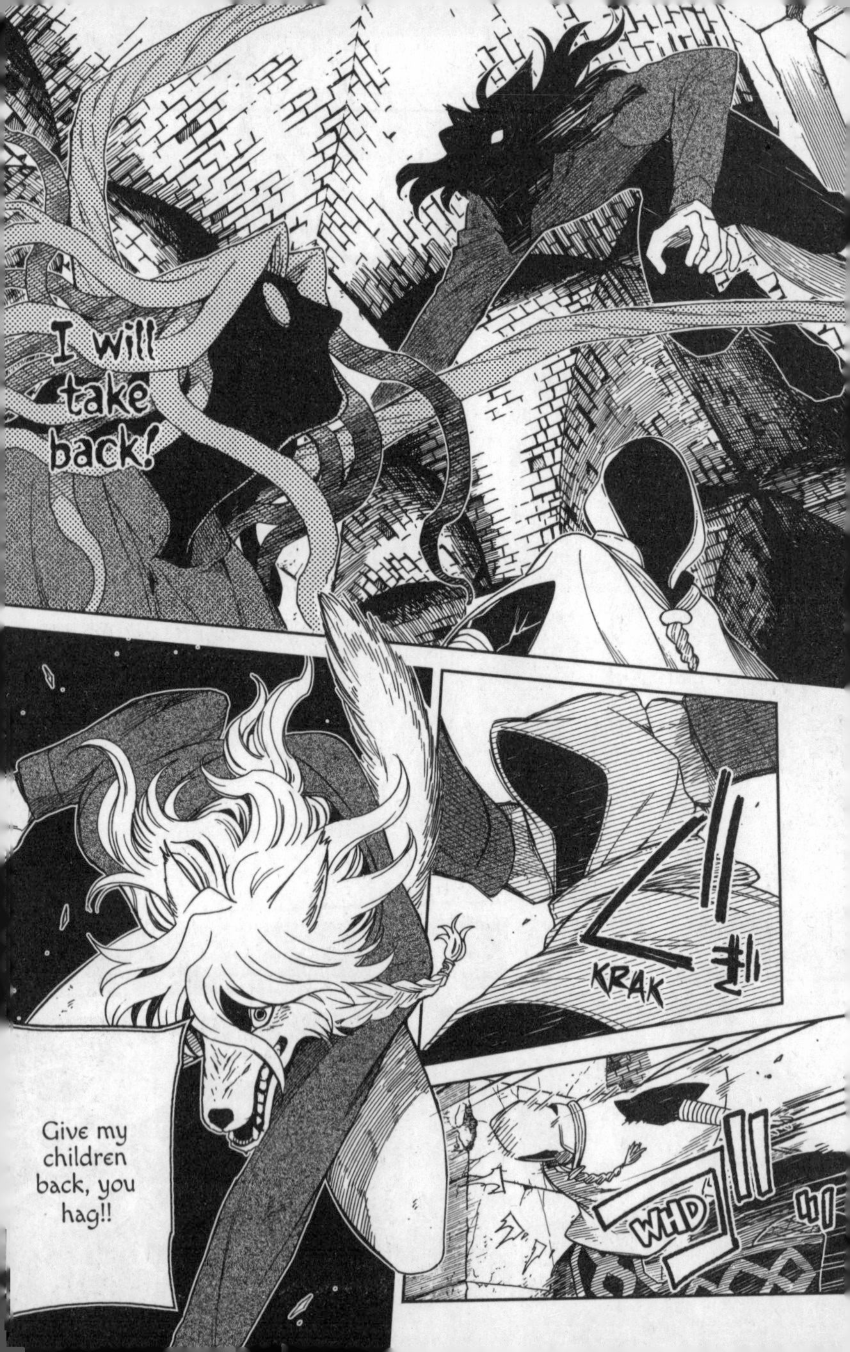
I will take back!
KRAK
WHD
Give my children back, you hag!!

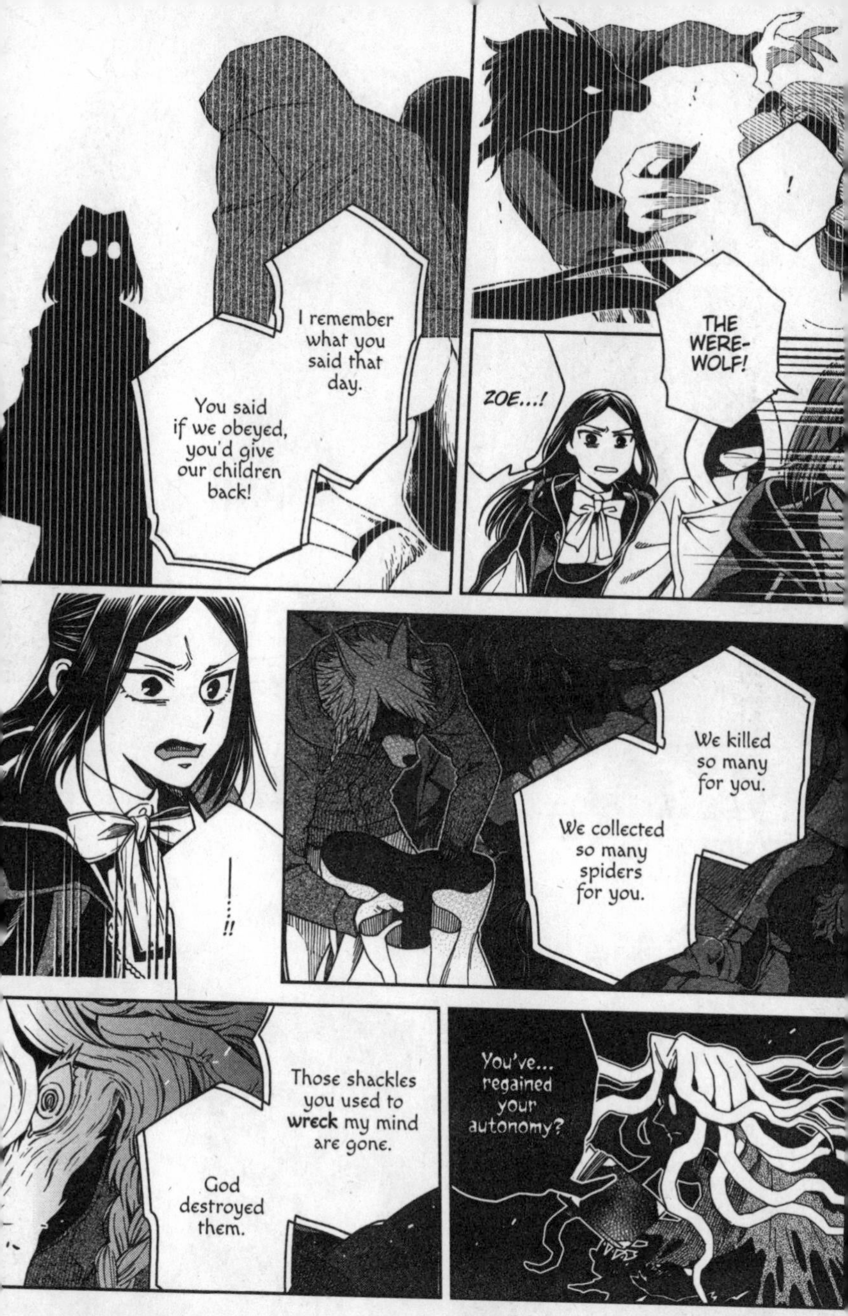
!
THE WERE-WOLF!
ZOE...!
I remember what you said that day.
You said if we obeyed, you'd give our children back!
We killed so many for you.
We collected so many spiders for you.
...!!
You've... regained your autonomy?
Those shackles you used to **wreck** my mind are gone.
God destroyed them.

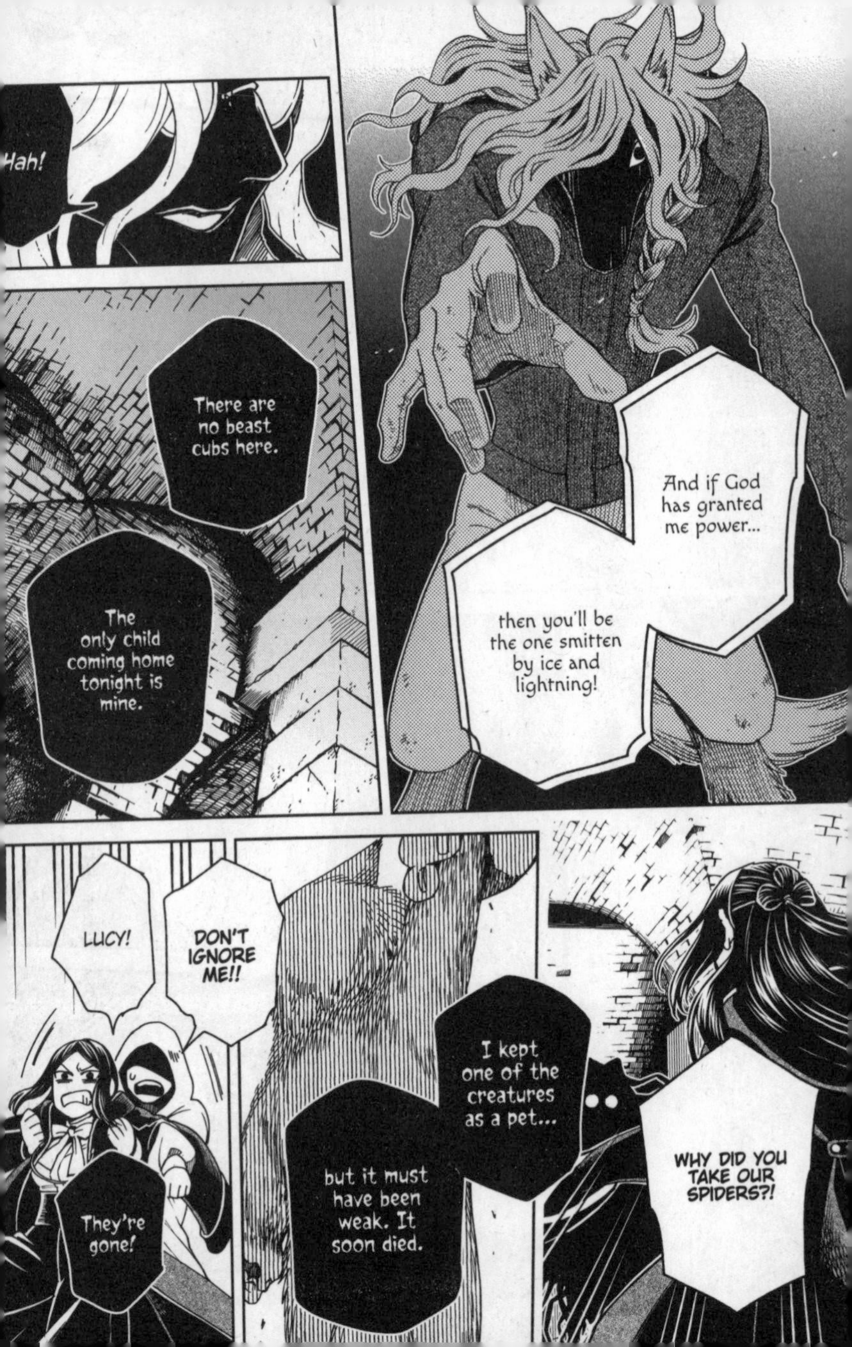
And if God has granted me power...
then you'll be the one smitten by ice and lightning!
Hah!
There are no beast cubs here.
The only child coming home tonight is mine.
WHY DID YOU TAKE OUR SPIDERS?!
I kept one of the creatures as a pet...
but it must have been weak. It soon died.
DON'T IGNORE ME!!
LUCY!
They're gone!

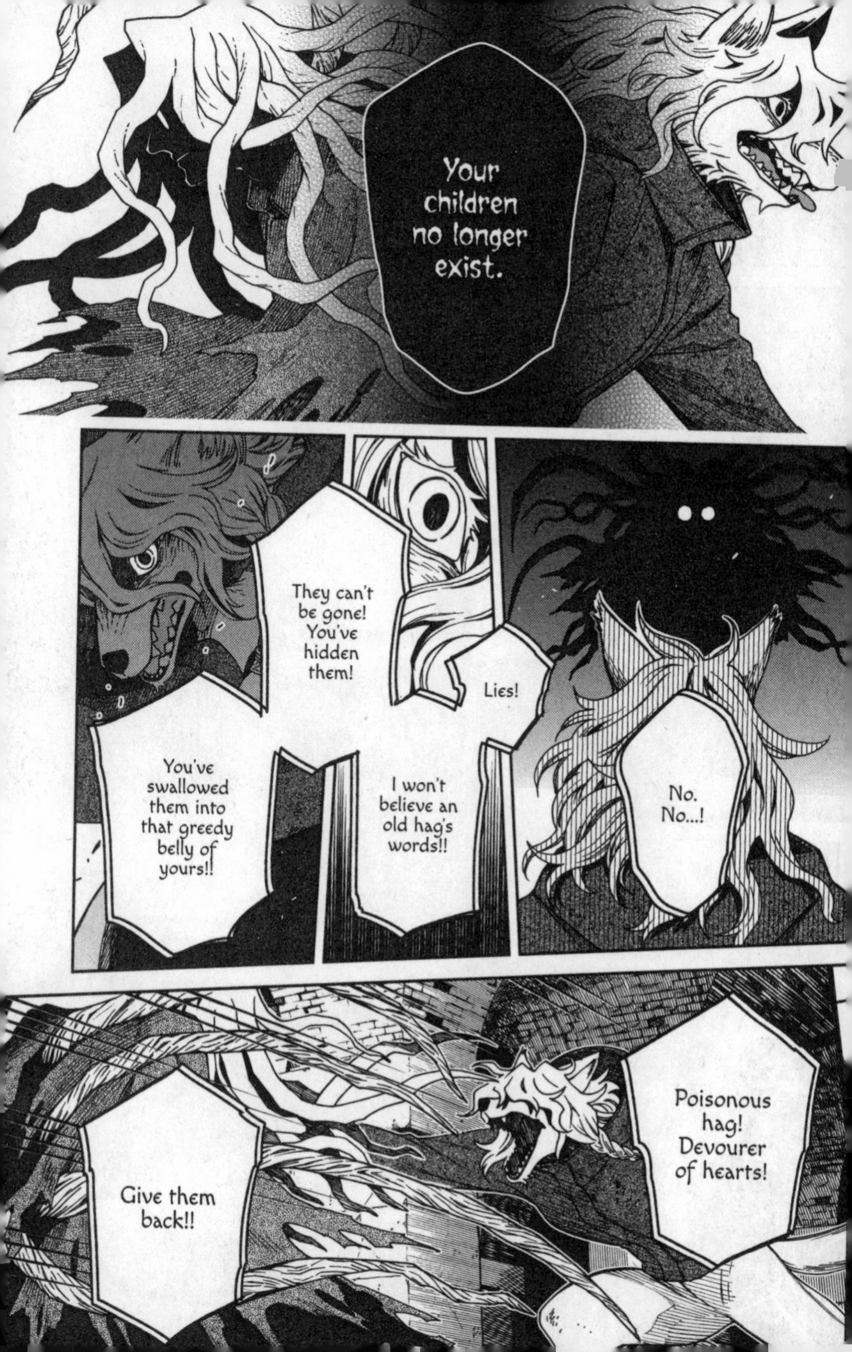
Your children no longer exist.
No. No...!
Lies!
They can't be gone! You've hidden them!
I won't believe an old hag's words!!
You've swallowed them into that greedy belly of yours!!
Poisonous hag! Devourer of hearts!
Give them back!!

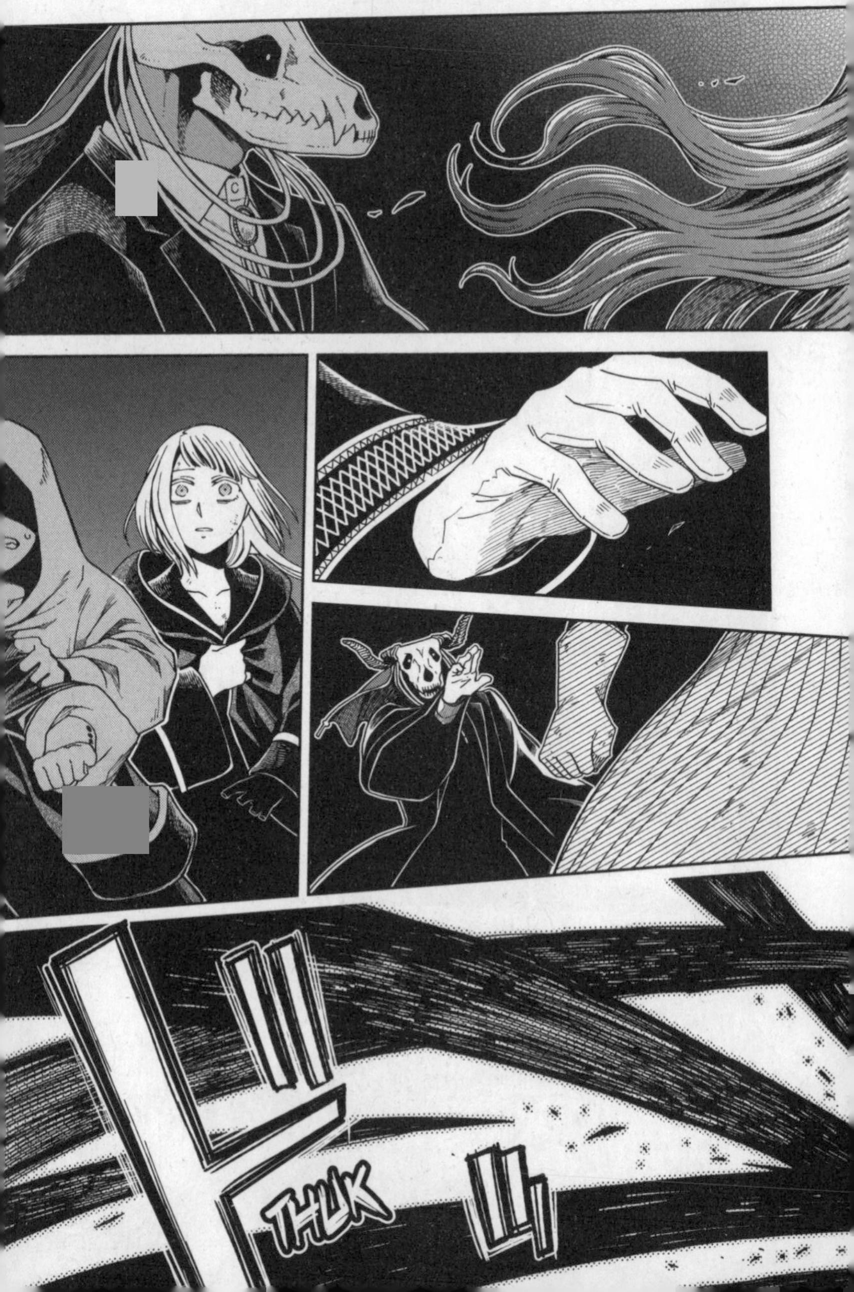
THUK

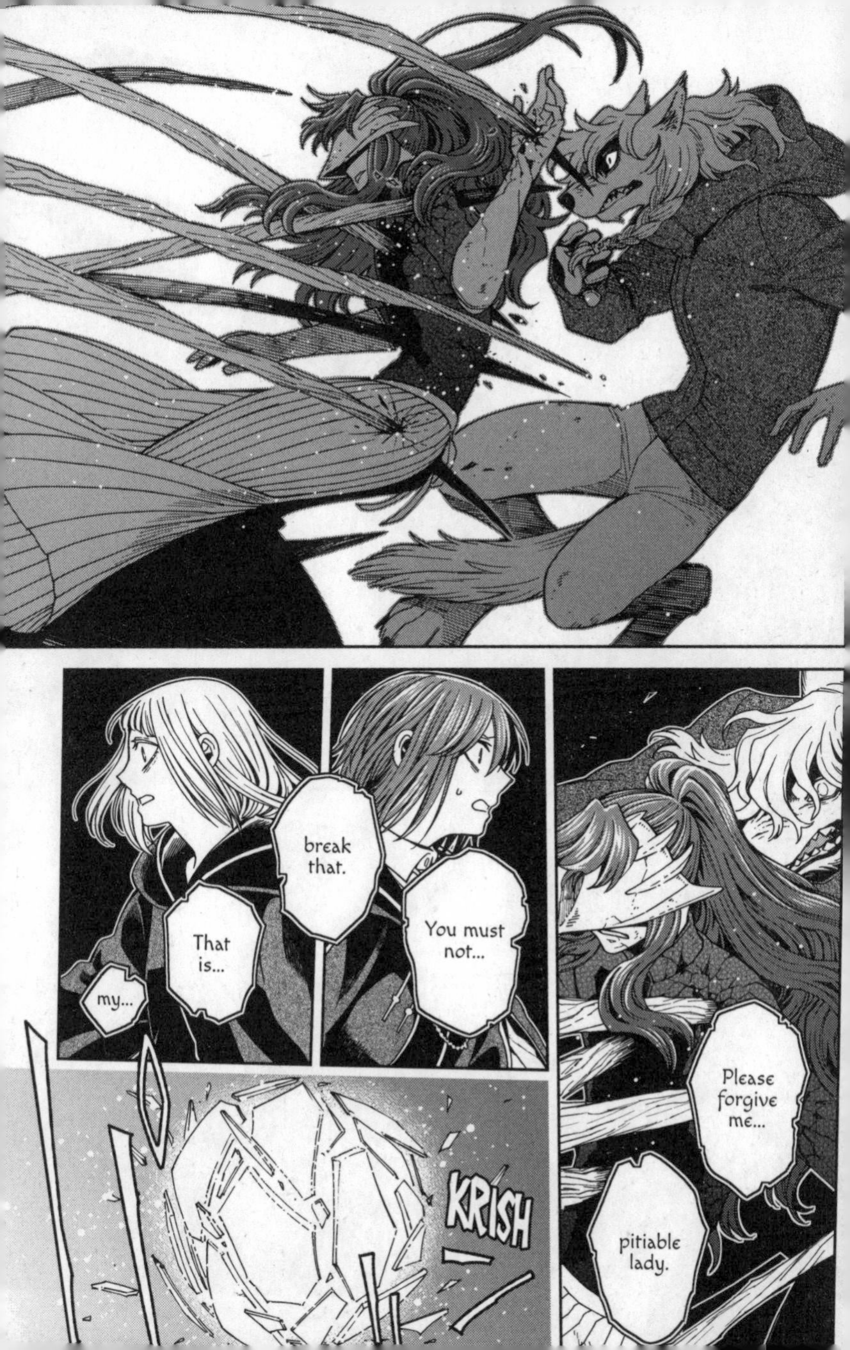
Please forgive me...
pitiable lady.
You must not...
break that.
That is...
my...
KRISH

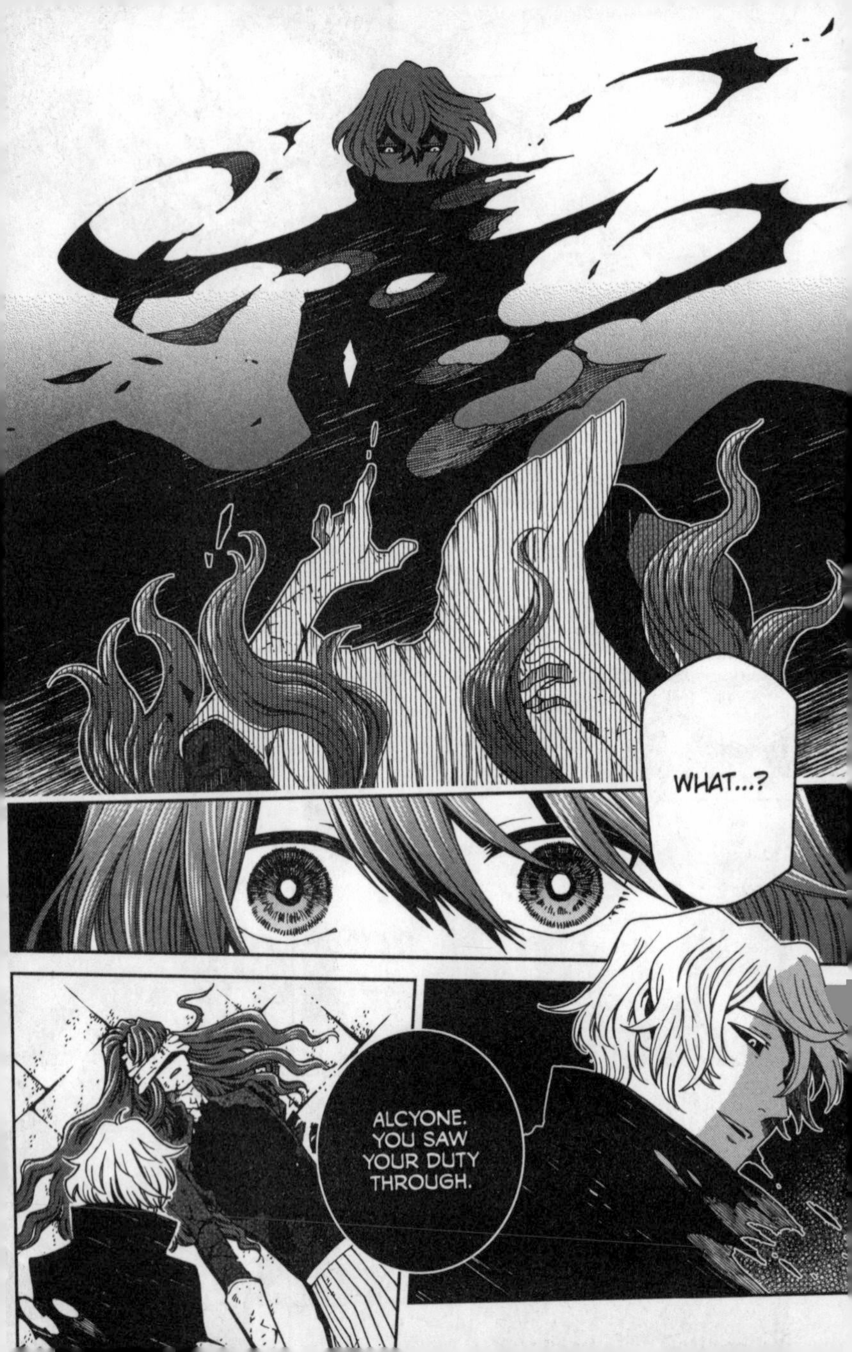
WHAT...?
ALCYONE. YOU SAW YOUR DUTY THROUGH.

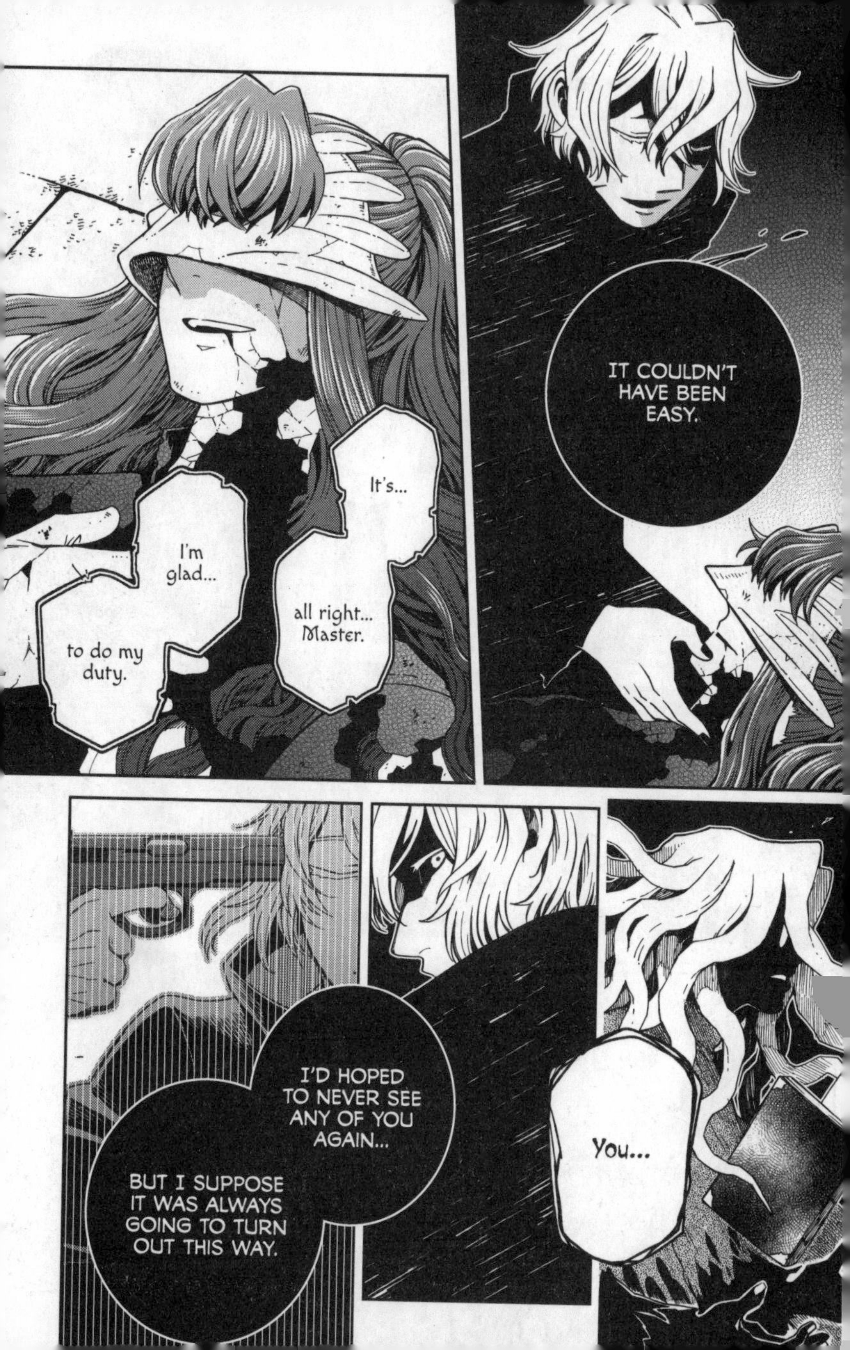
IT COULDN'T HAVE BEEN EASY.
It's... all right... Master.
I'm glad... to do my duty.
You...
I'D HOPED TO NEVER SEE ANY OF YOU AGAIN...
BUT I SUPPOSE IT WAS ALWAYS GOING TO TURN OUT THIS WAY.

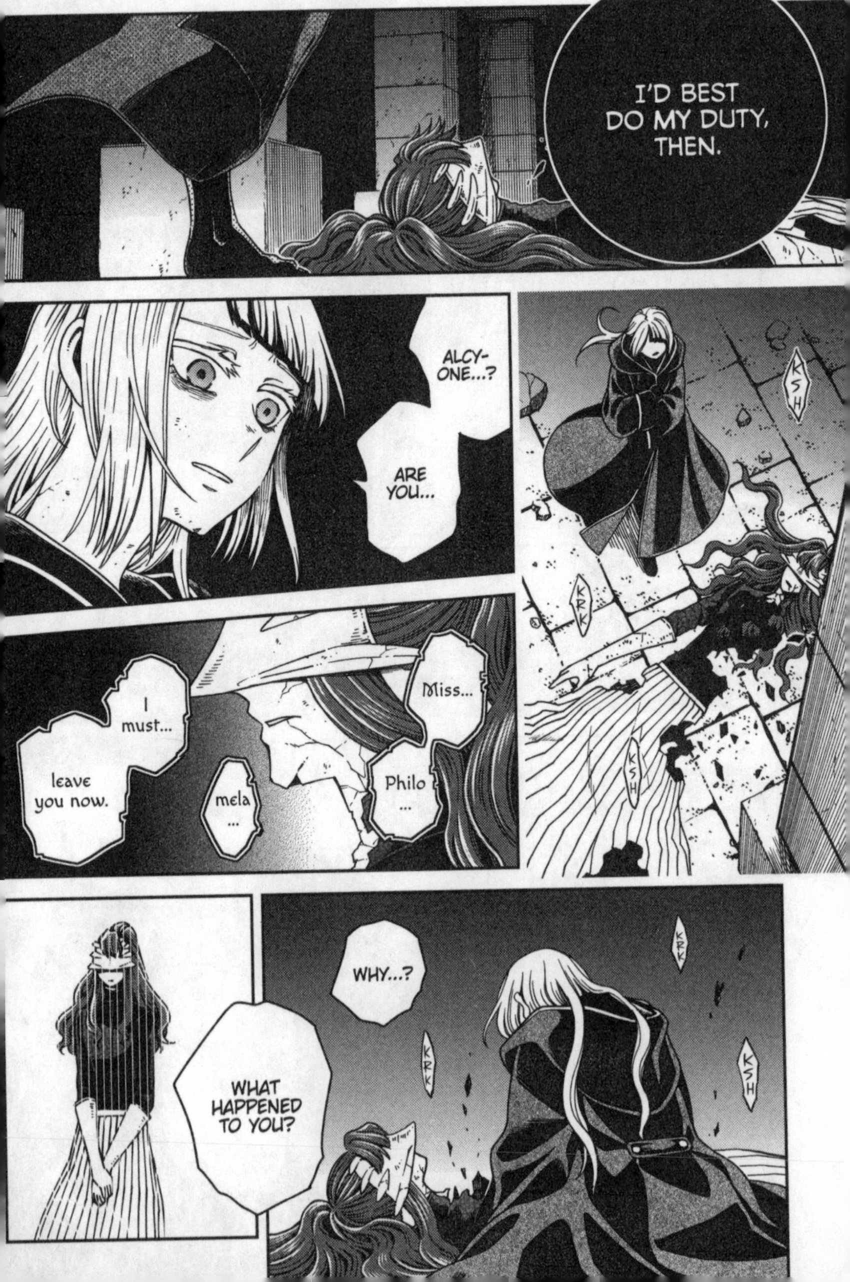
I'D BEST DO MY DUTY, THEN.
KSH
KRK
KSH
ALCY-ONE...?
ARE YOU...
Miss...
Philo...
mela...
I must...
leave you now.
KRK
WHY...?
KSH
KRK
WHAT HAPPENED TO YOU?

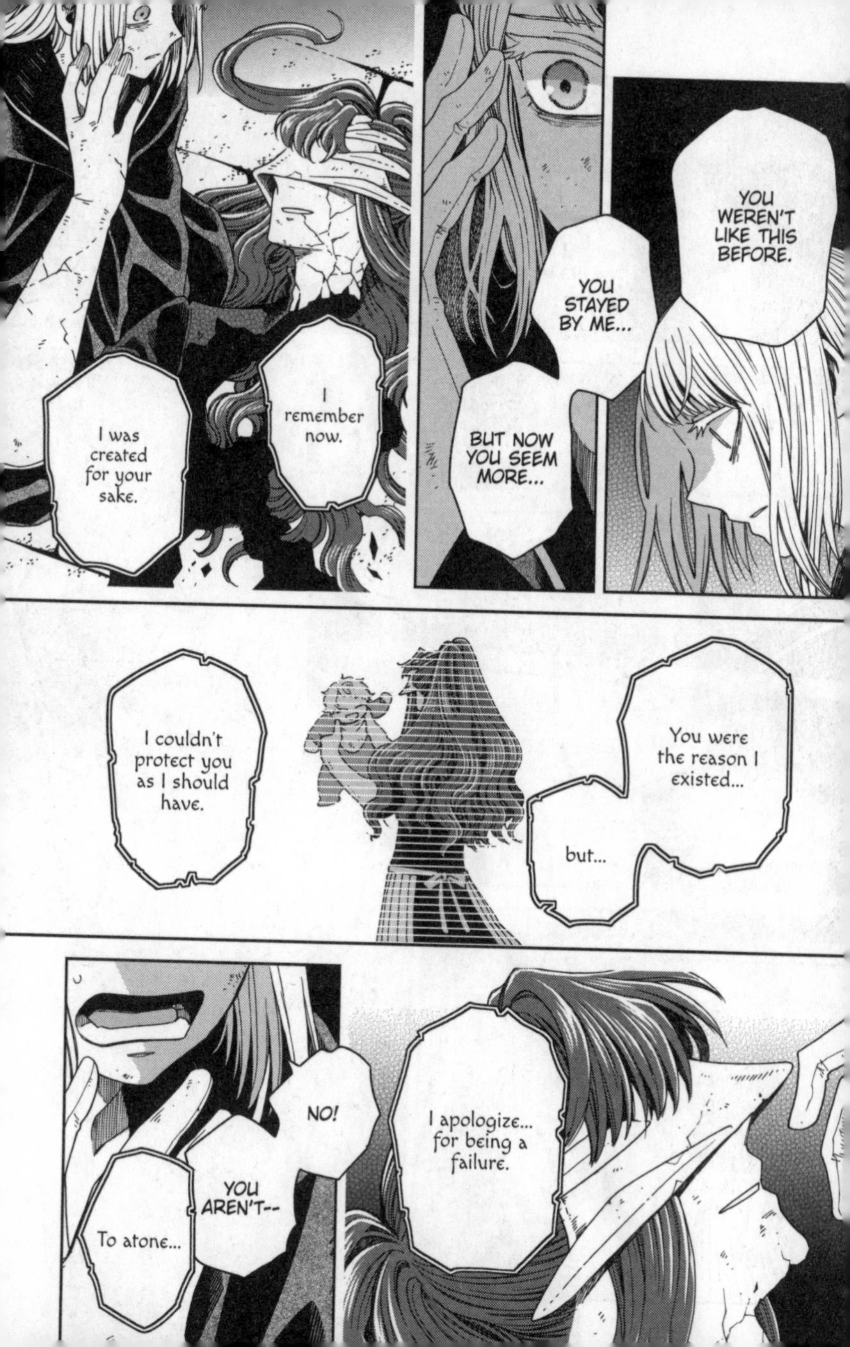
YOU WEREN'T LIKE THIS BEFORE.
YOU STAYED BY ME...
BUT NOW YOU SEEM MORE...
I remember now.
I was created for your sake.
You were the reason I existed...
but...
I couldn't protect you as I should have.
I apologize... for being a failure.
NO!
YOU AREN'T--
To atone...

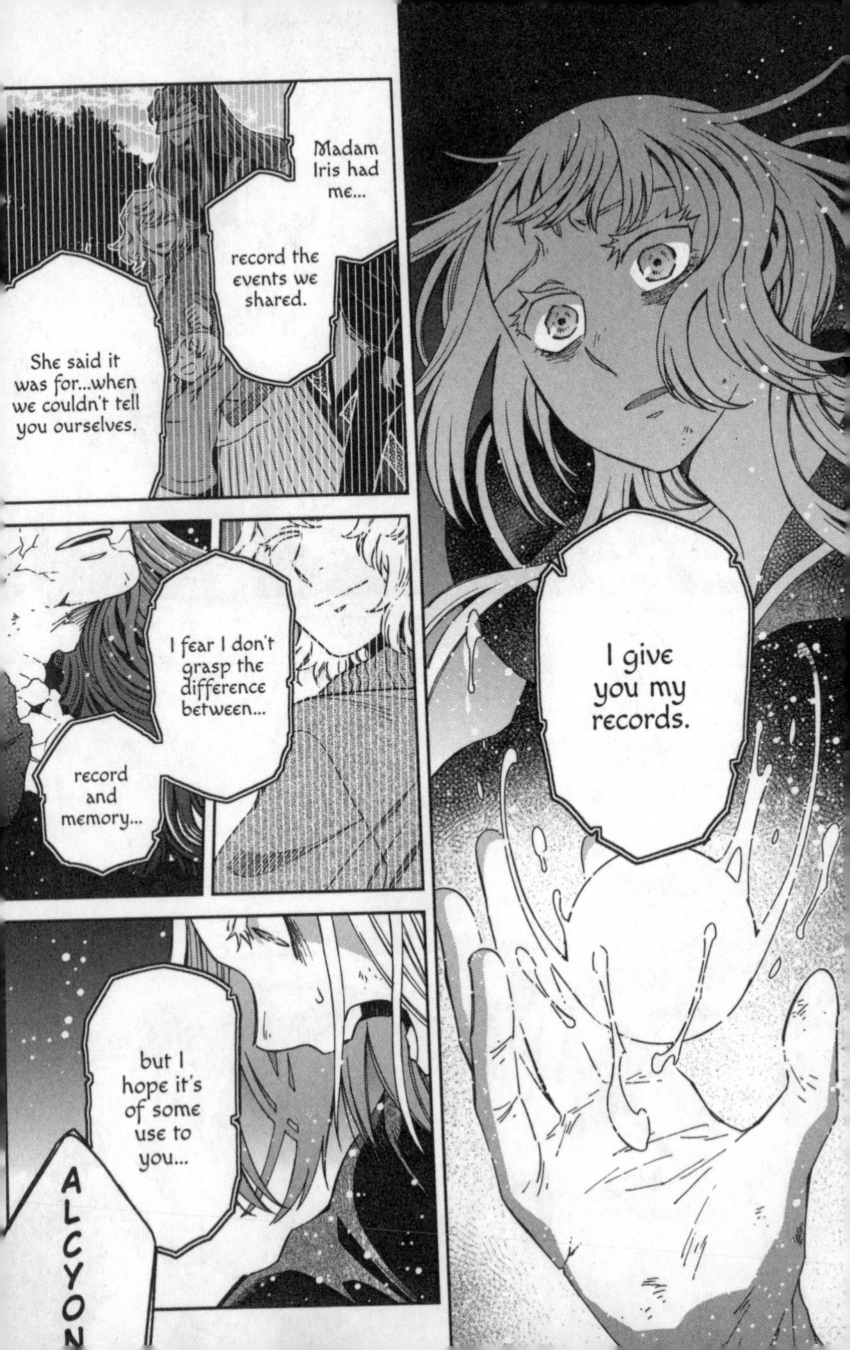
I give you my records.
Madam Iris had me...
record the events we shared.
She said it was for...when we couldn't tell you ourselves.
I fear I don't grasp the difference between...
record and memory...
but I hope it's of some use to you...
ALCYON

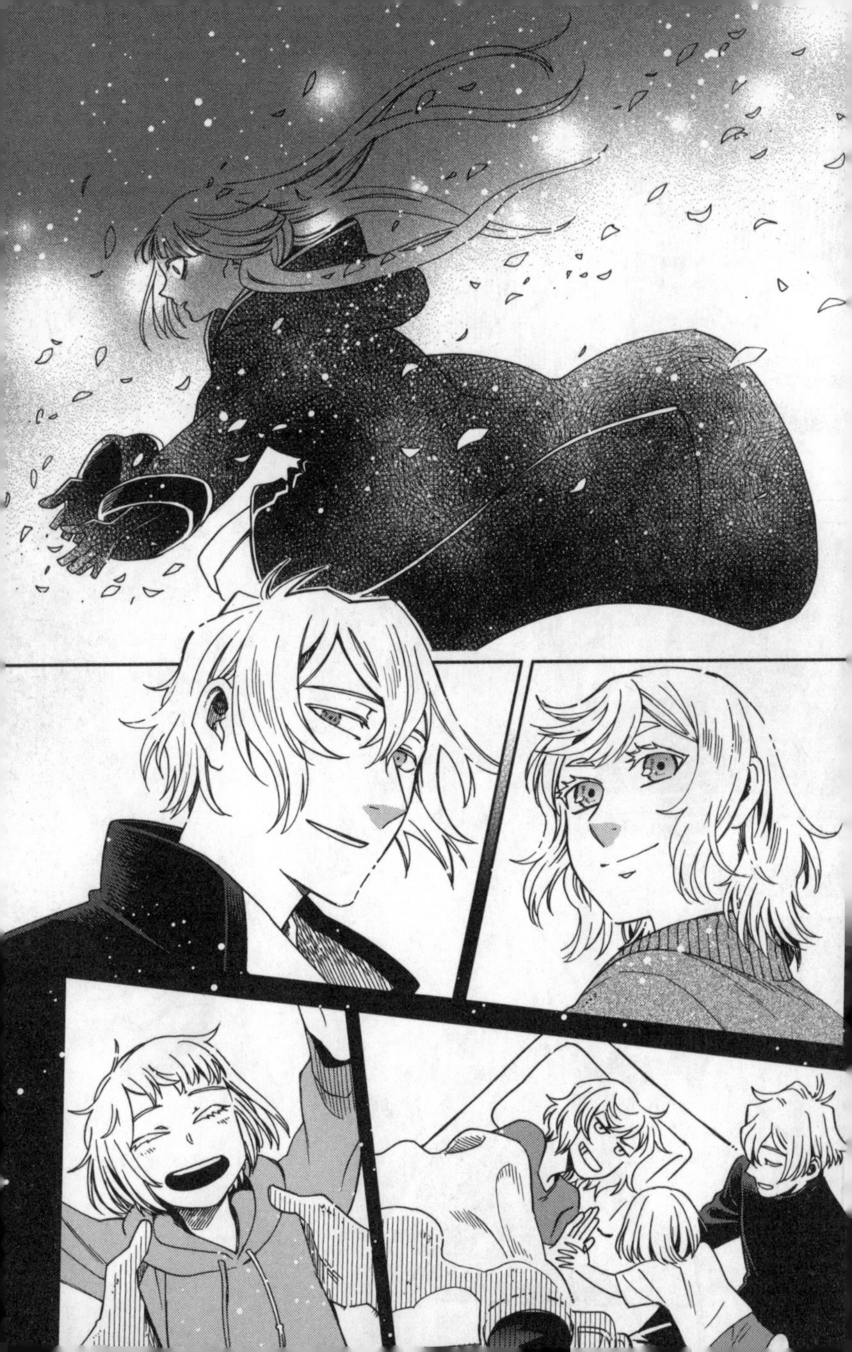

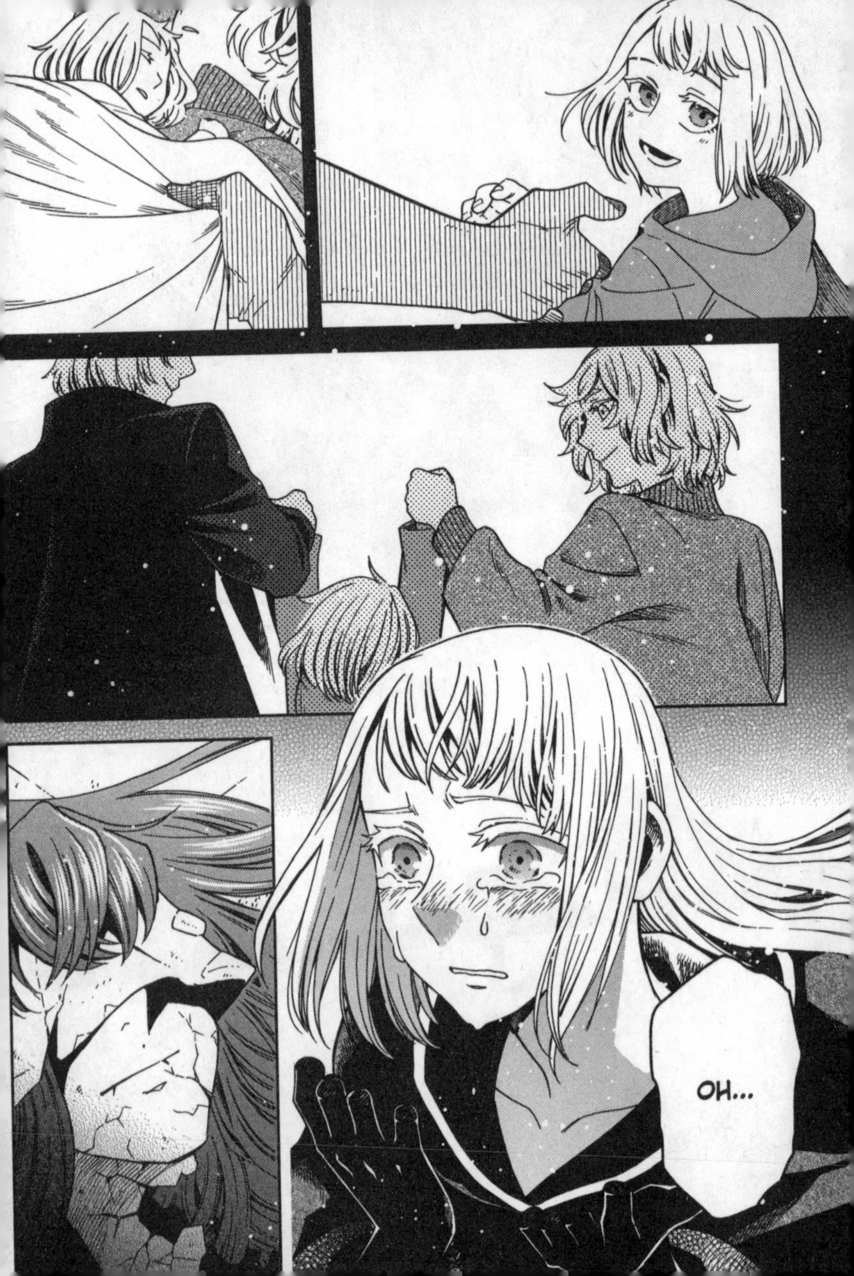
OH...

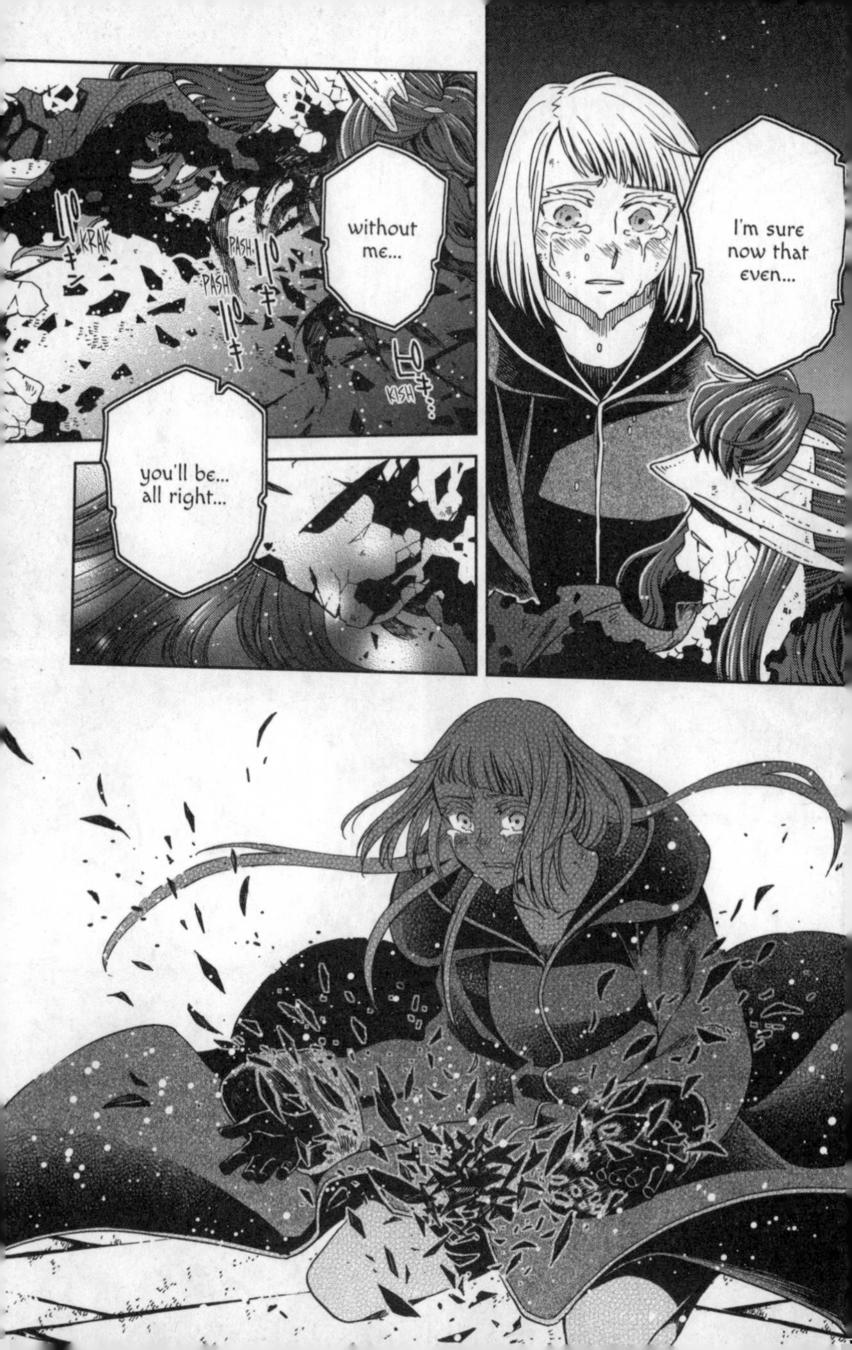
I'm sure now that even...
without me...
KRAK
PASH
PASH
KISH
you'll be... all right...

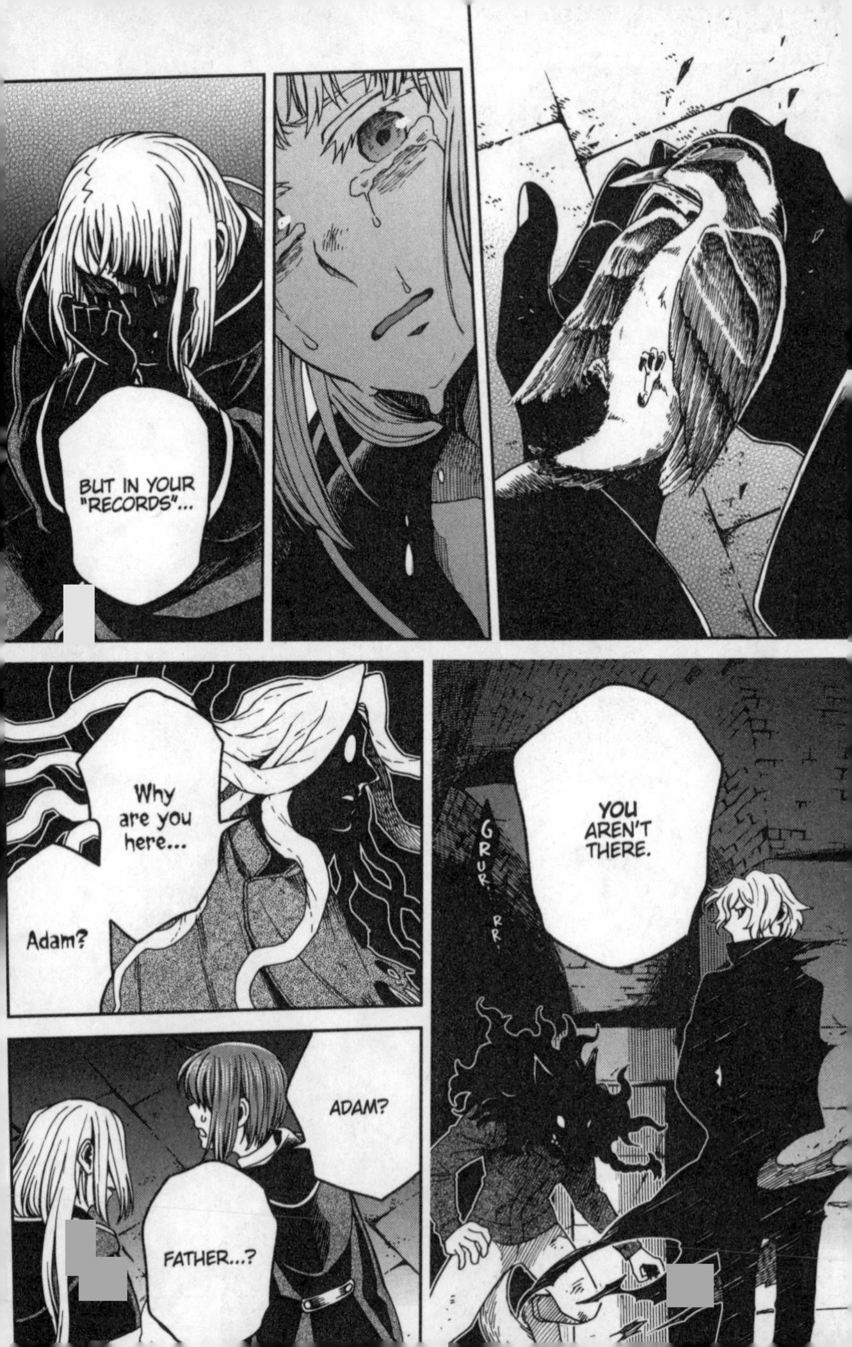
BUT IN YOUR "RECORDS"...
YOU AREN'T THERE.
GRUR RR
Why are you here...
Adam?
ADAM?
FATHER...?

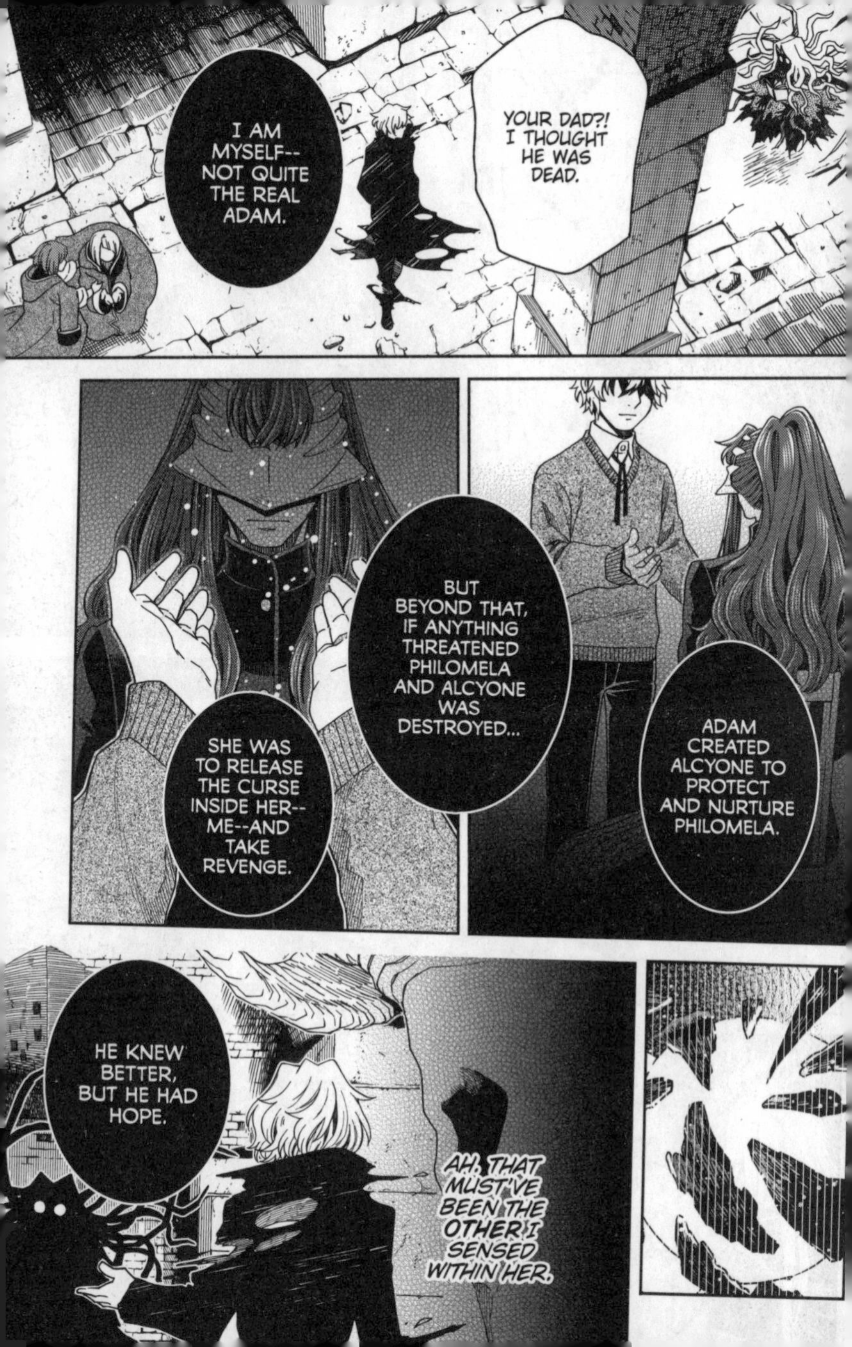

YOUR DAD?! I THOUGHT HE WAS DEAD.
I AM MYSELF-- NOT QUITE THE REAL ADAM.
ADAM CREATED ALCYONE TO PROTECT AND NURTURE PHILOMELA.
BUT BEYOND THAT, IF ANYTHING THREATENED PHILOMELA AND ALCYONE WAS DESTROYED...
SHE WAS TO RELEASE THE CURSE INSIDE HER-- ME--AND TAKE REVENGE.
HE KNEW BETTER, BUT HE HAD HOPE.
AH. THAT MUST'VE BEEN THE OTHER I SENSED WITHIN HER.

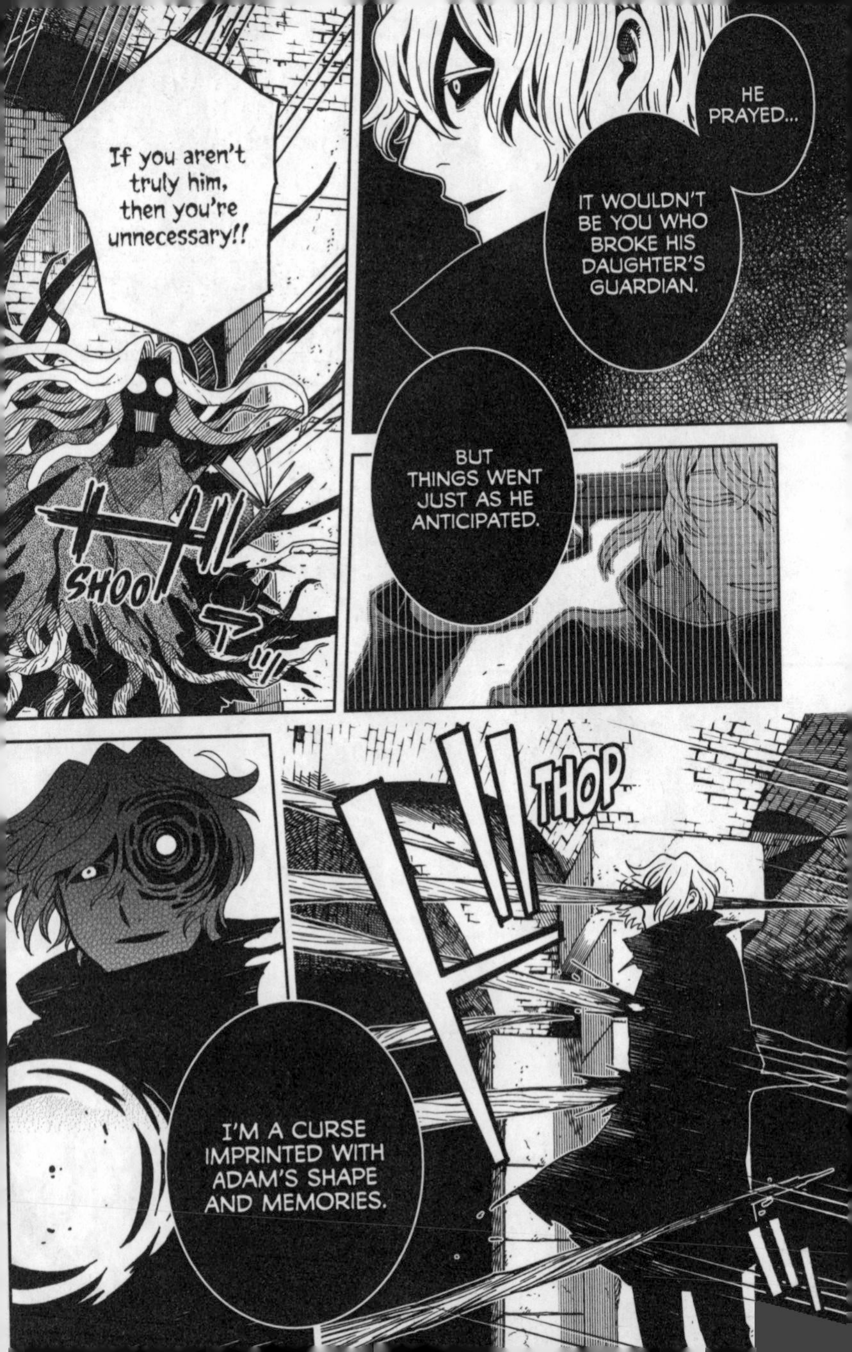
HE PRAYED...
IT WOULDN'T BE YOU WHO BROKE HIS DAUGHTER'S GUARDIAN.
BUT THINGS WENT JUST AS HE ANTICIPATED.
If you aren't truly him, then you're unnecessary!!
SHOOO
THOP
I'M A CURSE IMPRINTED WITH ADAM'S SHAPE AND MEMORIES.

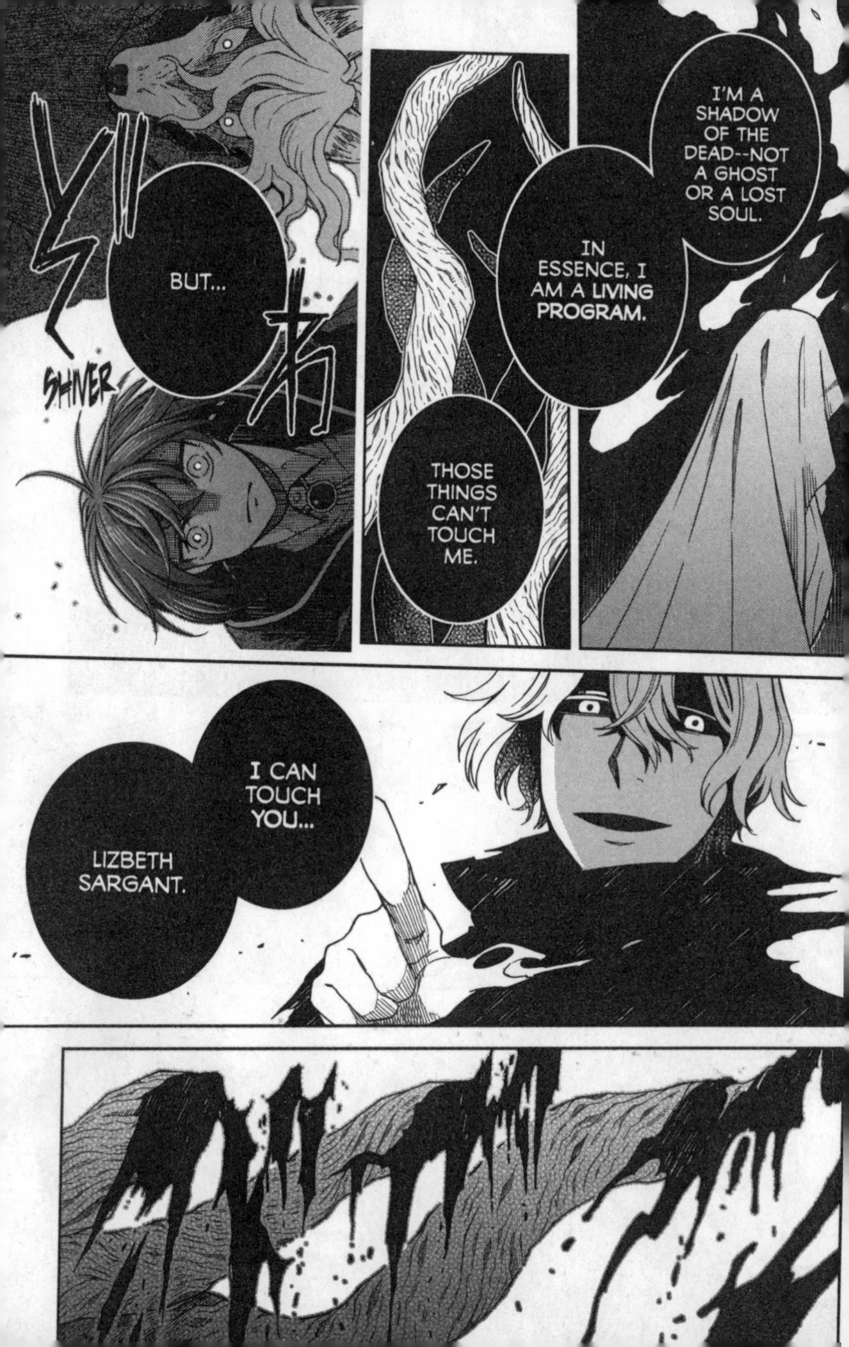
I'M A SHADOW OF THE DEAD--NOT A GHOST OR A LOST SOUL.
IN ESSENCE, I AM A LIVING PROGRAM.
THOSE THINGS CAN'T TOUCH ME.
BUT...
SHIVER
I CAN TOUCH YOU...
LIZBETH SARGANT.

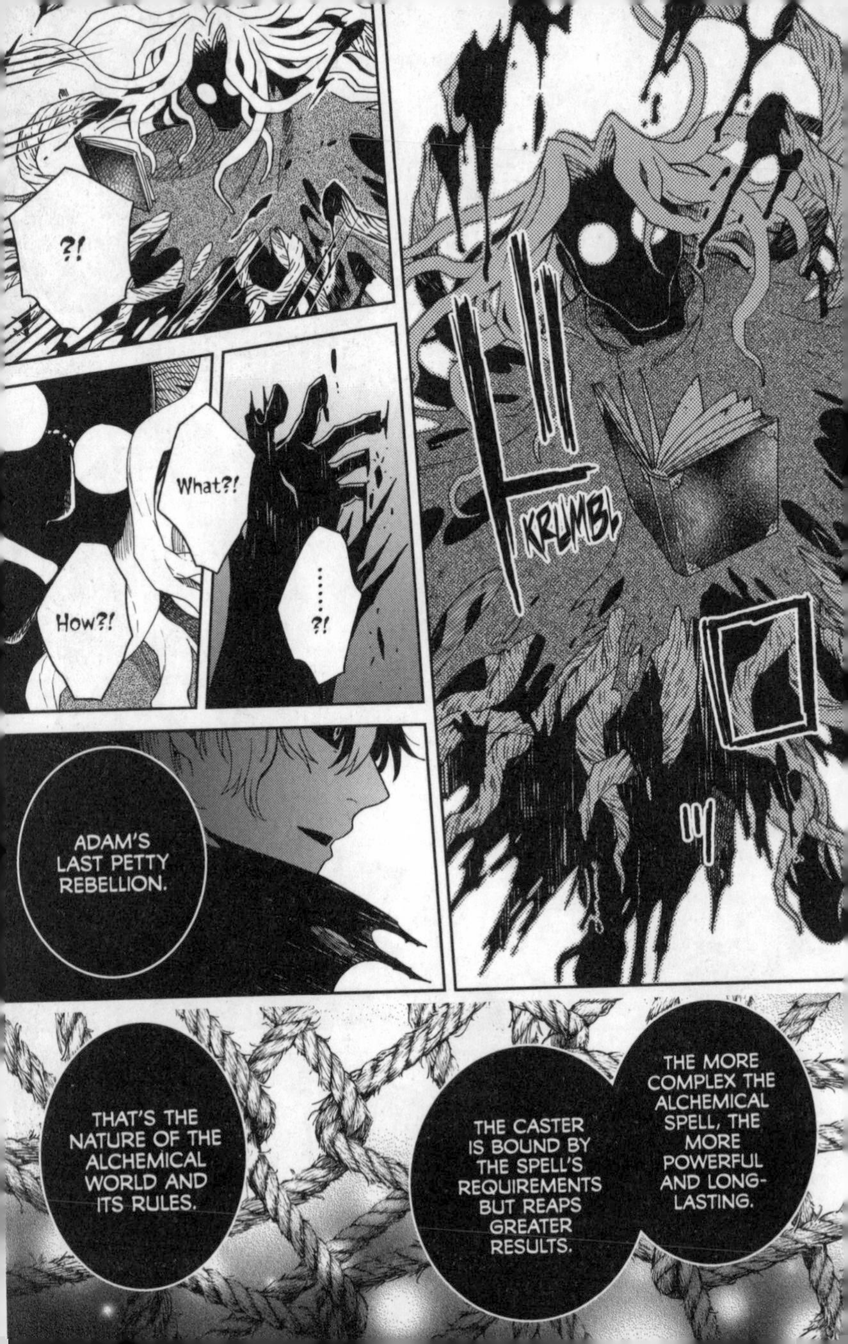
KRUMBL
!!
?!
!
......?!
What?!
How?!
ADAM'S LAST PETTY REBELLION.
THE MORE COMPLEX THE ALCHEMICAL SPELL, THE MORE POWERFUL AND LONG-LASTING.
THE CASTER IS BOUND BY THE SPELL'S REQUIREMENTS BUT REAPS GREATER RESULTS.
THAT'S THE NATURE OF THE ALCHEMICAL WORLD AND ITS RULES.

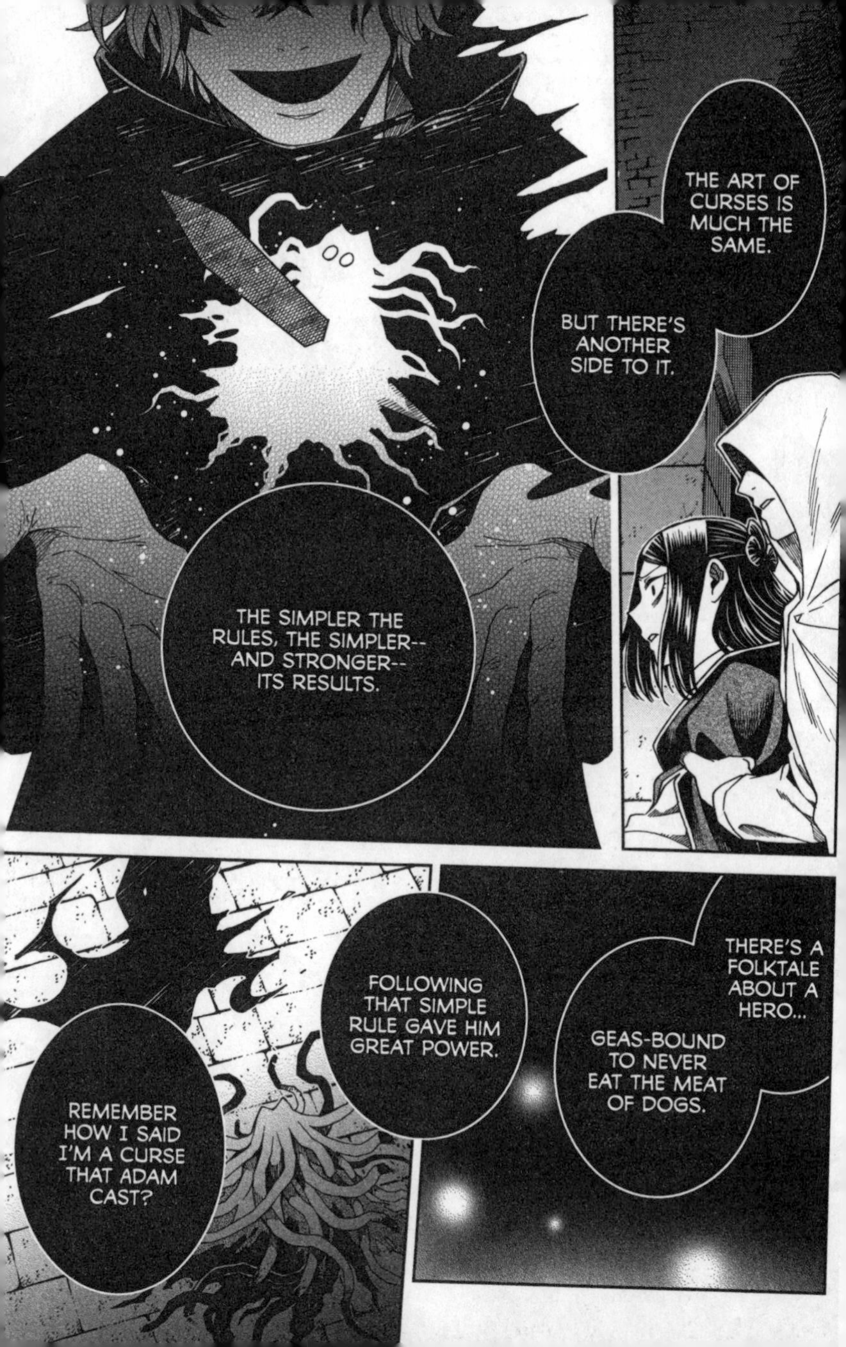
THE ART OF CURSES IS MUCH THE SAME.
BUT THERE'S ANOTHER SIDE TO IT.
THE SIMPLER THE RULES, THE SIMPLER-- AND STRONGER-- ITS RESULTS.
THERE'S A FOLKTALE ABOUT A HERO...
GEAS-BOUND TO NEVER EAT THE MEAT OF DOGS.
FOLLOWING THAT SIMPLE RULE GAVE HIM GREAT POWER.
REMEMBER HOW I SAID I'M A CURSE THAT ADAM CAST?

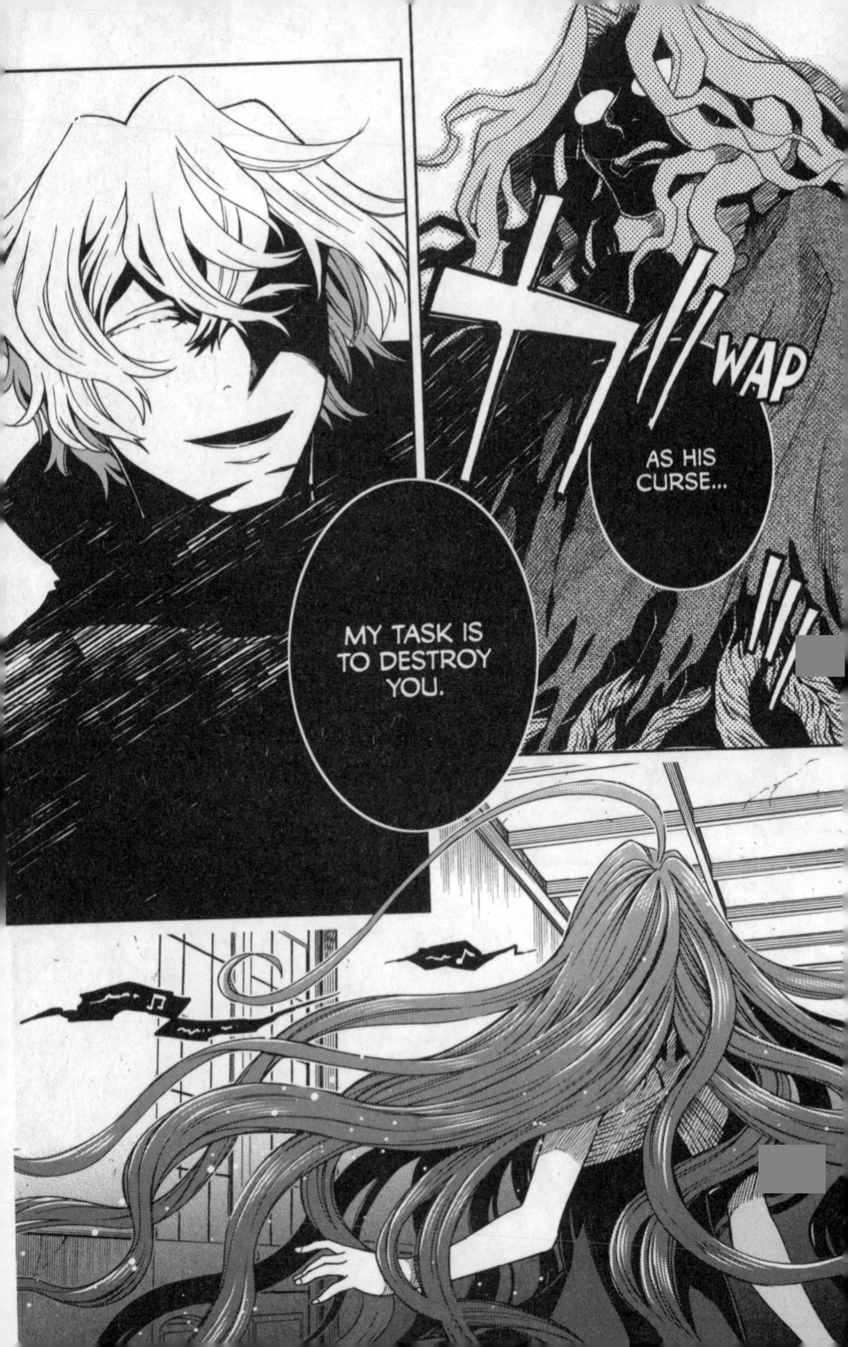
WAP
AS HIS CURSE...
MY TASK IS TO DESTROY YOU.

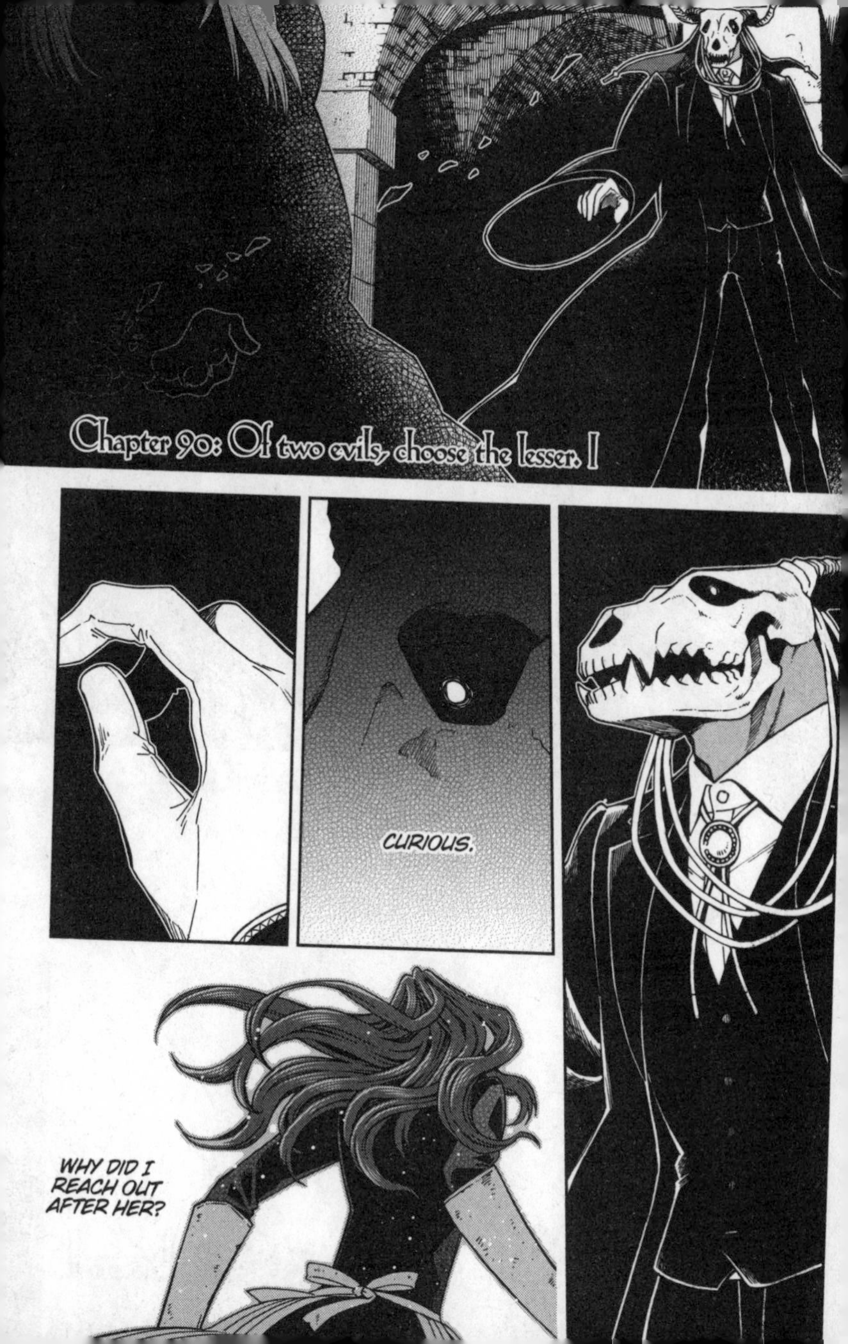
Chapter 90: Of two evils, choose the lesser. I
CURIOUS.
WHY DID I REACH OUT AFTER HER?

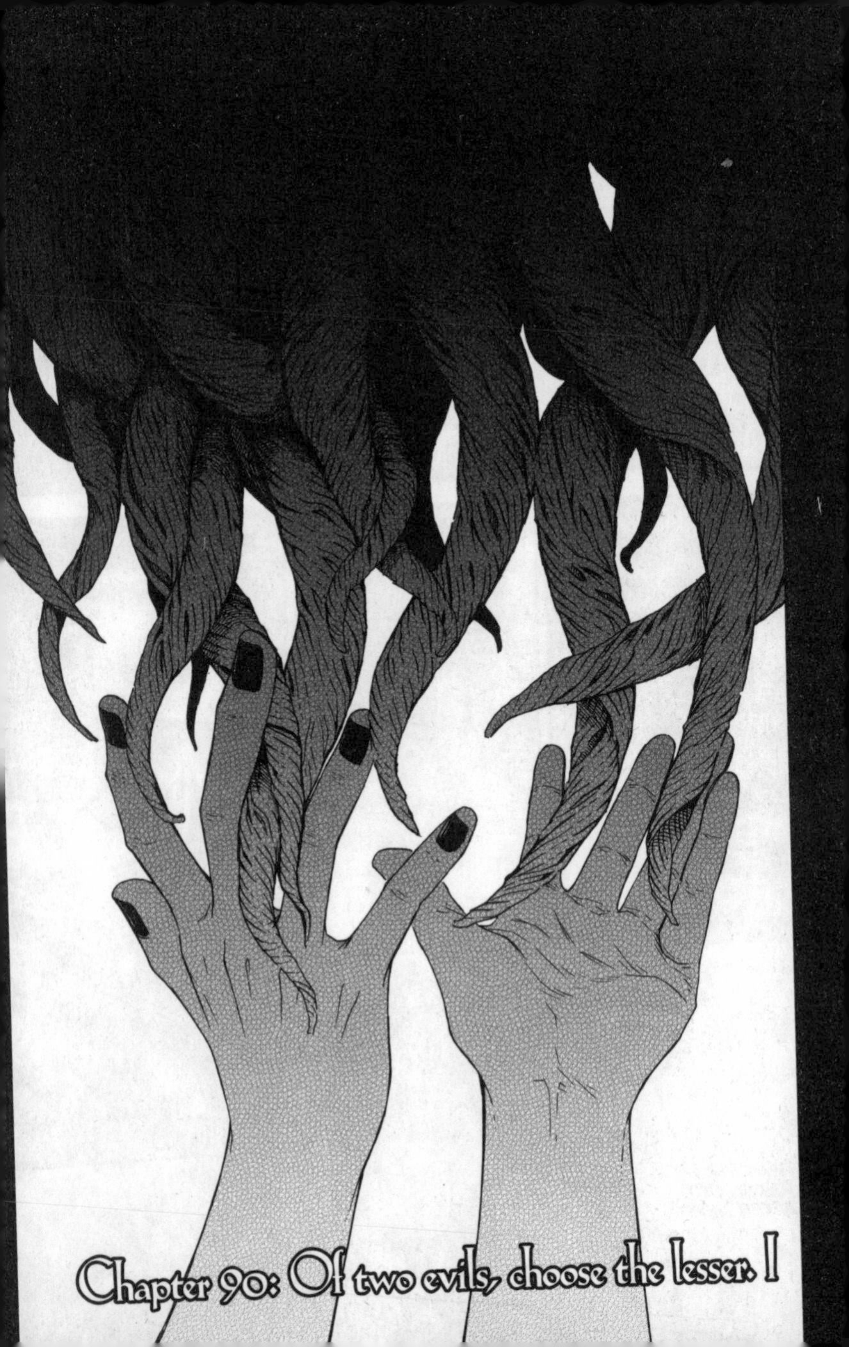
Chapter 90: Of two evils, choose the lesser. I

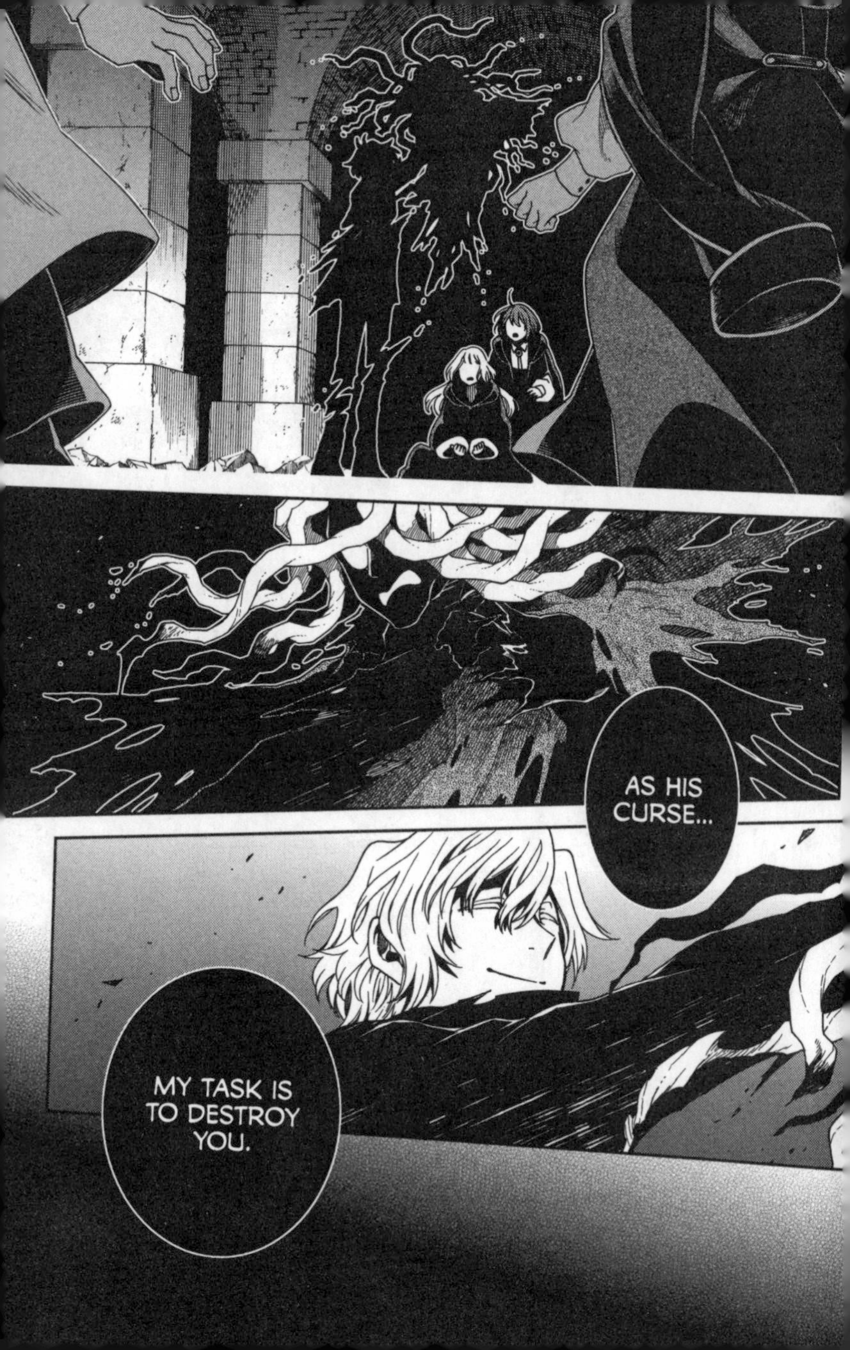
AS HIS CURSE...
MY TASK IS TO DESTROY YOU.

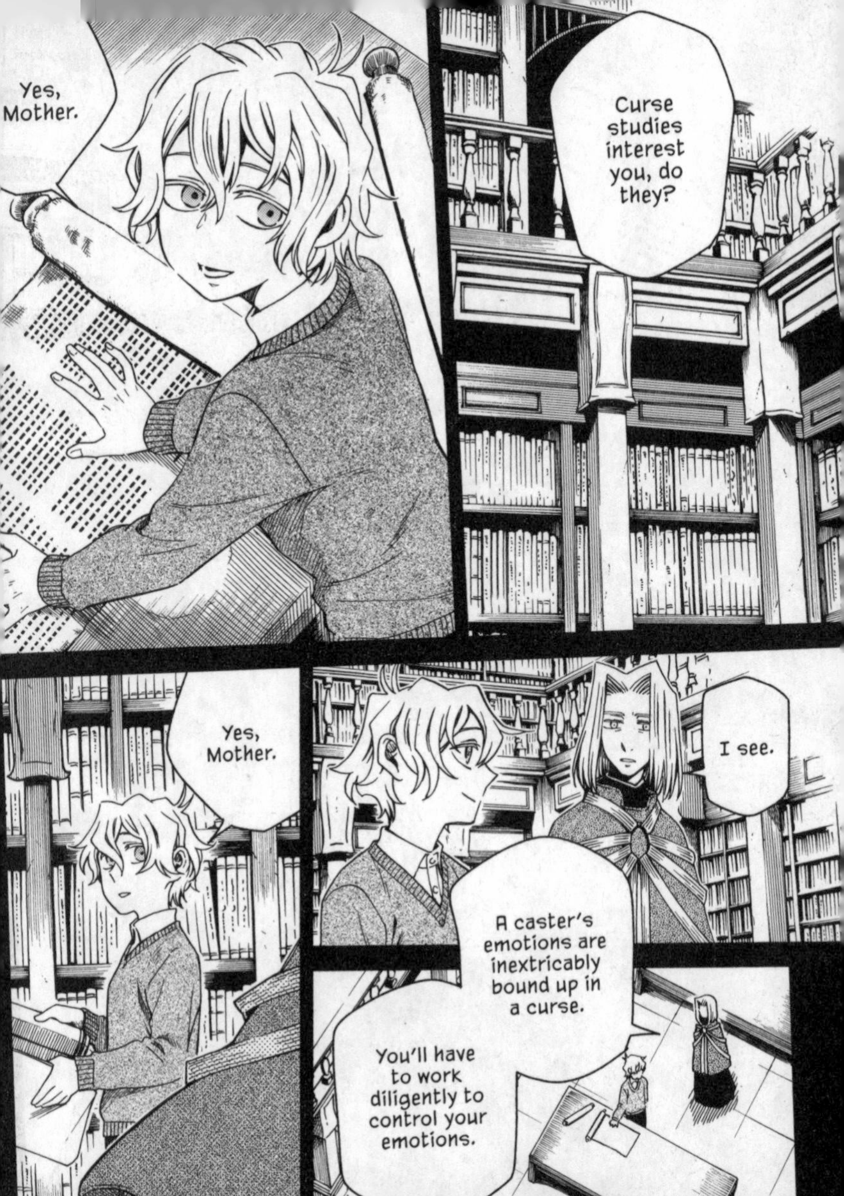
Curse studies interest you, do they?
Yes, Mother.
I see.
A caster's emotions are inextricably bound up in a curse.
You'll have to work diligently to control your emotions.
Yes, Mother.

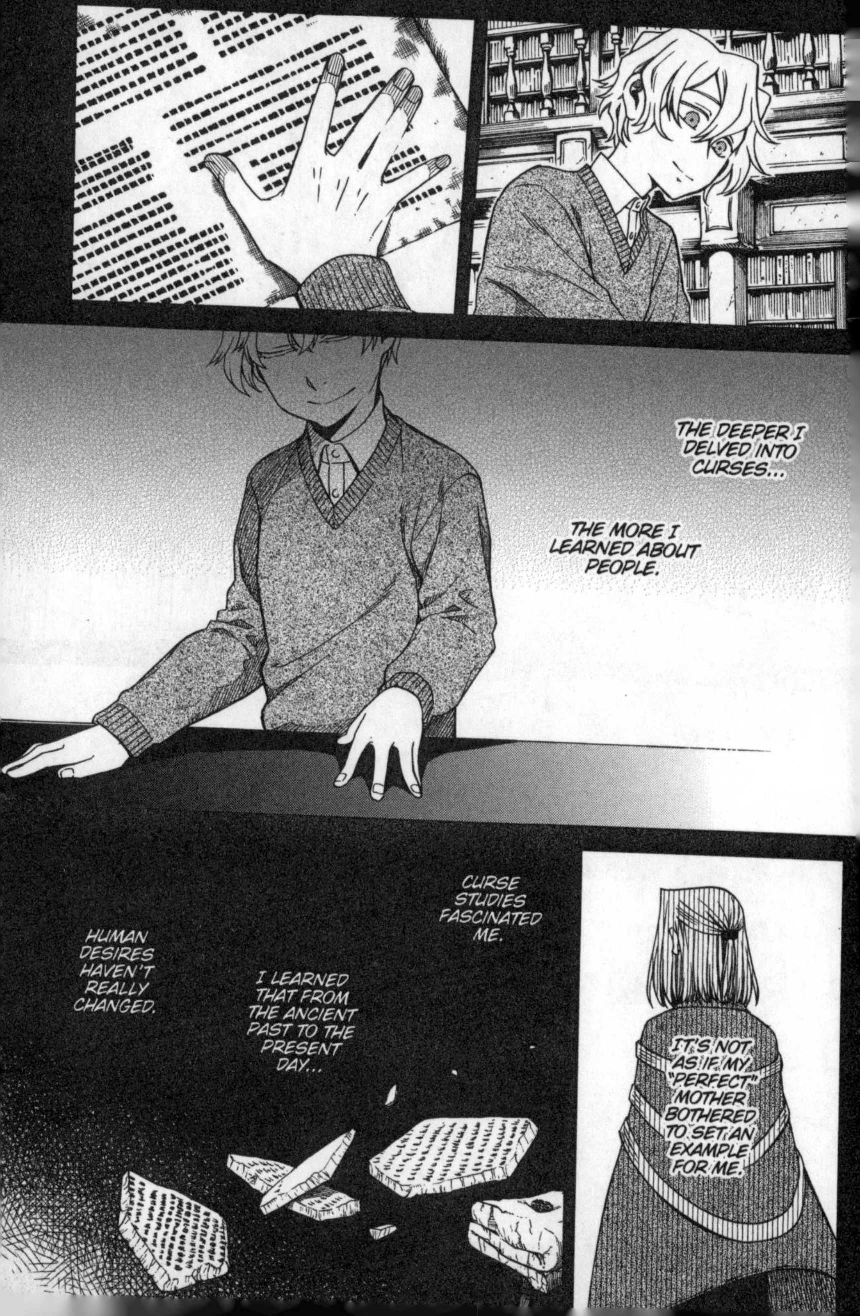
THE DEEPER I DELVED INTO CURSES...
THE MORE I LEARNED ABOUT PEOPLE.
IT'S NOT AS IF MY "PERFECT" MOTHER BOTHERED TO SET AN EXAMPLE FOR ME.
CURSE STUDIES FASCINATED ME.
I LEARNED THAT FROM THE ANCIENT PAST TO THE PRESENT DAY...
HUMAN DESIRES HAVEN'T REALLY CHANGED.

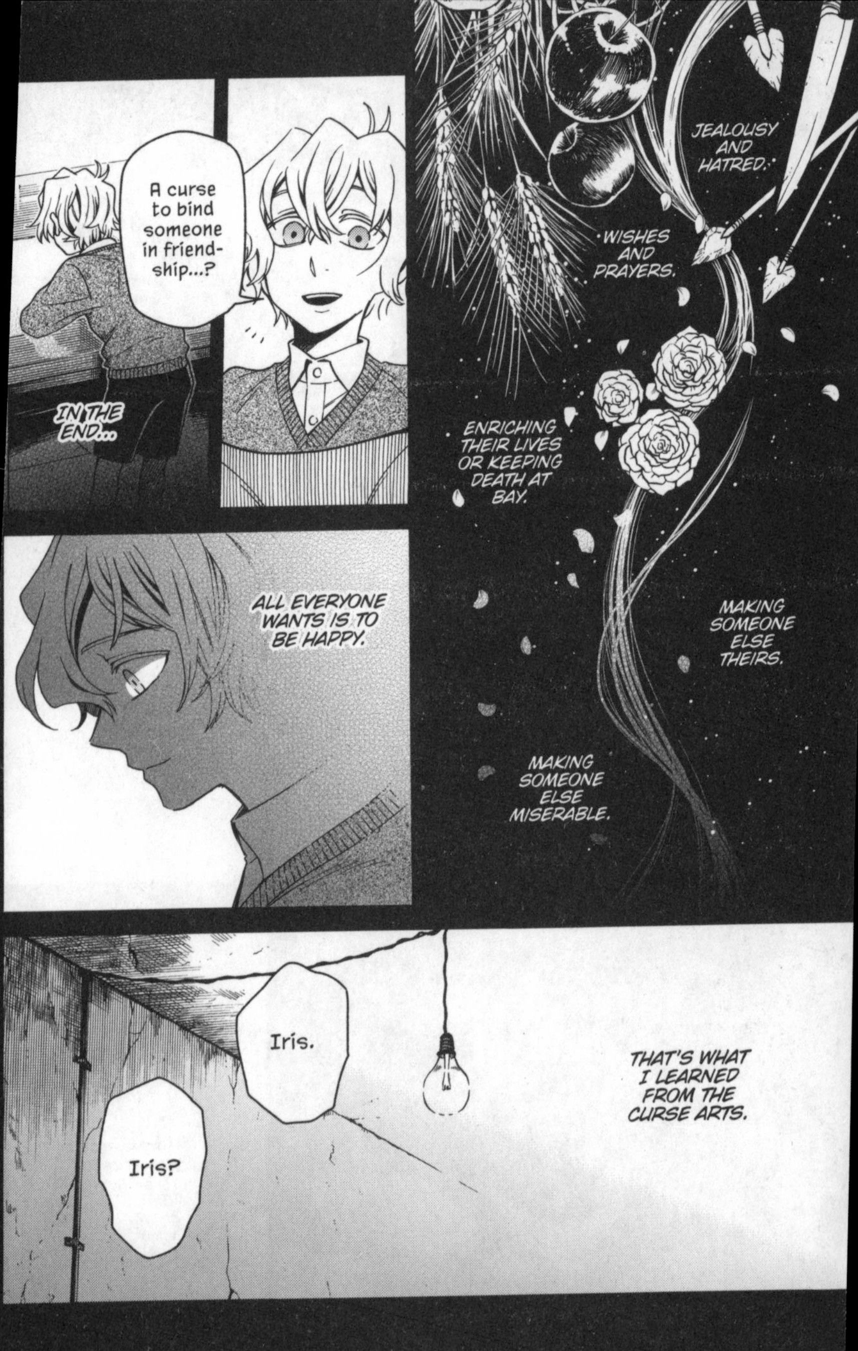
JEALOUSY AND HATRED.
WISHES AND PRAYERS.
ENRICHING THEIR LIVES OR KEEPING DEATH AT BAY.
MAKING SOMEONE ELSE THEIRS.
MAKING SOMEONE ELSE MISERABLE.
A curse to bind someone in friend-ship...?
IN THE END...
ALL EVERYONE WANTS IS TO BE HAPPY.
THAT'S WHAT I LEARNED FROM THE CURSE ARTS.
Iris.
Iris?

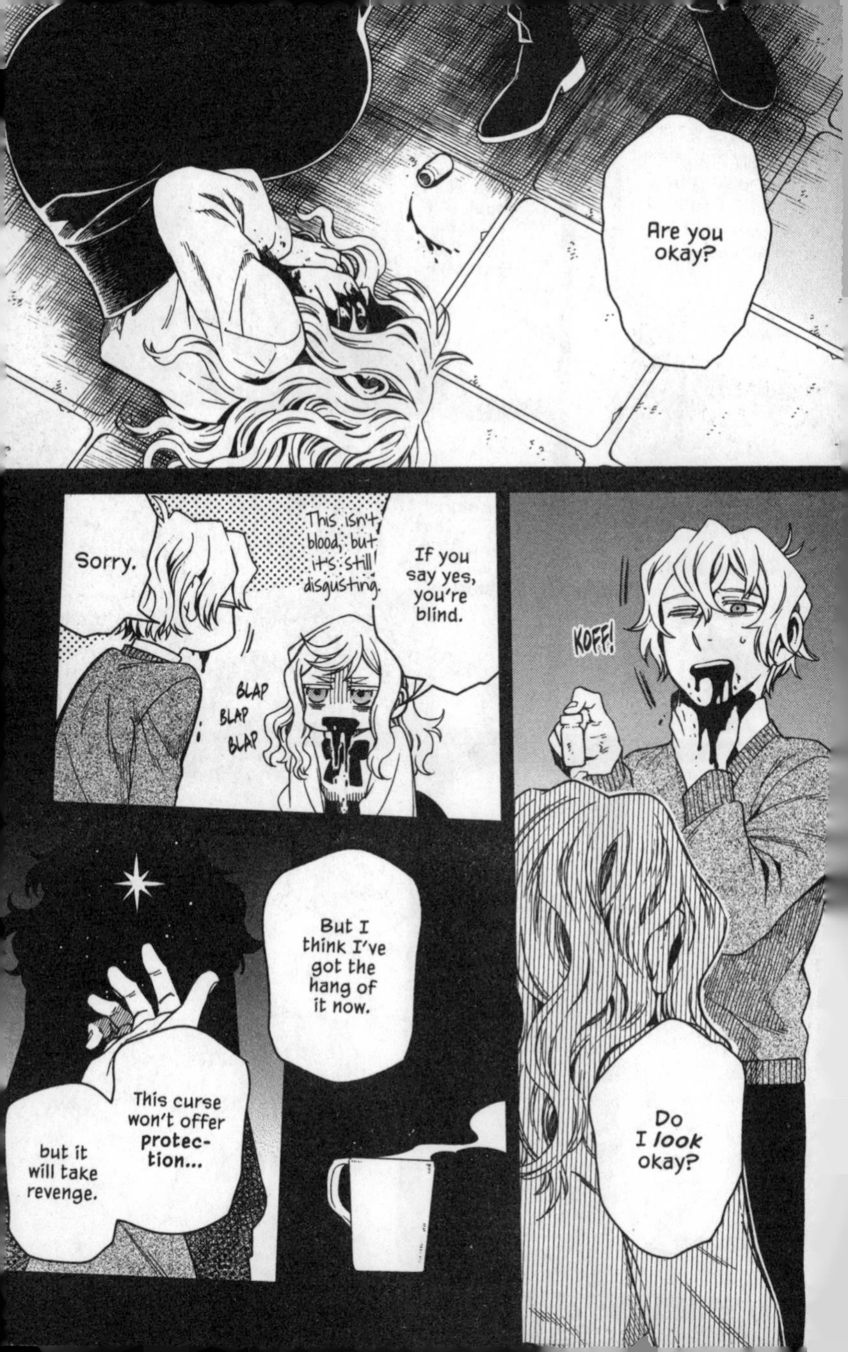
Are you okay?
KOFF!
Do I *look* okay?
If you say yes, you're blind.
This isn't blood, but it's still disgusting.
Sorry.
BLAP
BLAP
BLAP
But I think I've got the hang of it now.
This curse won't offer protection...
but it will take revenge.

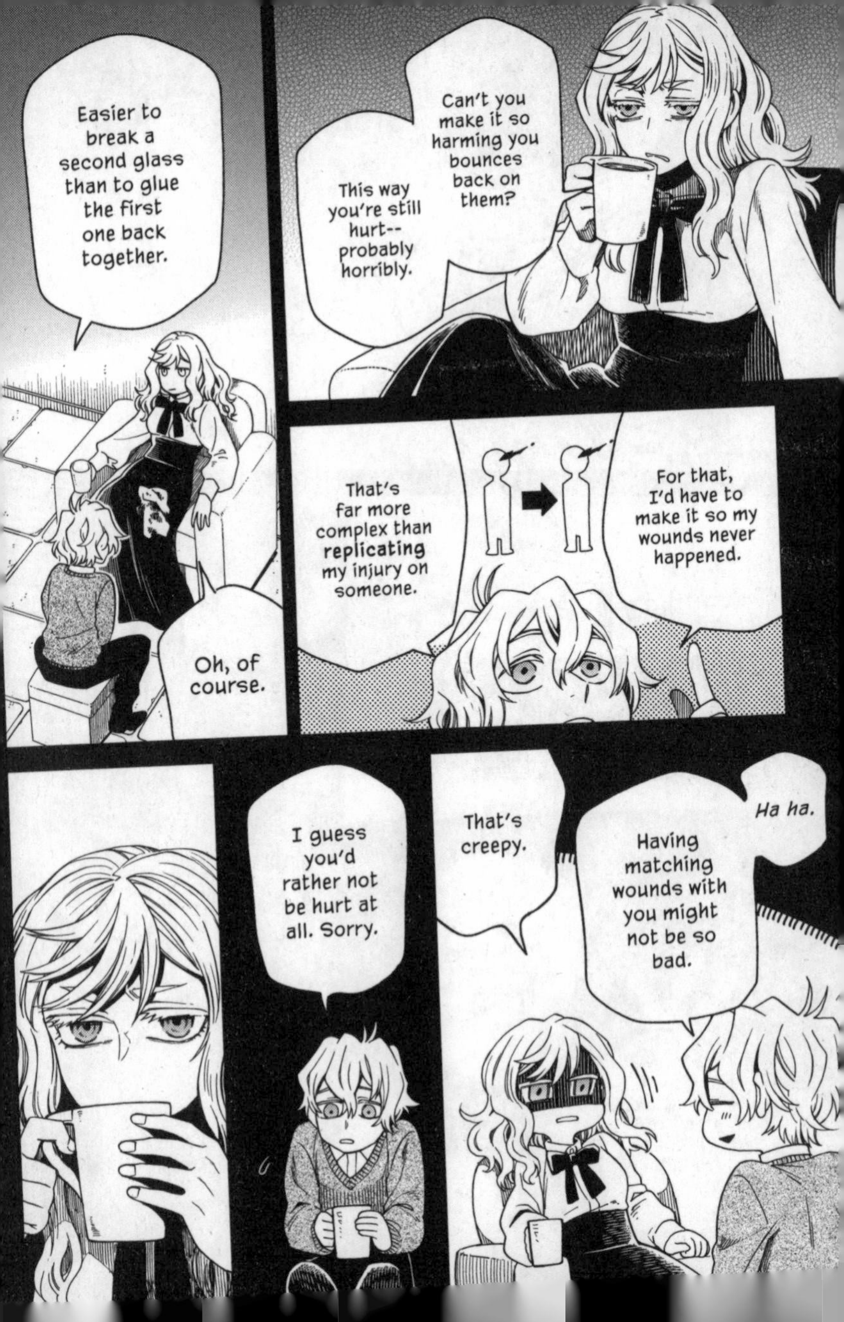
Can't you make it so harming you bounces back on them?
This way you're still hurt--probably horribly.
For that, I'd have to make it so my wounds never happened.
That's far more complex than **replicating** my injury on someone.
Easier to break a second glass than to glue the first one back together.
Oh, of course.
Ha ha.
Having matching wounds with you might not be so bad.
That's creepy.
I guess you'd rather not be hurt at all. Sorry.

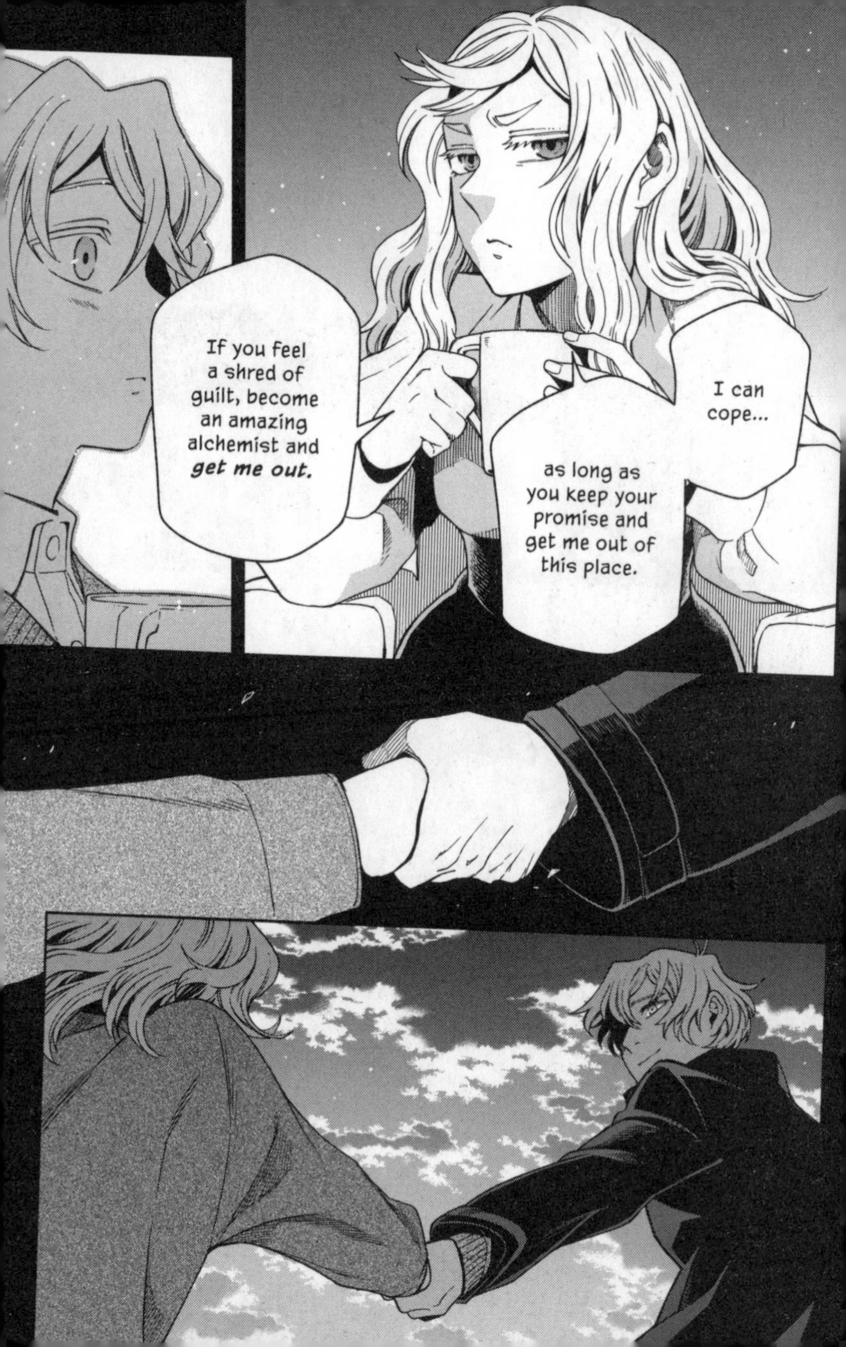
I can cope...
as long as you keep your promise and get me out of this place.
If you feel a shred of guilt, become an amazing alchemist and ***get me out.***

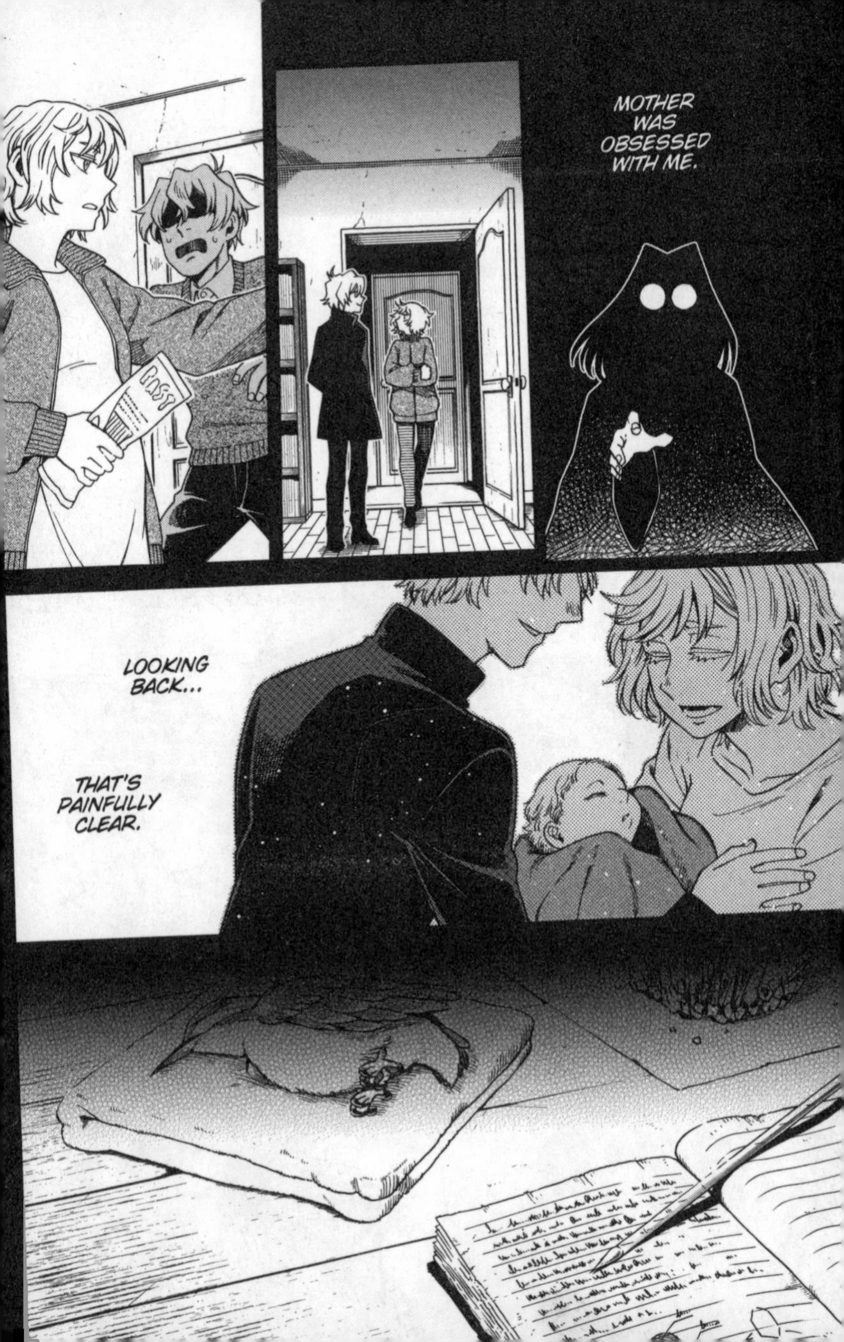
MOTHER WAS OBSESSED WITH ME.
LOOKING BACK...
THAT'S PAINFULLY CLEAR.

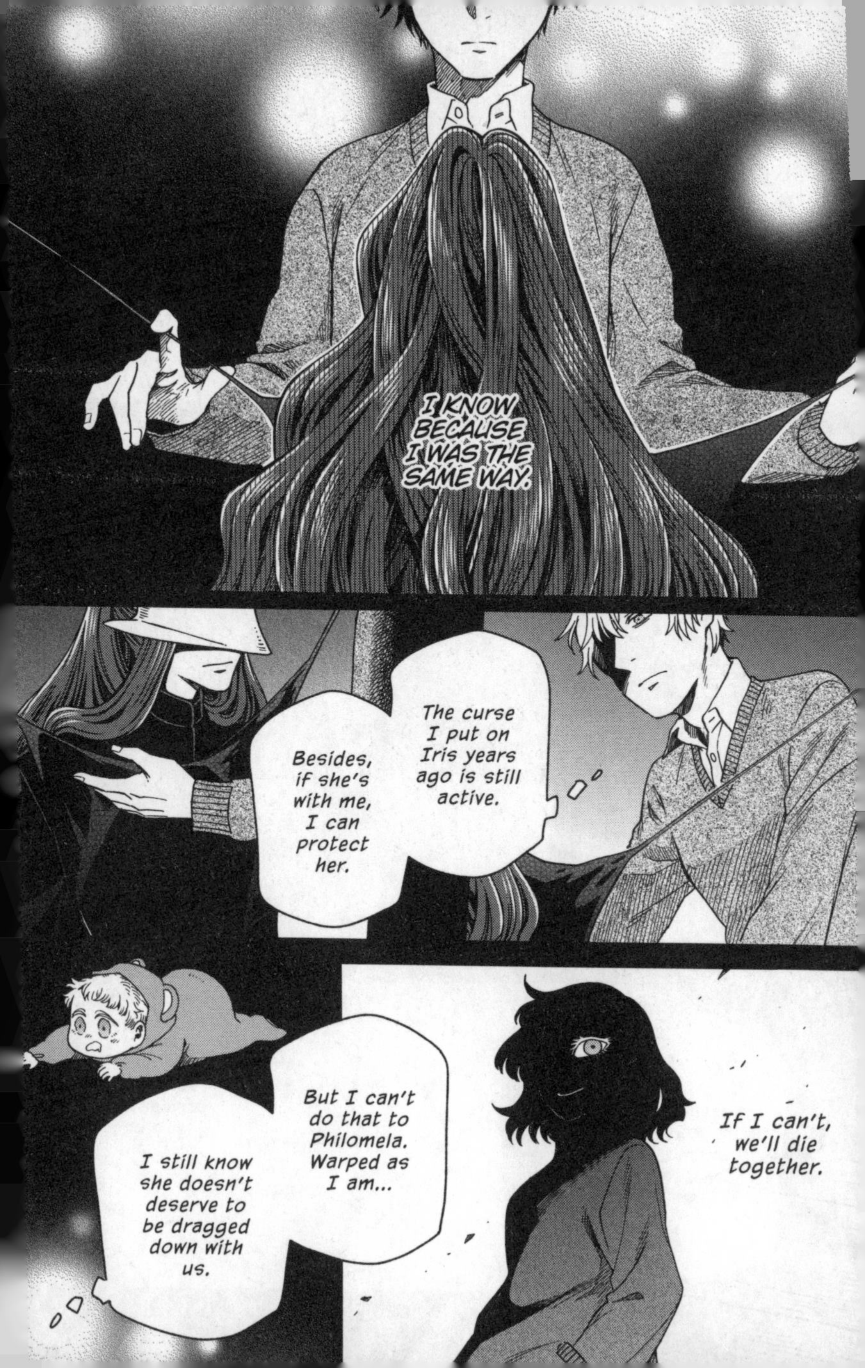
I KNOW BECAUSE I WAS THE SAME WAY.
The curse I put on Iris years ago is still active.
Besides, if she's with me, I can protect her.
If I can't, we'll die together.
But I can't do that to Philomela. Warped as I am...
I still know she doesn't deserve to be dragged down with us.

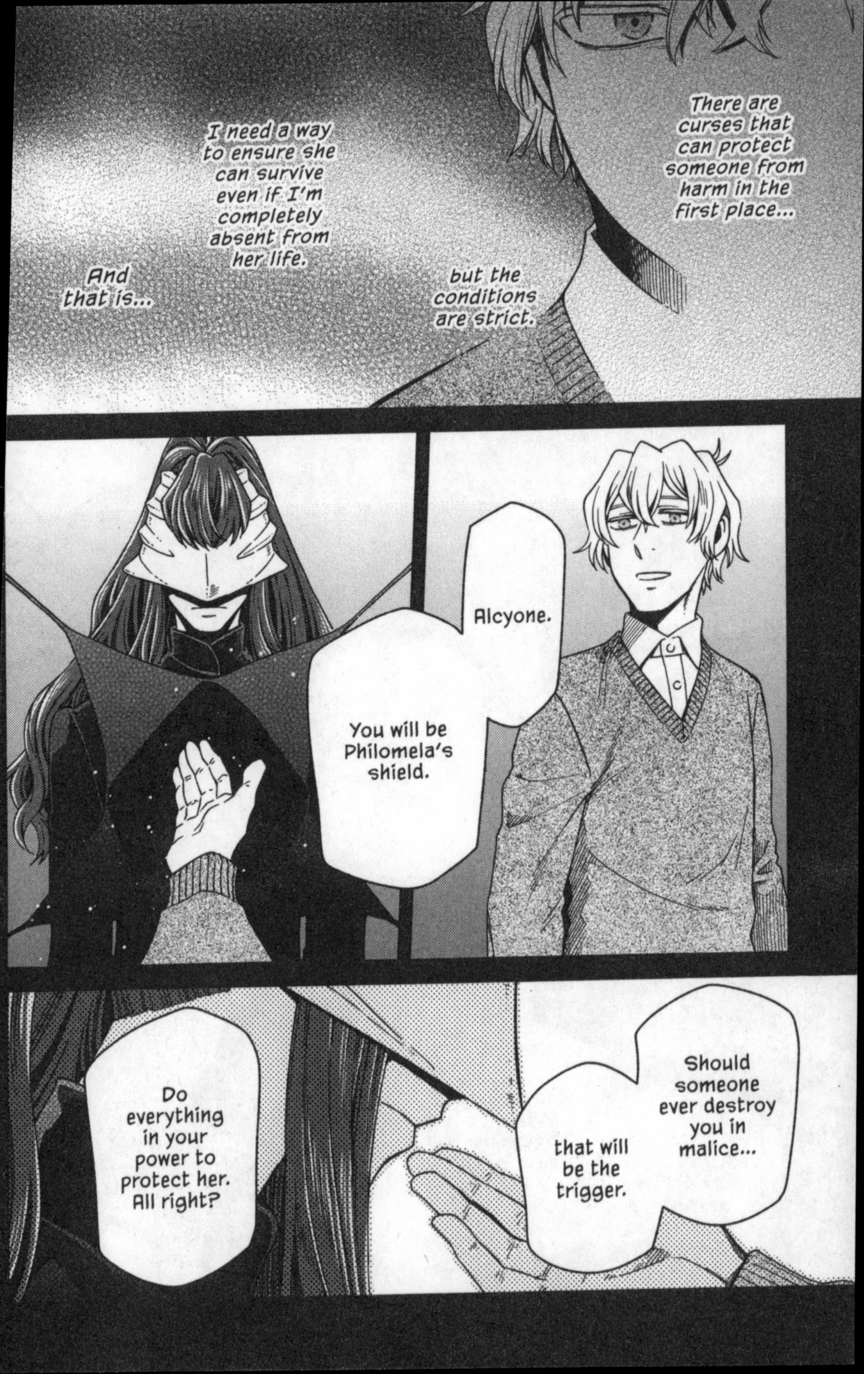
There are curses that can protect someone from harm in the first place...
but the conditions are strict.
I need a way to ensure she can survive even if I'm completely absent from her life.
And that is...
Alcyone.
You will be Philomela's shield.
Should someone ever destroy you in malice...
that will be the trigger.
Do everything in your power to protect her. All right?

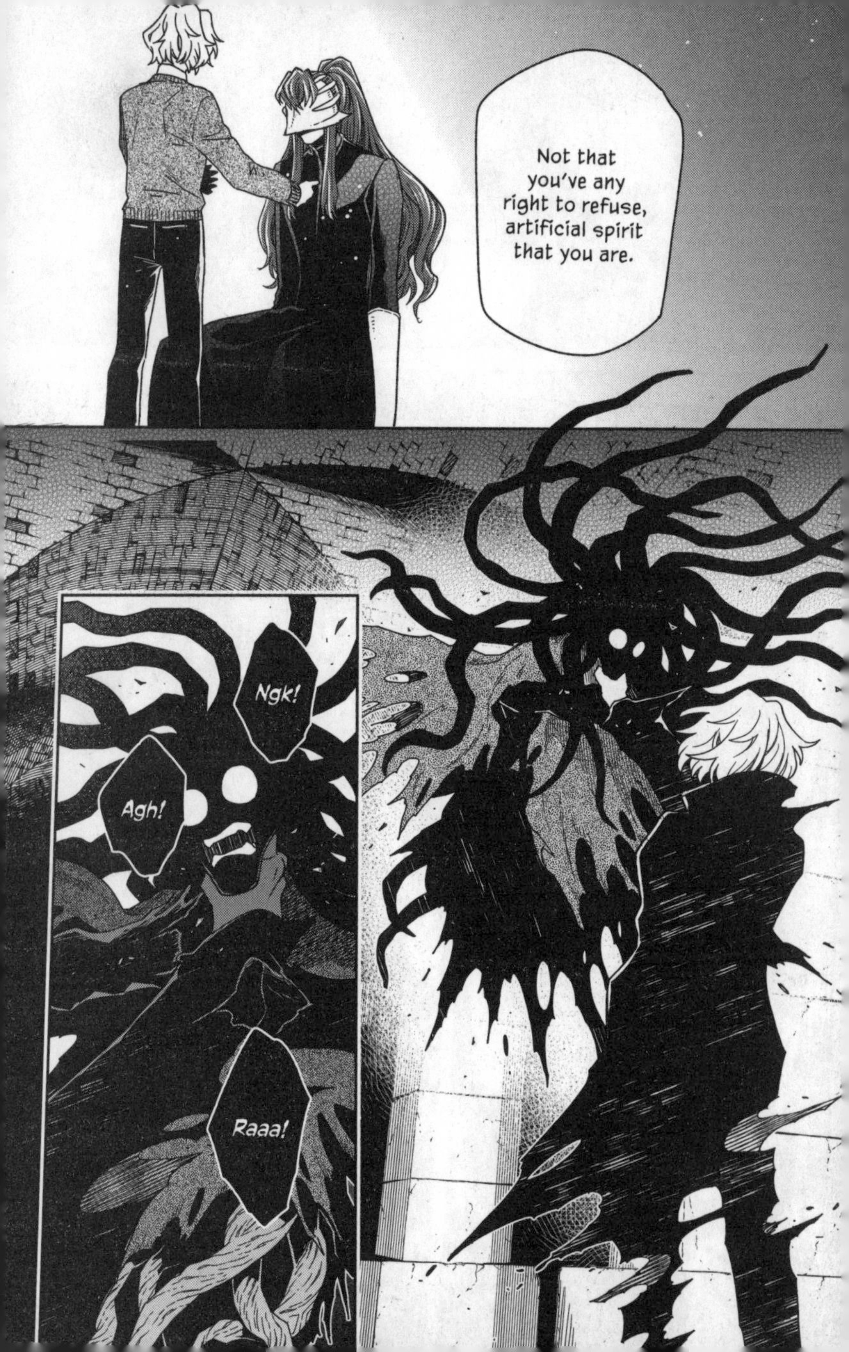
Not that you've any right to refuse, artificial spirit that you are.
Ngk!
Agh!
Raaa!

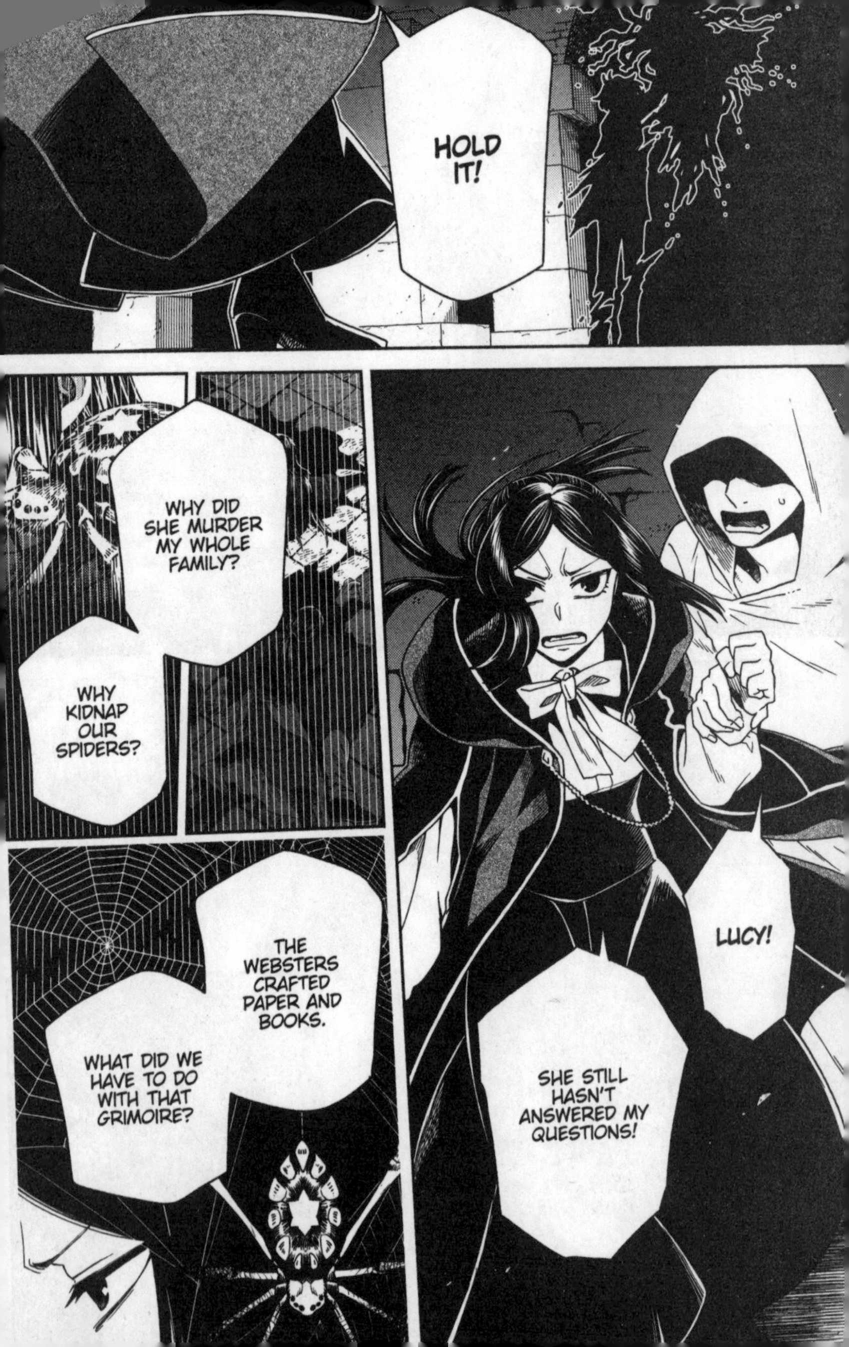
HOLD IT!
LUCY!
SHE STILL HASN'T ANSWERED MY QUESTIONS!
WHY DID SHE MURDER MY WHOLE FAMILY?
WHY KIDNAP OUR SPIDERS?
THE WEBSTERS CRAFTED PAPER AND BOOKS.
WHAT DID WE HAVE TO DO WITH THAT GRIMOIRE?

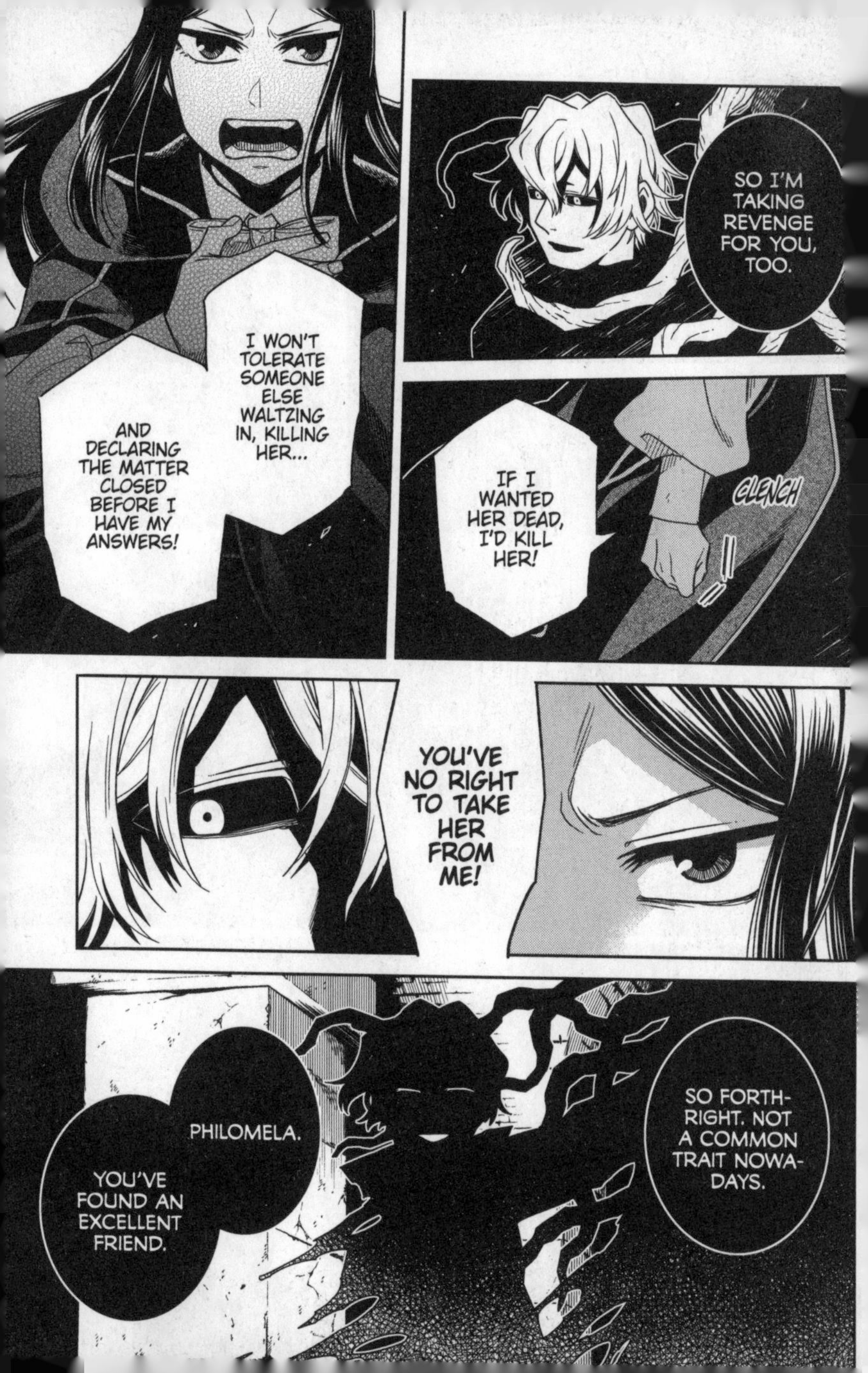
SO I'M TAKING REVENGE FOR YOU, TOO.
IF I WANTED HER DEAD, I'D KILL HER!
CLENCH
I WON'T TOLERATE SOMEONE ELSE WALTZING IN, KILLING HER...
AND DECLARING THE MATTER CLOSED BEFORE I HAVE MY ANSWERS!
YOU'VE NO RIGHT TO TAKE HER FROM ME!
SO FORTH-RIGHT. NOT A COMMON TRAIT NOWA-DAYS.
PHILOMELA.
YOU'VE FOUND AN EXCELLENT FRIEND.

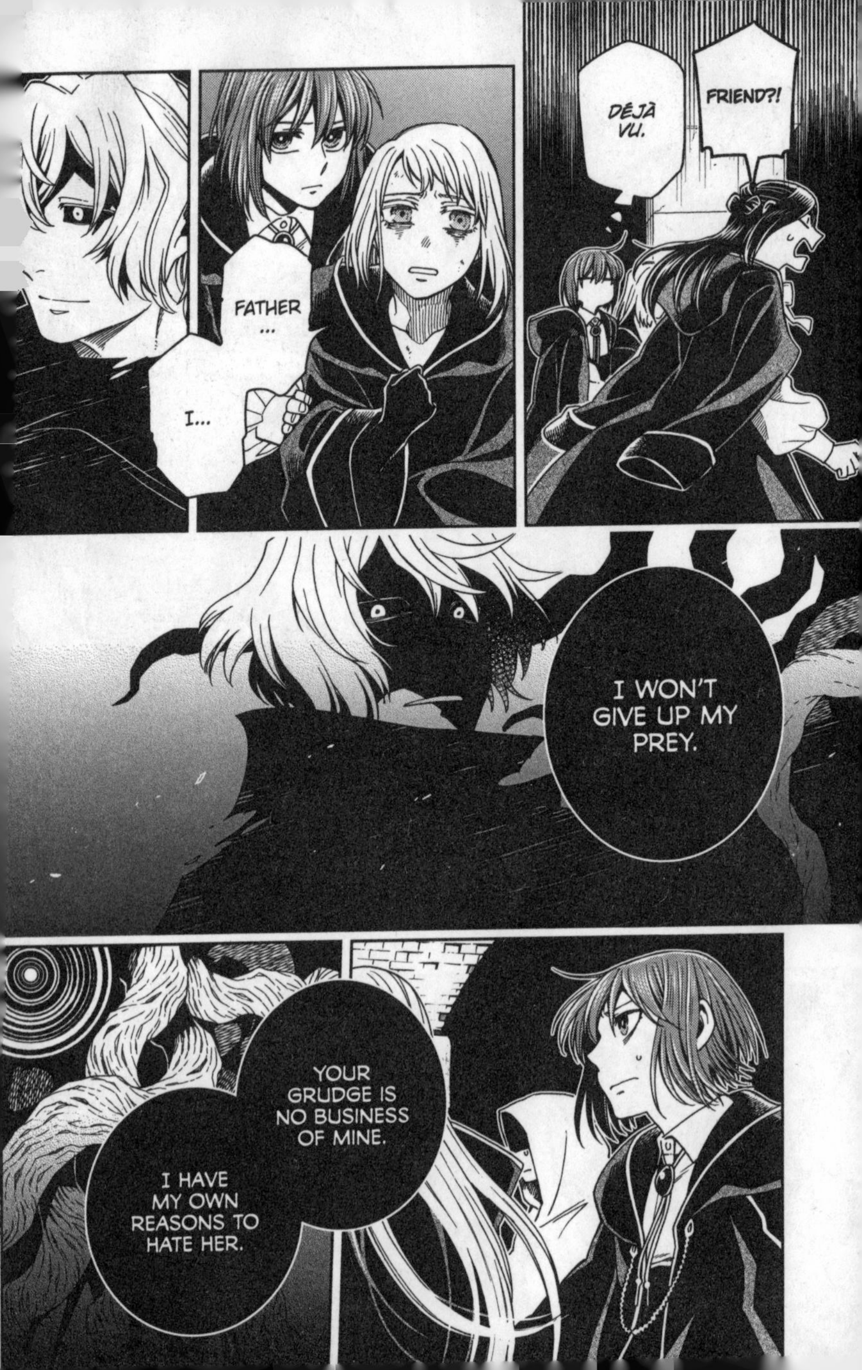
FRIEND?!
DÉJÀ VU.
FATHER ...
I...
I WON'T GIVE UP MY PREY.
YOUR GRUDGE IS NO BUSINESS OF MINE.
I HAVE MY OWN REASONS TO HATE HER.

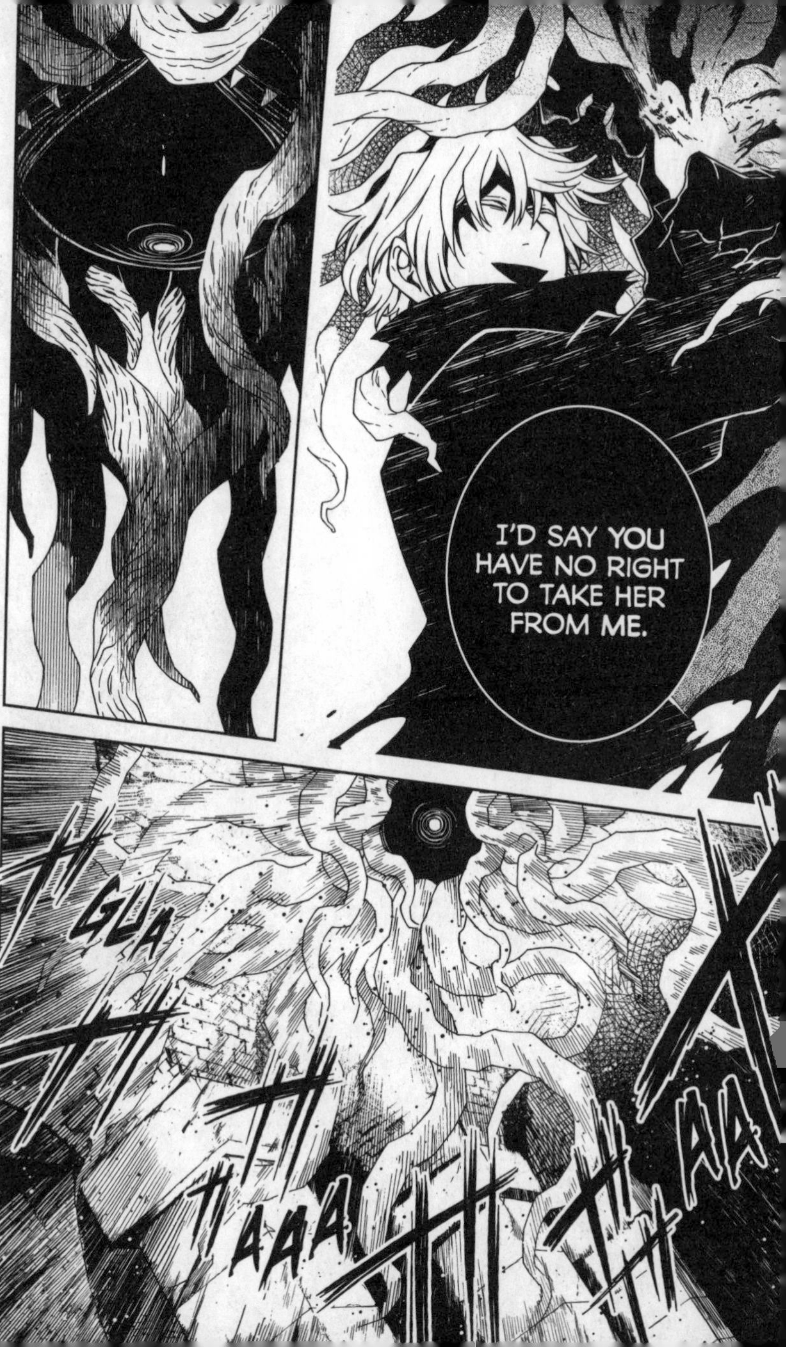
I'D SAY YOU HAVE NO RIGHT TO TAKE HER FROM ME.

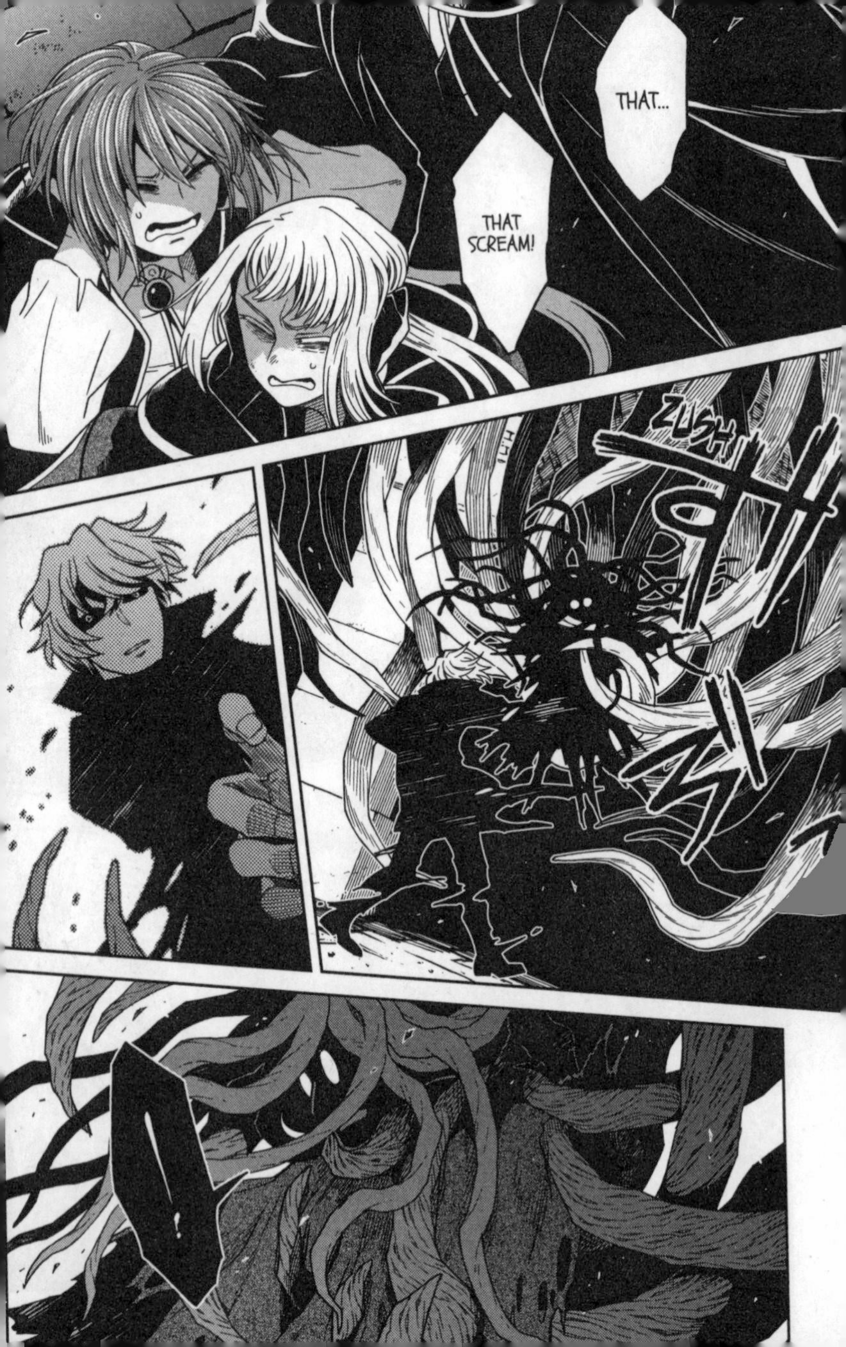
THAT...
THAT SCREAM!
ZUSH

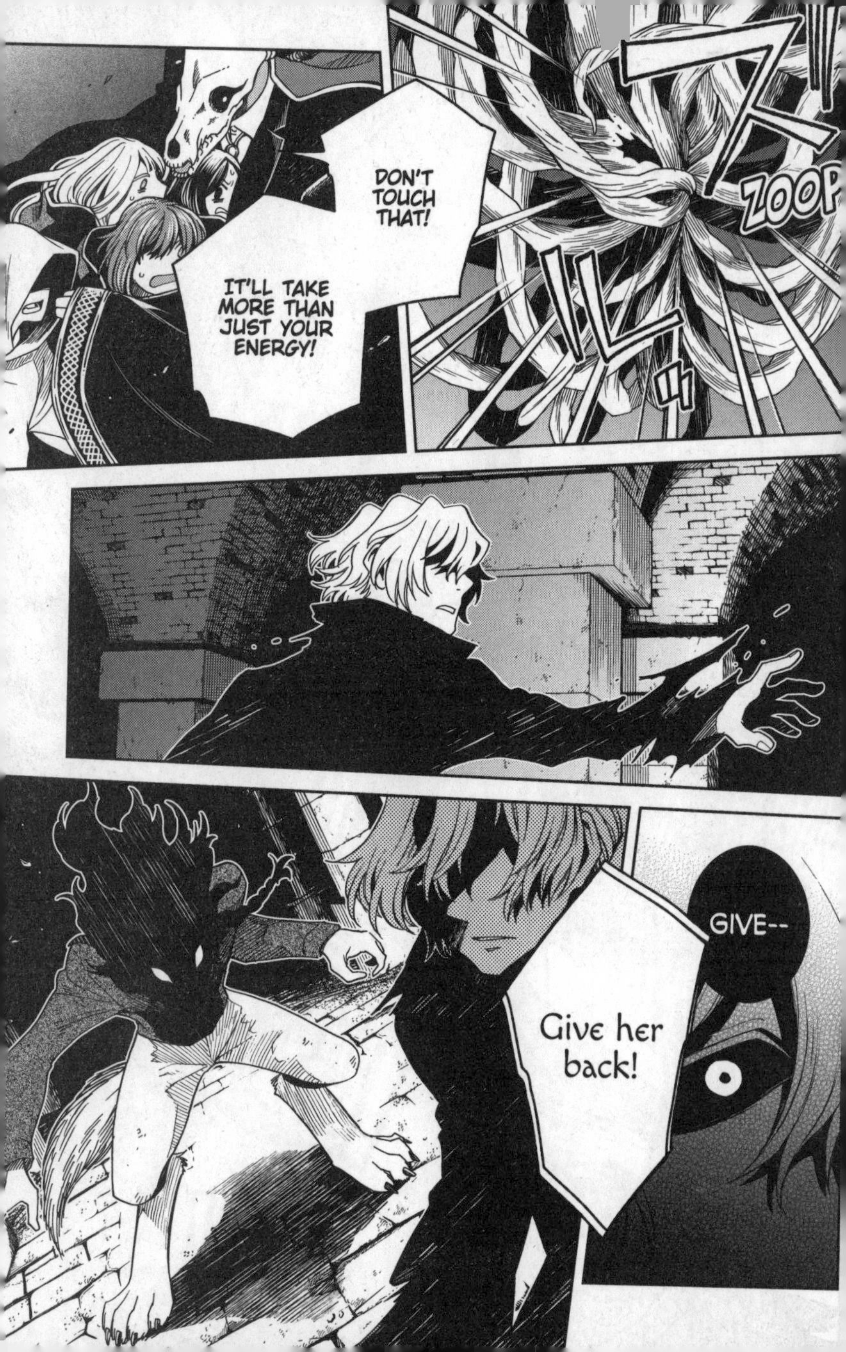
ZOOP
DON'T TOUCH THAT!
IT'LL TAKE MORE THAN JUST YOUR ENERGY!
GIVE--
Give her back!

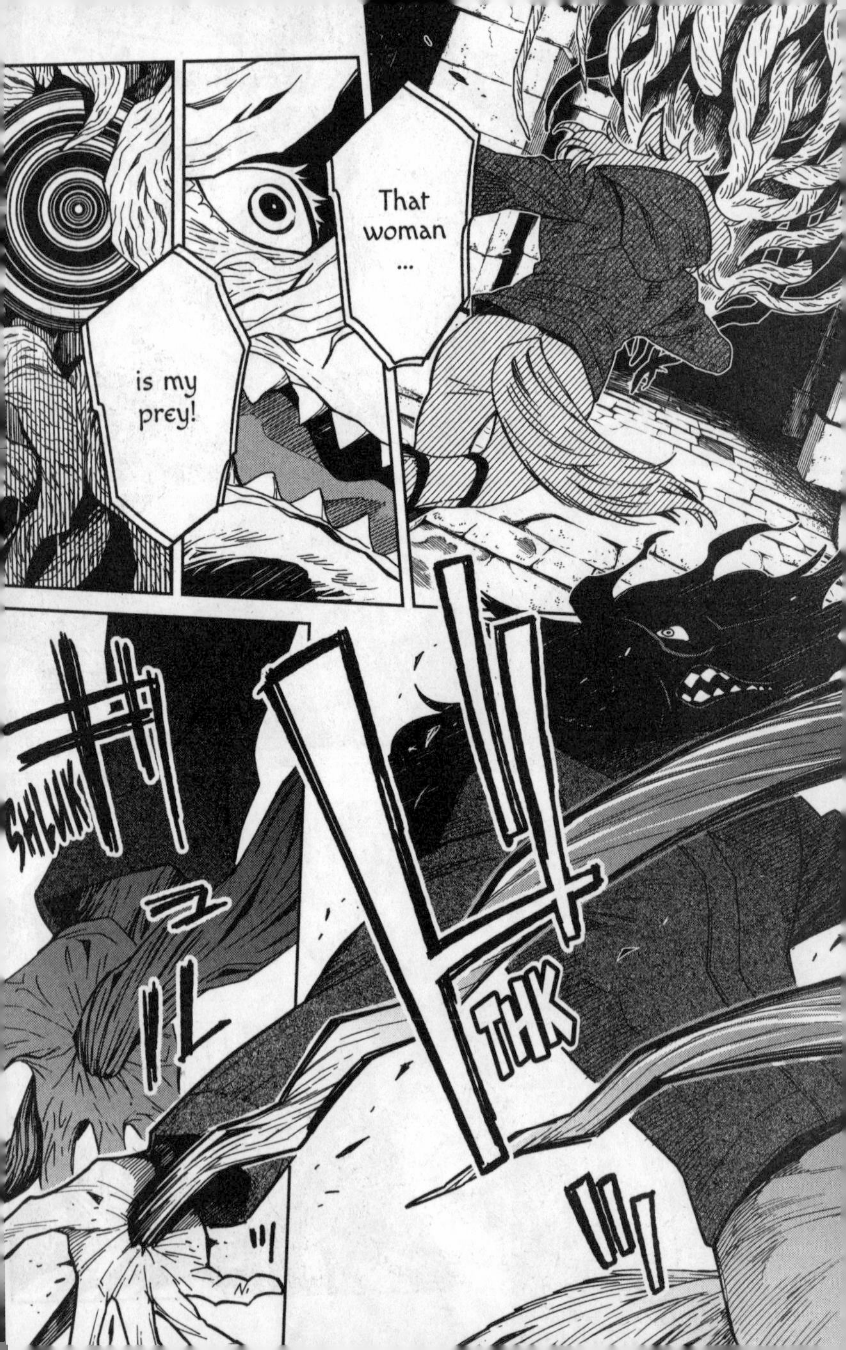
That woman ...
is my prey!
THK
SHLUK

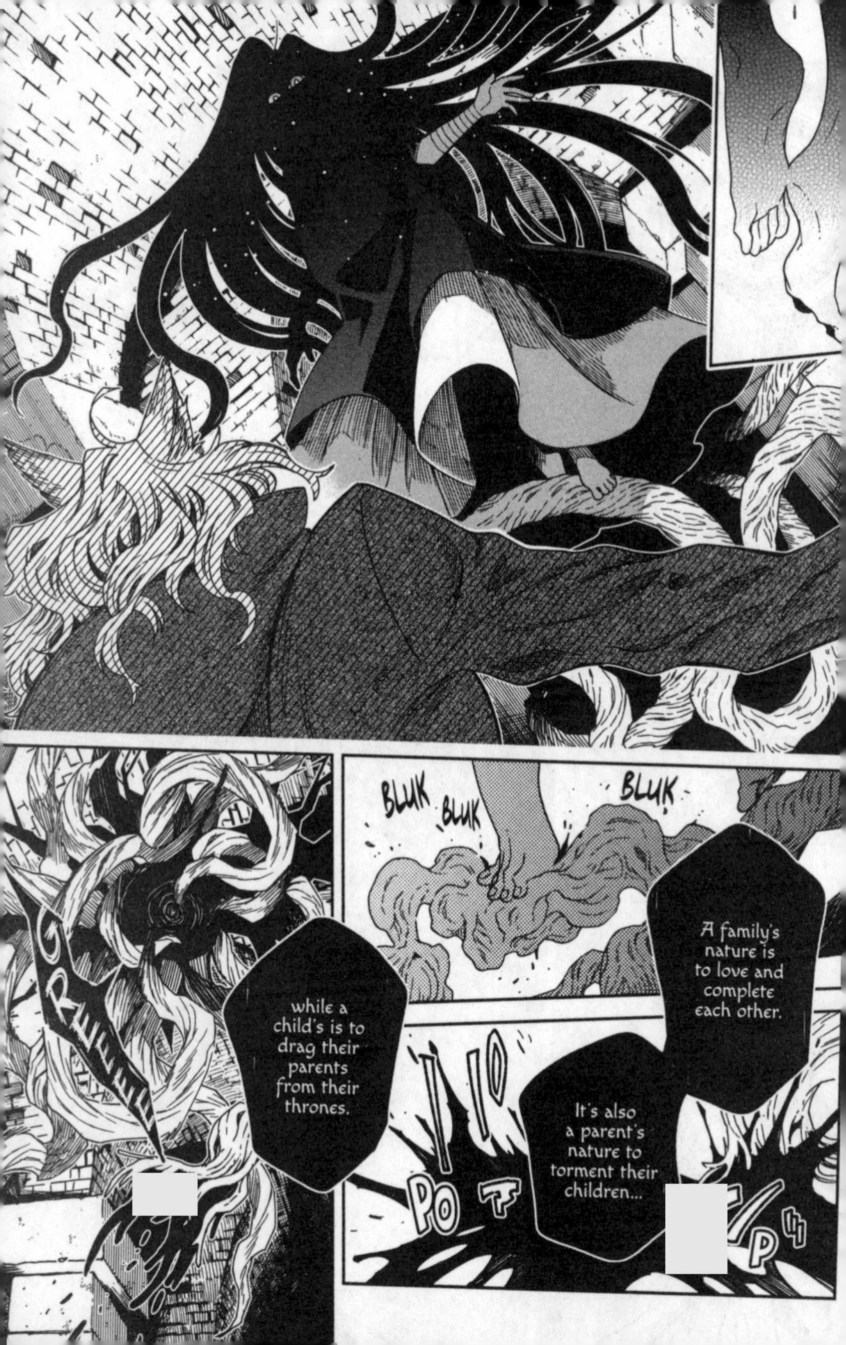
BLUK
BLUK
BLUK
A family's nature is to love and complete each other.
It's also a parent's nature to torment their children...
while a child's is to drag their parents from their thrones.

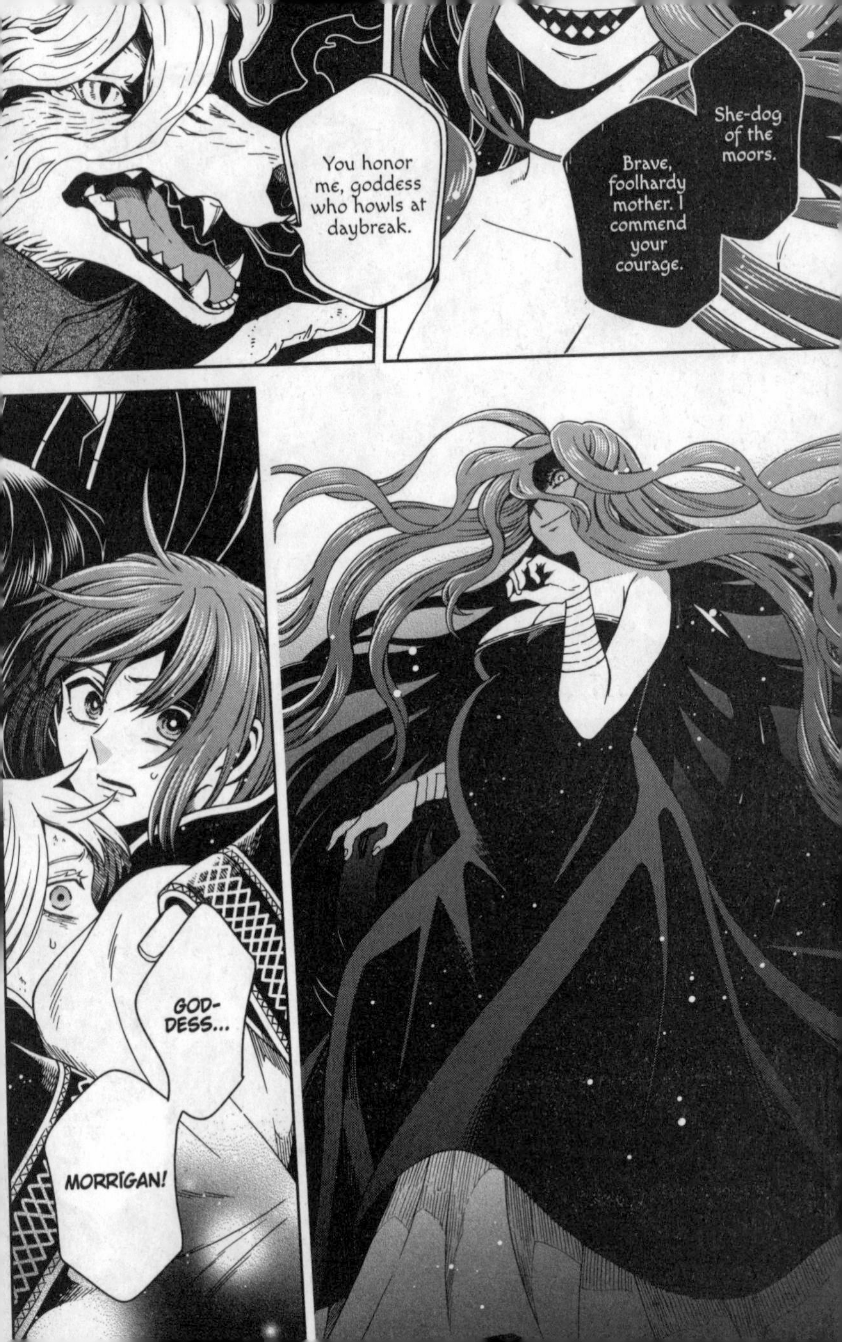
She-dog of the moors.
Brave, foolhardy mother. I commend your courage.
You honor me, goddess who howls at daybreak.
GOD-DESS...
MORRIGAN!

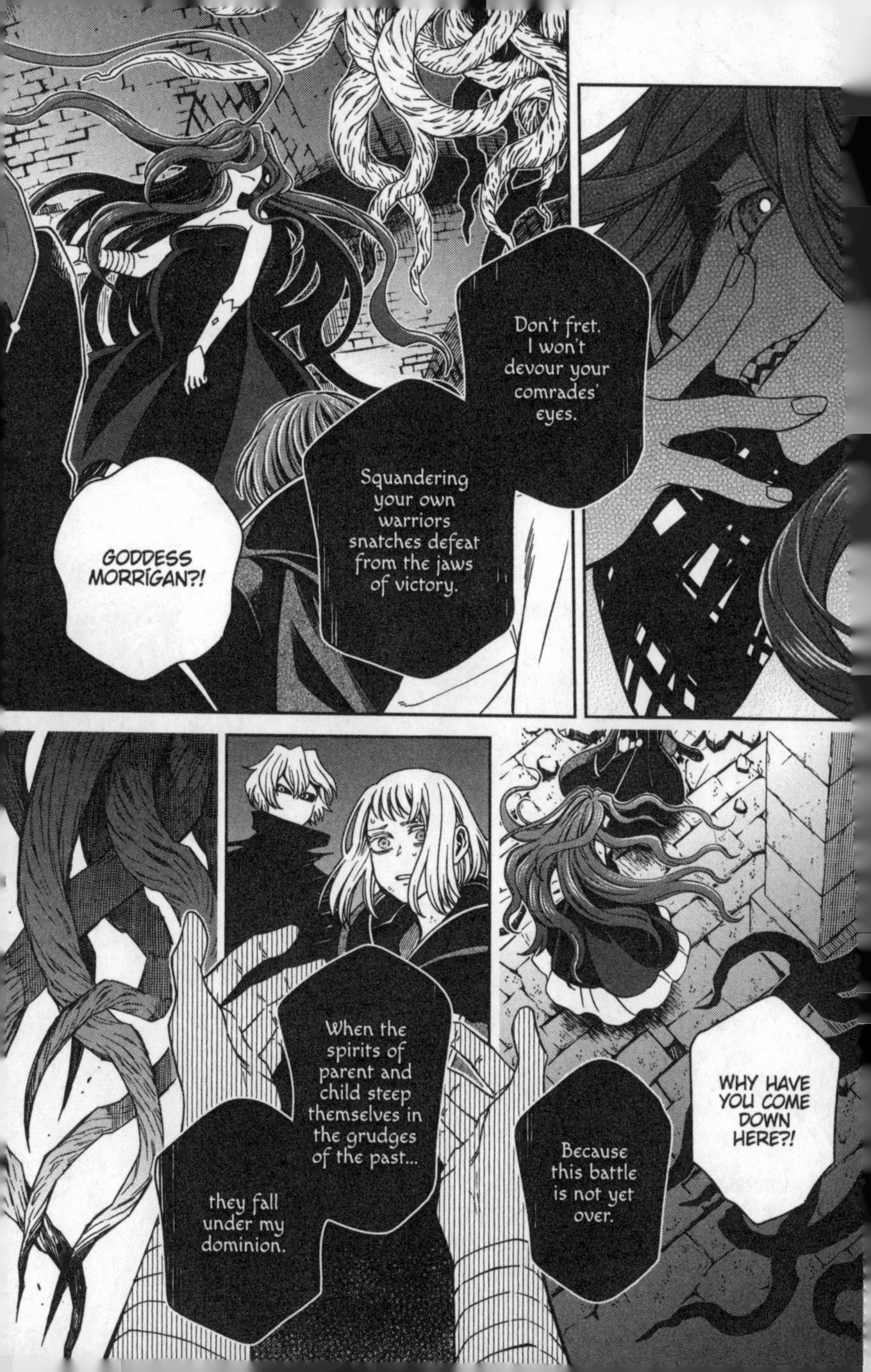
Don't fret. I won't devour your comrades' eyes.
Squandering your own warriors snatches defeat from the jaws of victory.
GODDESS MORRIGAN?!
WHY HAVE YOU COME DOWN HERE?!
Because this battle is not yet over.
When the spirits of parent and child steep themselves in the grudges of the past...
they fall under my dominion.

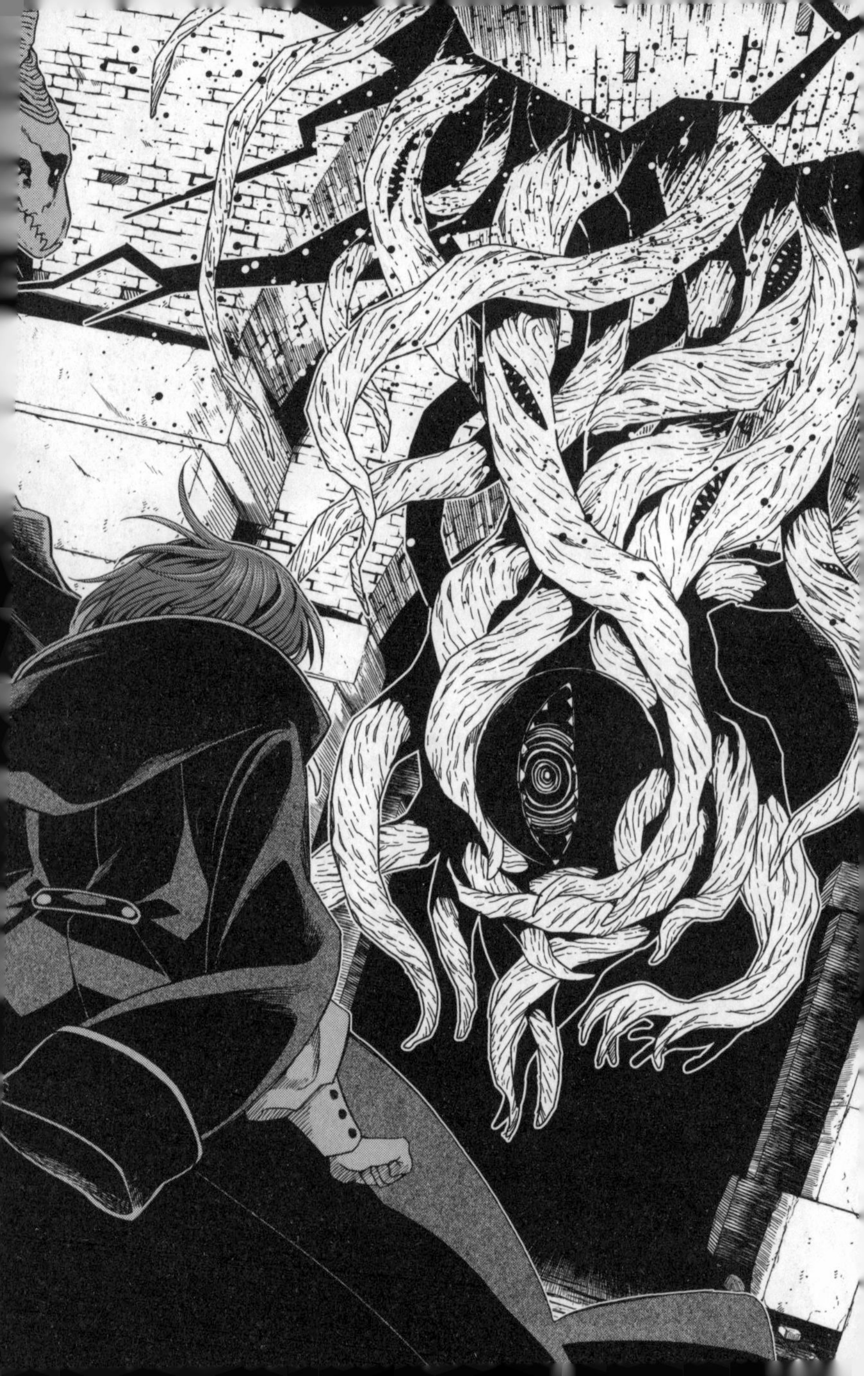

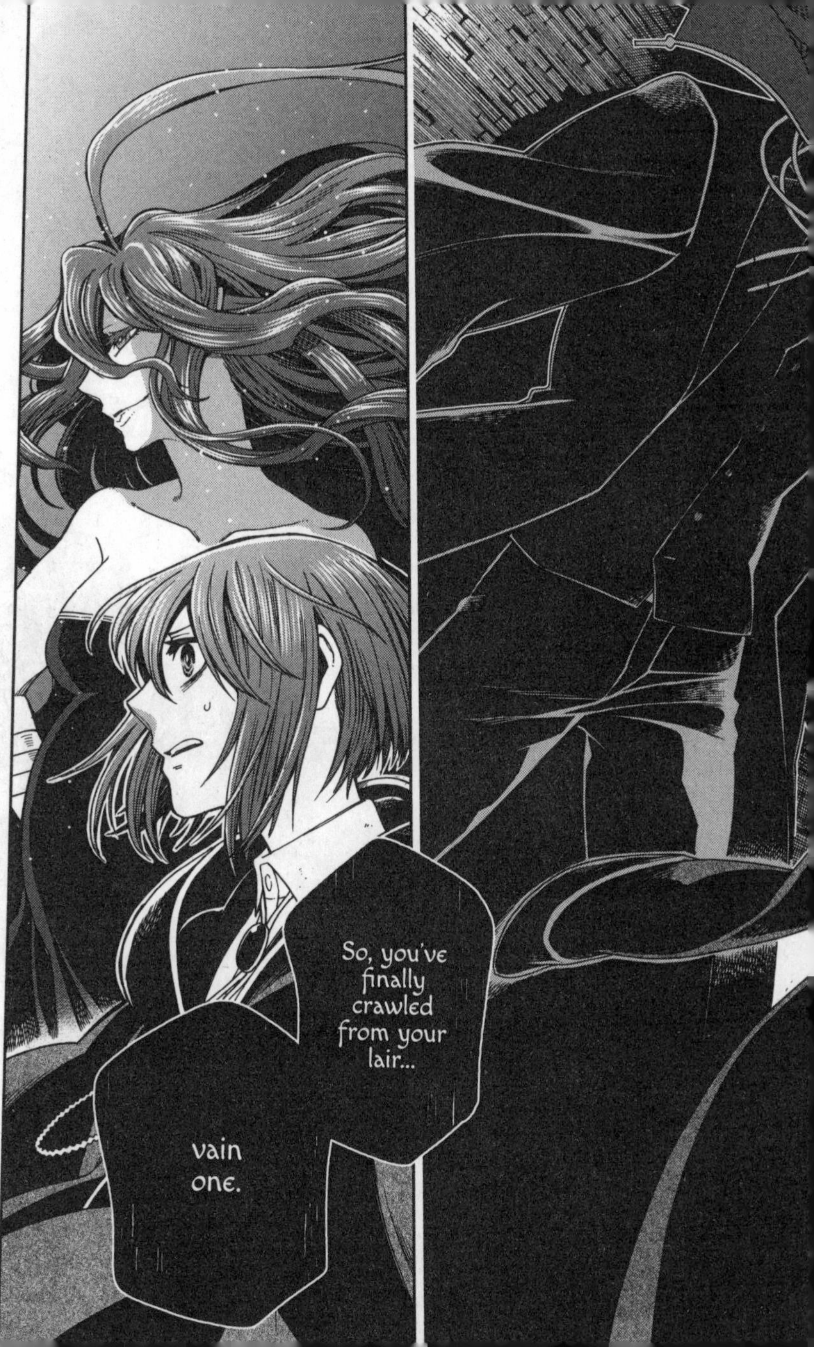
So, you've finally crawled from your lair...
vain one.

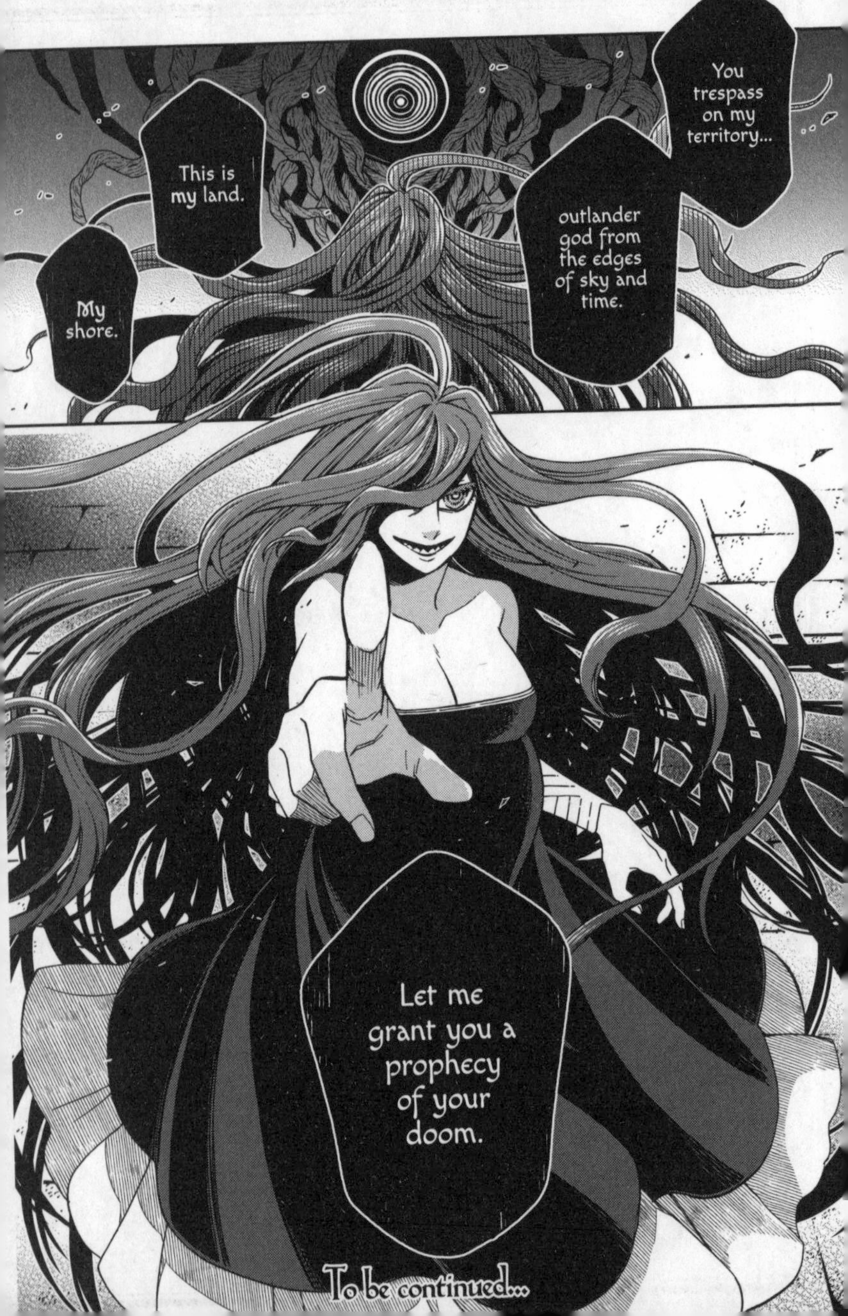
You trespass on my territory...
outlander god from the edges of sky and time.
This is my land.
My shore.
Let me grant you a prophecy of your doom.
To be continued...

The Ancient Magus' Bride

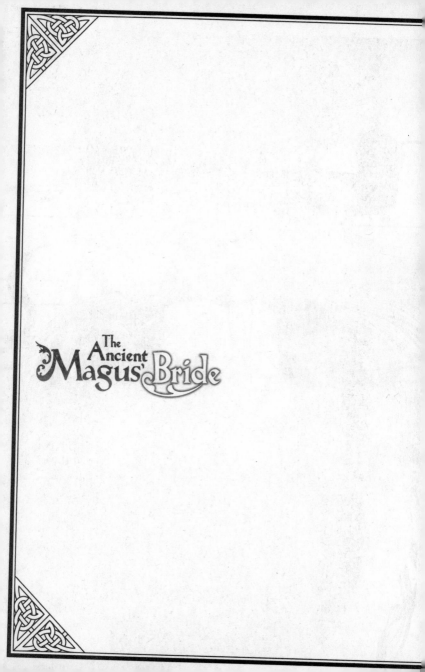

The Ancient Magus' Bride

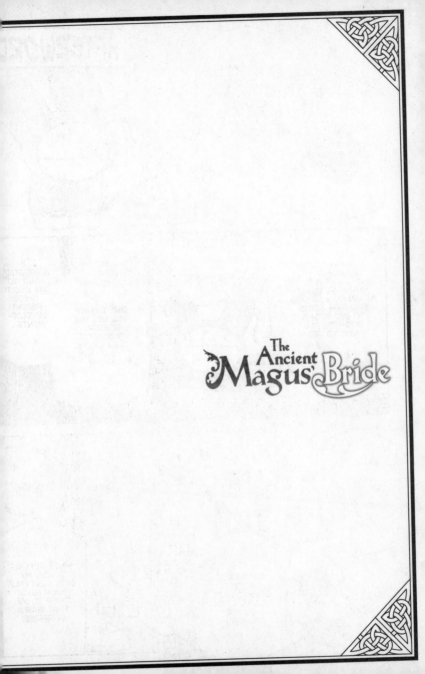

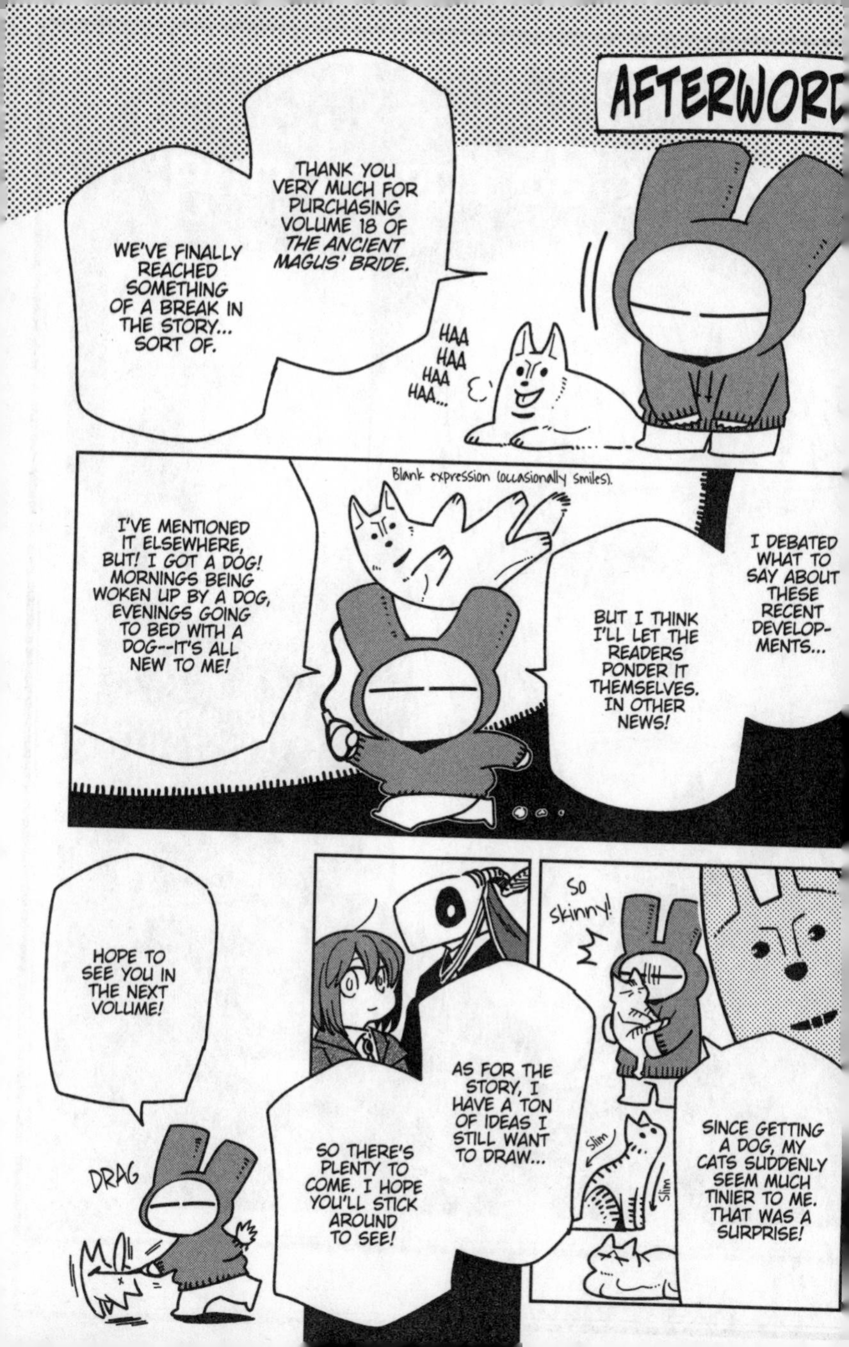
AFTERWORD
THANK YOU VERY MUCH FOR PURCHASING VOLUME 18 OF THE ANCIENT MAGUS' BRIDE.
WE'VE FINALLY REACHED SOMETHING OF A BREAK IN THE STORY... SORT OF.
HAA HAA HAA HAA...
I DEBATED WHAT TO SAY ABOUT THESE RECENT DEVELOP-MENTS...
BUT I THINK I'LL LET THE READERS PONDER IT THEMSELVES. IN OTHER NEWS!
Blank expression (occasionally smiles).
I'VE MENTIONED IT ELSEWHERE, BUT! I GOT A DOG! MORNINGS BEING WOKEN UP BY A DOG, EVENINGS GOING TO BED WITH A DOG--IT'S ALL NEW TO ME!
SINCE GETTING A DOG, MY CATS SUDDENLY SEEM MUCH TINIER TO ME. THAT WAS A SURPRISE!
So skinny!
Slim
Slim
AS FOR THE STORY, I HAVE A TON OF IDEAS I STILL WANT TO DRAW...
SO THERE'S PLENTY TO COME. I HOPE YOU'LL STICK AROUND TO SEE!
HOPE TO SEE YOU IN THE NEXT VOLUME!
DRAG

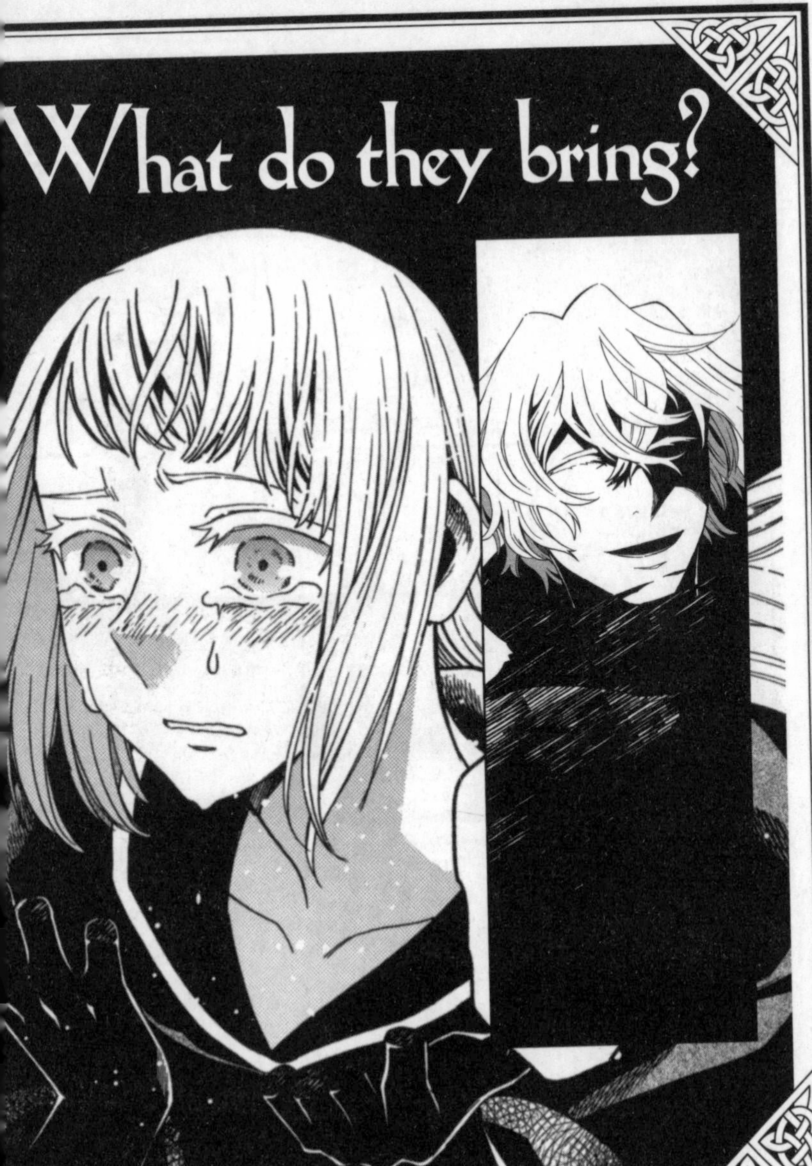
What do they bring?

Vol. 19 Preview

Curses. Chaos. Gods

Philomela had finally learned to unclasp her hands from prayer and reach out for help. Merging with the forbidden tome, Lizbeth gives in to her jealous obsession. And then there's the shadow of Adam's curse, aimed squarely at his mother. In the midst of the chaos, the Goddess Morrigan arrives to bring one family's story to an end...

This otherworldly fairy tale of romance and learning to accept the world continues in Volume 19!

The Ancient Magus' Bride

SEVEN SEAS ENTERTAINMENT PRESENTS

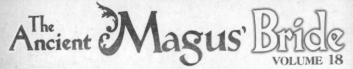

The Ancient Magus' Bride

VOLUME 18

story and art by **KORE YAMAZAKI**

TRANSLATION
Adrienne Beck

ADAPTATION
abet Reinhardt MacFarlane

LETTERING AND RETOUCH
Lys Blakeslee
Rachel Pierce

COVER DESIGN
Nicky Lim

PROOFREADER
Brett Hallahan

SENIOR EDITOR
Shanti Whitesides

PRODUCTION DESIGNER
Christina McKenzie

PREPRESS TECHNICIAN
Melanie Ujimori
Jules Valera

MANAGING EDITOR
J.P. Sullivan

EDITOR-IN-CHIEF
Julie Davis

ASSOCIATE PUBLISHER
Adam Arnold

PUBLISHER
Jason DeAngelis

THE ANCIENT MAGUS' BRIDE VOL. 18

Originally published in Japan in 2022 by MAG Garden Corporation, Tokyo.
English translation rights arranged through TOHAN CORPORATION, Tokyo.

Seven Seas press and purchase enquiries can be sent to Marketing Manager Lianne Sentar at press@gomanga.com. Information regarding the distribution and purchase of digital editions is available from Digital Manager CK Russell at digital@gomanga.com.

ISBN: 978-1-68579-577-1
Printed in Canada
First Printed: July 2023
10 9 8 7 6 5 4 3 2 1

READING DIRECTIONS

This book reads from ***right to left***, Japanese style. If this is your first time reading manga, you start reading from the top right panel on each page and take it from there. If you get lost, just follow the numbered diagram here. It may seem backwards at first, but you'll get the hang of it! Have fun!!

1
2
3
4
5
6
7
8
9

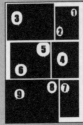

Follow us online: www.SevenSeasEntertainment.com